A PLACE CALLED APPOMATTOX

A Place Called
APPOM

Appomatox C.H.

ATTOX

William Marvel

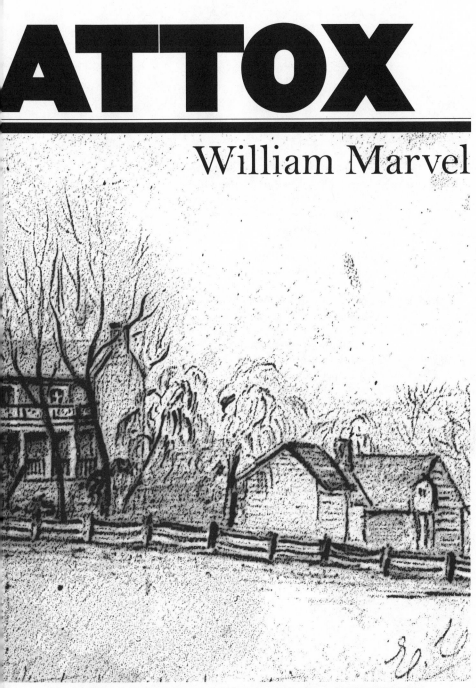

SOUTHERN ILLINOIS UNIVERSITY PRESS   CARBONDALE

Copyright © 2008 by William Marvel
First edition published 2000 by University of North Carolina Press
Paperback edition published 2008 by Southern Illinois University Press
All rights reserved
Printed in the United States of America
11 10 09 08   4 3 2 1

Library of Congress Cataloging-in-Publication Data
A place called Appomattox / William Marvel.
p. cm.
Originally published: Chapel Hill : University of North Carolina Press, c2000.
Includes bibliographical references and index.
ISBN-13: 978-0-8093-2831-4 (alk. paper)
ISBN-10: 0-8093-2831-3 (alk. paper)
1. Appomattox (Va.)—History. 2. Appomattox (Va.)—Social conditions. 3. Appomattox
County (Va.)—History. 4. Appomattox County (Va.)—Social conditions. 5. Appomattox
Campaign, 1865. 6. United States—History—Civil War, 1861–1865—Social aspects.
7. United States—History—Civil War, 1861–1865—Causes. 8. United States—
History—Civil War, 1861–1865—Influence.
F234.A6M37 2008
973.7'38—dc22   2007036486

Printed on recycled paper. ♻
The paper used in this publication meets the minimum requirements of American
National Standard for Information Sciences—Permanence of Paper for Printed Library
Materials, ANSI Z39.48-1992. ∞

FOR ZI,

my Appomattox companion,

who loved the old village

CONTENTS

MAPS & ILLUSTRATIONS

A section of

illustrations follows page 132.

PREFACE

For the majority of Americans, including the preponderance of those who witnessed the historic events there, the name "Appomattox" has signified only the place where our Civil War came to an end. It consisted, so far as most moderns know, of nothing more than a brick home and a courthouse that some manage to confuse with each other, all labeled with a name few can spell correctly on the first attempt. The greater part of the American people live and die without ever having seen this spot, although it represents the coupling between the two great halves of American history. Until recently the average adult citizen had been at least marginally familiar with the nature of Appomattox as a watershed in the flow of national affairs, and might have been able to locate it somewhere in central Virginia, but lately the mention of the name seems to produce more puzzlement than recognition.

Representative as it was of the average Confederate community, Appomattox assumed the typical postwar reputation of having sacrificed everything in a valiant effort to preserve an innocent and idyllic past. While the village certainly did typify the slaveholding South, that Lost Cause image did not apply in any of its details: for all the recollections of a South stripped of men to fill the army, rich and influential residents usually managed to avoid the front if they preferred, remaining at home or nearby while their poorer, older, and sometimes disabled neighbors bore the battle for those who had begun it. Among the lower classes total sacrifice had been common; among the gentry it was far more rare.

Appomattox also formed the scene of its own particular myth. Thanks to the romantic imaginations of men like Joshua Chamberlain and John B. Gordon, it became the place where enemies who had battled each other for four years suddenly laid down their weapons and welcomed each other as brothers, setting aside political and philosophical differences that had fermented into hatred. Neither was that image especially accurate.

This book will examine the lesser-known aspects of Appomattox Court

House. There will be little inquiry, for instance, into the details of the meeting of two great men in the McLean house: that brief incident has been done to death, and all the sources appear to have been mined; even if new information surfaced, it could offer little of historical significance. Instead, the focus will remain upon the citizens who peopled Appomattox, the soldiers who sojourned there, and the community they knew.

Go to Appomattox Court House today and you will find a scene that all but transports the visitor in time. Approaching the village at dawn from the west, in the old bed of the Lynchburg Stage Road, the pedestrian might just as easily be making his way to town during a quiet moment of the war that ended there. At considerable but justifiable expense the federal government has restored Appomattox Court House to a reasonable semblance of its pastoral former appearance, rebuilding important structures that had disappeared and rehabilitating the relics that survived. In acknowledgment of the most important event that ever happened there, park stewards have striven (with the controversial recent exception of an anachronistic stockade fence at the Peers house) to maintain the atmosphere of 1865 in the old village.

Yet Appomattox Court House existed before and after the two armies collided there. For those who lived in or near the village, the scenes of that famous April were merely incidental. The settlement served as a home and as a rural village center for thousands of Virginians black and white, poor and planter alike. The town sprang into existence the same year that Texas became a state, and it survived—albeit in gradual decay—until the reunited states had become a world power. During those years, Appomattox citizens watched as slavery consumed the national consciousness, dividing the nation and bringing on cataclysm of a magnitude none had ever imagined. That catastrophe ended, or began to end, in their dooryards. Then they witnessed the trials of Reconstruction and reunion, and they felt the pinch of industrial growth and demographic consolidation as their community was left behind by the bold new era the conflict had spawned. To tell the story of Appomattox Court House is to tell the South's story of the Civil War—a struggle that lasted not four years, but many, encompassing more than a lifetime between the first sectionalist rumblings to the last gasp of reactionary rhetoric.

A PLACE CALLED APPOMATTOX

THE TAVERN

John Raine might have been forgiven a touch of melancholy on the eve of his fiftieth birthday, for in the spring of 1845 the half-century mark served as an even greater reminder of man's mortality than it would in a more salubrious time. For Raine, however, the eleventh of April that year signified more than the last day of his fifth decade. According to a notice posted in the Lynchburg papers, that date had been chosen for the liquidation of property that he had once expected to tide him through old age.[1]

In the summer of 1839 Raine and his wife, Eliza, had bought half the interest in a twenty-year-old tavern on Clover Hill, overlooking the headwaters of the Appomattox River from one of the gentle hills of Virginia's Piedmont. The tavern had been built by Alexander Patteson to serve passengers on the stage line that he and his late brother had established between Richmond and Lynchburg in 1814; Alexander Patteson himself died in 1836, leaving the tavern and its 206 acres divided between his estate and his brother's, but in September of 1840 the Raines acquired the remaining half-interest for the same price of $1,525 that they had agreed upon for the first half. By 1839 stages stopped twice every weekday at the two-story brick tavern, and once a day on weekends; Raine lacked the Pattesons' advantage of owning both stage line and tavern, but his was the best-known stop between Buckingham Court House and Lynchburg, and regular travelers remembered Clover Hill as the old headquarters of the stage company.[2]

For all of that, Raine had not prospered. At his death he would be remembered as a man who suffered economic reverses through his own stubborn belief in the virtue of others, and before the Christmas of 1842 his fortunes had sunk so low that he appealed to his brother, back in Campbell

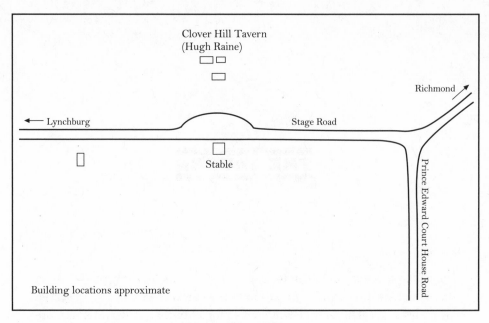

Map 1. Clover Hill, 1845

County, to pick up the lapsed notes on the tavern parcel. Hugh Raine allowed him $3,500 for the 206-acre parcel, and permitted him to stay on as manager of the tavern. Now, barely two years later, thirty acres around the tavern had been sketched into town lots, and Hugh Raine was advertising them for sale.[3]

Hugh was taking economic advantage of a political circumstance on which John had long hoped to capitalize. Clover Hill lay amid rolling farmland, isolated by twenty-five or thirty miles from any county seat. Patteson's tavern sat on the upper edge of Prince Edward County; a few hundred yards away, hugging the north branch of the Appomattox, the Sweeney family's apple orchard worked its way up a slope in Buckingham County. Interested delegates to the state legislature had been trying for decades to have portions of Prince Edward, Buckingham, Campbell, and Charlotte Counties carved off to form a new county, with Clover Hill as the seat. For obvious reasons Alexander Patteson had made the first attempt himself, in 1824, when he presented a petition to the General Assembly for a new county called "Fayette," but the attempt failed on a technicality.

By 1839 proponents of a new county had grown better organized, and on February 21 of that year Thomas H. Flood presented the House of Delegates with another petition from a committee (which included John Raine) representing citizens in extremities of the four existing counties.

These people were burdened with travel of as much as thirty-two miles each way every time they had to vote, attend militia muster, serve as jurors, or do any court business; they asked the delegates to create a new county with Clover Hill, the residence of John Raine, as the seat of justice, with a town of about forty lots laid out there. According to this memorial, the new county might be called Bouldin, Bolling, Appomattox, or anything else the legislature preferred. So certain was John Raine of ultimate success, despite the petition's failure in the 1839 session, that over the next two summers he signed the pair of interest-bearing notes for a total of $3,050 to gain title to the Patteson property, where he had apparently been managing the tavern for some time.[4]

Raine had good cause for his optimism, as the momentum for a new county was clearly growing, but his timing could have been better. Not until the 1841 session did the General Assembly entertain another petition on the subject, and that April voters in the affected precincts expressed their wishes in four nonbinding polls. All save Charlotte County returned majorities for the new county, but that did not convince the delegates; nor did another poll taken in April 1842, in which the Campbell County section tallied forty-five men for and forty-five men against the change. At that juncture the delay proved too much for John Raine, who had been unable to meet his mortgage notes; in December of 1842 he sold his Clover Hill holdings to his brother.[5]

Thomas Bocock resurrected the new-county bill in January of 1844, but a fellow delegate from Buckingham County by the name of Jones objected on the grounds that people had paid dearly for land at Buckingham Court House (where Jones, too, owned some real estate), and it would be unfair to diminish the value of their property by shaving off so much of their county. If the bill were to pass, however, Delegate Jones thought the new county should be called Jones, after an ancestor of his who had fallen at the head of a volunteer company at the battle of Guilford Court House. To the surprise and dismay of both isolated citizens and prospective profiteers, the assembly again voted the bill down on the argument that the sense of the voters had not been taken.[6]

Disgruntled residents called a meeting at Clover Hill for February 2. Gathering at Patteson's tavern, the local gentry formed standing committees to spread the gospel on the new county and to circulate more petitions. That April the various sheriffs opened the polls for yet another referendum, and this time the vote was overwhelming in all four counties. Just to be certain, the committees arranged a free, nonpartisan barbecue at Clover Hill in the fall, inviting speakers from among both the Whigs and the Democrats. In December a new petition was entered in Richmond by Samuel C. Anderson of Prince Edward County, who had proposed the name "Appomattox" the previous session, in place of Jones: the Appomattox River that flowed so majestically into the James, below Petersburg, originated with a trickling stream behind Patteson's tavern; early Virginians believed the name evolved from an Indian tribe, or sovereign, called Apumetec. This bill passed the House of Delegates by a margin of fifteen votes on February 6, 1845, and the state senate ratified it two days later.[7]

This was the news that John Raine had waited so long—too long, now—to hear. Less than a fortnight after passage of the bill, he and his son-in-law hosted an inaugural ball to celebrate the birth of the new county, hiring a local fiddler and one "blind Billy," who plied his flute for six dozen men and women who crowded into the tavern for a rare evening's entertainment. Raine provided a dinner as well (with champagne from time to time during the evening), doubtless commenting on the prosperity that would inevitably attend Clover Hill now that it had been designated the county seat.

On March 6 the justices of the peace within the proposed boundaries met at the tavern with the eight town trustees who had been appointed by the legislature to lay out the lots of the new county seat; each of the trustees had taken an oath to execute his office "faithfully and impartially." They adjourned to the sitting room, and over refreshments they determined how to position the county's buildings on the two acres the state had allowed them to take from the Raines. Without much debate they decided to arrange the town lots around a central square where the courthouse would be constructed, between the tavern and its stable. The jail would sit behind the courthouse. By the end of that day they had divided thirty acres of the old Patteson land into a prospective village, the vast majority of which one of those faithful and impartial men would soon snag for himself.[8]

Hugh Raine did not wait long. The tavern conclave had elevated Clover Hill from a pleasant stage stop on the old Buckingham Road to a destination for militiamen, lawyers, litigants, judges, and jurors, whose needs would vary from a noon meal or a night's lodging to a site for an office or even a home. Raine's notice for the sale of his lots appeared eleven days later in the *Lynchburg Republican*. If the weather turned inclement on April 11, he proposed the "next fair day."

April can be a wet season in Appomattox County, and the roads often turned to soup, as thousands of soldiers would learn two decades hence. Bad weather may have postponed the land sale, or wary speculators may have driven too hard a bargain, but in any case John Raine's birthday passed with the Clover Hill parcel still intact. On May 5 Hugh Raine again advertised his lots for sale, inviting the general public as well as his brother's creditors to an auction on Friday, May 9.[9]

The day before this scheduled sale, the county justices returned to Patteson's tavern to establish their government, electing a sheriff, a coroner, the commonwealth's attorney, and a clerk. They awarded the county attorney's position to Thomas S. Bocock, the Buckingham County delegate who had introduced the successful bill for the new county, and for clerk they selected his father, seventy-two-year-old John T. Bocock. The elder Bocock lived only twenty-five days longer, though, and after some political wrangling the justices filled the vacancy with Henry T. Bocock, another of the deceased clerk's sons.[10]

Even with the county government seated just the day before, bidding on the old Patteson tract fell short of enthusiastic, and John Raine saw his chance. Perhaps suffering from a measure of fraternal responsibility, he attempted to relieve his brother of what may have begun to seem a burden, and when the tavern did not sell he took it back himself, approaching another brother for enough cash to pay Hugh the same $3,500 he had invested some thirty months before. Now, at least, he and Eliza might bargain for some of the profits he had long hoped to draw from the increased value of Clover Hill land.[11]

Those profits proved small, at least for John Raine, who never paid off the note to his brother and soon lost his last grip on the Clover Hill dream. That summer there appeared at the tavern an aggressive young man by the name of Samuel Daniel McDearmon, armed with some grand ideas and supported by some wealthy relatives.

On August 1, 1845, McDearmon borrowed $2,070.40 from a bachelor uncle and strode into Clover Hill with plans to make his fortune there. At the ripe age of twenty-nine, McDearmon already had a finger in every conceivable pie that a new county could bake. Just the previous April the young Democrat had been elected to the House of Delegates, and the statute for the new county had named him as one of the eight trustees of the village at Clover Hill. He held a governor's commission as major in the state militia, and he also served as a deputy sheriff in both Campbell and Prince Edward Counties, while his brother was now a deputy in Appomattox County.[12]

McDearmon's political power derived at least partly from the money and prominence that came with his pedigree. His father, James McDearmon, was a Presbyterian minister who, like most professionals of that time and era, lived principally on the proceeds of farm income. As the only

child of an early settler, Reverend McDearmon enjoyed considerable property — hundreds of acres and more than a score of slaves — on an inherited
estate called Mount Evergreen, some seven miles southeast of the new
courthouse village. Given part of that land to make a beginning, Samuel
McDearmon had augmented that stake a decade before with his teenage
marriage to Mary Frances Philadelphia Walton, who came with a respect-
able dowry, and he cultivated friends who seemed willing to apply their
assets to joint business ventures. He already owned nearly 450 acres adjoining (and from) his father's plantation, besides holding 147 acres in trust
for a neighbor's estate, and near Mount Evergreen he owned a sawmill
that provided his most regular income.[13]

McDearmon may have approached John Raine at first, but when it came
to making an offer on the old Patteson estate he dealt with Hugh and the
third brother, known only as R. K. Raine; this last brother now held the
title. That fall McDearmon bought the tavern piece, evidently by taking
over the notes John Raine had signed in May: half the price of $3,500 was
due on November 1, 1846, and the balance a year later, with McDearmon's
father and brother-in-law securing the debt for him. That gave him the
30-acre village and the 176 surrounding acres, but he did not stop there.
In a frenzy of acquisition, he picked up a little over 60 acres about eight
miles southeast of the courthouse, as well as part interest in another parcel
there, and he bought 163 acres between the stage road and the north fork
of the Appomattox. In the course of 1845 he nearly doubled the acreage
that he owned, meanwhile more than doubling the value of his property,
and this was only the beginning.[14]

As McDearmon accumulated his little empire, county officials moved
ahead with their duties. Toward the end of the summer they determined
what specifications they wanted for the first municipal building — not a
courthouse, significantly enough, but a jail. Bidders had three options: a
stone building twenty feet by forty, with walls two feet thick; a brick structure of the same dimensions, with eighteen-inch walls; or a hewn-log jail,
solid oak, thirty feet long and eighteen feet wide. Proposals were invited
on court day in October, which, according to a longtime clerk of that court,
was held in the stagecoach barn across the road from the tavern. So far as
the county commissioners were concerned, a courthouse could wait until
spring.[15]

Samuel McDearmon could not wait. By November 1 he had secured the
deed to the Patteson land, and two days later appeared his first advertisement for a grand sale to be held on November 26. The entire thirty acres

of platted lots would be on the block, with no money down, on notes of six, twelve, or eighteen months with the appropriate bonds and security. The tavern and the remaining land were also available, for a third down and two annual payments on the balance.

"This is one of the handsomest locations in Virginia," promised his advertisement in the Lynchburg papers, "in the midst of a fine and healthy country, noted for its fare between Lynchburg, Farmville, and Richmond." Fever and other dreaded diseases had not visited Clover Hill in years, McDearmon asserted, and as the county seat the property had potential for either further speculation or as the location for professional offices and tradesmen's shops. If all went well, the terms on the tavern would not only satisfy his notes with Raine but more than compensate him for his entire cost, while any proceeds from town lots would be pure profit.

Nor was McDearmon the only one who hoped to cash in on the transformation of Clover Hill. Jacob Tibbs, a local farmer and veteran of the War of 1812, wished to divest himself of everything: 404 acres of good tobacco land, house, barn, outbuildings, furnishings, standing crops—even his pots and pans, and presumably his slaves and livestock as well. Tibbs hoped to move west, as numerous neighbors had and would. He was well past fifty and soundly established, with a wife less than half his age and two small boys, but the prospect of a good price in Appomattox and cheaper land west of the Mississippi lured him to the newspaper office with his notice. William Still, who owned another big tract with a tavern and a store about five miles up the stage road, advertised his property in the same issues.[16]

All did not go well, and especially for McDearmon. Neither Tibbs nor Still saw an offer tempting enough to carry them out of the county, but they had not strung their finances as thin as McDearmon had. Instead of gaining him a fortune, the advertised sale of McDearmon's purchase instead brought him disaster, and in more than one form.

The creation of Appomattox County had attracted at least one young lawyer who considered the new seat a good place to begin his career. Sometime that summer Coleman C. May took lodging at the tavern, and over the passing weeks locals learned that he was twenty-four years old, that he originally hailed from Staunton, and that he had never recovered the complete use of his left arm, which had long ago been broken at the elbow. May stood two or three inches short of six feet, with a burly frame, and he maintained a dapper appearance, dressing well and keeping both his dark hair and his red muttonchop whiskers neatly trimmed.

May seemed to own a little temper, however. On the day before the bidding was to open on McDearmon's land, the lodger and his landlord fell into disagreement over something—the board bill, perhaps, or the sale of a coveted lot—and their argument escalated in volume and fury. Deputy Sheriff William J. McDearmon heard his brother's voice and interceded on his behalf, swinging a cudgel at May and striking him several times. May had clearly not expected a fight that day: he was fashionably attired, wearing a black broadcloth coat and vest with striped trousers, and his crippled arm impaired his ability to defend himself. When the deputy continued to batter him, May produced a pocket knife, opened it, and stabbed his assailant once in the neck, severing the jugular vein. William McDearmon dropped to the floor, blood gushing through his fingers, while Samuel McDearmon retrieved a pepperbox revolver from its hiding place and shot May in the chest.

May staggered out the door as the tavern owner attended to his brother. There was nothing anyone could do for such a wound, and within minutes Appomattox County was short one deputy sheriff. An enraged Samuel McDearmon mounted a search party and posted a reward for the capture of "that murderer," insisting that May had killed his brother "without provocation." [17]

May was soon found, so badly wounded that the lack of a jail made little difference, but he survived long enough for a grand jury to indict him for murder. By the time he had fully recovered the freshly finished jail was ready for him, and in the spring he appeared before Judge Daniel Wilson Sr. Alluding to the blood, business, and political relationships that would complicate any effort to seat an untainted jury for the killer of Deputy McDearmon, defense attorneys appealed for a change of venue. Judge Wilson, whose own son would have partaken in the prosecution, agreed, and May's case was transferred to Amherst Court House, over thirty miles away.[18]

Flanked by four prominent attorneys, Coleman May emerged from the log jail at Amherst on August 21, 1846, and crossed the muddy yard to the old frame courthouse. Four days later a jury was finally sworn. The testimony dragged on for six days a week until September 3, when the defense rested. Obviously convinced that May had acted in self-defense, the jury returned a verdict of not guilty that same day. The judge ordered his release, but May's choleric manner had revealed itself over the past few days, and in a peculiar conclusion the judge also demanded, "on consideration of the circumstances developed in the course of this trial," that

{ THE TAVERN }

May post a substantial bond to assure his good behavior for the next year. May, who had already spent nine months in jail for a crime of which he was essentially innocent, provided security worth a total of $4,000 before disappearing forever from the scenes of his misery.[19]

Nine days after William McDearmon's death the court of Appomattox County convened, presumably in the old Patteson carriage house. There was little business to conduct, but before going home the court officers issued a formal document expressing their grief over the passing of the late deputy. They resolved to wear black badges of mourning for the next sixty days in honor of their departed colleague, whom they judged "humane and courteous to all, a man of unblemished character and unexceptionable conduct." Had that been strictly true, Deputy McDearmon would probably still have walked among them, but the opinion of the assembled officials was ratified at the tavern that same afternoon by a meeting of citizens who deemed the dead man "humane and just in the discharge of his various duties." Had it not been for the change of venue, some of those sympathetic citizens might have sat on Coleman May's jury, and those grieving court officers would have been administering his case.[20]

With the excitement of the tavern killing still fresh, few Clover Hill residents probably made the journey to Lynchburg the following week to hear their most celebrated neighbor perform. Joel Walker Sweeney, the man credited with inventing the American banjo, had come back at last from Europe, where he had captivated the Queen of England with his music; on the night of December 11 he appeared at a Lynchburg theater with a minstrel show touted as "the greatest Ethiopian extravaganza extant."[21]

Sweeney was the most accomplished in a musical clan that lived in a house beside the stage road, where it crossed the Appomattox, just a few yards from the stream and half a mile from the tavern. Without the least training he had mastered the violin and an obscure stringed instrument called the ban-jar, variations of which local slaves still crafted from a gourd and hardwood, after a traditional African design. As a young man Sweeney built something similar to the ban-jar but stronger, forming the sound-board by stretching a hide over a wooden frame; he also added a fifth string. Thus the banjo was born (or so the story goes), and Sweeney was soon touring the South with his new sound and a repertoire of songs, dances, stories, and animal impressions borrowed from the slaves he had known as a youth. Unsatisfied merely to invent an instrument, he then inspired an entirely new genre in entertainment, blacking his face for his performances and wearing a costume consisting of a garish waistcoat, gaudy trousers, and a top hat.

"Joe Sweeney was a fine delineator of the Negro character," recalled an Appomattox judge who was brought up a mile and a half up the stage road from the Sweeney place. "Raised as he was in the midst of them and possessing a quick observation and a keen sense of the ludicrous, he made his concerts very attractive, because his manners and language were so true to the original."

Although audiences outside the South were less likely to appreciate the accuracy of Sweeney's imitations, his humor and music proved universally popular. He took his show north, to the cities, and in 1842 he crossed the Atlantic, appearing at the Lyceum Royal Theater in London on February 6, 1843. Traveling for the next two years with Sand's Great American Circus, he played major cities in England, Scotland, and Ireland, including a reputed command performance for Queen Victoria. Not yet thirty-five, he returned to America with a sizable fortune, at least in Appomattox County estimation, including a gold-laden money belt that he said Her Majesty had given him.

Joel was the oldest in his generation of Sweeneys. Richard Sweeney could play nearly as well as his brother, and soon after Joel returned from Europe the two began appearing together. Sampson, their youngest brother, joined them eventually. The youngest Sweeney girl, Missouri, reportedly shared her brothers' talents but she kept from the stage lest it raise antebellum eyebrows. Joel's return performance in Lynchburg included no relatives, however, except those who sat in the audience.[22]

Samuel McDearmon was not among those who made the long trek to the Lynchburg theater, for he had already arrived in Richmond for the next session of the General Assembly. Although he no longer lived in Prince Edward County he had been elected to represent that district; if he was to continue a political career (and his business interests demanded that he do so), he could not resign on the mere technicality that he was not a resident of the county that had elected him.

As the coach carried him east, the freshman delegate likely thought of his dead brother, but he may have mourned almost as keenly the failure of his plan to turn a profit on the Clover Hill property. His brother's death and the search for his killer had put an end to the scheduled property sale, and by the close of 1845 McDearmon had peddled only two half-acre lots: one to Thomas and Henry Bocock and one to Hugh Raine, who may have reserved the parcel from the original sale. Both the Bocock brothers would want office and lodging space near the courthouse now; Raine, meanwhile, had long supposed that the new county seat could support a second tavern, and he began construction by winter.[23]

Early in his sojourn at the capital, Delegate McDearmon found himself asked to select the next governor, and as it happened he sided with the victor, William Smith: "Extra Billy" Smith, who earned that nickname through the additional payments he drew from an ever-expanding mail contract, would one day stand on the steps of the old Patteson tavern. McDearmon next forwarded a small sheaf of bills that dealt with administrative issues in the new county, including one to organize the militia there and to reorganize it in the four old counties. The male citizens of military age in Appomattox County were assigned to the 174th Infantry Regiment, which was divided into two battalions, and McDearmon retained his major's commission with the command of one of those battalions.[24]

McDearmon also presented the House of Delegates with a petition from Appomattox County men—his father chief among them—who wanted to eliminate the precinct elections for delegates there. That was a cheeky request in light of arguments posed for the very creation of Appomattox County, where voters had so long protested the lengthy journeys to their county seats to cast their ballots, but such a change would have worked to Mr. McDearmon's political benefit. If voters had to come all the way to the courthouse to exercise the franchise, the greatest proportion of votes would come from the immediate vicinity of the county seat, where McDearmon's business presence gave him a substantial advantage over candidates from outlying districts.[25]

Perhaps such an advantage was unnecessary, at least for the present. Even as McDearmon submitted the petition, his supporters were writing to the *Richmond Enquirer* and the *Lynchburg Republican* to suggest his nomination as the Democratic candidate for the first election of a delegate from Appomattox County. Two county citizens presently held seats from their respective previous counties—McDearmon from Prince Edward and Thomas H. Flood, a Whig, from Buckingham—but the new county was allowed only one representative in the next election.

The 1846 nomination was confirmed in a "nonpartisan" meeting held on February 5 at Appomattox Court House—the new alternative designation for Clover Hill—when a committee of thirteen political leaders from the various districts of the county decided on McDearmon over Flood. Once the committee had announced its decision, McDearmon was invited in from an antechamber where he had been waiting expectantly. He accepted the nomination "in a becoming manner," though it would have been insincere to express any surprise that he had prevailed in a county now so heavily weighted with Democrats.[26]

Attendance at the February caucus illustrated how political power might gravitate toward someone who lived near the county seat. Of fifteen participants who were prominent enough to merit identification by the Lynchburg newspaper, at least seven lived within an hour's easy ride of Clover Hill, and those seven included the richest and most influential.

Dr. Joel Walker Flood, the wealthiest man in the county, chaired the meeting. The good doctor could boast real estate worth more than $50,000: he owned some 2,500 acres of land, most of it surrounding the plantation he called Pleasant Retreat, two miles northeast of Appomattox Court House on the stage road. His son, Henry, who served on the nominating committee, lived three miles west of the county seat on a 1,700-acre plantation his father had just deeded to him the previous year. Between them, father and son owned a hundred slaves of taxable age (besides scores of children and elderly), some fine carriages that included an enclosed coach, and three dozen horses. For the pleasure of his new wife (who was also his close cousin), Henry Flood had bought one of the only five pianos in the county.[27]

The political wizard of Appomattox seemed to be Thomas Bocock, the thirty-year-old commonwealth attorney who had already served one term in the legislature. Bocock chaired the nomination committee, and his brother Charles, a young medical student who lived with him, served as secretary of the meeting. Another Bocock brother, Henry, was the county clerk; the eldest sibling, Willis, was still sitting as Buckingham County's second delegate in Richmond. Thomas Bocock owned a modest estate compared to the holdings of his social peers, but he was blessed with sharp instincts and a golden tongue. He connected himself to those who could do him some good, and at that very moment he was courting seventeen-year-old Sarah Flood, a not-so-distant cousin of his (his mother was a Flood) and the daughter of the Whig delegate whose name the committee had just rejected. The marriage would make him a brother-in-law of Democrat Henry Flood.[28]

The Whigs fielded no legislative candidate in Appomattox that spring of 1846; in a region so dominated by the Democrats it would have been a losing fight. In order to express their political differences, most men sought variations within the Democratic Party. McDearmon billed himself as a Locofoco Democrat: the nickname had been coined in New York City a decade before, when party regulars tried to stifle a reform faction by dousing the gaslights at a strategic point in their convention;

the reformers had foiled that ploy by producing some newly invented friction matches (called "locofocos") and lighting candles. Locofocoism had its philosophical roots in antagonism toward the privileged class that McDearmon was striving so diligently to attain. The irony of his Locofoco attachment was muted, however, both by the relatively moderate circumstances of his origins—at least compared to the Floods and Tidewater patricians—and by his efforts to improve his situation through business enterprise: Samuel McDearmon might have been ambitious, but he was no aristocrat, and it was the virtual aristocracy of the eastern seaboard that fueled Locofoco ire.

Tenets of the Locofoco doctrine included hatred of tariffs and banks, and McDearmon shared those prejudices. Tariffs favored only the industrialized North, while state banks holding federal deposits had precipitated the panic of 1837 with their rampant land speculation and inflated currency. Like most of his neighbors, McDearmon favored an independent U.S. treasury and the withdrawal of all federal funds from local banks: that would remove the banks from the bidding when it came to further speculation, and if McDearmon wanted to borrow money he would go to his relatives and friends.

Also like most of his fellow Appomattox citizens, McDearmon supported the annexation of Texas as a state, which had now been accomplished. That was not a Locofoco demand, but a Southern one, and there would be hell to pay as a result.[29]

Almost immediately after McDearmon's nomination some of the Democrats dissented, offering instead the names of Thomas A. LeGrand (a Baptist minister who had served on the nominating committee) and Zacheus Cheatham (a farmer, War of 1812 veteran, and militia colonel), both of whom were in their fifties. Only Cheatham showed any interest, initially casting himself as an independent Locofoco Democrat to further distinguish himself and to give his neighbors "the opportunity of selecting between men," but when the votes were cast at the end of April McDearmon was reelected without opposition.[30]

If McDearmon had no competition for the legislature, he did have some in his reluctant capacity as a tavernkeeper. Days before the April election, John Raine announced the opening of what he called the Clover Hill Tavern, with room and board for man and horse at $1.50 per day; individual meals were two bits, and a bed alone would cost twelve and a half cents a night. Raine invited all who had formerly partaken of his hospitality at the old Patteson establishment to stay with him at his new place, a two-story frame house a hundred yards west of the Patteson tavern and across the stage road, on Hugh Raine's reserved lot. Raine's house sat tight against the road, for his son had plans for a more spacious guest house in the middle of the lot.[31]

Raine's choice of name for his new hostelry probably irritated McDearmon, for the Patteson place had sometimes been called the Clover Hill Tavern, and Raine might enjoy some benefit from the confusion, at McDearmon's expense. For that matter, the new hotel would diminish McDearmon's trade whatever its name; that must have become evident within days, when rural denizens flocked to Clover Hill for the election. A few weeks later the summer season began, and wealthy Virginians started flooding into the mountains from the Tidewater and the Deep South: western Virginia was dotted with palatial resorts encircling warm mineral springs, and travelers flocked to them for the relief of every malady from ruptures to rheumatism, or simply to escape the yellow fever season on the coast. The Lynchburg coaches brought all such passengers through Appomattox Court House.[32]

The taverns at the county seat would also have shared profit from the patriotic excesses of the annual Fourth of July celebrations, the first of which was held at Appomattox Court House that year. These events drew listeners—and revelers—from every reach of the county. The officers of the county militia regiment all turned out, with many of their men; under the reorganization bill that Major McDearmon had inspired, the captains all cast ballots for new field officers. McDearmon's chagrin at losing some of the tavern trade that day may have been compensated by his election as lieutenant colonel; his fellow citizens instantly employed the new title whenever they addressed him.[33]

That Fourth of July began with threatening skies, but a big crowd surprised everyone. There was the customary reading of the Declaration of Independence, a speech or two (lacking one from the spellbinding Thomas Bocock, who declined a call to speak because of "indisposition"), and a barbecue that was followed by endless toasts. Appropriately enough, the deluge of liquid acknowledgments was begun by Dr. Flood, who urged the sons of Revolutionary soldiers to emulate the examples of their fathers. Samuel Walker, Samuel McDearmon's brother-in-law and his successor as major in the regiment, recognized Bartholomew Cyrus, the only Revolutionary veteran at the banquet.

"May his last days be his best," asked Major Walker. Although Cyrus was just short of ninety, he took a glass and returned a toast to the spirit of his own generation.

Such traditional reflections on 1776 ended early this year, though, for war with Mexico had commenced just two months before, and most of those who raised their glasses thereafter alluded to more immediate events, according to party platform. Less enthusiastic about James Polk's war, Whigs tended to praise generals or candidates of their own political persuasion. Colonel Benjamin Walker of the 174th Regiment, a Whig from the northern end of the county, commended Zachary Taylor; the major, who shared his brother's sentiments, hoped that Winfield Scott would be protected from President Polk's "assaults" upon him. Dr. William Christian called for speedy peace with Mexico and continued peace with Great Britain, with which Polk had been jousting over the Oregon boundary. With fluid metaphor, one brave soul toasted "Colonel T. H. Flood: long the Whig tide of Buckingham; surely not diked by Appomattox Locofocoism."

Despite his indisposition, Thomas Bocock could not let such remarks pass without comment upon General Scott, who had twice sought the Whig nomination for president and whose correspondence with Polk and the secretary of war alluded to both his dietary habits and his fear that the administration would be as dangerous an enemy as the Mexicans.

"We thank him for what he has done for his country," said Bocock, "and only wish that during the next presidential term he may take his 'hasty plate of soup' in privacy, without fear of enemies either in front or rear."

Court clerk Henry Bocock tried to steer the celebration away from partisan conflict with a toast to the ladies of Appomattox ("as patriotic as they are fair"), but once his brother had begun to speak he found it hard to stop. The commonwealth attorney next hailed John C. Calhoun, the patron saint of Southern radicals. Others shouted for Andrew Jackson, and for the state of Texas. Samuel McDearmon scoffed at the Mexicans and British alike. Whigs came back with Henry Clay, and the written record hints that the atmosphere grew strained, but a series of self-congratulatory toasts finally seemed to restore conviviality.

"The citizens of Appomattox," bellowed a young farmer. "May they ever be united: not to consider stage roads, or other highways, as constituting points for division, either in civil, military, or political point of view."

Zacheus Cheatham concurred, noting that with the election of its militia officers the county of Appomattox was fully organized at last.

"May union and brotherly love exist among us," he concluded.[34]

On court day, the Thursday after that first Fourth of July barbecue, the county commissioners awarded the lowest bidder a contract to build the new courthouse. It was to be a two-story brick structure, forty feet wide and about that deep, with four massive chimneys in the expansive Georgian style that Virginians favored from colonial times, but with a touch of Greek Revival in the cornice and the porch pediments that protected the front and rear entrances. The courthouse would radically change the face of the infant village, for it was to sit in the middle of the stage road, which would be divided to pass around it on either side. Travelers coming over the bluff from the Appomattox or trotting east from Lynchburg would be guided straight toward the opposing entrances to this new and most imposing edifice at Clover Hill.[35]

The name of this contractor would be lost to history in a fire that consumed this very building forty-five years after he completed it, but he soon had a platoon of carpenters, bricklayers, and laborers on the scene. Those who were not slaves, hired from local owners, would have taken lodging at one or the other of the taverns. That regular rent could only have helped Samuel McDearmon, whose income from the Clover Hill tract that year amounted only to the sale of a portion of two lots immediately south of the courthouse site. The partial lots had gone to Pryor Wright, an aging farmer with political aspirations; Wright had spent his six decades in isolated little plantation houses like the one he now owned, a few hundred yards to the south, and with a new brood of late-life children he thought he might like to live in a village, if only one would sprout.[36]

For the next five years, Samuel McDearmon moved every obstacle he could to assure that the village of Appomattox Court House did germinate, and at the same time he stretched his own credit, his father's, and that of anyone else he could enlist in order to buy as much of the surrounding countryside as he could persuade the owners to sell him. As neighbors died off, he approached each of their survivors with an offer of cash for their respective interests in the estate. When the sheriff auctioned off land, McDearmon bought it even if it meant going into partnership on it with someone else. Nor did he confine his speculation to the vicinity of the courthouse, allying himself with the sheriff to buy 626 acres on Cub Creek, picking up a gristmill and sawmill on the Falling River, and hedging his bets with a town lot in Farmville, the market center and eventual shire town of Prince Edward County.[37]

All the while, McDearmon hoped to finance the notes for these purchases with rent and lot sales at Clover Hill, or by the sale of the tavern parcel. No one seemed interested in the tavern, however, and lots moved slowly. On the western edge of the village, David Robertson built an old brick blacksmith shop on one side of the stage road and bought a partial lot on the other side where he built a massive stable, each of which he rented out for $25 a year; the Raines leased the stable for the use of their guests and the stage line. By 1848 the Bocock brothers had traded the single piece they had initially bought for six contiguous lots on the southwest corner of the courthouse, and that year they began the cellar of a typical Virginia farmhouse, not unlike Raine's new tavern: two stories tall, wide and shallow, with the front door in the middle of the long wall. Pryor Wright built a solid, square brick home on his adjoining lot fragments, just off the courthouse lawn.

The Raines, too, began construction of yet another tavern that year on their lot west of the courthouse. John Raine now shared his role of innkeeper with his oldest son, George, who would manage this latest establishment. Like Wright's house and the Patteson tavern, this house would be brick, with chimneys climbing up either side wall; children from the surrounding countryside watched as the bricks were formed and baked right there in the yard. It sat facing into a gentle slope south of the stage road, with its cellar largely above ground. The cellar contained the winter kitchen on one side and on the other a big room that could serve either as a dining hall or an additional bedroom; above this were two more floors, on each of which two spacious rooms faced each other across a central hallway. George Raine evidently intended to accommodate his own wife and three children in the house, while his father, mother, two brothers, two sisters, brother-in-law, and two nephews lived in the old stand; otherwise, he would never have found room for the traveling public.

Young Raine promised the best meals, round-the-clock lodging, and ample stalls for animals. To the undoubted relief of Samuel McDearmon, Raine abandoned the name Clover Hill Tavern and billed this house as the Raine tavern, throwing open the doors in the summer of 1849. Before the last of the mortar had cured, another of his uncles assumed the actual ownership of both the new brick tavern and the clapboard house that stood in front of it, alongside the road—where, if any rooms remained empty, they could rent to the tradesmen who had come to build the town or make their living in it.[38]

Samuel McDearmon hired some of those artisans himself, putting up a big brick store just a few yards east of the old Patteson tavern. Another young local entrepreneur, Benjamin Nowlin, swallowed enough of McDearmon's professed confidence in the future of the village to rent this building and fill it with merchandise, buttressing the McDearmon empire a little longer. By 1851 John Plunkett had established a second store in a frame building on the northwest corner of the town center, which McDearmon sold him along with a panhandle piece of the tavern lot.

That nearly completed the village. The Patteson tavern and its adjoining guest house filled up with clerks from the two stores, itinerant doctors, lawyers, clergymen, teachers, and as many as three saddlers, who repaired harness for both the stage line and individual travelers. McDearmon installed a onetime captain from his militia regiment as hotel keeper, and supplied a barkeeper for the little groggery he had thrown together between the tavern and the brick storehouse.

Then McDearmon built his own house, on a slope that looked down upon the village and the valley of the upper Appomattox from half a mile to the north. Inspired by the stately plantation houses of the Tidewater, he chose a broad Georgian design with a hipped roof, thereby achieving an architectural atmosphere that many of his neighbors must have considered pretentious in a backwater farmhouse, however popular it may have been along the lower James.[39]

Most Appomattox residents owned plain, quadrangular cabins or farmhouses, some of which had been expanded with equally plain, blocky additions. As the century reached its midpoint, half a dozen families lived in such houses within a mile radius of the village.

Three-quarters of a mile north by a farm lane sat the home of James Williams, a carpenter still in his twenties. Williams found considerable business at Appomattox Court House these days and was able to support his wife and son on an independent homestead. Except for professionals, sons of the very wealthy, and fortunate heirs, most young men with families found it necessary to either dwell in separate buildings on the family farm or to board in the same houses with their parents.[40]

Northeast of Clover Hill, on the stage road, lived the Sweeney clan, most of whom enjoyed life tenancy on their property rather than perpetual title: Samuel McDearmon now owned the balance of the rights. Wheelwright John Sweeney, born during the Revolution, lived in the old family home along the north bank of the Appomattox with his wife and their talented brood, who ranged in age from eighteen to nearly forty: Richard, Elizabeth, Missouri, and Sampson remained at home, and when Joel was not touring the country he stayed there, too. Just up the hill, these Sweeneys could see the tiny cabin where their uncle, Charles Sweeney, lived: two children still shared cramped quarters there with their parents. Downhill from John, through the orchard, Charlie's older son Robert, the left-handed fiddle player, had moved his little family into an even smaller cabin hard against the riverbank; Bob and his wife had found themselves parents of a baby girl at eighteen, just as Cousin Joel returned from his European tour.[41]

Cut by the north branch of the Appomattox and Plain Run, the thick

woods due east of Clover Hill had not yet been penetrated by home builders. South of the village, though, three farms occupied a ridge that rose
on the far side of Plain Run. To the southeast, near the road to Prince
Edward Court House, Reverend Thomas LeGrand's widow maintained
his farm with her unmarried daughter and her teenage son. Eleven slaves
helped them to work the land. Half a mile west on the road that followed
the ridge, which came to be called the LeGrand Road, lived her brother-
in-law Archibald LeGrand, whose wife bore him at least fifteen children
during their marriage. A little farther west, down the ridge and within
pistol-shot of Plain Run, sat a rambling farmhouse owned by John Sears.
This farm had come to him through his first wife, a sister of Archibald
and Reverend LeGrand. She had died in 1843, however, and now he was
married to a widow, Martha Nowlin, who had brought still more property
with her; through this marriage Sears would come into part ownership
of some village property that Martha's son prized. Sears also had seven
children surviving from his first marriage.[42]

John Sears reached the village by a farm lane that bisected his land,
crossing Plain Run and intersecting the stage road a third of a mile west
of town. Another farm road, parallel to Sears Lane and a few hundred
yards farther from the village, led to Thomas Trent's farm, which lay on
the opposite bank of Plain Run from the Sears place. Trent's wife died
in the spring of 1850; his oldest son was away from home, so he placed
most of his younger children with neighbors, keeping house thereafter by
himself, with one teenage daughter. Trent's brother, William, lived on the
old family homestead beyond Plain Run, about two miles from the courthouse.[43]

But for two little farms worked by Abednego and Arthur Conner, a
quarter mile beyond the last Sweeney cabin, and Willis Inge's house, a
little farther out on the LeGrand Road, that was the extent of Appomattox Court House as the second half of the nineteenth century began. At a
distance of two and a half miles to the east on the stage road, Dr. Flood
probably did not consider his home at Pleasant Retreat part of the village community; nor did his son, Henry, whose home lay a similar distance
from it in the opposite direction. Descendants of the Pattesons who once
owned Clover Hill still maintained farms a couple of miles north of the village, but their names seldom graced the store ledgers at the courthouse.
The Bocock brothers did frequent the town, but largely on court or political business, and except for Henry they spent most of their time on their
plantations up in the Stonewall District, some six miles away.[44]

For all Samuel McDearmon's talk of growth and prosperity, the frontier had not left Appomattox County that far behind; the oldest residents might still have recalled childhood anxiety over rumored Indian raids. Barely two dozen people, a slight preponderance of them slaves, occupied each square mile of the county. If the relative isolation did not satisfy the white residents they at least accepted it, while the slaves had no choice.

Three-quarters of the employed white males still supported themselves and their families by farming, with the usual sprinkling of doctors, lawyers, clergymen, teachers, and artisans, for many of whom the more technical calling merely supplemented their farm income. It was not unusual for that time and region that the county had more clergymen or tanners than lawyers, and fewer teachers than blacksmiths, shoemakers, or wheelwrights. The stage road provided a few jobs for drivers, hotel keepers, service employees, and related tradesmen. Illustrating the long-standing reliance on the plantation economy, some of those craftsmen were slaves, hired out by their masters, with a rare free black man working as a wheelwright or blacksmith. Half a dozen officials worked for the county government, and in the northern fringe along the James River there lived ten miners and foundrymen (two of them English immigrants and one a transplanted Marylander) who earned a marginal subsistence from an iron smelting operation. Like a number of prosperous farmers along the river, the owners of the iron foundry transported their supplies and product on the James River canal, which lay more than a dozen miles away from the courthouse by the nearest road.

Two subtle signs that things might be changing in Appomattox County were the numbers of retail occupations and skilled builders. Only one itinerant peddler still lived in the county, and even he kept a farm now, while twenty-seven citizens supported themselves as clerks or merchants. This was a new line of work, and it attracted the latest generation: a handful of farmers and millers kept stores in strategic locations, but twenty young men, averaging twenty-seven years in age, pursued retail trade exclusive of the more traditional sidelines.

Meanwhile, 66 of the nearly 1,000 white men who identified with a particular occupation in 1850 named a construction trade, from carpentry and masonry to joinery and cabinetmaking. In an earlier day too many men owned a modicum of such skills, and the demands upon them were too light, for many to have claimed the occupational titles, but now three men—probably perceived as aliens, hailing from Pennsylvania and New Jersey—considered themselves contractors.[45]

Few could have recognized such gradual trends at the time. For most of those who saw the sun rise over the valley of the upper Appomattox during the abbreviated presidency of Zachary Taylor, society still resembled a revered feudal past. Thriving on captive labor, vast fiefdoms dominated the landscape, interspersed with smaller freeholds that occupied proportionately smaller forces of bondsmen—or no bondsmen at all: upwards of half the county households included no servants. Unwritten law prescribed the relations between gentry, yeoman, and peasant, while more formal codes regulated the conduct of the slave. Life revolved around the crops, as it always had.

Most prominent among those crops was tobacco: Appomattox farmers reaped nearly a million pounds of the not-yet-noxious weed in the year President Taylor died. Antebellum Virginia was also cornbread country, and county farms grew 187,000 bushels of Indian corn that same year, yielding about half that volume of oats and still less wheat. The harvest included about 10,000 bushels each in Irish potatoes and sweet potatoes. Ten thousand hogs comprised the main meat source for local consumption, and 6,600 sheep produced not only mutton but nearly 15,000 pounds of wool. More than 4,500 beef and dairy cattle supplemented the rural diet.[46]

Horses remained the most popular motive power, with 1,719 spread across the county. The larger farms accounted for most of them: Thomas H. Flood, Dr. Flood, and his son, Henry, kept four dozen horses themselves, while the Walker brothers, Samuel and Benjamin, owned more than thirty; Samuel McDearmon paid taxes on thirteen at the height of his success, and those who owned any horses usually kept at least two or three. Most of that horseflesh was devoted to farm labor, harnessed either to wagons or plows; thanks to the efforts of Cyrus McCormick of nearby Rockbridge County, a limited number of more sophisticated agricultural implements were also available, at least for bringing in the grain crops. The more affluent citizens indulged themselves and their womenfolk with more comfortable horse-drawn conveyances, however: three different pleasure carriages sat hub to hub in Dr. Flood's stable, and two in Thomas Flood's, while Henry flaunted his fortune with the finest coach in the county. McDearmon owned three rigs when he first bought the Clover Hill Tavern, but within five years he had exchanged them for a formal coach and a light buggy. Some Appomattox families did not own horses, opting instead for oxen. Scattered farmers experimented with mules, but that hybrid was relatively new and rare in the county and would have been a rich man's novelty. The poorest did without animal power altogether.[47]

Militia service, which amounted by then to a leisure activity, only added to the medieval atmosphere of midcentury life. By statute the county regiment consisted of two battalions of eight companies apiece, which allowed for the election of four field officers and eighty company officers, for each company was authorized two first and two second lieutenants, as well as a captain. Companies usually fielded fewer than five dozen enlisted men, but the generous distribution of commissions helped to satisfy the Southern predilection for military titles. Once having donned the gaudy epaulets of a militia officer, a man customarily carried that rank to his grave, and the Piedmont teemed with men who luxuriated in being addressed as captain so-and-so, although in most cases if their swords ever drew any blood, it was their own.

While few of those officers who flourished on the parade ground at Clover Hill distinguished themselves on any battlefield, they could generally boast some distinction in their community. Militiamen elected their company officers, and captains elected the field officers. Social status tended to outweigh other factors, including apparently length of service, and the Appomattox regiment came out of its first election in 1846 with three field officers (the Walker brothers and McDearmon) who collectively owned $80,000 in real estate and 137 slaves. Companies were most often commanded by respected farmers or professionals, although those offices sometimes became available to the upwardly mobile: Joseph Godsey, a landless laborer when he was in his early thirties, eventually came to own one small farm and to serve as overseer on another, and on the way he was elected captain of an infantry company.[48]

Already content with his station, the true grandee seldom participated in the militia, but his son might accept a lieutenancy in the local company. If such a subaltern failed to meet even the militia standard of competence, however, or if he ignored enough musters, he could find himself replaced by a more enthusiastic candidate.

Scores of such eager young men, and some not so young, stepped forward when a company of volunteer cavalry was added to the regiment in the spring of 1848. Sixty-five men signed their names to the roll, donned new uniforms, and elected the twenty-five-year-old merchant Benjamin Nowlin as their captain. Nowlin's younger brother James, a doctor, rode beside him as first lieutenant when the company paraded before Colonel Walker for the first time, and not far behind followed Second Lieutenant Thomas Trent, who remained an able horseman at sixty-two. The troop enhanced that year's Fourth of July celebration with another parade, and Joel Sweeney brought some of his minstrel company to liven the festivities. Dr. Nowlin resigned before his three-year enlistment expired—as did Trent, whose wife was dying—and the other second lieutenant was removed for some unstated failing; the cavalrymen selected Sweeney, George Raine, and another young physician to replace them.[49]

Colonel Walker surrendered his commission just before the spring elections of 1849. Samuel McDearmon was chosen to fill his place without competition, for in the field grades it seemed traditional to elect men to the next vacancy above them; that assured more openings below, as well, with a chance for one captain to move up. Colonel was about as high as a militia officer could climb in an organization that never saw brigade musters, so when McDearmon sat at the head table on the Fourth of July that year, and presided over the festivities of the annual muster, he had achieved all the military glory that Appomattox County could offer. His economic star had also reached its zenith, had he but known it. For that matter, the fortunes of all his neighbors lay on the brink of an uncertain dimension.[50]

THE RAILROAD

Colonel McDearmon had taken a sabbatical from politics, leaving his seat in the House of Delegates to Henry Flood. During his sojourn at home, McDearmon funded the construction of a substantial building on an acre of land just south of the village, across the Prince Edward Court House Road. He carved the lot off from the Clover Hill parcel for a joint stock company that evidently hoped to found an academy there. No private school ever seems to have occupied the building, but eventually the overseers of the county poor took it over: here, probably, is where the most indigent Appomattox children learned their letters. Barbara Wright, a young local woman who suffered from skeletal deformities, devoted herself to their education from the inception of the new county.

Even with major construction projects, the county seat soon proved too idle for McDearmon. He evidently felt that his own economic interests were not being satisfactorily addressed by his successor in the House of Delegates, and during the first fortnight of 1850 the former delegate announced that he would challenge the incumbent. Come spring, he beat Flood nearly four to one.[1]

While McDearmon conducted this campaign, the fruits of national policies he had espoused five years before were threatening the very unity of the federal government. The first of the territory won during the Mexican War, California, had applied for admission to the union as a free state: Southerners, most of whom wished to see slavery expanded into the Mexican cessions, rankled at what they perceived as an abridgment of their own manifest destiny. As the fateful year of 1850 began, there came a call for a convention of Southern delegates in Nashville—where, many feared, the main topic might be the dissolution of the United States. Hinting broadly

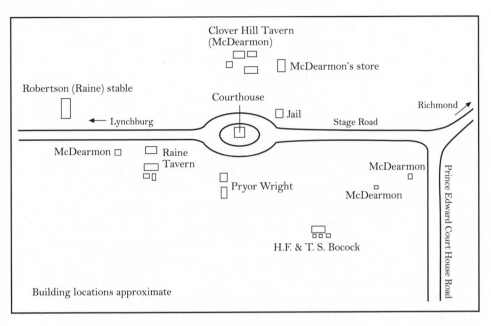

Map 2. Appomattox Court House, 1850

at secession if the slave states' rights were not recognized, the *Richmond Enquirer* maintained that the fate of the nation hung in the balance.

Somehow things did not go that far, at least just then. The most radical slave power advocate, Senator John C. Calhoun, and the most stubborn foe of the radicals, President Taylor, both died within a few weeks of each other. That freed Henry Clay, a slaveowning Kentucky Whig, to forward a five-point compromise measure that acknowledged the constitutionality of slavery and promised the South a fugitive slave law (which would enable slaveowners to retrieve their property in free states) in return for allowing California into the union, forbidding the sale of slaves within the national capital, and prohibiting slavery anywhere north of Missouri's long Arkansas boundary all the way to the Pacific. The compromise deflated the Nashville convention, and soon at least Whig newspapers in Richmond had returned to more fraternal descriptions of the Northern states.[2]

Secession, slavery, and compromise may have dominated much of the daily conversation at Clover Hill's taverns and stores, and Samuel McDearmon raged against Northern "aggression" as loudly as anyone, but the issue that most concerned Appomattox citizens—and their new delegate to Richmond—was internal improvements. By 1850 an old plan to build a railroad from Petersburg to Lynchburg seemed to have come to life, and its route would take it right through Appomattox County; in early December (just as McDearmon resumed his legislative seat in Richmond) the chief engineer of the Southside Railroad advertised for bids on grading and masonry along another sixteen miles of the road. That would bring it almost to Farmville by the first day of 1852. McDearmon would have wanted a hand in not only supporting that line but, if possible, in directing its course; he also harbored a special interest in building a plank road from Clover Hill to the James River canal at Bent Creek, all of which would require his attendance in the state assembly.[3]

No sooner had McDearmon arrived in the capital than he lent his support to a bill authorizing the state to subscribe to 60 percent of the Southside Railroad stock. Under previous incarnations that company had failed for lack of funds, and McDearmon was not about to let it happen again. The bill passed in February, and a few weeks later McDearmon met success in his campaign for a state-funded plank road to the county seat; plank roads served as Virginia's answer to its four-month mud season, though the expense of lumber by the mile precluded their use on any but main thoroughfares. It did not hurt McDearmon's political popularity that his advocacy of such internal improvements (at least within his district) preempted the traditional principles of his Whig opponents. In his role as a rabid sectional advocate, which may have contributed even more to his overwhelming victory, McDearmon also presented the legislature with a petition from the "Appomattox States Rights Association." The petition called for legislation to implement a policy of "nonintercourse" with Northern states, and it marked the militia colonel as a true Southern hotspur.[4]

Nonintercourse became the rallying cry of the fire-eaters whose rhetoric would help tear the country apart. *De Bow's Review,* a New Orleans monthly, began advocating social and economic separation from the North almost as soon as Henry Clay's compromise had been adopted: dissatisfied with the South's half of that bargain, its contributors argued for practical secession if the political variety could not be achieved. Under nonintercourse the South would seek freedom through industrialization — weaving its own cloth from its own cotton in order to "pay no more tribute to northern looms." Southern merchants would buy their own ships, to avoid the triangular trade that carried such high tariffs. Manufacturing would be expanded to relieve the dependence on Northern industry. Southerners would put an end to their Northern summer vacations. Perhaps most appealing to Colonel McDearmon, this radical doctrine called for the South to build its own railroads and plank roads. The petition from Appomattox failed to elicit the desired statutory revisions, but the sentiment lingered and grew; within a few years, the *Richmond Enquirer* was insisting upon "the declaration of our independence of the North in commercial, literary and other matters of equal importance."[5]

When McDearmon returned home that spring of 1851, he found his community momentarily unconcerned about national affairs, or even about local roads. Just now, Appomattox Court House was buzzing with the whispered talk of fever. Charles Bocock, who had just finished his medical education and had not yet reached the age of twenty-nine, had fallen ill soon after returning to Wildway, his brother Thomas's plantation nearly six miles from the courthouse. Thomas, finishing his second term in Congress, was still away at Washington when his youngest brother gave up the ghost on April 16.

Perhaps the young doctor had paid a fateful call—either social or professional—at the Raine house. The Raine family endured persistent hard luck: few of them would live out the decade. They had not yet emerged from mourning over the death of George's twenty-month-old daughter, the previous August, when his infant nephew turned sick. The nephew did not last long, and his grandfather followed him immediately. "Captain" John Raine perished on April 17 and was buried alongside his grandchildren in the family cemetery, just outside the village.[6]

Gravestones still standing in Appomattox cemeteries hint that the warm months may have been deadlier than winter in a day when so many outdoor privies sat near shallow wells. Typhoid, spread to water and food through contaminated fecal matter, periodically raged through the South —it was one of those "malignant diseases" that Samuel McDearmon had advertised as so conspicuously absent from Clover Hill. It was never altogether absent, however, nor very far away. Typhoid took the blame for killing some Appomattox citizens every year, and—along with unrecognized scourges like leukemia and diabetes—may have been responsible for some of the many unexplained deaths that Henry Bocock recorded each year. Typhoid was not invariably fatal once it lodged in the intestines, but some strains must have proven more virulent than others, for survival rates varied according to the outbreak. One family that lived north of the courthouse was all but wiped out by this ailment in the summer of 1857: Fanny Sears watched her little sister, her teenage brother, and both her parents die of it within a two-month period. Only fifteen herself, Fannie took her three younger siblings to live with their grandfather, near Walker's Church; her father's brother, meanwhile, died of the same disease a month later. Thirty-two of the 115 known causes of death in the county that year were attributed to typhoid fever.[7]

Respiratory complaints took an even heavier and more steady toll. During the summer of 1850 the assistant marshal of the census tallied 143 deaths in Appomattox County over the previous year, but he was able to record causes for only 92. Typhoid accounted for only 3 of them that year, and an assortment of other fevers took 9 victims. Consumption alone, meanwhile, killed 14 residents; other afflictions of the lungs, from colds, "cold plague," and "congestion" to pneumonia and pleurisy carried off another 17.

The sheer fragility of life flavored much of antebellum Southern culture. By the time they had reached their allotted threescore and ten, assuming they did so, most men had buried at least one wife, and almost any who had fathered children had also buried one or more of them. Children suffered the highest mortality of any age group: 28.6 percent of the white citizens who died between July of 1849 and the following June were under the age of ten; even more striking, 25.7 percent of the white mortality consisted of children aged one year or less. With little medical attention and crowded living conditions, slave children fared even worse: nearly 53 percent of the slaves who died that year were under ten, and more than 36 percent of the total had not passed their first year. During those same twelve months eleven Appomattox residents died of scrofula, a milk-borne tuberculosis that settled in the lymph nodes of the neck; all eleven of the victims were slaves, and most of them children. The overall rate of black mortality—which did not happen to include any of the county's 184 free blacks in 1850—ran almost three times higher than the proportion of white deaths.

Curiously, the records that yield so phenomenal an infant mortality do not demonstrate a correspondingly high rate of death associated with childbirth. The schedule that lists forty-eight infant deaths in 1850 also names thirteen women who died between the ages of fourteen and forty-nine, four of them white and nine black: only two of them, both slaves, died of "miscarriage" and "childbed fever." [8]

Newspapers and cemeteries, however, reveal motherhood to have been an especially risky undertaking. Henry Flood had gotten his first wife with child in 1838, when she was only fifteen; the girl perished barely two weeks after the birth of that baby, whom the grieving widower named Joel Walker Flood Jr. in honor of his own father. On the very day in 1845 that the new justices of Appomattox met to appoint their county officers, Willis Inge's young wife died at their home on the LeGrand Road; she left her husband and seven children, the last of them a newborn. The following spring John McKinney, who bought Samuel Walker's farm on the Oakville Road, lost his twenty-one-year-old wife a few days after the birth of their second child.[9]

Nor was childbearing the sole maternal peril. Like most Southerners of their era, Appomattox men generally sired large families that created enormous burdens for their wives. Maintaining a teeming household exhausted women who lacked domestic servants: those who survived the constitutional attrition of repeated pregnancies and the increased odds of complications in labor then found themselves susceptible, through chronic fatigue, to myriad lurking diseases. When John Sears's first wife died in 1843, shortly after her thirty-seventh birthday, they had eight living children between two years old and sixteen; three years later Temple and Martha Richardson still had ten children at home under the age of fifteen, including an infant, when Martha died at forty-two; Archibald LeGrand's wife, Caroline, expired from heart failure in June 1857, at the age of only forty-seven, a year after giving birth to the last of at least fifteen children over the previous three decades.[10]

Emotional fatigue sometimes turned deadly, too. Saluda Gilliam, who was ten years younger than Caroline LeGrand, died on the same day as that woman at her home near the Prince Edward County line: whether overcome by the endless drudgery of motherhood, by the agony of burying earlier children, or by postpartum depression following the birth of her latest child, she met her end by swallowing an overdose of opium.[11]

All of the widowers left by these women remarried, and some of them did so in desperate haste. Judging by the birth dates of their subsequent children, Willis Inge waited perhaps four months to take a second wife, choosing one who was more than a dozen years younger than his first one, while Archibald LeGrand married again only a few weeks after Caroline's death.[12]

Temple Richardson was fifty years old when his wife died. He mourned a little longer than Inge or LeGrand before remarrying, but when he did it was with plans for a second family. He found a woman more than two decades his junior, installed her among his remaining children, and greeted their first child by the fourth anniversary of his first wife's death; within another decade his household was dominated by the offspring of this second family.

Richardson's neighbors found little material for gossip in his productivity. Many Appomattox farmers married late, or began again with a new woman after the death of the first. Pryor Wright saw his last daughter born in his new brick house alongside the courthouse when he was sixty-three; Jacob Tibbs waited until his late forties to marry a woman in her teens, and they were still producing children after he reached his mid-sixties.

Whether bachelors or widowers, these settled farmers offered single young women financial security that most of their younger suitors had not attained (whatever other attractions they might have had), and in the early 1850s more than one sixteen-year-old girl consigned her future to a man pushing fifty. Sixteen was not especially young for a bride, anyway: in the decade before secession at least one girl of fourteen was escorted before a local minister, as well as several more who were only fifteen. Even wealthy planters gave their youthful daughters away to middle-aged men without a qualm, and considered them lucky if they had attracted a professional with a promising career. Thomas and Henry Bocock, respectively congressman and court clerk, and both over thirty, had chosen to pursue girls younger than eighteen. In 1838 Henry Flood married Thomas Trent's daughter, Mary Elizabeth, when she was only fifteen. She died a few months later from postnatal complications, and in the third summer after her death Henry selected another bride of the same name, his cousin Mary Elizabeth Flood, who was just sixteen.[13]

Samuel McDearmon's own daughter, who was only fifteen herself, had caught the attention of a mere store clerk ten years her senior, and McDearmon seems not to have objected. By the end of another year, she and David Plunkett would be married.

David Plunkett worked for his father in the new store just off the courthouse door. Plunkett's father also owned a store at Spout Spring, about seven miles down the Lynchburg Road, and late in 1850 or early in 1851 the elder Plunkett had bought a building and part of a lot from McDearmon on the southwest corner of the tavern, where he thought another mercantile establishment might offer Benjamin Nowlin some real competition.[14]

Plunkett's purchase had helped little with McDearmon's notes on the Clover Hill land, all of which had now passed their collection dates. Of the money he had borrowed from his uncle to launch his venture he had made only one small payment at the end of 1845; the uncle was now dead, but heirs in the form of other nephews wanted to see the estate reimbursed. He still owed R. K. Raine $2,300 on the notes for the balance on the tavern parcel, and he had paid nothing since 1848. Raine was taking the issue to court, as were a number of lesser creditors. Meanwhile, McDearmon had borrowed several hundred dollars more from William Trent, paying back a little over half of it, and upwards of $2,000 from his wife's brothers. For temporary relief he even appears to have dipped into the treasury of the local Masonic Lodge, of which he was guardian, for when he tallied his holdings to satisfy his creditors he reserved a debt of $290 to that lodge from his liquible assets. These debts and smaller notes would be due at intervals beginning the first of the year, and the gristmill that he now owned in common with another brother-in-law was starting to accrue its own debts. The $550 he realized in annual rent, principally from Nowlin's store, hardly met the interest on his debts.[15]

Still, McDearmon remained optimistic. If only the railroad would reach the county seat in time, his investments could still yield the profits he had hoped. The iron rails were already halfway to Farmville, and ought to reach Appomattox within another year or two, but debtors threatened to relieve him of his assets before they achieved their maximum potential value. His credit had worn thin on all fronts, and he needed cash for expenses that others might have charged. The previous spring he had borrowed $3,000 from his younger brother, an unmarried doctor. That had helped fend off importuning creditors for a time, and covered operating costs for the tavern and mill, but there was a bottom to that bucket.[16]

For Samuel McDearmon, the answer to entrepreneurial woes was more enterprise. Another opportunity offered itself in the summer of 1851, when the Southside Railroad first crossed the Appomattox River below Farmville. There, for the first time west of Petersburg, Chief Engineer C. O. Sanford encountered a serious topographical difficulty. Over the millennia the river had carved a broad valley with steep bluffs, and Sanford answered nature's impediment by designing a long timber-truss bridge atop towering brick piers. Each pier would stand over a hundred feet tall and at least one-third that wide; the breadth of the riverbottom called for nearly a score of them. A well-connected Prince Edward County investor joined with McDearmon and another partner to offer as low a bid as they dared on the masonry, and in August they learned that they had undercut everyone else; even the early newspaper reports of their successful bid implied some doubt of their ability to do the job properly at that price. Before winter, gangs of hired slaves were mixing mortar on the great flats of the Appomattox, beginning the supports for what would soon become both the first railway cantilever in North America and the highest railroad bridge of such length in the world.[17]

Within days of learning that he and his partners had won the contract for the great bridge, McDearmon also discovered some bad news. The next thirty miles of the railbed grading was being offered for bid, running from the bridge below Farmville to the James River, on the western edge of Appomattox County: perhaps McDearmon reviewed the layout and specifications with hope of further business, but even if he abstained from the bidding he could not have failed to notice that the proposed route carried the tracks three miles west of Appomattox Court House.[18]

That layout jeopardized everything McDearmon had worked for in the past six years, for a journey of three miles over Virginia's bottomless roads in winter or spring offered little of the convenience that would have augmented the value of courthouse property. To have recognized the disaster that had just befallen him, though, McDearmon would have had to own unusual foresight, for even many of those who were busy promoting railroads in 1851 did not realize the extent of the transportation revolution in which they participated. McDearmon may have been one of those who did, however, for his next step suggested that he wished to avert this calamity somehow, or at least mitigate it.

Two weeks before contractors accepted the Appomattox section of the railroad, McDearmon won appointment as the Democratic Party's designated spokesman for the Fifteenth Senatorial District, encompassing his own county, Campbell County, and the city of Lynchburg. McDearmon put that position to good use, and ten days later he was nominated for that state senate seat himself—wresting it, said some Whigs who may have wanted to divide the Democratic vote, from the duly chosen nominee. There followed two months of acrimonious journalistic skirmishing between the respective partisans of McDearmon and Lynchburg newspaperman Robert Glass (the other supposed nominee), with McDearmon painted as a "Simon-pure, logrolling, plank-road Democrat." One of McDearmon's critics accused him of forwarding the plank-road bill because "your town of Clover Hill, and your manufacturing mill at Bent Creek, we suspect, entered very largely into your calculations at that time—your private interest swayed your actions." On the very day of the election, December 8, McDearmon positioned supporters at the polls with documents purporting to prove his innocence of various opposition charges: Colonel Benjamin Walker, McDearmon's former militia commander and now his Whig contender for the senate seat, had assigned similar agents with instructions to respond in kind, and the two factions tangled with some nasty rhetoric before the votes were finally cast. The campaign raised sores that throbbed for months afterward, confusing party boundaries as McDearmon's father and his surviving brother, the Whig doctor, rallied to his defense.[19]

This election marked the first time that all adult male Virginians could vote—a new constitution having finally removed the ancient property requirement—but the additional voters worked few changes at the polls.

Overall, Appomattox Democrats savored their customary advantage that year: Thomas Bocock eclipsed his Whig rival for the district congressional seat, while his brother, Willis Bocock, eased into the attorney general's office in Richmond. But the would-be spoiler, Glass, siphoned off nearly a thousand Democratic votes in the senate race, and McDearmon barely squeezed into the senate with a plurality of just a dozen votes over Walker. However slim the margin, Colonel McDearmon was now Senator McDearmon, and if there were a way to reroute the Southside Railroad he was in a position to find it.[20]

McDearmon secured an assignment to the committee on roads and internal navigation as his first order of business. That took care of two of the major types of transportation; in an effort to exert control over the third, he voted against a charter for an extension to the Orange & Alexandria Railroad, which would connect Lynchburg with Charlottesville and, eventually, the Potomac. That connection would inevitably diminish traffic through Appomattox, especially after a planned route from Lynchburg to Tennessee came to fruition.

With less enthusiasm, McDearmon presented the senate clerk with a petition from some of his constituents in the southern fringe of Appomattox County: in the latest foray of the battle for power with the county seat clique, several dozen voters demanded a new precinct. They asked, too, for approval before the election of new judges in April, arguing that the precinct would serve at least forty voters who would never make the fifteen-mile ride to Clover Hill. McDearmon could muster no reasonable argument against it, though all the prominent names on the petition belonged to active Whigs, and the legislature authorized three new voting places besides Clover Hill.[21]

Even if it were not for the directly partisan motive, precinct elections would hurt the new senator on two counts. His victory against Benjamin Walker had come partly because his opponent's home and greatest political base lay on the James River, a dozen inconvenient miles from the polling place, while McDearmon lived at the hub of county affairs; then there was the economic damage to bear, for election day profits at the taverns and stores would suffer without those thirsty, tired citizens who did slog in from the backcountry to cast their ballots.

By the summer of 1852 the second store at Clover Hill had found its market, just outside the western entrance to the courthouse. John Plunkett stocked the two-story frame building with everything from powder, shot, and whiskey to sugar, starch, and silk. His emporium and the Raine tavern were the first things people saw as they emerged on the Lynchburg side of the courthouse. If they departed by the doors on the Buckingham side, they might turn toward Benjamin Nowlin's store as they made for the saloon beside the Clover Hill Tavern, but Plunkett even took part of that trade by selling whiskey from a barrel.[22]

The trickle of daily court business that helped support the two merchants turned into a little boom that August, when a man went on trial for a notorious robbery at Spout Spring. The newly elected presiding justice—Benjamin Walker—sat on the bench as idle spectators wandered in and out. Plunkett must have taken a big enough share of their refreshment money that Nowlin saw the handwriting on the wall. At first Nowlin tried to diversify, convincing his stepfather, John Sears, to buy into David Robertson's old blacksmith shop on the Lynchburg side of the village. Then he sought more control of the store, persuading a relative to become his partner in it by buying the building from McDearmon, whose financial plight dropped the price to a bargain. Mr. Nowlin had set his sights for greater targets, however; within a couple of years he sold out and moved to Lynchburg, leaving behind only his share of the blacksmith shop, for his stepfather's care.[23]

Over at the rival store, clerk David Plunkett indulged his interest in politics (he had already been appointed to the commission charged with establishing the county's new election districts), and the store offered a perfect podium. He read widely and late into the evening, buying expensive "adamantine" candles instead of the common tallow variety that cost less than half as much; Plunkett was also one of the few county citizens who paid $4 a year for the *Richmond Examiner,* rather than borrowing a tardy copy. The Richmond papers carried a little more national news than the *Lynchburg Virginian,* but Plunkett would have found the earlier and more complete coverage of the political activities at the capital even more attractive.

These days, David Plunkett also devoted a lot of time to Mary McDearmon, the only daughter of his near neighbor and new state senator. Mary was about to turn sixteen, which made her old enough for a Piedmont bride, and her father still posed no complaint; indeed, the senator allowed the young man to sign as his security on a $500 debt. On October 8, 1852, the couple was married by a visiting minister and took up housekeeping, probably right over the store.[24]

As winter approached, Senator McDearmon had more to think about than the prospect of becoming a grandfather by the time he turned thirty-seven. Construction of the railroad bridge below Farmville was taking longer than expected, which not only delayed the appreciation of Appomattox County property but cost McDearmon more than he had anticipated and prevented him from collecting timely payments from the rail company. Meanwhile, his cumbersome sheaf of debts climbed higher and faster. He had borrowed heavily to take part in the bridge project, and even his newest notes were about to come due. At the same time, his income grew less dependable, for every time he sold something like Nowlin's store it deprived him of regular rent thereafter. His name appeared frequently now as a defendant in courthouse documents, and people were beginning to talk.

Christmas brought no divine windfall, and McDearmon could no longer deny that the crisis had arrived. His debts approached $24,000, including most of the original notes on the Clover Hill Tavern tract. Courts had already rendered judgments on well over $4,000 of his debts, and he was then in litigation over nearly $2,000 more. His father and other relatives had backed him with their own cash and credit over the past seven years, and McDearmon began technically disassociating himself from his family members as a means of protecting them.[25]

He proceeded quietly, at first. One week into the new year, McDearmon advertised the dissolution of the Bent Creek Mills, in which two of his wife's brothers had been his partners. Virginia's hinterlands knew little of incorporation, so the three had merely to pronounce the venture undone to end the partnership, and the Walton brothers were able to continue the operation for a few more years. In the end they, too, would succumb to the fiduciary ripples of McDearmon's plunge: by the summer of 1854 Henry Flood complained to Thomas Bocock that they had spoken for his wheat in advance for a generous $1.50 a bushel, delivered, but now they could not meet the debt.

"I thought it was doing well," Flood lamented, "but it can't be got now."[26]

For the present, though, McDearmon had taken care of his in-laws. Next, a $2,000 bond for materials from his masonry suppliers in Prince Edward County was due on January 19, 1853, but instead of paying them off he persuaded them to sell him another $4,000 worth of goods on a demand note, which they might negotiate immediately. He had no means of paying the note, immediately or in the foreseeable future, but apparently he also lacked any intention of paying: even then he was concocting a document that approached the 1853 equivalent of bankruptcy.

With no convenient legal mechanism for either liquidation or protection and reorganization, McDearmon took refuge in the haven of matrimony. In a deed that covered eight ledger pages in the fine scrivener's script of the time, he gathered his property under the authority of two trustees who were, respectively, his brother and brother-in-law. He gave them license to sell everything to the best advantage, taking a 5 percent cut before turning the rest against his debts, but he noted significant exceptions. On the excuse that his wife "refused to relinquish her right of dower" in his estate, he transferred substantial assets to her name and withheld them from the deed, ostensibly to clear the title on the rest and offer it for the benefit of his creditors.

Once this document had been signed and recorded, McDearmon was reduced to effective destitution. The land, buildings, and businesses he had accumulated over a decade were gone from his control. That year he was required to pay personal property taxes on thirty-two slaves, five horses and mules (he had just conveyed eight others), five dozen cattle and sheep, three carriages, and hundreds of dollars in household furnishings. The next year his name did not appear on the tax list at all.[27]

Some of McDearmon's creditors may have wondered which of them would be paid first, since the pair of brother-trustees sat rather high on the list themselves, and if that did not arouse suspicion there was the manner in which McDearmon divided his debts into "classes." The first class, scheduled for the earliest discharge, consisted of notes and bonds on which the courts had already rendered judgments, and those for which his father, uncle, brother, or brothers-in-law had supplied either the actual cash or the security of their good names. The second class encompassed those creditors who were not related to him and those who had not yet had the foresight to file a civil suit against him; these could wait.

Because he had accumulated land in several different counties, the deed had to be registered in each county seat before any further actions were entered. McDearmon and his wife appeared at the Appomattox courthouse on February 17, and Henry Bocock read the entire 4,000-word document to her. Over the next three weeks they traveled to Campbell and Prince Edward Counties, where clerks repeated the ritual.

By the nature of their jobs, clerks tend to indulge in a little gossip, and it is difficult to believe that at least one of them failed to leak the news. Any pursuing creditors would also have encountered the trustee deed, which stopped them cold. Yet for some time McDearmon's sudden poverty appears to have remained more a matter of conjecture than common knowledge, at least partly because nothing changed in the village where he had so long held sway. He continued living in the misplaced Georgian manse, enjoying Mrs. McDearmon's newfound wealth, and for the moment the trustees advertised nothing for sale. They were prohibited from selling the tavern before the first day of 1854, when the manager's contract expired, or from delivering any of the rented lots until the same date, when all the leases expired.[28]

The prohibition against sale of the tavern allowed the trustees to wait until that building increased in value, for the railroad watchers expected to hear steam whistles by the beginning of 1854. Even if the tracks gave Clover Hill a wide berth, the passage of the train would bring the best prices anyone could hope for.

Southside Railroad stockholders were just as anxious as Appomattox landowners for the completion of their line, but McDearmon's economic demise only impeded the interminable construction of High Bridge, below Farmville. To expedite that segment Chief Engineer Sanford designed massive approaches to the bridge, consisting of earthen embankments extending out from the bluffs. That would not only obviate some of the time-consuming masonry piers, but could be undertaken even as the contractors topped off the towers they had begun. By the late spring of 1853 the herculean filling operation was under way.[29]

It was already too late for some, as it had been for McDearmon. George Raine found that business in Clover Hill offered no future, and with his younger brother he opened a resort hotel at Buffalo Springs, on the eastern slope of the Blue Ridge north of Lynchburg. Their widowed mother remained behind in the new brick house, taking a firmer hand than her late husband or son. She bought the new brick house and the old tavern from her brother-in-law, to whom she had been paying $700 a year in rent, and bought David Robertson's big stable, just across the road. She now headed the household, consisting of her youngest son, two grandchildren, and her married daughter, Sarah Horner. Sickness plagued that family, and Sarah, who had already lost the first of her three sons, would not live to see the second one buried: she turned twenty-five in April and was assailed by measles a few weeks later; in the middle of June she, too, was carried over to the little cemetery alongside the stage road.[30]

By 1853 Benjamin Nowlin had already begun withdrawing his village presence. The periodic Whig meetings in Appomattox no longer included his name, and he had resigned his commission as captain of the cavalry company. It would be another year or so before he sold the brick store and moved away, but he had started shopping for prospects in Lynchburg and had probably hired a manager for the store, or even rented it out. His manager, or tenant, may have been young Samuel Glover, whose father kept a stage-road tavern on the western side of the county: father and son coveted both Nowlin's store and the Clover Hill Tavern, and would own them both eventually. Meanwhile, at the direction of a new Democratic president, Glover took the postmastership of Clover Hill away from the incumbent Whig, who had been appointed by Zachary Taylor. Keeping the post office in the brick store not only earned a modest stipend for the clerk, but assured a certain amount of additional traffic through the front door.[31]

No record of Nowlin's Appomattox business activity survives, but one of the ledgers that David Plunkett kept still sits in the same building where he made the entries, and it suggests that during 1853 he spent the vast majority of his days alone in the store. In the entire first week of October only ten customers showed their faces: they bought a mere $10.87 in merchandise, more than half of which came from a single sale to a Lynchburg land speculator. Had it not been for payments of more than $130 on Samuel McDearmon's past-due account, made by one of the trustees or by someone who had bought some of the property, the week's receipts would not have been worth the trouble of watching the door. McDearmon still patronized his son-in-law's store, but most of the new purchases went under his wife's name.

It was primarily the village residents who came into Plunkett's emporium, looking for a pound or two of sugar and coffee, with an occasional visit from denizens of the surrounding countryside, who would stock up for weeks at a time when they came in for business at the courthouse. The Irishmen who lived out on the Buckingham Road dropped by more frequently for a dram of whiskey: Abednego Conner preferred to draw off a quart in his own bottle for twenty cents, while John Sweeney was willing to pay twenty-five for a full pint flask. The store kept a supply of yard goods and notions, from which the perennially bereaved Eliza Raine would replenish her stock of black velvet and mourning collars. One day when he was ailing, Drury Woodson, who lived a good four miles out on the way to Buckingham Court House, sent his son all the way in to Plunkett's store for a bottle of cod-liver oil, paying the substantial price of a dollar for that imported Yankee product. The most expensive item in the store seemed to be shoes, though, at $1.50 a pair.[32]

The store ledger hints that a couple of lawyers had opened offices in the village, or intended to open one in the near future. The first of these was John W. Woodson, a young lawyer and sometime teacher; he and his family lived on one of the old Patteson farms, a couple of miles north of the courthouse. Woodson made his first purchase at the end of October— a bucket, perhaps for the water with which to scrub up the little building just beyond the Raine family lot, where he would keep his law books and papers. His rental agreement for that lot evidently began on January 1, just as Samuel McDearmon had noted, and it was not until the first court day of 1854 that Woodson bought a hasp, hinge, and padlock for the building and a lock for the chest in which he could store a change of clothes. That was only a couple of weeks after Crawford Jones began sending his slave, Sam, to the store for a cotton handkerchief or a cake of "Yankie" soap. Until recently Jones, who was only twenty-three, had made his home on the family plantation out in the Walker's Church District; that was miles from the courthouse, and with the cheap rents McDearmon was asking there was no reason not to keep a little office.

It would take a lot of soap, sugar, and even shoe sales to produce enough profit for the Plunkett venture to prosper, and one way to increase the volume was to pry the postmaster's sinecure away from Samuel Glover. Even with Senator McDearmon's political connections that proved difficult, but before Franklin Pierce left office someone convinced him that David Plunkett was a much more competent man for the job—and incidentally a more active and loyal Democrat than Mr. Glover.[33]

The postal appointment may have been delayed so long because Plunkett's father-in-law had little time for lobbying beyond Richmond that first winter. Back in Richmond, undiscouraged by what he may have considered a temporary financial setback, Senator McDearmon lunged headlong into the battle for economic dominance in the Piedmont, fighting anew the Orange & Alexandria extension that would have favored Lynchburg, but simultaneously campaigning for another rail line from Appomattox to the Staunton River and a plank road, each of which would have made Appomattox more of a hub than a wayside. The *Lynchburg Virginian* pilloried him for his apparent betrayal of his constituents in that city, but the *Virginian* leaned to the Whig persuasion anyway; he still had another year before the senatorial election, and with the possibility of speculative salvation riding on these new transportation corridors, McDearmon was not to be diverted from his course.[34]

Across America, the midcentury transportation explosion made thriving cities of rural backwaters while sealing the doom of many a promising crossroads community. McDearmon sought the former fate for the village on which he had planted his hopes; if he seemed to use his political office to butter his own bread, he did so in an era when public servants had not yet learned to disguise self-interest. The city of Washington attracted representatives who made it their business to mold the national map for the benefit of regions in which their fortunes were invested, and any of them would have argued that they were merely taking a share of the prosperity they had assured for their constituencies.

One of those manipulators of manifest destiny in the national capital was Senator Stephen Douglas. Douglas had moved to Chicago, a relatively small port on Lake Michigan that he wished to see transformed into a rail-road metropolis connecting the Midwest and the Great Plains. That feat required Douglas to guide all plans for a transcontinental railroad toward northern Illinois. In 1853 he saw two major threats to his preferred route, one of which would have reached California by traversing the extreme Southwest along the Mexican border. With a terminus at New Orleans, or perhaps Memphis, this line would have thrown the attendant industrial and economic growth to the South. Douglas turned his prodigious mind to the task of luring Southern congressmen away from the project that would have borne the most fruit for their homeland, and the result was a bill for the organization of Kansas and Nebraska Territories as new states, with the residents of each territory to decide whether slavery should exist there.

Douglas's proposed Kansas-Nebraska Act drew the desired Southern support, but for all the wrong reasons. The implication that either of those regions could be converted into a slave state flew in the face of the Missouri Compromise and the Compromise of 1850, which had prohibited slavery north of latitude 36°30′. There may have been some slave-state congress-men who hoped the admission of a slaveholding Kansas would gain a new pair of senate seats for their peculiar viewpoint, but most seemed to rec-ognize that the terrain of Kansas and Nebraska did not lend itself to agri-cultural pursuits that could profit from slave labor. The principal victory, as they saw it, lay in the repeal of a federal law that purported to outlaw slavery anywhere, and the acknowledgment of "popular sovereignty" on that issue.

"The single aim of the Nebraska bill," wrote the editor of the *Richmond Enquirer*, "is to establish the principle of Federal non-intervention in re-gard to slavery." This same man freely admitted that slavery could not live in that region, which had been gruesomely misrepresented as the "Great American Desert." [35]

There were those who charged Douglas with courting Southern favor for his presidential ambitions, but the first and most obvious motive for his bill was the rail route to his home town, which required the organization of the two territories. To Douglas, that was worth stirring up a new turmoil over slavery, and even before the act became law in May of 1854 it did just that. In Wisconsin the first adherents to the Republican Party gathered in response to this potential expansion of slavery, and New England abolitionists took militant steps to assure that the more vulnerable territory, Kansas, would be settled by free-state voters. Both these developments would lead to more startling consequences.

As significant as the Kansas discussion was to the nation's future, and as much venom as it inspired in the North, Southern newspapers remained relatively silent and storefront debate appears to have died early. The *Enquirer* editor supposed that Virginians were still worn out from the political eruptions of 1850, but the truth may be that they saw Kansas as a victory against abolitionist doctrine, rather than submission to it.[36]

In Appomattox County, the Southside Railroad provided more grist for conversation than Kansas did. Slave gangs heralded its progress as they marched in platoons ahead of the rails, axes on their shoulders; they sang slow, mournful dirges as their blades rang on the tall pine trunks. George Abbitt, who would soon forsake his plantation for a conductor's berth on the Southside line, rented most of his field hands to the railroad for the clearing operation. The final spike went into the bottleneck bridge below Farmville on the last day of 1853, and on Tuesday, June 20, 1854, the tracks reached what would become known as Appomattox Station. By the end of June the line was open to the gorge of the James River, with a stage connection shuttling passengers over the remaining eighteen miles. One of the first passengers to ride the entire 124 miles reported that the engineers had "levelled hills, filled up valleys, and made the 'crooked places straight,'" but he expressed enormous anxiety while looking down from High Bridge. The entire passenger car fell ominously silent as the train tested the span, he noted.

"Too much like dancing upon nothing," recorded the adventurer. Still, he seemed pleased with the experience in the end. His impression of Samuel McDearmon's home district did not match the senator's vision, however: instead he revealed a cosmopolitan condescension when he described the train stopping for a meal at "a shanty in the woods at a place called Appomattox."

"We had as good a dinner as could be expected at such a place," this sojourner concluded.[37]

Outsiders passing on the cars might look down their noses at the Appomattox countryside, but those who lived there seemed to attach great value to the place, at least now that iron rails had linked it to Tidewater Virginia. The notes of the first whistle had not yet skirled over the treetops when landowners began offering their property for sale by the square mile. On the first of the year Fielding Jones advertised an undeveloped parcel of uncertain extent—600 or 700 acres, he supposed—accentuating its proximity to Concord Depot. That depot had not yet seen a train: as soon as regular rail traffic began, willing sellers started coming out of the woods. That summer at least three entire farms lying on or near the Southside Railroad went on the market, with auctions planned for September if private sales could not be arranged beforehand. Another county resident tried to hawk upwards of 900 acres of timberland. The railroad had been completed for little more than a year before some 6,000 acres of Appomattox land had been advertised in the newspapers, aside from the more common quiet purchases.[38]

Village property underwent a succession of changes now, too. Early in 1854 Willis Inge bought a couple of lots from Samuel McDearmon and erected a little shop. At about the same time, Benjamin Nowlin found buyers for his store in the persons of two eager young county natives. Joseph Abbitt and John H. Flood (son of Colonel Thomas H. Flood) had grown up in the same neighborhood along the Buckingham Court House Road; they probably paid the full market value of $1,250 for Nowlin's brick building and a thin perimeter of land. William M. Wright, who had bought half an acre from McDearmon beside the Raine stable, went into business with Charles H. Diuguid, a free black man. Diuguid opened a blacksmith shop in a new building on Wright's lot at the western edge of the village, barely a hundred yards from the competing shop owned by Sears and Nowlin.

At this juncture Samuel McDearmon, or the kinfolk who served as trustees of his estate, decided that the worth of his Clover Hill land had reached its peak. The bankruptcy remained thinly disguised: alleging that McDearmon wished to sell everything from the Clover Hill Tavern to his flock of chickens and move west, to Texas or Nebraska, the trustees proposed a final sale for October 5, 1854. Included were the Georgian house with the hipped roof and a number of undeveloped lots near the new Appomattox depot—where stood that hotel deemed a "shanty in the woods," three miles from the courthouse.[39]

In fact, that shanty in the woods also belonged to McDearmon, or rather to his wife. Eventually Mary Frances Philadelphia Walton McDearmon came into nominal ownership of nearly 500 acres in that vicinity, either as the equivalent of her "dower right" or through the surreptitious business dealings of her husband, who could own no more land without jeopardy of a judgment for debt. McDearmon built a new six-room Virginia farmhouse on that land, within a hundred yards of the Appomattox depot, and the couple moved in that summer; the colonel quickly suppressed any dreams he may have harbored about Texas or Nebraska. The glut of land for sale merely diluted the Appomattox real estate market, and much of it lay more attractively convenient to the railroad. Still, McDearmon managed to peddle the most valuable of his holdings. He sold the tavern to Samuel Glover, who had long kept another tavern on the stage road, beyond Spout Spring. The other significant sale completed as a result of McDearmon's October auction involved the 220-acre parcel with the prized manse: that went to neighbor Jacob Tibbs, a peripatetic trader in farms. Tibbs had sold one of his own homes a decade before, during a publicly proclaimed (but unconsummated) lust for westward migration.[40]

Provincial as they may have been, local residents would hardly swallow such marketing ruses neat. When the news circulated that McDearmon's advertised journey from Clover Hill had ended at the railroad, smirking yeomen and gentry alike began calling the depot vicinity "Nebraska." That winter the postmaster general formally recognized a community of that name, and appointed the unembarrassed McDearmon as its first postmaster at a stipend of $10 a month. McDearmon located the post office in the corner of his new store, right alongside the tracks.[41]

Residents plied the Nebraska joke on McDearmon with an evident lack of sympathy, for he spent the winter recuperating from fractures and lacerations sustained in the first major accident on the Southside Railroad. On Friday, November 10, the westbound train struck a cow and derailed between Rice's Station and High Bridge, injuring dozens of passengers as it slid down a twenty-five-foot embankment. One woman suffered a broken collarbone, and a young bride was trapped beneath the wreckage. The black fireman tried to jump clear, but the tender rolled over him; his was the only life lost, although the single passenger car was packed with more than six dozen travelers. McDearmon lay among the worst hurt, with a nasty gash ripped in his mouth and some ribs broken. He suffered no permanent damage save for the scars, but by the end of his convalescence he had decided not to run for reelection to the senate. Whether it was his financial situation or the alienation of too many district voters that prevented him from continuing in office, he announced in mid-January, to the delight of his antagonists, that he would be a candidate "under no circumstance." Except for functionary appointments, his political life was over.[42]

The senator's retirement did not entirely convince the opposition. Just before assuming his duties as postmaster, McDearmon found it necessary to defend himself against a charge that, in the wake of a speech at Lynchburg by Democratic gubernatorial candidate Henry Wise, he had hired some Irishmen to disrupt a Know-Nothing Party meeting at Appomattox Court House. With some heat, McDearmon replied that he had spoken to only one Irishman since Wise's speech.

Members of the new American Party were almost universally called Know-Nothings because of their professed ignorance of secret activities. In the South, this party had absorbed a significant proportion of the Whig faction, which had begun to disintegrate in the early stages of the battle over Kansas. Northern dissidents swung more toward the Republicans, but the Republican platform condemned the institution of slavery and opposed its expansion: radical Southerners perceived that the introduction of free states without a commensurate increase in slave states would doom the unpopular institution in Congress, and particularly in the Senate, where a delicate balance had been achieved. The Know-Nothing prejudice against foreigners—at least recent immigrants—struck a more appealing chord for those seeking a new party in the slave states. Some Virginia Democrats migrated to the American Party, but many of them were soon wooed back, along with a moderate reinforcement of disaffected Whigs. Inseminated with surviving elements of Whig doctrine and supported by most of the old Whig names, the Know-Nothings fielded candidates against the Democrats at each level of government in Virginia in 1855—and most of those candidates went down in defeat as their Whig predecessors usually had, at least in Appomattox County.[43]

Five men ran for the Appomattox seat in the House of Delegates, including the novice lawyer Crawford Jones, who, at twenty-five, spouted Democratic state-rights rhetoric worthy of John Calhoun. His competitors all had the advantage on him by more than a dozen years, and all were well known in the county: Robert Boaz, who had managed the Clover Hill Tavern for Colonel McDearmon; McDearmon's own brother and trustee, John, the physician; William Trent, a substantial farmer who lived a couple of miles south of the courthouse; and Nelson Kelley, a wheelwright in his late fifties. Squire Trent, a former Whig, ran without party affiliation, and Dr. McDearmon, who had also once voted with the Whigs, had now gravitated to the Democrats. Had Trent or McDearmon aligned themselves with the Know-Nothings they might have stood a chance in so populated a field, but the opposition had no one to rally behind and young Jones was chosen to go to Richmond.[44]

The only victory for the Know-Nothings in Appomattox that year came with the election of Thomas Flood to Samuel McDearmon's vacant senate seat. Colonel Flood enjoyed the respect of his neighbors in both parties. His kinsmen Joel, the wealthy doctor, and Henry were both prominent

{ THE RAILROAD }

Democrats, and according to the Lynchburg papers Flood even won the support of the outgoing McDearmon, whose economic interests reflected Flood's. Colonel Flood's son John now owned the Bocock brothers' house and their lots at the courthouse, had secured an interest in the brick store, and was bargaining with McDearmon's trustees for the entire quadrant of the village surrounding his house. Thomas Flood was one of the first trustees of the James River and Clover Hill Plank Road Company. If anyone wished more fervently than McDearmon to see Clover Hill prosper, it would have been John Flood and his father.[45]

Senator Flood prevailed in the senate race, and he succeeded Samuel McDearmon on the committee on roads and navigation, where he followed his predecessor's lead in railroad promotion. As soon as he reached the capital he presented a resolution calling for the state to lend the Virginia & Tennessee Railroad Company enough money to complete its route from Lynchburg to Bristol. That would connect Appomattox not only to Richmond and the sea, but to the Shenandoah Valley and the West.[46]

In this confused era of slave politics, the distinctions between the old parties began to blur. The same Virginians who sent Thomas Flood to Richmond now showed a more militant side when it came to choosing governors, congressmen, or a new president. The Know-Nothings put up a brave fight in the waning days of 1855, but Henry Wise, a former Whig now converted to a wrathful Democrat, became governor with a majority of more than 6 percent. Willis Bocock, elder brother to the Democratic district congressman, won reelection as the state's attorney general by an even wider margin. Their terms would carry through the last years of real peace in slaveholding Virginia.[47]

The political transmutations made themselves most evident as the House of Representatives attempted to seat a new Speaker that winter. The most likely candidate, Nathaniel Banks of Massachusetts, had entered Congress as a Democrat and had been reelected as a Know-Nothing. Sectional splits within parties kept him from gaining a majority, and he only won the office when the House agreed to a decision on a plurality vote. Speaker Banks then became a Republican, like so many other Northern Know-Nothings. Their Southern counterparts had nowhere to go for a national party, finding the Republican platform on slavery repugnant and the Whig Party defunct.

The disintegration of the Whig Party also destroyed any hope for a presidential contender to the Democratic candidate who would be simultaneously palatable to Southern voters and viable at the national level, and that polarized the presidential election over the issue of slavery. Since 1832 all but one of the Whig candidates had at least been born in Southern states, and had been introduced to slavery early, but in 1856 the Know-Nothing heirs of that party could recruit only that most obscure of even the accidental presidents, New Yorker Millard Fillmore. Habitual opponents of the Democratic Party nonetheless endorsed him, for if Fillmore was not a champion of slavery he at least posed no direct threat to it.

Old Whig loyalists like Benjamin Walker, Senator Flood, his son John, and Dr. William Christian—a lean, hawk-nosed man who lived between Pleasant Retreat and Wildway—met at Appomattox Court House on April 10, 1856, to praise Fillmore and choose delegates for a convention. Accustomed to defeat, they no longer had so much as a prayer in Virginia, or in the electoral college. Democrats overwhelmed the American Party in the South, and Republicans dominated in the North. In the end Fillmore took only one state, and Democrat James Buchanan, of Pennsylvania, assumed the presidency with a slaveowning Kentuckian as his vice president.[48]

In these unsettled times, national politics seemed to have abandoned the practical economic issues that troubled most Virginians. For many in Appomattox County (for now, at least), local improvements like the railroad and plank roads meant more than any philosophical debate over slavery; for some these improvements meant everything, because the value they added to their property offered the opportunity to sell out and move on. The pioneering instinct had not died out yet, and Samuel McDearmon's claimed migratory intentions had rung true enough until he relocated at the depot: not a few middle-aged men sold everything and moved their families westward to establish new farms on cheaper land, taking with them what would amount to a fortune in the new country. The Cawthorn, Thornhill, Lewis, and Woodson families all had relatives living in Missouri by the mid-1850s, while most other Appomattox emigrants gravitated to the open spaces of Texas. Obituaries of the less fortunate among them sometimes drifted back for tardy publication in the Lynchburg papers.[49]

The eldest daughter of John Sears undertook the pilgrimage to Texas, and came to regret it. Betty Sears married late for an Appomattox girl: she still lived with her father when she was twenty-one. But a year or two later a family named Tweedy moved into the county and settled near the Sears place along Plain Run. One of the Tweedy boys, John, married Betty and took her away to the big new state, where she bore their first child in the summer of 1853. That daughter was barely a year old before Betty conceived a son. She was still pregnant with that boy when John died and

{ THE RAILROAD }

she had to endure the exhausting journey back to her father's home in Virginia, trundling her toddler the entire way.[50]

The Widow Tweedy had returned to Appomattox Court House by the spring of 1855. The changes she observed then and witnessed over the next year might have given early promise of prosperity, but most of those changes resulted from someone's bad luck. The misfortunes began with Samuel McDearmon's collapsed real estate speculation. That disaster had benefited Benjamin Nowlin, for whom the purchase price for the brick store had evidently been rendered affordable by McDearmon's reverses. With the coming of the railroad, Nowlin was able to sell out almost immediately, allowing John Flood and Joseph Abbitt to move in. Samuel Glover had also benefited from McDearmon's bankruptcy. Then Pryor Wright died, at the age of sixty-four; Mariah gave up the brick home by the courthouse and moved her younger children, her married daughter, and her son-in-law into the old frame dwelling on the outskirts of town, offering the big house for rent if anyone would take it. In the wake of Benjamin Nowlin's departure, Betty Tweedy's own father now rented out that blacksmith shop on the lot he had helped Nowlin to buy.[51]

Eventually Crawford Jones and John Woodson also took advantage of McDearmon's plight, and by the end of 1855 both of them owned their office lots. Woodson's little shed occupied only a few square yards on the corner of the same lot as John Sears's blacksmith shop, so he sold the balance of the lot to John Plunkett, who apparently did nothing with it. Jones occupied a slightly more comfortable one-room building on lot 30, at the easternmost limit of the village, where the Prince Edward Court House Road joined the stage road.[52]

Immediately across the Prince Edward Court House Road from this lot, just outside the platted village boundary, a new house sat atop the hill that sloped down to the Appomattox River. Another of those two-story, rectangular Virginia farmhouses, it faced the courthouse across a grassy triangle that belonged to no one: where the Buckingham Road veered north, a village lane continued straight toward this new residence, cutting this little gore off from any practical use. Inside the house lived Dr. William B. Abbitt and his wife, Sarah. Down the Prince Edward Court House Road from them, in an even bigger new house toward the academy building, lived John Moffitt, a saddler who had once boarded at the Clover Hill Tavern.[53]

The circumstances that brought Dr. Abbitt to the new house lacked the tragic touch of some other village transactions (although the young doctor had bought the place only after McDearmon's desperation became evident), but John Flood had acquired the Bocock house as a consequence of his sister's early death. Thomas Bocock, who had married the girl a decade before, soothed his grief with a new bride half his age and instantly began another family. The bridegroom likewise devoted himself to his congressional career in Washington, where he lost a close race for Speaker of the House; his recent marriage, to the daughter of Congressman Charles Faulkner, had certainly done nothing to harm his political standing. The plantation he called Wildway lay barely five miles from the county seat, so he saw no need of retaining the village house. Court clerk Henry Bocock evidently stayed on as a tenant, though, and the expansive yard rang with the voices of his growing brood.[54]

On the northwesternmost corner of Appomattox Court House, as the commissioners originally laid it out, stood the new home of Lorenzo Kelly, a thirty-five-year-old bachelor who had built the house for himself, his mother, his grandmother, and his younger siblings. The youngest Kelly boy and a girl were still children, while the four older sons all followed their father's trade as wheelwrights and carriage builders. Neal Kelly had died but recently, and the presence of the family enterprise illustrated Lorenzo's leadership. Three years hence, Leonard and Lawrence would elope simultaneously with local girls, but Lorenzo and Lawson would stay behind to look after the family.[55]

Death had also struck again at the Raine home, where Eliza Raine remained with her youngest son, Charles, and her dead daughter's two surviving boys. The elder of those, nine-year-old Ezekiel, passed away on April 16, 1855, just four years after the dual deaths of John Raine and Ezekiel's brother. It may have been some comfort to this woman that a granddaughter was born at her son's resort hotel that same day, but sixteen months later, in the summer of 1856, that latest granddaughter also died. The fifty-one-year-old Mrs. Raine, who had buried six members of her family in as many years, expired within a fortnight of the infant.

The Raine house and tavern fell silent thereafter. From Lynchburg, heirs squabbled without resolution over the late widow's estate, turning on John Raine's brother for a share of the Clover Hill property. As befit so unfortunate a family, the only Raines who returned to Appomattox Court House now arrived in coffins. George Raine would be carried back to the family cemetery less than four years afterward, dead at the hands of his son-in-law; another grandson found a grave there the next year, and Eliza Raine's youngest son, Charles, would come home at the end of 1863, having given his life for a nation that did not yet exist when he last turned his back upon the village.[56]

THE CRISIS

By the autumn of 1856, the plank road had connected Clover Hill with the James River, by way of Oakville. The roadbed lay twenty feet wide, with eight feet of that covered in thick boards on timber runners. That would have been a much more valuable asset a decade previously, when the James River canal offered the easiest and cheapest bulk transportation to Richmond, but the canal was already deteriorating: three years before, a serious rupture had forced passengers to shuttle around the Bent Creek segment in wagons, one of which had overturned and catapulted the occupants down the embankment, with injuries all around. The state completed a toll bridge over Bent Creek in 1853, so farmers on the Appomattox side could reach the canal more easily, but this eleventh-hour amenity saw little traffic. The hooting of the railroad whistles a mere three miles from Appomattox Court House signaled the impending obsolescence of the Oakville Road and the canal. Some shrewd villagers already seemed to understand that the fate of the county seat had also been sealed, and they began casting about for more promising pastures.

Robert Boaz, the former militia captain who had managed the Clover Hill Tavern for Samuel McDearmon, followed McDearmon to his little Nebraska. Early in October of 1856 he secured the postmastership there, which McDearmon had exchanged for a job in Richmond; within a month Boaz heard that the rail agent's position at the depot would also be vacant soon, and he solicited Congressman Bocock's influence for that appointment, as well.[1]

Even the court clerk threatened to abandon his bailiwick. Henry Bocock was approaching forty now, but his wife was in her mid-twenties and they had five children between the ages of one and eight. Their two older boys

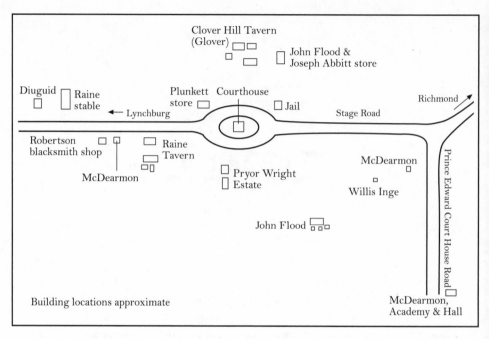

Map 3. Appomattox Court House, 1855

were ready for school and might have benefited from the educational opportunities of a more vibrant community. Bocock had held the clerkship at Appomattox Court House for eleven years now, but when the Farmer's Bank of Lynchburg offered him an executive opportunity he decided to take it. He broke the news to the county justices on court day, November 6, and within hours everyone had heard about it. The following day the courthouse filled with citizens who wished Bocock to stay; as people of their century so often did, they elected a chairman and secretary, adopted a resolution of regret at the prospect of losing their "most excellent Clerk," and elected a committee to convey their hope for his reconsideration. Bocock would have had to know of this gathering, so the committee was probably unnecessary unless the county officers also wished to communicate a confidential raise in pay, but everyone observed the formalities and Bocock changed his mind, at least for the present.[2]

As the new year of 1857 began, it looked as though Attorney General Willis Bocock might be planning to leave the county. Hours after renewing his oath of office in Richmond he boarded a train for Marengo County, in distant Alabama, where on January 10 he ended just under half a century of bachelorhood. In the manner of Virginia gentlemen since long before George Washington, the eldest Bocock brother saw to both his romantic and his economic interests at the same instant by marrying a wealthy widow. The attorney general then returned to Richmond, probably without the former Mrs. Mourning Smith Gracie; he stayed only long enough to resign his post and wrap up his paperwork, after which he rejoined his bride in southwestern Alabama. He would be back, periodically: like many of Alabama's ruling class, the new Mrs. Bocock was a native of South Carolina, and she may have enjoyed visiting among the eastern gentry; that, or Bocock's own stubborn attachment to his homeland, drew him back to Appomattox County from time to time, but in the three decades that remained to him he would eventually come to think of himself as an Alabamian.

Bocock's younger brother, John, a Presbyterian minister, followed him out of Virginia about the same time. Reverend Bocock, who had been pastor of a Lynchburg congregation, accepted a similar post in the District of Columbia.[3]

Henry Flood also moved, but not far away. For over a decade he had lived three miles west of the courthouse, but his father's home lay the same distance east of it and they owned a substantial part of the countryside in between, so the Floods were village figures if not village residents. Henry may have been as ill-equipped to manage a plantation as he had been to satisfy his legislative constituents, and apparently the agricultural life lacked the allure for him that it did for his father, the doctor. Henry had been trained as a lawyer. He had evidently practiced little, but the law, politics, and business seemed to inspire him more than the plow, and in his fortieth year he decided that his destiny lay in Lynchburg. He accepted the post of director for the same Farmer's Bank that had tried to recruit Henry Bocock, and he opened a formal law office at last.

Then, or soon thereafter, Flood left the house at Rocky Farm for a more comfortable home in the city. He and his cousin-wife had produced only one child, a boy who died in infancy. Joel Walker Flood Jr., Henry's only issue by his first child bride, remained behind at Pleasant Retreat, with Dr. Flood and his wife; this boy had lived with his grandparents since childhood, and that was his real home. Besides, he was about to pack his trunk for the fall session at Emory and Henry College, deep in southwestern Virginia. Dr. Flood had presented Henry with Rocky Farm as a gift, but it was the teenage grandson who showed more interest in working it, and although Henry might have sold the plantation at some profit he maintained it for the son to whom he had been little more than an uncle.[4]

Even as such rooted citizens sought more fertile soil, others embraced Clover Hill with better faith in its future. In the fall of 1856 David Plunkett signed a deed for the hilltop home of Dr. William B. Abbitt, moving his growing family into the more spacious quarters from the cramped apartment over his father's store. Dr. Abbitt merely moved to the other side of the north branch of the Appomattox, taking up the old Sweeney homestead. John Flood showed some confidence when he bought half of Nowlin's store, the Bocock brothers' home, and most of the surrounding lots. Artisans and lawyers still wandered into the village to try their luck on a small stake, and at the beginning of 1857 someone took the Clover Hill Tavern from Samuel Glover, who had more interest in the brick store. From the platted James River town of Diuguidsville, better known as Bent Creek, came Wilson Hix, a portly veteran of the War of 1812. He had been a substantial member of that community in more than a physical sense, for he had served as postmaster there for most of the previous two decades, but Bent Creek's sun began to set as soon as the railroad started to supersede canal traffic: the Walton brothers' gristmill, a blacksmith shop, and a wheelwright shop constituted most of the working village, and Hix's portion of those structures had recently burned down. On February 1 Hix notified the postmaster general that he would have to resign because he was moving, sending the message through his former brother-in-law Thomas Bocock, who wangled a new appointment to that office for Hix's oldest son.

Trailing a household of thirty souls, children and slaves included, Hix lumbered into the village a few days later and took possession of his new enterprise. With his white hair, chin-strap beard, and broad girth, Hix looked as though he ought to find a seat on the porch of the tavern and spend the rest of his days smoking his pipe there, but his plans did not include retirement. He may have seen more than sixty winters, but Wilson Hix was still an active man (as the toddler clinging to his wife's skirts so loudly proclaimed), and his ambition survived undiminished.[5]

Hix subscribed to the old school of finance: he paid cash for his purchases, and spent most of his time looking for ways to accumulate that cash. That attitude allows for some hard bargaining when the other party has mortgaged everything on speculation, which is how Hix came by the tavern: competition for lodgers had ended with the death of Eliza Raine and the closing of her hostelry, and Hix saw a chance to haggle for a business that might actually make a profit.

The onetime owner of the tavern, McDearmon, had been reduced to a salaried position with the Shockoe tobacco warehouse in Richmond, for which he served as the second inspector. McDearmon harbored no apparent intention of leaving Appomattox County permanently even after his promotion to first inspector, in April, but transportation limitations required that he board in the city. That might have eased any mortification he suffered over his new station in life, which appears to have been little enough, and during this enforced absence he retired from the militia, although he retained the social capital of his title the rest of his days.[6]

McDearmon's new job reflected the importance of tobacco in Virginia, and Appomattox produced more of it than most counties in the Old Dominion. Farmers there were cutting back on the land they devoted to wheat, corn, sheep, hogs, and beef cattle and giving it over to bigger tobacco crops; when they sold out, they advertised their land on the sole draw that it was good for tobacco. On the hillside overlooking the Appomattox River Dr. Flood maintained an old tobacco prizery, so called because of the twist in provincial dialect that converted "pry" into the verb "prize," meaning to press, or force: here the cured tobacco leaf was compressed into hogsheads by means of a levered plunger. In past years the filled hogsheads were rolled onto wagon beds and taken up the plank road over a dozen miles to the canal; by 1857 such prizeries packed more than one and a half million pounds of the noxious weed annually, and much of it rolled eastward on the railroad.[7]

The tobacco plant tended to burn out the soil in which it grew, but it enjoyed a prominent place in the history of Virginia agriculture. Cultivation of *Nicotiana tabacum* played a major role in the early settlement of the colony, once the habit of smoking took its firm hold on British society, and that vital crop also exerted considerable influence on the future of slavery. Two hundred years before Samuel McDearmon accepted the inspectorship at Shockoe, a sharp, sustained drop in tobacco prices had driven most of Virginia's yeomen farmers from the competition, and those who harvested vast tracts with a ready supply of cheap labor made the great fortunes thereafter; such opulent planters naturally came into political power as well, and it was these seventeenth-century grandees who replaced Virginia's labor force of indentured servants with one of Africans consigned to perpetual slavery.[8]

From there, slavery had migrated to other colonies that had since become states — and, especially with the emergence of the cotton industry, into new territories. Now the territorial expansion of the institution had become the single most pressing question faced by the American people, and the final campaign of the war of words had already begun. In March the Supreme Court finally ruled on the decade-old case of a slave named Dred Scott. Scott represented the geographical progression of the institution that bound him; his original master had taken him from his native Virginia to Alabama, where he tried cotton planting, and later he had moved his family, slaves and all, to Missouri. A subsequent owner took Scott to Wisconsin Territory, where slavery had been prohibited by the Missouri Compromise.

In the course of rejecting Scott's plea for freedom, the Court declared the Missouri Compromise unconstitutional. The Kansas-Nebraska Act had already repealed that legislation, but to the antislavery faction of the North the important element was the reason behind that decision: the Missouri Compromise could not stand, the Court decreed, because Congress had no right to interfere with slavery in the territories. That interpretation emasculated the growing Northern majority in Congress, which now included a significant percentage of Republicans who wanted to forbid slavery in all territories. The Northern press howled over a proslave high court, and Republicans profited from the public outrage, which worsened as the smoldering question of Kansas drifted back into the forum. The South bridled in turn. Virginians resented the intrusion of abolition sentiment as vigorously as any. The *Richmond Enquirer* spent the spring describing North and South as two hostile camps whose differences would probably come to a head with the election of the next president; if the party of abolition should prevail, the editor argued, the only answer would be secession. By autumn the *Enquirer* was encouraging its once-moderate readers to throw off the yoke of union if, before the next presidentiad, congressional "Black Republicans" should succeed in drawing another boundary line against slavery.[9]

That summer a book appearing under the name of a renegade North Carolinian purported to prove how slavery engendered all of the South's evils, economic and social. Hinton Rowan Helper's *The Impending Crisis of the South* argued that slavery contributed to every disadvantage from illiteracy to the relative shortage of rail service. His book was banned in much of the South, where citizens remembered bloody slave revolts with active dread, and in its place the loyal Southron would have read *Cannibals All! Or Slaves without Masters*, by Virginia's own George Fitzhugh. Fitzhugh attempted to demonstrate that slavery provided a more efficient society and a more desirable quality of life for the laborer than anything the mills of Leeds or Lowell had yet developed; universal poverty and unrest would be avoided in the North only so long as cheap land lay open in the West, he contended, while the South's slaves lived lives of "carefree" security.[10]

Not always had Virginians felt so defensive of slavery. A quarter of a century before, in the wake of Nat Turner's rebellion, the General Assembly had seriously considered emancipation. Even Charles Faulkner, who would become Thomas Bocock's father-in-law, had advocated gradual abolition as a delegate from Martinsburg. The debate always ran against the problem of removing the slaves as they were freed, but the idea remained alive until midcentury. Antislavery rhetoric and abolition doctrine from the North had subsequently alienated such moderate Southern minds, transforming nationalistic Whigs like Faulkner into Democrats of a sectional turn and eliminating any possibility of internal solutions. As the editor of the *Enquirer* noted, sectional antagonism had grown so palpable by 1857 that few people would have been welcome to inspect the conditions of both Northern factory operatives and Southern slaves. An objective visitor to Appomattox County might nevertheless have questioned Fitzhugh's benevolent assessment of human bondage; even so far from the notorious Deep South plantations, slaves lived in perfect destitution, and died off nearly twice as fast as the white population.[11]

That summer of 1857 a number of them were dying from typhoid, along with their white neighbors. The spring and early summer turned hot and dry, with the grass and crops browning on the stalk. Typhoid appeared early, perhaps as wells went dry and the children charged with fetching water sought less trustworthy sources, or possibly it originated with a stagecoach passenger. The stage line had always helped spread contagious diseases: in 1851 a traveler at the Clover Hill Tavern infected the manager's daughter with smallpox, which she passed on to Mariah Wright and William Trent; a pest hospital on Squire Trent's farm had arrested that plague, but the Richmond Road still offered the same threat. Arthur Conner, who lived a mile east of Clover Hill on the stage road, became the first typhoid victim on March 31, and by July a full-blown epidemic had developed in the eastern and northern reaches of the county. It struck black and white without distinction, laying entire families low, and this year's outbreak fell with a unusual virulence, killing thirty-two men, women, and children. Once the bacillus entered the mouth, it found its way to the small intestine and settled in. The illness lasted for weeks, beginning with chills and high fever, and if the patient did not succumb to pneumonia or other complications there was always the danger of severe hemorrhage from, or perforation of, the bowel; this is what tended to kill typhoid victims.

Two of Robert Cheatham's slaves died by the first of June, and a third died in August. Samuel Cawthorn's wife passed away on August 18, and two of his brother's slaves perished over the next three weeks. Typhoid took two of Washington Hunter's slaves over the same period, seven miles west of the courthouse. A couple of miles north of the village, some of the dozen or so slaves Henry Patteson had inherited from his father began showing signs of typhoid in July, and on August 12 one of the women died.

Three miles east of the village, it seemed for a time that Edward Sears's family would be wiped out. The first to die, on July 1, was little Ellen Sears, whose frail constitution could not withstand the onslaught. By then her father had come down with it, and her mother—who had just given birth to a baby boy—began quaking with chills soon afterward.

On the final Sunday in July Drury Woodson's oldest daughter, Amanda, attended services at New Hope Baptist Church, near her home and three miles from the village, where she learned that Ned Sears had sunk "very low" with fever. When she related the news to her sister, who was away at school, she never mentioned the dead child, but perhaps she observed the restraint of a society that dared not invest much emotional stock in the youngest and most vulnerable members of society. She did, however, take particular notice of two of the teenage Walker boys—one of whom, she observed, had also been sick.[12]

Less than a week later, Ned Sears lay dead. Eight days after that Susan Sears, who named her new baby Edward, after his dead father, gave up her fight against the illness, and her son William breathed his last on September 1. The infant somehow avoided infection, and the three other children all recovered. Their mother's parents took the four orphans into their home at Walker's Church, about ten miles southeast of Clover Hill. Meanwhile, the epidemic still swirled around Appomattox Court House. Jeremiah Sears died with typhoid on October 2, and six weeks later Dr. Robert Patteson lost one of his field hands to it. Two more of Henry Patteson's slaves, Peter and "Joice," perished within a month after that, at least one of them to a diagnosed case of typhoid. The *Lynchburg Virginian* reported somewhat prematurely, on November 4, that the raging fever had "subsided," but shortly afterward the epidemic finally did end just about where it had begun—on the stage road, just east of the courthouse. On November 5 Dr. William B. Abbitt breathed his last at his home on the Sweeney place, and on November 20 the death of twenty-year-old John Plunkett ended the outbreak.[13]

Southerners of that century had grown accustomed to passing their lives amid pestilence, but the long, hot summer of 1857 exacted its tribute in spirit, as well. While Northern abolitionists concerned themselves with the position of slaves in the Southern community, the slaves had their own society within the confines of their condition, and their realm suffered from some of the same evils as the parent culture. While the white farmer worried over the drought and the epidemic, and perhaps conveyed that stress to his slaves, the blacks endured their own concerns and pressures aside from those applied directly by their masters. In at least one instance that year, internal conflict turned to tragedy among the serried cabins of an expansive Appomattox plantation.

Since his father's death, Crawford Jones and his mother owned more than five dozen slaves. Two of them fell into dispute over something—one of the slave women, suggested a county official four decades later—and one Tuesday after the middle of August the older of them, Reuben, killed his competitor, who was known simply as Jim. According to the Dred Scott decision, a slave could not sue in court, but apparently one could be tried there, and Reuben was. The verdict came swift and sure, so in the end the Joneses lost not only one prime hand, but two. On November 22, after three months in the jail, Reuben was taken across the branch of the Appomattox directly behind the Clover Hill Tavern, to be hanged on the opposite hillside. As his was the county's first execution and it happened to fall on a Sunday, the slope behind the tavern attracted a crowd worthy of a Fourth of July celebration.[14]

Only days after the murder, in the faraway city of New York, a bank with Ohio connections went out of business. Ordinarily that should have had little effect on Appomattox County, but this was the most respected bank in its home state and its failure created a panic on Wall Street—what would become known as the panic of 1857.

Thanks in part to the Democratic hostility to a national bank, there existed too few controls over the banking systems of the individual states. Those systems varied from state to state, with some banks regulated by a central state authority, some operating on their own under special state charters, and some enjoying "free banking," which allowed anyone with sufficient capital to found a bank by posting stocks and bonds with state officials. A few states permitted all three varieties, and Virginia was one of them. The General Assembly had just chartered the Appomattox Savings Bank in 1856, with eight local shareholders. Banks of that era printed their own notes, which passed for legal tender with anyone who would accept it, and the greatest support for banking regulation arose from the fear of inflation, as independent banks met growing demands for cash by simply running off more currency.

A new phenomenon known as the "demand deposit" added another stratum of danger, for a depositor might appear at the teller's window at any moment and ask to have an account receipt or a sheaf of bank notes redeemed for gold or silver coin. When depositors grew suspicious of their banks they would be very likely to do that, and once that had started it was almost impossible to stop: if someone holding hundreds of dollars in a certain bank's notes, or substantial savings deposits, happened by the building and saw a queue at the door, he was certain to fall into that line before the bank had distributed all its specie. Since the bank could not call in all its outstanding loans, it was bound to fall short somewhere along the way, and in most cases early on. On September 25 the Bank of Pennsylvania suspended specie payments in the face of such a run, and the crisis worsened as depositors across the country demanded hard money. To protect themselves during the panic, most banks refused to distribute specie until fears had settled.[15]

In Richmond every bank suspended specie payments by mid-October, and most of those in the Piedmont did so within another week, but by the end of the month the calm seemed to have come, at least in Virginia; now Richmond newspaper editors boasted over how well the South had fared, turning the financial crisis into just one more round in the cold war between the sections. The *Enquirer* spent more than a few smug words on Northern indebtedness, alluded to the economic plight of the North's sudden masses of unemployed, and used Virginia's rapid recovery from this Yankee-induced panic as more evidence of the superiority of a slave economy.[16]

Virginia's self-congratulation proved hasty. Thanks to Wall Street speculation, the price of tobacco depended largely upon what New York buyers were willing to pay for it, and in their cautious condition they were not willing to pay much that autumn, when the crop came to market. Warehouses in Richmond soon bulged with the bountiful harvest. Counties where tobacco reigned supreme, including Appomattox, suffered acutely. Almost immediately a plantation at Pamplin's Depot, bordering both Charlotte and Prince Edward Counties, went up for sale: with money so tight that the market would have been abnormally depressed, the owner, one Steptoe, could only have been persuaded to sell by his own financial straits. In crowing over the merits of his farm he mentioned the proximity of a tobacco factory, but he named his harvested tobacco along with the tools and livestock he was willing to throw into the bargain.[17]

Falling prices created a local depression that lasted into the winter, crushing the more fragile enterprises and squeezing them all. By February 2 the boasted tobacco factory at Pamplin's Depot had gone out of business. Even Sheriff William Paris, a neighbor and occasional business associate of Samuel McDearmon's from his days near Evergreen, lost everything he had: extensive indebtedness forced Paris to put his 1,300-

{ THE CRISIS }

acre plantation on the block, slaves and all, and still he defaulted on his official accounts, prompting the state treasurer to call in $30,000 in bonds that Paris's supporters and deputies had signed to assure the faithful discharge of his duties.

A universal shortage of funds prompted unusual solutions. As rare as horse theft was in Appomattox County, it may have been an acute need for cash that motivated someone to lead a horse out of Willis Inge's stable, on the LeGrand Road, in the dead of night on January 29.[18]

Bankruptcies rebounded across the county, and into adjoining counties, as more farmers found themselves unable to repay their loans and mortgages, and at the upper terminal of the credit chain the new lending institutions accumulated the greatest losses. The new director of Lynchburg's Farmer's Bank, Henry Flood, thereafter devoted his talents to a new grocery and commission business, and to his legal practice. His cousin John, the erstwhile Clover Hill entrepreneur, ceased to supervise his interest in the brick store, and moved to Lynchburg himself, to join Henry's new firm; within a couple of years he would sell everything he had accumulated in the village.[19]

During that winter McDearmon's brothers-in-law arrived at the same economic extremity that he had reached five years before. Hampered by the unsatisfied portion of McDearmon's debts to them, and finished off by the tobacco crisis, they composed trustee deeds not unlike the one McDearmon had signed, consigning their property to the payment of their creditors. At the traditional spring auctions they offered the Bent Creek mill that McDearmon had abandoned to them, with 228 acres, as well as an Appomattox farm they had acquired and a Lynchburg tobacco factory, complete with a store of tobacco, slaves, horses, mules, and wagons. Finally, James Walton turned his own home over to retire his debts. In a few short years McDearmon had bankrupted his name, if not his household, and had shown his wife's brothers the road to failure. His distant job may have become more of a blessing than an inconvenience now, and not merely for the steady salary.[20]

While Appomattox reeled with economic woes, the city of Washington struggled over Kansas. Opposing factions in that state had created rival governments, one of which lobbied for admission as a slave state while the other wished Kansas to become free soil. The proslave legislature, based in Lecompton, had submitted its constitution in the autumn of 1857, and President Buchanan gratified Southerners by advocating adoption. Senator Stephen Douglas defied the president, who was a member of his own party; as the author of the doctrine of popular sovereignty, Douglas denounced the Lecompton constitution as a fraud on the majority of citizens in Kansas, and demanded that those people have an opportunity to approve or reject it themselves, before Congress decided the matter. Having won the allegiance of Southern Democrats with his legislation organizing Kansas Territory, Douglas lost their loyalty when he refused to wink at its admission with slavery. Thenceforth there would be Douglas Democrats and Southern Democrats, with further subdivisions in the Southern wing, leaving the Republicans of the North with a plurality of the votes. That simple mathematical observation would cost Douglas his coveted presidency and invite national cataclysm.

That would come later. By the time Virginians read Douglas's speech, they had also read Governor Wise's pessimistic address to the General Assembly. Alarmed by the panic of 1857, in December of that year the governor advised retrenchment in the transportation plans that were linking the western counties of the state. He proposed a tax on state bonds, as well, which could only discourage even private investment in those projects. This was the sort of politics that provoked real interest, and delegates bickered through February and into March over continued state aid for railroad expansion, as the Orange & Alexandria extension staggered toward Lynchburg.[21]

Politics of any variety provided the Virginian his perennially favorite diversion. One Amelia County resident remembered a few years later that antebellum Virginians would discuss politics anywhere two of them met, save during a church sermon. As their great-grandchildren might one day argue the merits of an athlete, these planters would compare their recollections of vote counts on congressional bills, or debate the advantages of legislative alternatives. Democrats and Whigs always engaged in warm verbal combat, and as the Whigs degenerated into Know-Nothings, and later into an all-encompassing opposition party of little effectiveness, Democrats would heartily belabor each other on the finer points of contention between their party's competing factions; if they could find no disagreement, they would pose the hypothetical position of their opponents and sally forth against that.[22]

One of the more coveted political offices in Virginia was that of county sheriff. Once upon a time, before the new constitution of 1851 was adopted, the high sheriff owned considerable power: he was the senior justice of the court, appointed by the governor, and his office carried a certain financial return through the patronage of the office, for the nominal sheriff seldom performed his assigned duties personally. After 1851 the sheriff was elected directly by the people, with no judicial authority, but the fees of office remained, if not the contractual profits from the appointment of deputies.[23]

During economic crises, such fees would only increase while private businesses teetered uncertainly. That, and his natural attraction to politics, probably persuaded David Plunkett to trade his clerking job at the store and seek the vacant sheriff's office. In March of 1858 he abdicated the position of postmaster, which alone had contributed substantially to the volume of business, and set about the campaign trail. Young Samuel Glover snapped up the abandoned postmastership, while the man operating the tavern between the stores, dropsical Wilson Hix, challenged Plunkett for the shrievalty. A third candidate, a relative transient, prevented anyone from securing a majority, but Plunkett won with a plurality of nearly 45 percent. That substantially freed him from the store, which he and Joseph Abbitt Jr. bought from his father.[24]

Interrupting the political season that year was the annual outbreak of fever that seemed to lend Southern life such a morbid undertone. Typhoid surfaced again here and there, and one of Elvira Woodson's classmates wrote that it had struck with particular vengeance in her neighborhood. "Some of our most noble looking and healthy young men have died since I came home," she lamented.

The biggest news at Appomattox Court House that spring came when Dr. Joel Walker Flood died, at the age of sixty-nine, on April 17. In nearly half a century at Pleasant Retreat, which his father built for him in 1810, Dr. Flood had become the largest landowner in the county, until he gave nearly half his estate to his only son. Five years after presenting Henry with Rocky Farm and the slaves to work it, he had still accumulated more slaves than any man in the county save one, and between the 121 slaves at Pleasant Retreat and the 68 at Rocky Farm the father and son owned more than anyone. This grand estate would now fall under the supervision of either Henry Flood, who had not proven particularly adept at anything yet, or of Henry's nineteen-year-old son, Joel Walker Flood Jr.[25]

Within two years of Dr. Flood's death more than half of those 189 slaves were gone—sold either to account for Henry's losses in the 1857 panic and the subsequent depression, or to settle the doctor's estate. Henry served as his father's executor, bringing a friendly suit against all the heirs, who included his father-in-law, Thomas H. Flood, and his own son, Joel Jr. A decree came from the court eight months after old Dr. Flood died: so casually did Virginians treat such formalities as the settlement of a quarter-million-dollar estate that one of the attorneys even questioned, in rural Virginia syntax, whether "H. D. Flood don't want an order confirming [the] division."[26]

Whether Henry Flood obtained a court order or simply relied upon his father's recorded will, he retained twenty-seven of his field hands, who remained in the slave cabins at Rocky Farm. His son Joel, who continued to live with his grandmother at Pleasant Retreat, inherited twenty-five of Dr. Flood's slaves, while the widow Eliza Flood kept thirty-three. The sudden reduction in their chattel family allowed them to offer less crowded housing than most Appomattox slaves endured—less crowded, for that matter, than many of the county's poorer white citizens, like the Sweeney and Conner clans, two miles down the stage road.

Edward B. Harvey, a modest farmer from Cub Creek with a little family of his own, also owned a small slave family consisting of a man, woman, and infant who enjoyed a private cabin. Their ideal accommodations were not common, however. The average slaveowner kept either one or two servant women or a few field hands, but those with a dozen or more usually lodged anywhere from four to eight people in each slave cabin. John Johnson, the one man who had more slaves than Dr. Flood in 1850, still owned the most in the county ten years later, and his ninety-five people lived in fourteen cabins; the traditional slave cabin consisted of a single room with a loft, or two separated rooms with a common chimney, and each of those served six or seven persons at the Johnson plantation. John Isbell's twenty-seven slaves lived a little more closely in just four cabins, while a widow named Nancy Webb packed fifteen souls into two little hovels. More benevolent owners like Benjamin Walker built eighteen cabins for his seventy-seven slaves, reducing the density to barely four per dwelling, and Congressman Bocock supplied one house for every four people (at least after the depression winter), but even so prestigious a planter as Senator Thomas Flood put six or seven in each house. At Pleasant Retreat, after Dr. Flood's demise, the fifty-eight combined slaves of Eliza Flood and young Joel enjoyed seventeen cabins; Henry's workforce at Rocky Farm could spread out even more, at three to a unit, in nine houses. Even the best slave cabins offered insufficient protection against the elements, for after an 1857 blizzard one of Virginia's most progressive farmers noted that the floors and beds of his slaves' new, well-framed houses were covered in snow blown through the sheathing.[27]

Despite George Fitzhugh's characterization of slave life as "carefree," the housing conditions alone imply a misery that was only aggravated by the high death rate among slaves. A portion of that death rate may have been directly attributable to the inadequate living quarters, for just in the cold months of the winter of 1860 four slave infants died from being smothered or "overlaid," evidently by adults who tried to keep them warm as they slept in serried confinement. No white babies met that fate.

Mortality among free blacks did not come close to that of their enslaved brethren, although the number of free blacks declined during the final years of slavery: the marshal of the 1850 census counted 185 in Appomattox County, but a decade later only 170 remained. Migration may have contributed to the decline, for slaves freed in Virginia were supposed to leave the state, and the growing sensitivity over slavery left freedmen bearing the brunt of local hostility. Assimilation, or more likely simple error, accounted for at least one of the missing blacks, as an uneducated "mulatto" boy of 1850 named Joseph Staples had become a white overseer by 1860.[28]

Some bondsmen worked their way to freedom by following a trade for wages, and sharing it with their masters; occasionally they managed to buy the freedom of their families, as well. In 1854 Charles Diuguid, the freed slave of William Wright, established a blacksmith shop at Clover Hill with the help of his former owner; with income from the smithy Diuguid bought and "married" a black woman decades younger than he was. They began having children—a new one about every year—but his wife remained a nominal slave and all his children were born into slavery, at least until the Civil War was well under way.

Fanny Berry, who was raised as the slave of George Abbitt, four miles south of Appomattox Court House, remembered in her nineties that one community of blacks named "Umbler" lived in Appomattox who "wasn't never slaves." [29] The extended family of Claiborne Humbles, a sixty-year-old shoemaker, had grown to seventeen children and grandchildren by 1860. The family included one son-in-law, although one of Claiborne's daughters had conceived seven children without an official mate and the other had borne one, when she had barely reached her teens, before taking at least a nominal husband. Mrs. Berry may have been nearly correct in her recollection that the Humbles people had always been free, for no whites in that region bore their name; the same was true of the twenty-three free McCoys. The recently freed slave generally adopted the family name from the home plantation, like the dozens of Furgusons and Christians. No Humbles offspring carried any white blood, however, and maintaining such ethnic purity in their culture required long absence from white interference, so this family may have been among the earliest freed in that part of Virginia. Nearly all the McCoys, Furgusons, and Christians were listed as mulatto by white officials, and they may have owed their names as well as their freedom to guilty white ancestors.

Most free blacks lived, as these four families did, in their own enclaves; only twenty-one lodged with white families. Although antebellum Southern society (or postwar society, for that matter) would have roundly condemned the suggested blood relationship, two free mulatto toddlers named William Dener and Richard Tanner lived in a home with two young white women who shared the same last names.[30]

Like other census marshals of his century, Thomas J. M. Cheatham recognized only two racial descriptions among the slaves and free blacks: black, for those of purely African origin, and mulatto, which apparently also covered the fractional pedigrees that he and his neighbors might have denominated as quadroon or octoroon in an advertisement for sale or recapture. In so noting those slaves with a degree of mixed blood, Cheatham inadvertently hinted at the unspeakable secret that Southern women, in particular, tried to ignore. Several citizens, well known at the courthouse, owned slave families in which all the adults, male and female, were "black," but in which one or more—and sometimes all—of the youngest children could only be described as "mulatto." Whether the fathers of these children were the owners themselves, their elder sons, domineering overseers, or imposing neighbors, there were clearly many white men in Appomattox County who looked on silently as their own children were raised in bondage.

In the waning days of slavery George Abbitt, a railroad conductor and farmer, owned twenty human beings. Seventeen of them were black men who tended his plantation while he worked on the railroad. One of the others was a black woman, thirty-six years old, and the last two were teenage mulatto girls—including, it seems, one who would take the name Fanny Berry. George Abbitt had a son about the same age as these girls; according to Fanny Berry, Abbitt also bore a fondness for his young slave women, and especially for one called Sukie. Seven decades later, Fanny told the story of Sukie pushing Abbitt's hindquarters into a boiling vat of soap as she resisted his advances, and when Fanny reached her teens she, too, had to fend off a white assailant. Some of their sisters in slavery were not so fortunate: a few miles down the Southside tracks, one of Nicholas Pamplin's five black slaves gave birth to a mulatto girl in 1859. Up in Oakville, Charles North kept nineteen people between the ages of six months and sixty years, of whom only one young boy could be characterized as mulatto. In the southwestern corner of the county, Thomas L. Cheatham kept thirty-five slaves up to the age of sixty-five, but only a year-old girl had any white blood. In the same vicinity, millwright John J. Hannah, whose wife had borne him no children, owned a black teenager and a twenty-five-year-old black woman with two mulatto children under the age of three.

Of William Trent's eleven slaves, all who were over twenty-one were black, including two women in their thirties and forties, while all but one of those under that age were mulatto. Jacob Tibbs also owned eleven people, all of whom Assistant Marshal Cheatham considered black except a four-year-old boy: he apparently resulted from some white man's attention to one of Tibbs's two slave women, who were in their early twenties. Henry Flood's twenty-seven slaves ranged between the ages of one and eighty-five, with several mulattos, but all those older than twenty-eight were black. Of Samuel McDearmon's ten remaining slaves, all of whom were in the legal custody of his father, only a three-year-old girl exhibited obvious signs of racial admixture: presumably her mother was one of McDearmon's two thirtyish black women.

Even the county clerk, Henry Bocock, owned a woman who had evidently been seduced or assaulted by a white man. Bocock's thirteen slaves were all younger than their mid-forties: two were women, in their early thirties, and all of them were black save one mulatto girl, who was born about 1852.

In technical terms, "mulatto" would denote the child of black and white parents whose respective heritage had been racially homogeneous. Despite a certain preoccupation in the antebellum South with the shade of a slave's skin, the census officials of 1860 employed the word in the popular sense, to describe any racial combination: as far as they were concerned, any degree of white blood turned a black slave into a mulatto, with no further fractional progression officially recognized. That leaves no means of documenting similar miscegenation between white men and mulatto women. There is, however, no reason to believe that it happened any less frequently. The habit of coupling with slaves had not developed recently, either: both Thomas Bocock and Eliza Flood owned mulattos in their sixties; John Johnson had two whom he respectively estimated at seventy and eighty, while William Diuguid and Caroline Jones each kept slaves who had been conceived by white fathers well before the Revolution.[31]

The plight of Southern slaves only worsened with the national tension over slavery and its expansion. Northern rhetoric condemning the peculiar institution sometimes took a tone that raised the specter of slave insurrection in Southern minds, and the horrors of Nat Turner's rebellion lingered fresh in the memory of any Virginian over the age of forty: some commotion at George Abbitt's plantation in the final months before the Civil War provoked Sarah Abbitt to race into one of her buildings scream-ing that "the niggers is arisin'." Because of such paranoia, slaves traveling alone had to carry passes—or, if they traveled the railroads, two passes, one of which remained at the station for the company's protection. Slave patrols now scouted the roads at night, hunting for runaways as well as for those whose more sinister prowlings lacked the motivation of individual escape: Southern whites feared the implications of a midnight rendezvous between slaves far more than the flight of a desperate bondsman deter-mined to taste freedom. One September night in 1859 a slave of Benjamin Walker's, who had been hired out by a lumber contractor, was caught driv-ing a load of timber that the contractor said belonged to him. Consider-ing the circumstances, he fared well. Whatever exculpatory testimony this slave might have given would have been inadmissible in court anyway, and he drew a summary sentence of twenty lashes—for the theft, apparently, with no punishment for having been away from his assigned lodging. A month later that same slave might have had cause to tremble as his fate was decided.[32]

Slaves suffered not only from increased surveillance and official restric-tions in the reaction to antislavery agitation, but from the shrinking tol-erance and shortened tempers of their white neighbors. On a hunting ex-pedition late in the spring of 1858, a young man named Jennings passed by the home of Dr. William H. Abbitt—the "other" Dr. William Abbitt, who lived near the railroad. He took offense at something one of Abbitt's slaves said or did—or did not say or do—and Jennings leveled his shot-gun at him. The slave ducked into the Abbitts' outdoor kitchen, where a black woman was cooking, but the enraged Jennings fired a round into the building anyway; the object of his anger bounded away unhurt, while the unsuspecting woman fell seriously wounded in his place. Whether she died or not would have meant little to Jennings, for even in the unlikely event that a jury found him guilty of any wrongdoing it would only be a matter of paying for the damages to Dr. Abbitt's property.[33]

While Virginians clamped the shackles a little tighter on the slaves they held, they held fewer of them. Old Dominion planters had long re-lied upon good prices for slaves down in cotton country as an option for immediate cash in a crisis, and, although Virginia still contained more slaves than any other state, three decades of exporting excess labor had shifted the focus of slavery southward. Deep South newspapers warned that the border states (of which Virginia was still one) would be lost to the slave power through the attrition of their chattel population. Appomattox County itself lost a couple of hundred slaves between 1850 and 1860, and many of them may have been sold south in the wake of the financial panic: the auction block represented the slaveholder's economic salvation, and the slave's personal dread.[34]

Muttered speculation about resuming the African slave trade inspired editorial comment that seemed to confirm the fears for Virginia's loyalty to the slave South. The trade had been terminated by the U.S. Constitution in 1808, but the more fervent proponents of slavery insisted that it should be reopened as a means of reducing slave prices, which in turn would broaden the opportunities for ownership and enhance, rather than constrict, political support for slavery. Virginians lacked the zealotry of Alabama and South Carolina firebrands, and in June of 1858 the *Richmond Enquirer* sneered at a proposal for the Southern states to secede and open their ports to slave ships.

"Virginia had better consider whether the South of a Northern Confederacy would not be far more preferable for her than the North of a Southern Confederacy," advised the Richmond editor. Bolting the union would merely leave the South vulnerable to at least an economic recolonization by European powers, he concluded—apparently doubting that the slave states could cling together, given their sharp political differences.[35]

The *Enquirer* represented the political philosophy of Governor Wise, and Governor Wise was the man most Appomattox citizens had supported in the election of 1855. That devotion to the union must therefore have been fairly prevalent in the county, howevermuch it may have been predicated on a belief that the antagonistic Republicans of the North could be contained through political coalitions. By the late spring of 1859, after the elections, there even developed the suspicion (at least along the northern tier of slavery) that the Republican Party might not be the abolitionist coven the South had feared.[36]

For Congressman Thomas Bocock, 1859 began as a most promising year. He returned to Wildway in the spring, regaling the district with a moderated version of his renowned rhetoric to counter the presence of his sole Opposition rival. The voters not only sent Bocock back to Washington with a resounding mandate but elected as governor Bocock's stubbornly unionist congressional colleague, John Letcher. Bocock's popularity at Appomattox Court House won him every ballot cast there, while three-quarters of that precinct's 200 voters supported Letcher; the rest sided with the Opposition candidate—who leaned even more stridently for preservation of the union.

Bocock therefore looked confidently forward to another chance at winning the Speakership of an undivided House of Representatives that December. Early in August he suffered a personal tragedy when his only son died of what appears to have been whooping cough, a few days short of his second birthday. Barely a month later his brother Henry lost an eight-year-old daughter to scarlet fever, and they buried her at Wildway, but neither loss left the incumbent congressman idle for long: at only twenty-four his wife yet promised many more children, and the profession of politics allowed little leisure for mourning. In early September he agreed to speak at the annual fair of the Lynchburg Society of Agriculture, of which his former father-in-law, Senator Flood, served as the Appomattox County executive.[37]

By the time the agricultural fair convened, everything changed in the political world. Where thousands of fuming hotspurs had failed in their efforts to inflame Southern fear of Northern abolitionists, one old man with a handful of fanatical followers succeeded. On the night of October 16 John Brown, one of the antislavery variety of murderers who had infested the Kansas frontier a few years before, led some of his sons and a few ardent abolitionists of both colors across the Potomac River into Harpers Ferry, Virginia. Here two railroads and two rivers connected; the place was still more significant for the beauty of the surrounding mountains than for any strategic value, but Brown had his eye on the U.S. armory there. He and his accomplices carried weapons for themselves and weapons for the first of the slaves they hoped to lead in armed rebellion.

They killed a few citizens, beginning with a black employee of the railroad station, and kidnapped a few more, meanwhile freeing their victims' puzzled slaves. Militiamen forced the would-be insurrectionists onto the armory grounds, where they herded their hostages into the brick fire house, barricading the doors with the engine and knocking out a few loop holes. More militia companies arrived from both sides of the Potomac, and others started from as far away as Richmond; finally Colonel Robert E. Lee, of the U.S. Army and Virginia, came to take command. When Brown refused to surrender, Lee hurled a detachment of U.S. Marines against the engine house. They broke through, killed ten of Brown's companions and wounded numerous others, including Brown, and captured all but a couple of stragglers.

Brown's raid seemed to justify the direst apocalyptic pleadings of fire-eating slave power spokesmen, and shattered Southerners' remaining credence in Northern promises to leave slavery alone where it existed. Brown went to the gallows proclaiming that his country could never atone for the sin of slavery except with the shedding of blood. If that was not true before his raid, it was more likely now, and Brown himself could take the blame for that.

Slaveholders in general and Virginians in particular shuddered at the prospect of their most horrible nightmare coming to life, and accolades addressed to Brown in the more radical Northern newspapers implied an approbation that most of those above the Mason-Dixon line did not feel. To those who read this applause, though, it seemed that the Republican campaign to exterminate the mainstay of the Southern economy had now escalated to a war for the extermination of the Southerner. In the weeks after Harpers Ferry, Virginia newspapers focused suddenly on rebellious slaves, closely investigating the case of a Bedford County slave who killed his overseer and taking particular notice of a slave near Harpers Ferry who was sentenced to hang for inciting his fellows to revolt.[38]

In Appomattox County, the line between Democrats and the so-called Opposition Party dissolved almost instantly. Six days after Brown was hanged, staunch Whigs-cum-Americans like Senator Flood, Benjamin Walker, and Clover Hill attorney John Woodson joined with lifelong Democrats such as Zaccheus Cheatham and court clerk Henry Bocock in a grand public denunciation of the raid and raiders. They did not stop there, either—condemning as well the leadership of the Republican Party.

"The wicked instigators and movers in the crusade are yet at large," resolved the inevitable local committee, "occupying places of influence and power in the Northern states." The gathering averred a love of the United States derived from "hallowed memories of the past" but warned that the most loyal among them saw that the old confederation might have to end. "We here declare our purpose to make common cause with the people of the Southern States, and to abide by and maintain our just rights and nothing less than our just rights in the Union if we can, out of the Union if we must."

The Brown raid inspired dozens of new volunteer military companies across Virginia, including a cavalry troop in Lynchburg named after Governor Wise. These cavaliers drilled on a plain high above the James River, wearing bright red jackets and gaudy blue trousers reminiscent of Her Majesty's hussars. Their brilliant garb may have caught the eye of some would-be Appomattox officers: at the courthouse meeting Lewis Isbell, a bachelor lawyer who had lived at Clover Hill for more than a decade, announced the formation of a special volunteer rifle company, raised not explicitly to protect the populace from murder and rapine in the event of servile revolt, but to defend the "rights and privileges and immunities of the Southern people." Organization of this elite troop progressed as far as finding a native Virginia factory where a sufficient quantity of cloth might be bought for uniforms.[39]

Thomas Bocock could not attend the courthouse demonstration, for he had resumed his seat in Congress, where he took an early role in a marathon battle for Speaker of the House. The Thirty-sixth Congress could boast no majority party: Northern Republicans held a solid plurality even against the combined strength of Southern and Douglas Democrats, with the swing votes held by men who still considered themselves Know-Nothing, or even Whig, in party affiliation. The Speakership had to be awarded on a majority vote, and that was where the trouble lay.

Bocock knew the numbers by heart, for all the good it did him. In caucus his party chose him for its initial champion, but on the first ballot he came in behind Ohio Republican John Sherman. Sherman fell short of a majority, missing even a couple of votes in his own party, but Bocock lacked the support of Douglas Democrats. Without them he could not win even if every Southern Democrat and every member of the Southern Opposition Party cast a ballot for him.[40]

While party operatives scurried about the floor of the House chamber, trying to strike another deal, a slave-state congressman introduced a resolution designed to unite Southern solons of all parties with, he hoped, a few Douglas Democrats. He proposed that no House member was fit to be elected Speaker if he had endorsed Hinton Helper's *Impending Crisis of the South*. A majority of Republicans had done just that, including Sherman, and in the wake of the Harpers Ferry raid those endorsements of Helper's antislavery diatribe seemed dangerously close to approval of John Brown's incursion. When Sherman defended himself with the customary avowal that he never intended to interfere with slavery in the states, Southern congressmen pointed out that he had never offered a word of reproach for the disciples of abolitionist violence, either. Lucius Quintus Cincinnatus Lamar, of Mississippi, raged at the "black" Republicans for their disregard of the Constitution he cherished, and without which he said he would consider the federal government his enemy. The "gentlemen" of the House came to the brink of blows on more than one occasion.[41]

Democratic Party operatives perceived the simple addition of Bocock's dilemma, and soon enough his name dropped from discussion. Eventually a former Tennessee Whig drew almost the entire Southern vote—some-

{ THE CRISIS }

thing Bocock had been unable to do—but without the Northern Demo-crats he, too, fell short. Clearly the Congress was no longer divided by party, but by section, and hereafter all relevant questions would be decided that way. The charade dragged on for nearly two months, to the disgust or amusement of most who followed the saga, and if the conflict accom-plished any good at all it was to prevent this volatile body from making any new laws. If the government that governed least governed best, as a Massachusetts recluse had recently suggested, then the first session of the Thirty-sixth Congress was proving itself to be one of the best.[42]

At last John Sherman could see that he would never gain any ground either. He withdrew his name, having already achieved enough notoriety to win a seat in the U.S. Senate within the year, and on February 1, 1860, he and Bocock escorted the new Speaker to the podium. The House had chosen William Pennington, a Republican from New Jersey with conser-vative Whig credentials.

"The House could have done worse," observed the formerly Whiggish *Lynchburg Virginian,* but with the new political alignment the *Virginian* would have preferred to see Bocock wielding the gavel.[43]

The man at Appomattox Court House who might have been the most intrigued by the maneuvering at Washington, aside from the court clerk whose brother had a part in it, would have been Sheriff David Plunkett. As it happened, the sheriff never learned the outcome: in the wee hours of Friday, January 16, Plunkett expired in his home, where the ill-fated Dr. Abbitt had once lived, near the triangular intersection of the Prince Edward and Buckingham Roads. He had barely reached his thirty-fourth year, and had been ill for less than a week; no one knew what had killed him.[44]

At his death Plunkett left his twenty-two-year-old widow with four children under the age of five. With no income she could hardly live on her own, so she moved into her parents' new home at the depot, sharing cramped quarters with her three younger brothers and her mother; Samuel McDearmon still remained absent most of the time, at the Shockoe ware-house in Richmond. To bring herself a little income, Mary Plunkett rented the Clover Hill house to George Peers, one of her husband's deputies.[45]

Congressman Bocock's loss probably caused the owner of the Clover Hill Tavern some regrets, as well; as the husband of Bocock's late sister, Wilson Hix would have enjoyed not only a certain prestige but a level of political connection that no one in the county (least of all Wilson Hix) seemed bashful about using. The death of Sheriff Plunkett at least relieved Hix of his only real competition for that authority, and soon enough he had secured the vacant office, selecting his oldest son as his most trustworthy deputy and appointing Daniel Gills, his future son-in-law, as his other assistant.[46]

Nothing had been resolved in Washington by the selection of a Speaker for the lower House, and the national temper merely awaited another excuse for collision. In Appomattox County that fitfully slumbering fury seemed less obvious, and with the passage of a few weeks attention turned once again to the details of daily subsistence. Spring came, and with it the rains that washed the typhoid bacillus into the water supply for another long, anxious season; these days, the typhoid trail followed the rail corridor rather than the stage road, as the preponderance of travelers—and potential carriers—shifted to that method of transportation. This season's outbreak claimed its first victim by March 28, killing a boy named Zack Pamplin, of Pamplin's Depot. Zack was the second of three sons of Nicholas Pamplin who would die of typhoid within two years.

The railroad had become nearly as dangerous as horse-drawn conveyances. In mid-nineteenth-century Appomattox someone was killed or seriously injured by horses every year: Joseph Abbitt Sr. suffered some broken bones and internal injuries one evening in the spring of 1858 when his horse threw him on the way from his son's house at Appomattox Court House to his own home, five miles north of the village. Two slaves were killed in separate accidents in the spring of 1860 when the horses they were holding ran away with them, and those who worked teams in the fields and woods faced lesser injuries every day. Now that it had lost its novelty in the county, the railroad offered equal peril to passengers and passersby alike. In the summer of 1857 a black man drove an oxcart over the tracks in front of the westbound passenger train near Pamplin's Depot and lost three of his master's oxen, besides breaking his own hip. A couple of years later the Southside cars killed both a local resident and a railroad employee within six months of each other. One stone mason, a longtime resident of the county, fell beneath the wheels of the evening passenger train at Pamplin's Depot just before the Harpers Ferry raid; a young conductor who had grown up in Appomattox met a similar death the following March.[47]

Life came cheaply in a society that relied on primitive medicine and pocket pistols, as Clover Hill residents were reminded on the afternoon of May 25, 1860. Seldom did they encounter any cause to recollect the Raine family that had owned the nucleus of their village: their seedy frame tavern and the curtained windows of their brick guest house occupied a forlorn quadrant of the county seat. George, the eldest and most active son of unlucky old Captain John Raine, had moved the survivors of his

72   { THE CRISIS }

family westward in search of better fortunes, and with the completion of the Virginia & Tennessee Railroad he opened yet another hotel in the border town of Bristol, Tennessee. His teenage daughter, Alice, married a man from Lynchburg who followed her father to Bristol, fell into a dispute with him there, and killed him. The casket returned to Appomattox County over the same rails that had lured Raine away, and from the depot at Nebraska a wagon rattled his remains the three miles back to the family cemetery. Anyone standing in the yard of what had been the Raine tavern could have seen the team and the mourners crest the rise west of the village before turning down toward the grave. Once the prayers were said and the shovels began plying the grim red earth, Charles Raine may have stopped for one last look at the village where he had grown to manhood.[48]

If young Raine did saunter through the village that dismal Friday afternoon, he would have been among the last to find Henry Bocock attending to paperwork in the courthouse. Bocock had tendered his resignation once again, and this time he was not turning back. As he had intended to join Henry Flood in the Lynchburg banking industry four years before, he now followed Flood as a grocer and commission merchant in that city. George Peers sought the county clerkship once Bocock had cleared out. Peers had more than a decade of experience as a deputy behind his thirty years, and the people elected him although, unlike his predecessor, he had not trained as a lawyer. By June Peers had assumed the duties he would exercise for most of the next five decades.[49]

The village Peers saw on his short walk to work would still have seemed sleepy to a Richmonder, but it more resembled the town Samuel McDearmon had anticipated—too anxiously—fifteen years before. Peers lived in the late Sheriff Plunkett's house, on the hill overlooking the Appomattox and on the eastern border of the village. From his southern windows he could see the new home of John Moffitt, a former saddler who had gone to work for the railroad; Moffitt's house had burned down in the winter of 1858, but he had just completed its replacement.

As Peers left his house, he would pass Crawford Jones's law office on his left and William Rosser's cabin and shops on his right. Rosser, a carriage maker, had arrived in 1858 and bought a modest home beside the jail from Willis Inge. There he established his business, as well, and that summer he employed three men (likely John Rosser and two of the Kelly brothers) at the substantial wages of $25 a month.

Adjacent to Rosser's buildings, a lane branched off the stage road, passing a little frame cabin belonging to Inge and leading to the yard of the classic Virginia farmhouse built by the Bocock brothers—now occupied by

Lewis D. Isbell, the commonwealth attorney. Beyond that, this lane continued down the slope toward Plain Run, to the enlarged log cabin where Pryor Wright's widow Mariah lived with her daughter, son-in-law John Rosser, and her granddaughter. Alongside the courthouse, just across the road, Pryor Wright's brick house stood dark and empty. On the other side of the courthouse loomed the decrepit old jail. The mercantile house of Robertson & Glover, a big brick structure, sat behind the jail and beside the Clover Hill Tavern, which sprawled across two lots with at least four buildings. Crowded onto the end of one lot, Plunkett's store still flourished on the northwest corner of the town square: Plunkett's surviving partner, Joseph Abbitt Jr., managed the business. In the shadow of the store, a few feet to the north, Thomas Smith operated a little saddlery where, with two assistants, he assembled $2,000 worth of leather goods a year; their prosperity encouraged both Smith and his principal harness maker, John Oden, to take wives that year.[50]

Leaving the village for Lynchburg, a traveler would first encounter the old Raine tavern right on the left-hand edge of the stage road, its two-story front porch leaning threateningly; the neater brick house, now unoccupied, lay a few yards behind it. A hundred yards out on the stage road, and fifty yards north, rose a shabby two-story house with a stone chimney on the west gable: lawyer Isbell and his Lynchburg colleague, John Flood, acted as trustees of the property, where lived a succession of tenants. The frame house where Lorenzo Kelly lived with his mother and younger siblings stood a hundred yards or more north of this dwelling, and no passerby was likely to take much notice of it. More conspicuous was the Tibbs plantation, with Colonel McDearmon's architectural erratic perched atop the rise across the ravine behind the Kelly house.[51]

John Woodson's little law office lay on stone pilings south of the road, not far beyond the new Raine house and just before the small-but-sturdy brick blacksmith shop belonging to John Sears and Benjamin Nowlin. This shop was probably where the freedman Charles Diuguid practiced his craft. In 1854, with the help and formal partnership of his former master, Diuguid had bought a half acre from the foundering McDearmon just outside the town boundary, north of the stage road. On that half acre he patched together a flimsy building in which to work or live—or both— but by 1857 that shack had disappeared. The brick smithy remained, as did Diuguid's reputation as the local blacksmith.[52]

The brick shop offered the last sign of industry in the village. A little past it, and opposite, the old Raine stable echoed unused, its touted hundred stalls yielding only the faintest odor of horses long gone. Next lay

Sears Lane, drifting southward from the stage road toward Plain Run and the Sears plantation, passing the Raine cemetery on the way. Parallel to that, and a few hundred yards farther west, Trent Lane turned off to Thomas Trent's home. The plank Oakville Road veered northwestward opposite Trent's wagon track. So far as local residents cared, that represented the limits of Appomattox Court House. For the next two miles one would see nothing but standing corn, wheat, tobacco, or unharvested forest.[53]

A parasite struck the wheat fields that spring, destroying much of the crop, but tobacco prices had risen sky-high even in the face of rampant production. As Thomas Cheatham circulated the county with his census questions, most planters admitted to substantially larger estates than they had owned a decade before, and if there were fewer slaves it remained clear that this prosperity could not survive without their labor. The people Cheatham enumerated therefore reacted much as their cotton-state counterparts did when the Democratic Party nominated Stephen Douglas for president. Thanks to a walkout by the more radical Southern delegates, who failed at their Charleston convention to hammer down a platform plank protecting slavery in the territories, the Little Giant of Illinois won his party's endorsement on the first ballot of a second convention, at Baltimore. That June ballot included a single vote for Thomas Bocock and a scattering for other slave-state candidates, but Douglas was the party's man and that set the South against the party.

Unwilling to support the only man who was simultaneously able to win and willing to watch over their interests, Southern Democrats put their faith in a competing Democrat from Kentucky, Vice President John Cabell Breckinridge. Appomattox County went with them, albeit without the Deep South demands of victory or secession. More moderate forces in the Upper South assured defeat by forwarding a third nomination for John Bell of Tennessee, on a Union ticket proclaiming no platform save the preservation of the union as it existed, slave and free. Against a unified Republican Party, the factionalized South did not stand a chance at the presidency.[54]

Perhaps doubting that the election of a Republican would inevitably push the South out of the union, most Virginians clung to the constitution and hoped for the best, although most of them would vote for the perceived secession candidate, Breckinridge. The soaring indignation of the autumn and winter softened with summer. No volunteer rifle company stood ready to battle the abolitionist invasion, but between a legislative reorganization and the impetus of John Brown's foray the state militia had revived, and once again the 174th Regiment trod the fields of Appomattox Court House.

Abiding by new militia laws aimed at greater training and efficiency, the Appomattox regiment spent two days of the last week in August drilling and parading on the gentle slope behind the Clover Hill Tavern. A participant judged tavern owner Wilson Hix "kind, jovial, agreeable, and hospitable"—which he ought to have been, with so much trade coming his way. Between visits to the tavern for meals and incidental refreshments, the militiamen elected a new slate of field officers from their wealthier leaders. These four officers differed from their predecessors in that all of them would soon accept wartime commissions, however brief and undistinguished their service proved to be. An interested journalist described the colonel, forty-one-year-old Wyatt Abbitt, as "just the right kind of man for a hard fight," but Colonel Abbitt never found the opportunity to test that evaluation: eventually he would take command of another militia regiment that was never called to arms. Abbitt's three field officers would join regular line regiments, but only one of them would ever accompany his unit under fire.[55]

One of the officers elected during that summer muster, Joel Walker Flood Jr., had just reached his majority in more ways than one: in January he had turned twenty-one, and at the militia gathering he was selected as the senior major. Two years after the settlement of his grandfather's estate, this young man owned nearly twice as much property as the other three field-grade officers combined, and through his grandmother he controlled as much as he owned. The same correspondent who flattered Colonel Abbitt considered the raven-haired Major Flood "a fine looking officer" with the material for a true soldier. In the war that would come he would squander two chances to demonstrate that capacity, and in active service he would never attain so exalted a place as the one he held in Sheriff Hix's back pasture.[56]

It seemed like old times at this last peacetime muster. The most fermented version of the previous year's apple crop made its way down hundreds of throats, and brash boasts carried across a clear summer landscape. The crowd laughed and sang as the last two healthy Sweeney boys—cousins Sampson and Robert—accompanied the fifes and drums on their banjo and violin. The Sweeneys had seen some sad times lately, and more would come. Their father had died in a fall just prior to Christmas in 1857; his widow, Tabitha, the mother of the banjo players, had succumbed to the attrition of nearly eight decades of rural life the past January. Dick died on tour in Washington later that year, and at that very moment the fabled

{ THE CRISIS }

Joel lay failing with his final illness in Allen Conner's house, visible on the hillside just across the narrow Appomattox.

Listening to Sam and Bob working the strings of their instruments, the observer for the Lynchburg newspaper could not help but praise their skill.

"The Sweeneys are indeed a wonder," he remarked. The crowd evidently agreed, but their music reflected the influence of an era that would soon pass from the earth, taking with it them and the life they knew.[57]

THE PARTING

One of the mail bags that arrived during the Clover Hill muster carried letters of appointment from Governor John Letcher, who tried to achieve political balance in selecting county commissioners for the presidential election. He chose a former Whig, Thomas H. Flood, a unionist Democrat in Flood's cousin, Henry Bocock, and Crawford Jones, a fire-eating radical. Many in Appomattox evidently shared the moderation and tolerance displayed by Letcher (a Douglas Democrat who had carried a 207-vote majority in the county the year before), for when a John Bell congressional elector came through early in October that constitutional unionist drew a patient crowd at the courthouse.[1]

The three-way split in the Democratic Party, which otherwise might have attracted Southern Whigs, merely assured the election of the Republican, Abraham Lincoln. No sooner did that probability arise than the governor of South Carolina began advocating secession and mobilization if Lincoln did win. Some Virginians concurred, but even most of the hard-line defenders of slavery adopted a softer tone when it came to dissolution of the union. Home to campaign for reelection early in November, Thomas Bocock tried to persuade a Danville audience that Virginia ought to remain in the union and act as mediator between the national government and any Deep South states that did secede.

The ever-cautious *Lynchburg Virginian* applauded Bocock's advice, but that sentiment failed to carry Appomattox County, and when the citizens cast their votes it was largely for Breckinridge, the slave Democrat. Of the 794 men who exercised the franchise that autumn, 563 chose Breckinridge and 221 voted for Bell, who carried Virginia by just 358 votes. Only

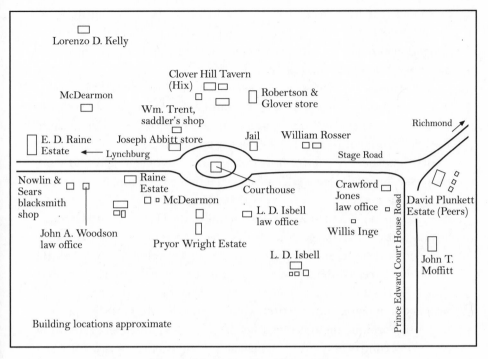

Map 4. Appomattox Court House, 1860

ten Appomattox residents backed Douglas, and not a single Lincoln man could be found in the entire county.[2]

Lincoln nevertheless prevailed nationwide. South Carolina called its secession convention as threatened, but still Virginia hesitated. Trouble soon surfaced over the U.S. forts in Charleston Harbor, which South Carolina sought to acquire—the hard way, if necessary. In the North, fervent union men clamored for the reinforcement of those forts, but a lame-duck president declined to act at all. Clinging to the theory that his state's rights could better be achieved in the union than out of it (and perhaps reflecting that his political ambitions could be more easily realized in the U.S. Congress than in any other), Thomas Bocock enlisted all the aid he could to persuade his constituents. He apparently even lobbied indirectly for restraint among South Carolinians after their state formally voted to secede.

Three days before Christmas the congressman's brother, Reverend John Bocock, sat at his desk in Georgetown and scratched off a letter to a fellow Presbyterian minister in Columbia. Remarking that he had just spoken with "a friend" who had spent part of the day advising President Buchanan on the forts (his brother Thomas, no doubt), Reverend Bocock explained that Buchanan's forbearance had cost the president dearly in the North. That, Bocock suggested, put South Carolina under "a Sort of obligation of honor" not to make an unprovoked attack against the federal bastions while Buchanan remained in office.

"If a collision of arms can be avoided," Bocock wrote, "all may yet be well. . . . The collision will drench the continent in blood, as well as deeply stain the honor of Carolina, as an ungenerous return for the great sacrifices the President has made to show her kindness." [3]

Reverend Bocock's letter had probably not even been delivered when the post commander at Charleston changed the complexion of the crisis by ferrying his garrison from the vulnerable quarters at Fort Moultrie to the more defensible Fort Sumter, in the middle of the harbor. South Carolinians raged over the movement, considering it an act of aggression rather than simple defense, and the Buchanan cabinet wrangled over it. While the president regretted the transfer, he refused to order the garrison back to Moultrie. His secretary of war, former Virginia governor John B. Floyd, resigned in nominal outrage over what he considered a breached promise to South Carolina, though Floyd's departure may have been hastened by a growing controversy over his mishandling of federal funds.

The days following Fort Sumter's occupation saw secession conventions meet in the Gulf states, and on January 7, 1861, Governor Letcher called the Virginia assembly into extra session and proposed a peace convention of all the states. Delegate Crawford Jones, of Appomattox, made it clear that he preferred voting for secession while the iron remained hot, and when he reached Richmond he submitted a bill allowing Appomattox County to raise $6,000 to arm all its militia and volunteer companies. Such radicals still failed to propel the Old Dominion out of the union, and the assembly merely called for a February 4 election of delegates to a secession convention. At Washington, meanwhile, Congressman Bocock supported a resolution calling on all members of Congress to resign so the people could choose new representatives who might be better able to resolve the conflict.

Though Virginia clung to the union by a broad majority, Appomattox County lay in the southern Piedmont, which harbored most of the state's slaves and, consequently, most of its more radical secessionists. The county therefore sent secession-minded Lewis D. Isbell as its representative to the state convention at Richmond—where, toward the end of February, convention members still declined to put secession to a vote. While the convention wrangled, delegates to a peace mission met at Washington and bought some time with a complicated compromise proposal aimed at holding the Upper South in the union if not enticing the Deep South to return. Congress failed to endorse the constitutional amendments they forwarded, however, and in so doing gave that much more ammunition to the disunionists.

In Southside Virginia that winter secession fever infected a substantial minority, and especially among the young. One recent Virginia Military Institute alumnus, teaching school near Walker's Church and mooning over his neighbor's teenage daughter, threatened to "go South" for the anticipated fight at Fort Pickens when she seemed to reject him. The ploy bought John Moseley a measure of temporary solicitude, but his nationalistic ardor would long outlast the affection of his beloved young lady.

The state elections were still scheduled that spring; on April 4 some of the more conservative of the former Whigs around Clover Hill sought out their old champion, Thomas Flood, to replace that fervently secessionist incumbent, Crawford Jones. Flood agreed to run, but after one full month of the Lincoln administration even he seemed sympathetic with secession. The *Lynchburg Virginian* still discouraged disunion, though, equating secession with the horrors of the French Revolution, and most of the state's citizens remained hopeful. On April 8 the Richmond convention sent a last-ditch delegation of three prominent Virginians to take one last peace measure to President Lincoln, but they failed to gain an audience with him until April 12.[4]

By then it was too late. Before dawn on that day a South Carolina mortar shell exploded over Fort Sumter, and even as the Virginians met with Lincoln the war had begun. The president called upon the three the following day, after Fort Sumter had surrendered, and informed them that he intended to call upon every state for troops to quash the rebellion. The trio hastened to telegraph that information ahead of Lincoln's formal appeal for 75,000 militia, and as early as Sunday morning, April 14, the word had reached Lynchburg. It had been a gloomy week, with rain and snow on April 12 and more rain the next day, but the news that Sunday proved more depressing than any precipitation. William Matthews Blackford, a Lynchburg banker and an old Whig, heard of it as he emerged from church. Blackford preferred the protections of the Constitution, and presumed they would be lost with secession.

"Of *course*," he had written the previous week, "I take it for granted that the free institutions we now enjoy are to be destroyed. Freedom of speech even now in the Confederacy is portentously abridged." Despite his own misgivings, he doubted that his state would ever tolerate federal coercion of the new Confederacy. "If this be true Virginia will secede at once," he noted in his diary that day. "No unionism can stand this."

Blackford's instincts struck the mark: Lincoln's call for troops had changed everything. The next day a secession meeting in Pittsylvania County passed a resolution supporting a call for secession by no less persistent a unionist than Thomas Bocock of Appomattox, erstwhile representative to the U.S. Congress.[5]

The indignation spread from the Potomac to the Rio Grande. In Nashville, Tennessee, a gathering of transient Virginians resolved to head home for service in their native state. Sampson Sweeney, who had taken his own banjo on the road after Joel's death the previous fall, was among those who raised his hand. Back in Appomattox County, even the women grew excited over the prospect of Virginia joining the Confederacy to repel the federal invasion. Indignant that Lincoln would ask Virginia to contribute 2,000 men to subdue the South, Drury Woodson's oldest daughter wrote her sister of the "glorious news" that Virginia would inevitably secede: Amanda Daniel had heard about it after attending Sunday services at New Hope Church, near her father's home, and she reveled in her brother's prediction of a bloody battle at Fort Pickens, in Florida.

Appomattox citizens like the Woodsons had other things to worry about. Mrs. Daniel mentioned, for instance, that their brother, James Woodson, had driven a 1,200-pound load of tobacco to market and received only $2.30 per hundredweight; after expenses he had come home with only $20, and Amanda wondered how her father could afford to pay for the year's meat supply, which was due in May. She also commiserated with her sister, Elvira, who had evidently made a bad bargain as a schoolteacher in Buckingham County, and it seemed that the entire Woodson clan was worried about Elvira's frail health that wet April as she perambulated a much longer daily route than her contract had called for.[6]

Perhaps the common folk greeted war fever as an opportunity to forget their personal and family problems. Recruiting began almost immediately, and fifty Appomattox men had volunteered within ten days of Mrs. Daniel's letter. James E. Robertson, a young farmer from Spout Spring, the eldest son of Clover Hill investor David Robertson, and the longtime captain of his militia company, almost instantly persuaded forty-nine local men to join him in a new company for active service in the field; another twenty-one signed with him early in May, assuring that he would become captain of this company, as well.[7]

As soon as the Virginia convention passed an ordinance of secession, on April 17, a Bedford County planter named Richard Radford sent agents into the adjoining counties to solicit companies for a cavalry regiment.[8] Appomattox County harbored many accomplished horsemen whose heritage fitted them for, and attracted them to, the cavalry, and while they embraced Radford's would-be regiment they rejected his recruiter. Instead they clove to their robust, raven-haired neighbor, Joel Walker Flood, who had commanded a battalion of the militia regiment at its encampment behind the Clover Hill Tavern the previous August. Barely twenty-two, the aristocratic militia major was already one of the wealthiest men in the county by virtue of having inherited more than half the sprawling estate of his grandfather, Dr. Flood. Such wealth allowed an aspiring officer to offer certain inducements that might not only attract volunteers to his company but engender an ephemeral loyalty: in the volunteer regiments company officers were usually appointed after an election among the recruits, just as the militia commissions were allotted, and the majority was more likely to cast its vote for a candidate who could buy everyone dashing uniforms, or provide a little pocket change.

Despite his personal worth, the prospective cavalry captain solicited contributions from his neighbors and relatives to help equip the company. Thomas Bocock gave him ten dollars toward that end, and other prosperous farmers would have been hard-pressed to refuse something, with the countryside in such a bellicose frenzy.

Flood's cousin, nineteen-year-old Robert Bolling Poore, helped him to organize the company. Poore, who had also been raised by their grandfather, came fresh from a year at the Virginia Military Institute; his familiarity with drill and discipline far surpassed that of his cousin, whose entire military education had consisted of no more than a couple of raucous annual musters. When it came down to the balloting Flood was elected captain, and Poore the first lieutenant.[9] Rotund William H. Trent, known to his neighbors as "Buck," garnered enough votes for second lieutenant. The position of third lieutenant—a rank unique to the Confederate army in the early days of the war—went to Dr. Charles E. Webb, whose brother Clifton became one of the sergeants.

Except for Lieutenant Webb, all the officers lived within such easy distance of Appomattox Court House that they thought of it as "their" village, and a plurality of the young men whose homes lay within sight of the courthouse chose Flood's cavalry company over the two infantry units forming that spring. Samuel A. Glover left his brick store to ride with Captain Flood, followed by his clerk and younger brother, William. Lafayette Meeks, whose father had just bought the old Plunkett store from Joseph

Abbitt and David Plunkett's estate, signed his name to the roll, as did Jacob Tibbs's oldest son, Thomas. From the ridge south of the courthouse came Thomas E. LeGrand, who left his widowed mother and widowed sister behind. Just down the slope from the village another widow, Mariah Wright, watched her son Fountain amble up to join the other youths, who included two of his cousins. From out beyond New Hope Church came Amanda Daniel's youngest brother, James Henry Woodson, whose family was facing such a lean year.

These anxious cavaliers ranged between eighteen and twenty-four years of age, as did two-thirds of those who rallied to Captain Flood's side that May, but not all his recruits proved so young. Over on the hillside east of the north branch of the Appomattox, Allen Conner and his cousin Bob Sweeney, the left-handed fiddler, found enough inspiration to leave their families and take horse, though both were in their mid-thirties. Even with no conscription law to prod them, five men between thirty-five and forty-one were stirred by either enough patriotism or enough domestic dissatisfaction to go to war with Joel Flood.[10] Ten Appomattox citizens in their forties took up arms that spring—as well as Robert Martin and James Overton, both of whom had turned fifty-five by the time they signed with Captain Robertson.

Confederate fever struck deep and wide, infecting unlikely sympathizers. Charles Diuguid, the Clover Hill blacksmith whose skills had only recently bought him his own freedom, had married a young slave woman, and because of her status each of the children she so quickly bore him entered the world in at least technical bondage. Motivated by an exaggerated feudal fealty or a desire to ingratiate their white neighbors, they chose the name Jeff Davis Diuguid for a son she bore on May 17.

Thus mesmerized, Virginians took to the polls on May 23 for popular ratification of the convention's secession ordinance. No one expected anything but handy approval, and in Appomattox County every man of the 805 who cast a ballot voted for disunion; that unanimity would come back to haunt citizens who wished, four years hence, that they could claim unswerving national loyalty. By election day Captain Flood had collected pledges from nearly enough men to compose an entire company. The next day they gathered in the yard of his house to sign formal enlistment papers and elect their officers, after which each man mounted a horse that he had provided for himself. Confident now that he would be their captain, Flood swung into the saddle and started for Lynchburg at the head of sixty-eight troopers, exactly one-quarter of whom would not survive the war.[11]

Many of those who marched off to war that spring had earnestly sought to avoid the conflict. Barely three weeks before he recruited the county's earliest volunteers, Captain Robertson himself had signed the April 4 letter to the unionist moderate, Thomas Flood, urging his candidacy for the legislature. So had Samuel Glover, Clifton Webb, and Allen Conner, all of whom had since ridden away with Captain Flood: their last effort at moderation having failed, they were among the first to step forward in the defense of their home state. Even William Blackford, the longtime Lynchburg loyalist, chaired a committee of overage men like himself, whom he wished to mobilize as a reserve military company, and within weeks all five of his sons had enlisted in the Confederate army. As so often happens, some of those who preached the loudest for the actions that precipitated war gave the recruiting officers the widest berth. Crawford Jones, who had clamored for secession since the beginning of the year, waited for ten months (until the eve of Confederate conscription) before seeking an appointment in a gentlemen's company of stay-at-home artillery; commonwealth attorney Lewis Isbell, whom George Peers remembered as an "avowed secessionist," never joined the army at all, though many men older than he carried a musket or a sword.[12]

Virginia's northern border became the battlefront, and the new Confederate War Department began recognizing regiments as quickly as sufficient companies arrived at their respective rendezvous. The company that Thomas Mathews raised, the Appomattox Grays, went to Camp Lee, at Richmond, where it became part of the 18th Virginia Infantry. That regiment traveled north in June to Manassas Junction, some twenty-five miles southwest of Washington, but when the Grays departed the Richmond rail station they left behind Charles Gilchrist, a young artist who had fallen ill. On June 6, just thirty days after he and his brother had enlisted together, Gilchrist became Appomattox County's first sacrifice to the Confederate cause.[13]

Captain Flood's Appomattox Rangers mustered into Confederate service at Lynchburg on June 3 and soon followed the 18th Virginia to Manassas, where the companies of Colonel Radford's regiment had been ordered to report. As Union forces concentrated around Washington, the Rangers moved forward for picket duty near Fairfax Court House. Like most of the Confederate cavalry in that vicinity, Radford's men had armed themselves with a motley collection of sabers, pistols, and shotguns, most of which had long hung over their mantles at home.[14]

James Robertson's company, optimistically known as the Appomattox Invincibles, also took the cars to Richmond. There it was incorporated into the 44th Virginia Infantry, under Colonel William Scott. On July 2 that regiment started by rail for the insurgent counties of western Virginia, where in his first campaign Colonel Scott managed to cast a pall over his reputation and to embarrass the proud new soldiers under him. During the battle of Rich Mountain, as a ragtag Confederate army tried to hold back four big Union brigades, Scott was expected to defend a key intersection with his regiment; instead he put his regiment into ignominiously premature retreat, burning a vital bridge without ever having sighted a Union soldier, and his flight contributed to the capture of several hundred Virginians. Second Lieutenant Charles Raine of the Lee Battery was one of those who barely escaped the affair at Rich Mountain. With his captain and three men, Raine fled through the rain-drenched forest when Yankee soldiers swarmed over their position, finding his way to freedom without encountering any of his neighbors from Appomattox, all of whom had flown over the mountains ahead of him.[15]

While the opposing forces prodded tentatively at each other in western and northern Virginia, the folks at home found the incentive to continue mobilizing. Henry Wise, who had served until recently as governor of the state, earned a commission as brigadier general on the strength of his political popularity; he soon began stumping his way across Virginia looking for volunteers to fill his brigade—which, in Roman imitation, he styled a "legion." As the Confederacy used Wise's appeal for a recruiting draw statewide, so Wise used his old political cronies locally, and he let it be known that Colonel Samuel McDearmon, the still-bankrupt former state senator, had his authority to raise a battalion in Appomattox, Amherst, Buckingham, Campbell, and Nelson Counties. George W. Abbitt, who had also tried to encourage Thomas Flood to lend his cooler temper to the state assembly, joined his younger brother, William, in recruiting a company for McDearmon's battalion.

Dr. William H. Abbitt (not to be confused with Dr. William B. Abbitt, who had died in the typhoid epidemic of 1857) was also a major in the 174th Virginia Militia, which meant that he owned a certain measure of respect among the members of his battalion. Although Appomattox County had been sifted for nearly 200 recruits already that spring, the Abbitt brothers were able to find more than threescore more men willing to serve a year in the field. Schoolteacher Robert Hannah and William Plunkett (younger brother of the late sheriff) helped raise the core of the company, in return for which Hannah became the first lieutenant and Plunkett the first sergeant. The recruits from Appomattox included a couple of sixteen-year-old boys and John W. Lawson, an ambrotype photographer who had once been hailed into the Appomattox County courthouse and fined the phenomenal antebellum sum of $41.37 for practicing his profession without a license. Adopting the fashionably noble cognomen of Liberty Guards once there were enough of them, the volunteers voted unanimously to join McDearmon's prospective battalion. On June 8 they paraded with the militia at its regimental muster behind the Clover Hill Tavern; the ranks of the 174th shrank quickly in the face of such patriotism.[16]

Henry Wise was not the only former governor trying to raise Virginia troops: John B. Floyd, who had resigned the previous December as secretary of war, competed for recruits in southwestern Virginia while Wise — once a fervent unionist but now an unmitigated secessionist — canvassed the central and western counties. Most of Virginia west of the Alleghenies was lost to the Confederacy, however, and Wise had to troll all the way from Chesapeake Bay to the Kanawha River for enough men to complete the Wise Legion. It was generally understood that the legion would operate in the mountains of western Virginia, to cow dissenting civilians, encourage loyal ones, and to repel Yankee forces that had crossed over the Ohio River. Captain Abbitt's company gathered again at Appomattox Court House on June 19 before starting west, across the Blue Ridge and into the contested Alleghenies, in search of General Wise. These sons of Appomattox found him deep in what would soon be called West Virginia. Colonel McDearmon went with them, but without donning a uniform: he had failed to raise the rest of his battalion, and the best spot he could find for himself was as a volunteer aid to the general.[17]

With the departure of this fourth company, Clover Hill grew even more quiet than it had been before Lincoln's call for troops. No more patriotic speeches rang from the courthouse steps, and no companies of volunteers mustered in the road. The Fourth of July, now an alien celebration, produced no festive militia gathering (although two more young men enlisted that day, perhaps in confused nationalism). The pastoral humor of county life assumed more somber tones, for 250 of the county's men and boys were gone from the presence of their families — one in eight of their gender — and one in five of them would never return.

One of the horsemen serving under Joel Flood became the first Appomattox citizen to lay eyes upon Yankee soldiers. Early on Wednesday morning, July 17, the vanguard of a Union army 35,000 strong marched into the village of Fairfax Court House, halfway between Washington City and the Confederate stronghold at Manassas Station. A South Carolina colonel pulled his pickets out ahead of the variegated host (for uniforms had hardly become uniform by the summer of 1861) and took position at the rear of his retreating brigade. Two companies of cavalry—one of them Flood's—galloped ahead from Colonel Radford's main camp to cover the flanks of this rear guard. All day the Confederate brigade backed toward Centreville, on the Warrenton Turnpike, and as the sun set that day the opponents settled in within sight of each other. Behind the Confederates lay Bull Run Creek, and after midnight Radford's cavalry rode back to guard Mitchell's Ford.

The next day a Federal brigade advanced on Blackburn's Ford, just downstream from Mitchell's. Radford's companies came under artillery fire that hurt no one, and the infantry drove away the little Yankee excursion. For the next two days the Appomattox Rangers helped to monitor activity at the fords, eventually drawing an assignment with General David Jones, who commanded a brigade covering McLean's Ford, at what was then the farthest reach of the Confederate right flank.[18]

General Jones made his headquarters in the home of the man for whom the ford had been named. Wilmer McLean, a stout farmer in his upper forties, occupied a big, airy house that he called Yorkshire, atop one of the rolling hills of Prince William County. Broad shade trees dotted his yard, which looked down on Bull Run over open pastureland and cornfields agleam with bright tassels. The views and the comfort of the site attracted the binoculars of more than one officer. General Pierre G. T. Beauregard, commander of the Confederate forces at Manassas, had made his headquarters there during the skirmish at Blackburn's Ford, and some of the first Union shells had landed in McLean's lawn. One of Beauregard's staff captains, Edward Porter Alexander, bore a distant relationship to Mrs. McLean, and he used his kinsman's parlor chair for a telescope rest during that engagement. McLean's barn had been dedicated to hospital space on the evening before Blackburn's Ford, and soldiers milled about his property. He had taken his family away to some undisclosed refuge, but after the halfhearted Federal incursion was thrown back he returned to Yorkshire to keep an eye on his estate and to assist the Confederates with his knowledge of the terrain.[19]

Joel Flood and his few dozen Appomattox Rangers, whose numbers had already dwindled from measles and typhoid, may have witnessed the arrival of General Joseph Johnston at the McLean house around noon of July 20. Johnston had arrived ahead of his troops from the Shenandoah Valley, who were coming in on the Manassas Gap Railroad; these reinforcements would bring Confederate strength closer to that of the invaders, and as the senior officer Johnston would take over the army.

Beauregard had concocted a plan to cross several brigades at the downstream fords to attack the Union left, while another force drove headlong toward Centreville. He gathered seven brigades around McLean's house, and sent two more to cross even farther downstream. David Jones received his orders a little after seven o'clock on the morning of July 21, and soon thereafter his three infantry regiments waded across McLean's Ford, followed by a battery of Louisiana artillery and Captain Flood's Appomattox horsemen.[20]

Upstream, nearer the Warrenton Turnpike, Beauregard left only two brigades to defend several miles of Bull Run. Captain Thomas P. Mathews and the Appomattox Grays, of the 18th Virginia, stood guard over Ball's Ford. By the time David Jones had started his men toward McLean's Ford, the pickets at Ball's Ford heard firing on the Warrenton Road, and the ominous noise of wagons: the Yankees had chosen the same morning to make their own attack. They had also planned the same combination of movements as Beauregard, and while Jones began his march on the Union left at Centreville, a similar flank attack was bearing down on the Confederate left, beyond the turnpike.

From an observation perch, Captain Alexander detected Federal bayonets glinting on the Confederate side of Bull Run, well upstream, and he signaled that the army was flanked. A single brigade contested the assault valiantly but was driven inexorably back toward the turnpike. Beauregard called off his own flank attack, bringing Jones back to the safe side of the creek and speeding reinforcements to the left of his line. Two more brigades joined the lone defenders late in the morning, but before noon all three were thrown across the turnpike by the growing Union strength.

The beleaguered refugees backed up a long slope toward the white frame home of Judith Henry, glancing anxiously behind them for help. Finally a single strong brigade of five Virginia regiments, under Thomas Jonathan Jackson, arrived atop Henry House Hill and formed in line of battle. The disorganized troops took shelter behind Jackson, who would never afterward be able to shake the nickname "Stonewall," and the enemy paused to align for another assault. Two Union batteries rolled up to the brim of the hill and began hammering Jackson's line, incidentally killing Mrs. Henry as she lay in her bed. Fifteen Federal regiments and a battalion of Marines poised to sweep eight Confederate regiments from the hill, but then the tide turned. Dressed in blue uniforms, one of Jackson's regiments moved brazenly toward the Union batteries until it came within musket range. The gunners held their fire until the Virginians leveled their weapons, but by then it was too late: most of the crews and horses went down before the volley. The Marines and New Yorkers who had been assigned to support the guns instead took flight.

Now, as most of the downstream Confederate units shifted up to the turnpike, the 18th Virginia shucked its equipment and dashed toward Henry House Hill, arriving just in time to come upon the abandoned Union artillery. The Virginians turned some of the pieces upon the retreating Yankees, who scurried up the hill on the other side of the turnpike, heading back in varying degrees of haste for the road by which they had arrived. With that the 18th Virginia, including the Appomattox Grays, turned up the turnpike in an unsuccessful attempt to catch the demoralized enemy on the far side of Bull Run.[21]

Meanwhile, Beauregard directed David Jones to march back across McLean's Ford—his third such march that blistering summer day—to assist adjoining brigades in an assault upon Union troops in their front. Jones did so, placing his artillery on a hill with the Appomattox Rangers in support, but enemy artillery leveled a crossfire at the Louisiana guns and advancing infantry drove it away. With it went Captain Flood's company, and that was as close as his cavaliers came to action that day. They had no wounds to lick while the frightened Yankees scrambled back to Washington, but the same could not be said for their neighbors of the Appomattox Grays. Ten of the fifty men who had followed Captain Mathews from home were already on the sick list (and four of those would die), while Mathews and three of the remaining forty fell in their charge down Henry House Hill. A bullet in the spine crippled Mathews; Andrew Leach, a transient laborer who had boarded with a family near Pamplin's Depot, was killed outright in the charge. Elijah Chism, a cabinetmaker from south of Appomattox Station, was carried from the field seriously wounded; he would live only five more weeks, leaving a wife and two young children. Robert Meadows, erstwhile bricklayer, suffered a less serious wound. In his entire regiment, Mathews was the only officer injured, and his company absorbed a quarter of the regiment's casualties.[22]

By the time news of the battle of Manassas reached Richmond, so had Samuel McDearmon. Savoring his old militia title, Colonel McDearmon used it to imply a certain authority in the current conflict. Introducing himself as one of General Wise's aides, he told a newspaperman of his observations in the valley of the Kanawha. Either he or the journalist exaggerated at will: in McDearmon's rendition of a July 16 skirmish below Charleston, Wise's estimate of enemy numbers rose from 200 to 300, while his count of Union dead swelled from 8 to anywhere between a dozen and 18; McDearmon's version of the July 17 fight at Scary Creek counted enemy casualties at somewhere between 250 and 400, while Wise's official report came closer to the actual Union loss of 31 killed, wounded, and missing.[23]

Wise complained as early as July 18 that measles had assailed his legion, and one furloughed soldier carried it back home; writing to her sometime sweetheart, one of Spencer Gilliam's daughters said that the soldier had infected her sister, and so she expected to come down with it any day. Measles did not take much hold on the absent sons of Appomattox, but their old plague — typhoid fever — followed them into the camps. That disease had already struck down three men in the Appomattox Grays before the fight at Manassas, and it returned to the same company a month afterward. Henry Dickerson died from it on August 24, right in the camp at Centreville, and James Calhoun went to the Culpeper hospital when he began showing symptoms of it; Calhoun died on September 12. Someone may have carried the disease from the home county, for it had also taken hold around Pamplin's Depot, where Nicholas Pamplin lost another son to it on September 14: the families of both Calhoun and Dickerson lived near Pamplin's Depot and would use that station when they traveled to or from Richmond. The Appomattox origin of the outbreak may also be corroborated by its simultaneous appearance in the ranks of William Abbitt's Liberty Guards, in western Virginia: John Farrar succumbed in the big hospital at White Sulphur Springs on September 14, and Presley Wooldridge died nine days later in camp near Sewell Mountain, where the 46th Virginia lay under arms. That company lost two more men to typhoid that autumn, including First Lieutenant Robert Hannah. Even Captain Abbitt suffered from it.[24]

By then, typhoid had also surfaced among the Appomattox Rangers. In the advanced picket camp beyond Fairfax, the illness left more than one company shorthanded, and it killed two of Captain Flood's men early in October. The first life lost among those who had mustered in Flood's dooryard was that of Lafayette Meeks, the eighteen-year-old son of Clover Hill's newest storekeeper. Meeks thus became the first of the village citizens sacrificed in this war. The surgeon pronounced him dead on October 4, after weeks of painful illness, and friends hurried his body home by rail, through Richmond. Two days after Lafayette's death, Francis Meeks retrieved his son's remains from Appomattox Station and drove the coffin back to his new store. In the field behind the store lay the fresh grave, and there they held a little service among the neighbors. County clerk George Peers attended the interment that Sunday, along with William Daniel Hix, the son and deputy of the aging sheriff. Few of Appomattox County's casualties would see so formal a funeral, for this was the first immediate reminder of the deadliness of the war they had undertaken; nor would so many mourners of military age again stand about a grave in civilian clothing.

Captain Flood may have attended his deceased trooper's funeral, as well. This strapping young officer had come home ailing himself, late in August, and there he remained as summer turned to autumn and autumn into winter. The nature of his complaint never found its way into the records, but whatever indisposition brought him home, it may have been lovesickness that kept him there.[25]

Three weeks after the battle of Manassas, Charles J. Faulkner was arrested in Washington City as he tried to make his way back to his home in Martinsburg, in northwestern Virginia. The former congressman had recently returned from Paris, having resigned as ambassador to France, and Secretary of State William Seward viewed Faulkner as a secessionist. As 1861 wore on, the former minister languished in various military prisons in Washington, New York, and Boston Harbor, but his family sought refuge within the Confederacy. His son, Boyd, joined a Virginia battery; Faulkner's wife and youngest daughters, meanwhile, left Martinsburg to live with one of his married daughters in unoccupied Virginia. That married daughter was Anna Bocock, the young wife of Thomas Bocock of Wildway.

Thus came Ella Faulkner to Appomattox County, where she would spend the rest of her life. She had just turned seventeen and bore the accomplished grace of a girl raised in world capitals. She spoke French fluently, as well as three other European languages, and could play an international repertoire on the piano. Like all her siblings and her mother, she put the local girls to shame on the dance floor. Ella quickly caught the eye of Captain Flood, who was perhaps the only young man in the county with any chance of winning her. Tall, powerful, and swarthy, Flood claimed lineal descent from Pocahontas—which, with his inherited fortune, made him a socially attractive bachelor. Beyond that, he owned the gallant distinction of his uniform (although he had effectively abandoned his post), and he enjoyed the excuse to visit Wildway frequently on political, agricultural, and even family business, for his stepmother and Thomas Bocock's first wife had been sisters.[26]

Between funerals and festivities, some Appomattox civilians exercised a domestic brand of patriotism. Those who had not yet expressed their nationalistic ardor by donning a uniform occasionally took it upon themselves to protect the country from enemies within, and passing strangers tended to arouse the suspicions of such hearthside sentinels. When a young German passed through Appomattox late that summer, he became the subject of some pointed questions. His broken English apparently failed to satisfy his inquisitors, who promptly lodged him at the jail, but it would hardly do to keep him there at county expense, so the court directed the sheriff to remove the prisoner to the capital. Billy Hix escorted the suspected Yankee to the Richmond provost marshal early in September. That was the last anyone heard of the stranger, whose name no two officials ever spelled the same, but Deputy Hix used two of those spellings to collect duplicate delivery fees.[27]

While the folks at home danced, mourned, and rid the countryside of potential subversives, the men at the front faced cold, rain, disease, and superior numbers. In western Virginia General Robert E. Lee came to supersede General Wise, but he arrived too late to save the mountains for the Confederacy, and the government assigned him elsewhere. General Wise went back to Richmond, for a later assignment on the North Carolina coast, but his legion remained behind for weeks, lying in damp Allegheny camps and falling sicker all the time.

Union occupation of the Kanawha Valley posed a direct problem for the agrarian society east of the Blue Ridge. Lacking any capacity for cold storage of food, Southern society relied upon salt, or brine, to preserve each season's meat supply. Virginians customarily obtained their supplies through the salt mines of the Kanawha region or those at Saltville, Virginia; eastern Kentucky provided some salt, too, but it was a long journey over the mountains, with no handy rail, river, or canal transportation to central Virginia. Other than Louisiana, southwestern Alabama, and small evaporation operations on the seacoast, no other significant source of salt existed in the South. By the autumn of 1861, therefore, only Saltville, deep in southwestern Virginia, remained to supply a demanding market.

By late September, Southern newspapers had already begun to worry their readers over the salt supply, leading the movers and shakers in larger communities to convene proactive meetings. Local patricians gathered in Lynchburg early in October to organize as wholesale distributors for the surrounding counties, and within a month men like John Flood, Henry Flood, Robert Boaz, and that old captain of the War of 1812, John Johns, had negotiated a contract with the new owners of the Saltville mines to provide salt for the city and four nearby counties, including Appomattox. The committee had to reconvene a few days later, though, to assure that the price of that salt would be reasonable. The lowest prices far exceeded what provincial farmers had been accustomed to paying, but speculators soon began driving those figures skyward. By the middle of December, the suppliers had fallen short of their contractual promises, and country citizens had to flock back to Lynchburg for another caucus. In the end the shipment came through, arriving at the depot all at once on the first of what Appomattox residents (and most other Confederate citizens) would come to know as "salt days," and each family sent a representative to fight the crowd for its share.[28]

Samuel McDearmon also arrived on the Southside train, albeit from the opposite direction. Evidently his brief experience in the wilds of western Virginia had soured the former militia colonel on active military operations. It may also have discouraged his confidence in an invulnerable Confederate army, as the mountain campaign had not shown the best of Southern mettle.

It may have been a lack of faith in his government's ability to survive that prompted McDearmon to divest himself of the rest of his property at Clover Hill. New speculators had surfaced in the village, and McDearmon allowed his trustee (and brother), John, to sell everything to them. Francis Meeks took the two long, empty lots behind his new store (and it was on the nearest edge of lot 15 that he had buried his son). Sheriff Wilson Hix, though heading into his upper sixties by now, seemed as interested in accumulating property as he did in consolidating political power, and he picked up two of McDearmon's more valuable parcels on the corner of the courthouse, across the stage road from Meeks's store. The lot between the former Raine taverns and Hix's new corner piece went to the heirs of the Raine estate, represented principally by Lieutenant Charles Raine of the Lee Artillery.[29]

Young Raine, now a father himself, endured his second bloody affray in western Virginia as 1861 drew to a close. A Union force of Midwesterners and renegade Virginians made an attempt on one of the Confederate citadels in the Alleghenies on the morning of December 13, and Captain Pierce B. Anderson's Lee Battery composed half the artillery on the Southern side. Union and Confederate generals alike saw more than double the actual numbers of their respective enemies, but the odds made little difference to the fifty or so men who died that day. Believing himself significantly outnumbered, the Federal general withdrew; the Confederate commander reported that he had repulsed an overpowering host. Among the killed lay Captain Anderson, whose death elevated Lieutenant Raine to command of the battery.

As the smoke of battle cleared around Camp Allegheny, the 44th Virginia marched to the scene from Monterey, too late once again to aid the Lee Battery but at least marching in the right direction this time. As they filed into line along the mountainside, Captain James Robertson and his Appomattox volunteers must have wondered whether their miserable months in the mountains would ever avail them the opportunity to prove their martial worth, either to themselves or to the folks back home. Captain Robertson's men had been more fortunate than their later compatriots from Appomattox: at least sixteen of their neighbors in other regiments had already gone under the sod, and only two of them had been killed by Yankee bullets. Corporal Peter Pamplin made his way home from Manassas to die of typhoid, as his two brothers had before him, on Christmas day, and typhoid killed another of the Dickerson boys in camp at Manassas four days later. Yet all of Robertson's company remained with the regiment, trudging the border counties and enduring the cold, rainy winter with a spartan diet.[30]

These men's families doubtless suffered for them, or for the absence of them, but the aristocrats of Appomattox greeted the Christmas season as gleefully as ever. The sheriff's son, twenty-four-year-old William Daniel Hix, provided some additional holiday festivities by asking the hand of Fannie Sears, whom typhoid fever had orphaned four years before. The bride's entourage consisted of her grandmother, her friend, Bettie Ford, and her next-door neighbor, Sarah Evelyn Gilliam. On Christmas Eve the bride, groom, and witnesses stood together at the Clover Hill Tavern; Fannie wore a deep purple dress that Evelyn Gilliam thought unbecoming, while the bridesmaids attended her in silk traveling dresses, Evelyn's gown looking more décolleté than late December customarily invited. The Reverend John Bocock—back from his Georgetown sojourn—blessed a union that would last nearly half a century. After the ceremony the entire party removed to the young deputy's little house, and on Christmas morning they drove out to Wildway, where they spent the day and enjoyed a sumptuous dinner. Joel Flood took advantage of the holiday to visit the Bococks there, and the Faulkner ladies, as well, and after dinner he invited the entire crowd to Pleasant Retreat, where his grandmother entertained them and kept everyone overnight.

The Sweeneys, or what was left of them, followed along. Sam Sweeney had returned from Tennessee, and perhaps his more talented sister, Missouri, accompanied him as he played for the grandee's party. Cousin Bob Sweeney had ridden off with the Appomattox Rangers; young Charlie remained home yet, but he had not been so well blessed with the family gift.

The war had not yet stripped the county of interesting young men. Besides Captain Flood, there was Boyd Faulkner, who had somehow severed his connection with the 1st Virginia Artillery, and he followed the party from Wildway to Pleasant Retreat.

"Boyd Faulkner and I pretended to be very much taken," Evelyn Gilliam informed her fiancé, "but neither could flirt with the other." Miss Gilliam also mentioned a young doctor who had driven her to the party, as well as Crawford Jones, who escorted her home afterward.

"I didn't fancy either particularly," reported the coquette. "They are fast boys." That assurance may not have proven very comforting to her intended, who had just marched his company to Winchester to join his old professor, Stonewall Jackson.[31]

As 1862 opened, Confederate officials were already fretting over spring, when new military campaigns would inevitably begin. The U.S. government had already begun girding for a long war and had been enlisting three-year regiments since summer. In the South, many soldiers had volunteered for a single year, and those enlistments would begin running out by the end of April. Freshly elected to the Confederate Congress, Thomas Bocock inquired of the adjutant general how Virginia's troops stood, only to learn that all but a single infantry battalion and a few artillery companies out of more than six dozen regiments had enlisted for only twelve months. By the end of June, these men would be able to go home. Bocock made his inquiry in preparation for voting on a bill that would allow the president to call upon the states for troops to serve for the duration of the war, or at least for three years. Official attention turned to filling up the regiments already in the field, which had suffered so heavily from diseases; that would put more muskets on the firing line, without awarding thousands of new commissions to superfluous officers.[32]

On some fronts, the war did not pause for winter. In January a Union division under Brigadier General Ambrose Burnside appeared off the North Carolina coast, and by early February Burnside's troopships lay inside Albemarle Sound, looking for a strategic landing spot. Expedition telescopes settled on Roanoke Island, which now fell under the command of Henry Wise. Wise, whose demands for the return of his legion had been partially met, kept his headquarters at Nag's Head, on the Outer Banks; to reinforce Roanoke's defenses he ferried over four companies of the 46th Virginia, including William Abbitt's Liberty Guards, from Appomattox. Neither Captain Abbitt nor his brother George, the first lieutenant, accompanied their men, who arrived on the island under two other brothers, Second Lieutenant John Lawson (the ambrotypist) and Third Lieutenant James Lawson. Their company landed on the beach just in time to be gobbled up, with hundreds of other defenders, by Burnside's victorious troops, and in a twinkling a full score of Appomattox citizens became prisoners.

Besides such losses, Confederate ranks had endured staggering attrition. The strength of the Liberty Guards at Roanoke offered a good example of the effects of death, disease, details, and discharge over the course of eight months: seventy men from Appomattox had enlisted in the company between June and January, yet only twenty of them were present with it when it was captured on February 8. Mortality alone had reached such proportions that it had already begun to affect the spirits of the folks at home; on the same day that the Liberty Guards were captured, a morose Sarah Evelyn Gilliam recorded that two of her male cousins were already dead.[33]

Hospitals bulged with the sick, while many had been sent home to either recover or die. Some took advantage of indefinite medical furloughs to linger with their families, while the War Department seemed to have forgotten them. Joel Flood had been absent nearly six months from his company, which was only two months away from mustering out, but still he delayed returning. At the front, his men grew discontent with his long sojourn at home, and their indignation could not have softened when Sam Sweeney showed up at the camp in Centreville to enlist with them, carrying the story of Flood's Christmas gala and his romance with Ella Faulkner. The fetching Miss Faulkner had all but anchored him to the county, but he must have felt a twinge of guilt as he woke each morning to the comfort of his plantation bedroom; the only solution was to marry her and go back to the army. Thomas Bocock acted as father of the bride, providing Ella's trousseau, and they were married on February 20.

Thomas Bocock owned ample cause to celebrate that weekend. Just two days before the wedding, the Confederate House of Representatives had elected him Speaker of that body. The habitual candidate for that office in the U.S. Congress, which he never attained, Bocock had to change his allegiance in order to win the chair, but he would hold it as long as his new nation survived.[34]

With the army so depleted and enlistments expiring, Congress could not withhold authority to fill up the old regiments with long-term troops, and by late February hundreds of Virginia officers started turning homeward to look for recruits. Lieutenant George Abbitt was among the first to reach Appomattox, and he went directly to work: within a few days of his homecoming he had conceived his fifth child, and inside of three weeks he had enrolled thirty new infantrymen from the home county—more than enough to replace the lost prisoners, including some good officer material. That was fortunate, for thus far the war had been hard on officers: a year after the first frenzy of recruiting, only one of the four county companies would remain under its original captain. Lieutenant Abbitt's brother, Captain William Abbitt, was himself on the verge of resigning his commission on the excuse of poor health.[35]

By now the authorities were thinking ahead to less voluntary methods of recruiting, and those within earshot of official whispering could sense the approach of universal conscription. With his seat in the House of Delegates, Crawford Jones enjoyed such advance warning, and perhaps as an antidote he obtained authority to raise a company for "local defense" with a commission as captain.

Local defense forces consisted of those who could not join the field armies—and of those who did not wish to do so. There were plenty of those: Jones held a valuable public office, but he also managed his mother's estate; Thomas J. M. Cheatham, the assistant marshal of the 1860 census, savored the company of a bride less than half his age; James Williams, who as a carpenter had helped build the village of Appomattox Court House, still supported his family on a modest income; twenty-year-old Boyd Faulkner, though a fervent secessionist at his father's office in the Paris legation, had already seen some field service and had apparently not cared for it. John J. Tibbs, meanwhile, was only sixteen years old—as was Samuel McDearmon's middle son, also named Samuel. John Worley, John Wingfield, Norborn Whitehead, and Marshall Pendleton all suffered from serious respiratory ailments.

These were the sort of patriots attracted by Captain Jones's appeal. Relatively few of his volunteers came from Appomattox, for he recruited all the way between there and Richmond, but it was his Appomattox constituents with whom he officered the company. With his few weeks of artillery experience Boyd Faulkner became his first lieutenant, young John Tibbs one of his second lieutenants, and Cheatham his first sergeant; he made McDearmon's son a corporal. Thomas Landrum, a newcomer who had turned the old saddler's shop at Clover Hill into a barroom where some of the recruits may have been persuaded, accepted the other post of second lieutenant. Captain Jones attached himself and his would-be artillerists to the 3rd Virginia Artillery for Local Defense, which never ventured beyond the confines of Richmond. Many of the members may never have even been called from their homes.[36]

Aside from these daintier volunteers, local recruiters convinced more than ten dozen additional Appomattox men to join the field armies in the month of March alone. Impending conscription may have played a role in that success, but it failed to explain the enlistments of those outside the anticipated age limits of any impending draft law. Older volunteers were persuaded by Governor Letcher's call for enrolling the state's militiamen and handing them over to the Confederate authorities. John Woodson, the lawyer who kept a little office at Clover Hill, was two weeks shy of his thirty-eighth birthday when he wrote to the secretary of war asking for permission to raise a company of heavy artillerymen. Speaker Bocock's endorsement that Woodson was "Southern in feeling and devoted to the cause" allayed any suspicions about the formerly cautious Whig, and four days later Judah Benjamin relayed his approval.

According to Bocock, Woodson had already enticed thirty or forty men, but he seems to have lost their loyalty early in March when over a hundred members of the 174th Militia formed their own company of heavy artillery under Captain Robert Kyle, a Tower Hill farmer the same age as Woodson. Not to be denied his commission, Woodson instead snared an appointment as captain in the quartermaster corps, with an assignment to Camp Winder, at Richmond.

Dozens of Appomattox men in their forties took arms that month, opting for organizations with established reputations in the wake of the more indiscriminate militia call. Lewis Megginson, on the other hand, was barely fifteen when he signed up with James Robertson's Appomattox Invincibles.

Captain Robertson, whose company had been detached from the 44th Infantry to form part of the 20th Heavy Artillery Battalion, was the last of the 1861 captains still serving with his men: Thomas Mathews had resigned over his wound, typhoid fever had removed William Abbitt from duty, and Joel Flood had still not gone back to the front. Robertson, who had shown such a talent for drawing recruits in that first April of the war, repeated the feat early in March when he persuaded another fifty-one men to join him. Among those who followed him back to Richmond were Lorenzo and Lawson Kelley, who left their teenage brother to care for the women of their family: the war had evidently curtailed the market for their custom-built carriages even more effectively than the railroad had. Eventually the War Department broke up Captain Kyle's company, discharging the underage boys and overage men with the authority of the Conscription Act; the survivors went into Robertson's company or into the 19th Heavy Artillery Battalion.[37]

The only men from Appomattox who had seen any real combat so far were the Appomattox Grays of the 18th Virginia, who had gone in at the tail end of the fight at Manassas. Recruiters from that regiment found particularly good hunting in the southern reaches of the county; storekeeper Thomas Gilliam joined first, on Washington's birthday, and brought in a few men himself. The Harvey clan, from below Evergreen, provided five men for the company, which already boasted four members of that family. James G. Harvey Jr., who appeared to be looking for a commission, enlisted his own father and his uncle, Edward B. Harvey. Edward, a man in his upper thirties, left a young wife, a toddler, and an infant daughter to go to war with his kinfolk. The Harveys infected much of their district with a familial patriotism: rather than go with the militia, Thomas Wooldridge enlisted with two of his teenage sons; the two Cawthorn brothers from the neighborhood of Bethany Church each contributed a son, as did the Lee brothers. Five Dickerson cousins had gone off with the Grays in 1861 (two of whom had already died from typhoid at the Manassas camps), and two more joined that spring; nine Appomattox County Dickersons would eventually serve with that company, and four of them would die in uniform. Those who joined the 18th Virginia suffered more, in fact, than any other Appomattox soldiers: of the 115 residents who eventually fought with that regiment, 34 perished during the war, for a death rate approaching 30 percent. The Grays differed from most other units, too, by losing more men to bullets than to bacteria, for only 16 of the 34 died from disease. The spring recruits of 1862 met the worst luck of all; 33 men and boys followed James Harvey back to duty that March, and fewer than half of them would live to see the war end.[38]

John Tibbs's brother Thomas, now a lieutenant in Captain Flood's company, also arrived home in February on recruiting service, though perhaps not in time to attend his commander's wedding. He found the county just about picked clean of men who were willing to leave home. Around the courthouse village only Charlie Sweeney agreed to ride with him, and Tibbs had to scour the county to come up with enough recruits to justify his furlough. The cavalry may have lost its romantic allure by then, or perhaps Captain Flood's continued absence from the army had diminished his popularity as a commander, but Lieutenant Tibbs was combing a county that had already put more than 400 men into uniform—one-fifth of its entire white male population. A few of those men remained at home, but most had left their families and their occupations, and the strain was beginning to tell. Tibbs took just a dozen men back to the regiment, not including Captain Flood.[39]

Jefferson Davis detected the decline in volunteering and took the political risk of requesting Congress to enact a conscription law. The Richmond solons agreed to do so, retreating into secret session lest their debate lend the enemy any useful information about Confederate military strength. The Congress at Richmond proved as contentious as any that ever convened in Washington, but for politicians they moved with remarkable speed and near-unanimity on the president's request: the greater part of the nation's armies, after all, would begin to dissolve by the third week in April. On the fifteenth of that month, the House of Representatives passed a law — with only two dissenting votes — that called every man between the ages of eighteen and thirty-five into military service. Their decision became law the next day.[40]

Having imposed mandatory military service on the country, the congressmen immediately fell into argument over the exemption of all those important citizens whom they had not really meant to draft. The war effort required railroad workers, foundrymen, wagon makers, tanners, shoemakers, niter manufacturers, and an assortment of artisans whose skills had been scarce enough in the South before the war, and the general population needed the services of agricultural specialists such as millers and salt producers. A few industrial craftsmen had already joined the army under the threat of militia mobilization, but their neighbors drafted petitions to the adjutant general and secretary of war seeking their release. The War Department later refused to grant discharges to volunteers who had waived their exemptions, but blacksmith Thomas Wooldridge and Richard Austin, who operated the only foundry in Appomattox County, were sent home in the spring of 1862. Between occupational exemptions at the national level and the exemption of state and county officials, reluctant young men enjoyed a variety of opportunities to escape the army. Court clerk George Peers, Deputy Sheriff William Daniel Hix, and William Durphy, section master on the Southside Railroad, never knew any fear of the enrolling officer, nor did any of the militia officers, so long as their regiments remained uncalled.[41]

Those who owned their own plantations, and especially the larger ones, could also breathe more easily. Throughout the war, Southerners in plantation country would fret over the growing preponderance of slaves to white adult males, and that concern had already gripped the residents of and near Appomattox Court House. John McKinney, who lived a couple of miles up the Oakville Road, joined Captain Kyle's company as his second lieutenant when it appeared the militia would be mobilized, but within a few weeks he regretted the decision and sought a discharge — both for personal reasons and on the grounds that too many white men had already departed that agricultural district. He persuaded Thomas Bocock to write the secretary of war a note on the subject, alluding to the large number of slaves in their neighborhood: McKinney and the two elderly planters on either side of his farm owned nearly a hundred slaves among them, with only themselves and one teenage boy for resident white males. It was barely a year into the war, yet Bocock remarked that their county was "drained" of white men. McKinney submitted his resignation two weeks later, and a few weeks after that he went home for the duration, obtaining an appointment as the county enrolling officer to insure against more stringent conscription requirements.[42]

For all the exemptions of skilled or connected civilians, the Conscription Act put a sudden end to dreams of discharge for the thousands of twelve-month volunteers then under arms, unless they fell outside the age limits and chose to avail themselves of that exit. What followed, among most of the units that had reached the end of their terms, was a flurry of reenlistments followed by open campaigning for new commissions at every company headquarters. Each company reorganized about a month before its term expired, with Captain Robertson's men taking the first turn among the Appomattox companies late in March. Robertson retained the command and Samuel Overton, from Bent Creek, became his first lieutenant.

A month later the 2nd Virginia Cavalry chose new officers, and it probably offered no surprise to Joel Flood when the Appomattox Rangers rejected him; they also refused to reelect his cousin, Lieutenant Robert Poore, who had held the command during Flood's long absence. Both these young lairds went home, while Dr. Charles Webb and Thomas Tibbs took their places. The Appomattox Grays continued a Richmond man as captain but gave all the lieutenants' slots to men from the Evergreen District of their own county: young James Glover Harvey and his fresh recruits, Thomas Gilliam and Edward Harvey, sewed the insignia of first, second, and third lieutenants on their collars. In the camp of the 46th Virginia, so depleted by the disaster at Roanoke, the survivors of Company B elected George Abbitt to fill the vacancy created by his brother's resignation; they also accepted Abbitt's candidates for subordinate office — William G. Coleman and William S. Hannah — both of whom had just come from home with him.[43]

Lieutenant Coleman's younger brother, Samuel, had been among those who enlisted when George Abbitt first came looking for recruits that February, but soon after arriving at Richmond he had thought better of it. Samuel had been married to Captain Abbitt's sister, Amanda, for five years now, but they still owned no home of their own. About the time Samuel joined his brother-in-law's company, Amanda's father gave her more than 200 acres of land a mile west of Appomattox Court House, adjoining a much smaller piece that Samuel had inherited. With the prospect of owning his own farm, Samuel Coleman thought more about returning home, and that determination crystallized after the spring elections left him without a commission. In accordance with the conscription law, he advertised for a substitute—someone who was ineligible for the draft himself but willing to serve in the soldier's place for a personal consideration. Such a person came forward, and before summer began the young husband and his wife had settled into a small frame house on the gift land, just west of the Oakville Road and alongside the stage road. With them came Amanda's personal servant, Hannah Reynolds, who had been with her for years.

The Colemans had no children yet, but the new home seemed to inspire them, and within a few months Amanda became pregnant. Her other brother, William, had resigned his commission and come home to resume his medical practice, which may have prompted Samuel Coleman to consider that profession; having enjoyed little taste for the military accomplishments of one brother-in-law, he soon began studying the occupation of the other. While the hostile armies glided away to war without him, the aspiring physician turned his attention to his pharmacopoeia, his family, and his farm, from which the sun rose each morning behind Appomattox Court House and set each evening beyond Appomattox Station, burning its way over gently rolling pastures and cool, perennially peaceful forests.[44]

THE CRUSADE

The armies strode mightily over Virginia's landscape that spring. Fearing that stronger Union forces could easily slip around his Manassas defenses, General Joseph Johnston decided to withdraw to a safer position near Richmond, and early in March Confederate soldiers began filing out of their winter camps. Instead of pushing ahead to dog Johnston's withdrawal, Union commander George McClellan began ferrying most of his army down Chesapeake Bay to Fort Monroe, at the tip of the peninsula between the York and James Rivers. That peninsula, ever after capitalized by veterans as *the* Peninsula, led straight to Richmond.

The Yankees bluffed for a time, leaving the impression that their movement to Fort Monroe amounted to a feint so the Confederates would feel obliged to divide their forces between the two fronts. For a time Johnston did just that, holding his main body on the Rappahannock while detachments contained the host at the tip of the Peninsula. At the same time, Stonewall Jackson started maneuvering in the Shenandoah Valley with an independent force, tying up additional Union troops. Early in April, however, McClellan started his gargantuan army up the Peninsula, and Richmond authorities scrambled to meet it.

George Abbitt's company of the 46th Virginia stood among the first to confront the Union advance. Rejuvenated with the spring recruits, several companies of that regiment lay waiting for orders at Richmond after the February fiasco on Roanoke Island, and the momentarily orphaned battalion had already been ordered to Yorktown by the time McClellan's vanguard left Fort Monroe. John Magruder, a brigadier with barely 10,000 men under his command, faced McClellan's entire army below Yorktown, and the depleted 46th Virginia offered some of his first reinforcements.

The Appomattox Grays of the 18th Virginia had lagged behind on the withdrawal from Manassas, and came along a few days later, while the Appomattox Rangers remained on the line of the Rappahannock with the 2nd Virginia Cavalry, screening that front after Joe Johnston pulled back to face McClellan.

James Robertson's company, also swollen with new recruits, lay in camp near Richmond as McClellan's army gathered at Fort Monroe. The War Department had decided to detach the company from the 44th Virginia and transform it into heavy artillery; with the Union army concentrating at Old Point Comfort, it seemed likely that Norfolk and the navy yard would come under attack, so Robertson took up his veterans and his recruits for service there.[1]

Johnston's army marched through the capital to meet the enemy, stalling the Federal advance for weeks. Through the rest of April McClellan encircled Yorktown with siege artillery, and not until early May did he force the outnumbered Confederates to give up the old town where, just eight decades before, the last British army had surrendered to Washington. Johnston began backpedaling to Richmond, unable to do more than delay his opponent while looking for a chance to strike him a fatal blow. A sharp fight at Williamsburg produced a few dozen casualties in the 18th Virginia on May 5, as McClellan tried to harry Johnston's rear guard, but from there it was a steady retreat to Richmond.

As the sprawling Union army crept up the swampy Peninsula, alarmed Confederate authorities again hastened to mobilize enough men to stop it. They abandoned Norfolk, and brought that city's defenders to the capital, among them James Robertson's new heavy artillerymen. Given its reputation for stationary duty, barracks housing, and reliable meals, heavy artillery became a popular arm of the service that spring, as the conscription law went into effect. Two of the three straggling patriots who enlisted from Appomattox County in April chose a heavy artillery regiment, including Drury Woodson the younger, who had given up teaching school to be a Baptist preacher but now faced conscription. Richmond needed heavy artillerists at the moment, for great earthen batteries surrounded the city, and their guns required a certain amount of skill that the infantry did not demand. Within a few weeks, Captain Robertson's company was assigned to the brand-new 20th Virginia Battalion of Heavy Artillery, with a permanent (and not uncomfortable) assignment to a new fort below the capital.[2]

No one looked forward to any easy duty just now, though, and the War Department wanted as many bodies as it could collect for what promised to be an apocalyptic struggle for the capital. Willing bodies proved a little more scarce than they had a year before, and the secretary of war found himself the subject of an indignant petition when he tried to order up the 3rd Virginia Artillery for field duty. The officers of that regiment almost unanimously signed a memorial reminding the government that they had enlisted "for Local Defense in and around the city of Richmond," and they protested any assignment elsewhere. They had not minded wearing government clothing and sleeping under government blankets, but not until the enemy came within sight of the capital did they intend to man any guns. It was true that the 3rd Artillery had enlisted under those restrictions, but official Richmond did not expect such able-bodied men to howl against taking up arms in so acute a crisis, and with little hesitation Secretary of War George W. Randolph—himself a Virginian and a field veteran—summarily disbanded the regiment. That left Richmond one regiment short, but it freed about a thousand men for assignment to other commands, or threw them back into the draft pool.[3]

Conscription seemed not to hold much terror for most of those in the 3rd Artillery. Captain Crawford Jones still held his seat in the House of Delegates, and his mother owned enough slaves that he might escape the army under a clause that allowed the owners of large plantations to remain at home. His first lieutenant, Boyd Faulkner, could depend upon his brother-in-law, Speaker of the House Thomas Bocock, for any strings he wanted pulled, and Second Lieutenant John Tibbs was still too young to be drafted. The only officer in Jones's company who might have worried was Second Lieutenant Thomas Landrum, but the enrolling officers failed to molest him, either, and he returned to Appomattox Court House and the little barroom on the courthouse square. Of the Appomattox men, only Samuel McDearmon's son and namesake remained on duty; McDearmon would not turn seventeen until the latter part of July and obtained a discharge as a minor, but his father escorted him to the camp of the 46th Virginia that spring and presented him to Captain Abbitt as a substitute for William, whom the father needed at home for his lumber business. Abbitt saw nothing wrong with that, and the youngest McDearmon male assumed his brother's place in the ranks despite a lame foot. Some of young McDearmon's compatriots from the 3rd Artillery drew orders to new commands rather than discharges, but for the most part they seemed to ignore their new assignments.[4]

Back in Appomattox County, other citizens were neglecting their military obligations, as well. At about the time McClellan captured Yorktown, Sheriff Hix's deputies apprehended two deserters, neither of whom were local men. The sheriff directed his chief deputy, his son, to take them to Richmond, where he collected $51.30 for mileage and expenses. The traffic in deserters had not become nearly so profitable as it would, but this was a beginning.[5]

By the end of May the enemy lurked within sight of Richmond's church steeples, and on the last day of the month General Johnston finally launched his long-awaited attack. Striking an isolated wing of McClellan's army at Seven Pines, Johnston hammered for two days, falling wounded himself on the first day. While he failed to capture or scatter that fragment, he did stun McClellan long enough to add another month to the campaign. As usual, the Appomattox Grays were the only local men in the fight, and one of them—John Singleton—went down with a wound that would kill him in six weeks.

The battle of Seven Pines was perhaps most important because it propelled Robert E. Lee to field command of what he began calling the Army of Northern Virginia. McClellan licked his wounds for more than three weeks while Lee organized a new plan of attack, striking the Union right wing at Mechanicsville on June 26. The next day George Pickett's brigade charged against formidable Union works at Gaines's Mill, and the 18th Virginia suffered the preponderance of his heavy casualties; the regiment had the same bad luck on June 30, at Glendale, and in those two battles three Appomattox men died, including one of the Cawthorn boys who had enlisted less than four months before. Second Lieutenant Thomas Gilliam, the shopkeeper who had come into the regiment with Cawthorn, went home with an ugly wound from Gaines's Mill.[6]

Lee's seven-day campaign drove McClellan's army to Harrison's Landing, on the James River. Richmond remained safe for the moment, and despite the bloody week on the Peninsula it appeared that home posed a greater threat to a Southerner's life than did the battlefield. Sudden epidemics of illness had blossomed in Appomattox County, and they gripped the civilian population with at least as mortal a grasp as camp life did the soldiers.

Typhoid raged again, killing even more than had perished in the typhoid year of 1857. Henry Inge, who lived just east of Appomattox Court House, lost three children to that plague in less than four months, including a boy who was in the army. Nathan Hancock also lost two soldier-sons to typhoid that year. More than a dozen soldiers swelled the typhoid toll, but the civilian victims alone outnumbered those of 1857. In all, fifty-five men, women, and children from Appomattox County succumbed to that disease in 1862.

Scarlet fever struck at Appomattox Court House that summer, as well. In his sixtieth year Wilson Hix had sired one final son, George, who had not yet reached school age by June of 1862, and for whom the only nearby playmates were the children of Hix's slaves: George evidently chose to associate with a little girl named Maria, perhaps sharing some plaything that each of them tasted, and by the end of the month both of them were dead. Within a few weeks the disease made its way across Plain Run to John Sears's farm, where it killed both of Elizabeth Tweedy's Texas-bred children.

As the war entered its first full calendar year, Appomattox residents died in far greater numbers than they ever had before, and the mortality of white citizens nearly tripled. In 1860, 57 white people and 119 slaves died within the county; in 1861, 98 white and 121 black residents died; in 1862, white mortality rose to 161 and black deaths to 156, marking the first recorded year in which more whites had died than blacks.[7]

Wartime mobility appears to have played a strong role in this deadly trend. The folks at home were falling victim to contagious diseases, and just as they transmitted those diseases to the army through furloughed brothers, husbands, and sweethearts, those soldiers brought their own epidemics home with them. That would help to explain the soaring proportion of white deaths, for when the soldiers came home they were not likely to be so intimate with their slaves as with their kin. Yet the blacks also suffered from contact with the infected soldiers, albeit to a lesser degree, for their own death tally rose by nearly a quarter between 1860 and 1862; some of the field hands had also been away with the army, working on fortifications, and several died from diseases contracted during that experience.[8]

Meanwhile, the absence of so many husbands (and potential husbands) tempered the local birthrate. By this second year of the war the death toll had nearly approached the number of births, momentarily sealing any chance of a general population increase. The 303 births in 1860 and the 351 in 1861 had added substantially to the county census, with only 176 and 219 deaths, respectively, in those years, but by 1862 births had dropped again, to 328, while 317 residents died. Soon deaths would significantly outnumber births, and the county would be losing souls.[9]

A decline in weddings aggravated the dropping birthrate. The romantic inclinations that had drawn so many of the early volunteers from Appomattox County also drew some of them into marriage, but not in numbers sufficient to make up for the random alliances of more peaceful days. The last year before the war, twenty-six couples had married, but in 1861 only eighteen did so, and not all of them with an eye to starting families: late that year Colonel John Harris, a War of 1812 veteran, took as his last wife a widow nearing fifty; a few weeks later young Andrew Paulett married a neighbor in her early teens, right after he was discharged for disability from the 46th Virginia and just before going away with the 18th Virginia, but they seem to have produced no children in the interim.

By 1862 ministers had lost half their antebellum marriage revenue, for only thirteen weddings went into the county register. Seven of those involved soldiers, including Joel Flood and two other officers: most enlisted men apparently found married life too expensive, or too precarious, to undertake while they remained in the field. Chauncey Ferguson, who had been captured at Roanoke Island, took his first bride in May, while at home awaiting exchange; his comrade James Franklin, who was in the same fix, did likewise the same week. William Jones hired a substitute to take his place in the Appomattox Rangers, then came home to marry his sweetheart. A Lynchburg soldier assigned as a hospital steward in his hometown came to Appomattox to get married, while the other bridegrooms were men of prime military age who never donned a uniform.[10]

It may not have been the reluctance of prospective husbands alone that prevented so many from approaching the altar. Later in the war Elvira Woodson wrote to a Danville friend of a sudden flurry of marriages in her family's neighborhood, near New Hope Baptist Church. Her friend replied that a woman who "maryes" in such uncertain times was "walking right in to trouble with her eyes wide open." Elvira herself, who was nearly twenty-six years old at the time, rejected all suitors until more than a year after the war ended.[11]

Among those who appear to have spurned the attentions of lonely soldiers was the fickle Sarah Evelyn Gilliam, who had already admitted to John Moseley that she had originally accepted his offer of marriage in order to spite another beau. She wrote to him sporadically during the first year of the war, alternately professing her regard for him and complaining about nearly everything he wrote to her, and once or twice she inquired after another officer in Captain Moseley's company. Moseley came home in March 1862 looking for recruits, but Sarah's letter of February 8 was the last he stored with his personal papers, and it would appear that the engagement ended during that furlough. In April the young captain went back to his regiment, the officers of which elected him major the following month; Sarah eventually married a young man who never served in the army, and she perished after giving birth to their second child.[12]

Those women who already were wives and mothers, and whose husbands had gone off to war, faced daunting duties. Hundreds of Appomattox County children went fatherless during the war, at least temporarily. In the 46th Virginia, the four officers of Company B alone—Captain George W. Abbitt and lieutenants John D. L. F. Patteson, William Coleman, and William S. Hannah—said good-bye to at least eighteen children under the age of twelve, and they fathered more during the war; Patteson would die in battle, in fact, just five days after the birth of his last child. But these officers also left their wives with better resources than the enlisted men could provide their families. Abbitt, Coleman, and Patteson all owned substantial farms, with slaves to work them and brothers to look after their affairs, while Hannah owned a mill in partnership with his surviving brother. The enlisted men generally lacked so secure a support system. All four officers also managed periodic furloughs home to attend to critical family business, while their men seldom enjoyed such a privilege.[13]

In these times the men who dared to begin or expand their families were more often wealthier farmers, whose situation or age protected them from the Conscription Bureau. Securely ensconced at Rocky Farm, which he had renamed Eldon, young Joel Walker Flood soon had his teenage bride with child. Up in the Stonewall District, forty-two-year-old Albert Thornhill greeted a new son whom he named Albert Beauregard, in honor of the hero of Manassas; Willis Inge had turned fifty in the spring of 1862 when his son, Stonewall Jackson Inge, was born. Nothing remained certain in the Confederacy, however, and before the end of 1862 the Confederate Congress extended the age limit for military service to forty-five. Those with as many slaves and as much property as Flood and Thornhill could still rest easy, but the draft seemed more certain at the lower strata of county society and at least half a dozen citizens who had been discharged as overage in the summer of 1862 either reenlisted or returned to the ranks under compulsion.[14]

While the latest draft law reached a greater segment of the population, it also exempted those in myriad occupations. Officers, clerks, engineers, conductors, station agents, and section masters of the railroads could not be called up, and the companies could designate a couple of expert track hands for every eight miles of track. One editor per newspaper and any certifiably indispensable printers were exempted, which did no one in newspaper-free Appomattox County any more good than the escape clause for pacifist religious sects, but the provision for active ministers and doctors who had been practicing for five years relieved a few county residents. Even more availed themselves of the exemptions for shoemakers, tanners, blacksmiths, wagon makers, millers, and millwrights.[15]

The residents of Appomattox Court House, many of whom had settled there specifically to ply skilled trades, took full advantage of these exemptions. William Rosser, whose blacksmith shop sat near the county jail, hammered the war away there—and later in Richmond, for the Ordnance Bureau. The enrolling officers collared his brother John, a wheelwright and buggy maker, but retained him in Richmond only long enough to take his name down. Soon enough he came back to Appomattox County, bought the academy property at Clover Hill from Lewis Isbell and John Flood, the trustees, and moved his family out of his mother-in-law's house; thereafter, Mariah Wright and her last daughter lived alone in the old home below the courthouse. Willis Inge's oldest son, Caswell, had already enlisted in the army but was detailed as a blacksmith; John Oden, a Clover Hill harness maker at the beginning of the war, had also enlisted in one of the new heavy artillery battalions in the spring of 1862, but the War Department put him to work in Lynchburg for the rest of the war, sewing harness for the artillery and the Quartermaster Department. Details like that freed thousands of Confederate soldiers from their muskets: when General Wise objected to the lame and underage Samuel W. McDearmon serving as a substitute for his older brother, William, their father rescued the elder boy from the ranks of the 46th Virginia by personally addressing the secretary of war about a contract to supply wood for the Southside Railroad; the company commander's complaints at losing such an able-bodied young man failed to impress anyone.[16]

To assure agricultural production, the latest conscription law allowed one adult white male to remain on the farm for every 500 head of cattle or sheep, and for every 250 head of horses and mules. It was with a closer eye to security than production, however, that the act also authorized another adult male for every plantation that employed twenty slaves.[17]

With such a law, Joel Flood hardly needed to worry, since he managed both his own and his grandmother's farms, with scores of slaves between them. Captain Flood must have felt a touch of conscience that summer, as wounded men began coming back from the front with news of neighbors killed, but either he could find no military office that seemed worthy of his service or he preferred not to leave his domestic responsibilities for an indefinite term; his grandmother was aging, and his wife would not turn eighteen until July. Yet he had spent most of his year's enlistment away from his men, and although no citizen would have dared mention it to him there must have been talk and he must have suspected it. After consulting with his connected relatives, he resolved his dilemma by offering to serve as an unpaid volunteer aide on the staff of Brigadier General James

Kemper—a relation by marriage to the Bococks, and by extension to the Faulkners and Floods. Reverend John Bocock served as a chaplain in Kemper's brigade, which had already seen a lot of fighting; service there would yield the requisite danger to satisfy Southern pride, and, once he had had enough of that, Flood could go home whenever he wished.[18]

As the Army of Northern Virginia lay watching McClellan's huge camp at Harrison's Landing, a second Union army gathered to threaten Richmond from the north. With calculated courage, Robert E. Lee detached part of his understrength army and sent it north under Stonewall Jackson. Jackson chastised the Yankees at Cedar Mountain on August 9, then moved toward the old Manassas battlefield to face the bulk of the new Union army under John Pope. Lee soon deduced that McClellan's army was abandoning its foothold on the Peninsula to return to the northern tip of the state, and eventually he sent most of his other troops to follow Jackson, grouping the divisions under the command of James Longstreet.

The 18th Virginia, including the Appomattox Grays, belonged to Longstreet's corps—a circumstance that contributed to their exceptional mortality. Longstreet trailed Jackson in the march to Manassas, following a roundabout route via Thoroughfare Gap to disguise his arrival. Jackson kept Pope's army busy all day on August 29 and throughout much of August 30, fighting against heavy odds from behind an unfinished railroad cut, and Pope pounded away in the full confidence that he had Jackson's fragment trapped. On the afternoon of the 30th, when Longstreet pitched into Pope's left flank, that hapless commander came to a rude awakening.

Appomattox County was well represented in Longstreet's flank attack. Pickett's division, including his old brigade with the 18th Virginia, would go in with the first wave, but Pickett would not be with them: he remained at home, recovering from a wound he had suffered at Gaines's Mill. Leading the division this day was James Lawson Kemper, who counted volunteer Joel Flood among his aides. And on Longstreet's right sat the cavalry, with the Appomattox Rangers under Charles Webb, waiting for the kill.

Kemper's division swept up Chinn Ridge, driving away Union infantry and artillery and aiming for Henry House Hill, where the 18th Virginia had gone into its first fight more than a year before. Under their Richmond captain, the Appomattox Grays slammed into an Ohio brigade supported by a battery of artillery. The Yankees backed away stubbornly, only to be replaced by others, and the Confederate onslaught veered toward the Warrenton Turnpike. General Kemper observed that his first two brigades needed help, and he sent Captain Flood to his third brigade to order it in.

Those who had been with the Appomattox Grays since the beginning could see, a few hundred yards to their right, the spot where they had driven the 1st Michigan Infantry in roughly the same direction thirteen months previously. That view flickered out with the setting sun, though, and eventually enough Federals formed on Henry House Hill to bring Longstreet's attack to a halt.

While the infantry struggled for the heights, Virginia cavalry raced to cut off the enemy's retreat. Beverly Robertson's brigade swung around the Union left, approaching the fords of Bull Run, and Robertson sent the 2nd Virginia ahead to scatter what appeared to be a stray troop of Union horsemen. That stray troop represented the vanguard of an entire brigade, however, and when Colonel Thomas Munford led the 2nd Virginia forward he ran into the 1st Michigan Cavalry, trotting toward him with drawn sabers. He ordered his own bugler to sound the charge, and the two regiments clashed head-on. A second Union regiment assailed Munford, who pulled out of the contest; Robertson sent in two of his other regiments, which drove the Yankees over Lewis Ford, but the fighting ended there.[19]

In the gloaming the Confederates counted their casualties. Complaining of a lack of timely support, Colonel Munford enumerated every man he had lost, and two of Captain Flood's young recruits from the southwestern corner of Appomattox County lay among them. William Mann had been killed outright in the charge, and Robert Cheatham was crippled by a bullet through the shoulder, near the neck. That same quadrant of the county suffered in the Appomattox Grays. By firelight Third Lieutenant Edward Harvey jotted down the names of four neighbors who had fallen in the assault on Chinn Ridge. His nephew and superior officer, James Glover Harvey, had been wounded in the hip, although not badly enough to warrant any official notice; Robert Jennings, a farmer with a family to support, was shot through the leg but would recover; Corporal Daniel Dickerson had been "slightly" wounded, according to Lieutenant Harvey. The lieutenant entered the same notation alongside the name of William Wooldridge, who had enlisted the previous March with his brother and father. The father had since been discharged as too old, and the brother had died; William went home for a little furlough to heal his Manassas wound, but two weeks later both he and his father fell ill, and by the middle of September both of them lay in their graves.[20]

The latest sacrifices on the plains of Manassas had ended Pope's campaign, and he withdrew to the outskirts of Washington. The battle there had also served to convince Wilmer McLean to leave his farm beside Bull Run, where opposing armies had collided on two successive summers. McLean had collected hundreds of dollars from the Confederate government for rent on his house and barn, which had been filled with surgeons and their attendants until the March evacuation, but those revenues hardly balanced against the danger and uncertainty of life near the front: it seemed that if his home was not infested with Confederate soldiers or under fire, it lay behind enemy lines. With his wife pregnant again, he had good reason to seek at least temporary refuge. McLean had been speculating profitably in certain scarce commodities, chief among them sugar, and he could live just about wherever he chose. Through some source he learned that the two Raine taverns at Appomattox Court House were for sale, and with ready cash he could demand a reasonable price.[21]

Sometime between the autumn of 1862 and early 1863, McLean visited Clover Hill to inspect the property. He found at least the big brick house suitable for his family, but he wanted a little more yard space; for that he apparently spoke to Wilson Hix, who had recently acquired the corner lots adjoining the Raine houses. By the time George Peers entered the property assessments the next June, McLean owned the taverns and all but a fragment of four surrounding lots. Until Mrs. McLean gave birth her husband would not be likely to move her to the relative isolation of Appomattox, but, satisfied that he had found a safe haven for his family, he returned to his investments. That spring he traveled all the way to Mississippi and enlisted the aid of General Johnston, his Manassas acquaintance, to retrieve a shipment of Louisiana sugar that had been detained in Vicksburg.[22]

With his defeat of Pope, Robert E. Lee continued northward, crossing the Potomac River into Maryland and relieving Virginia momentarily of the ravages that drove such men as Wilmer McLean from their homes. Boldly dividing his army in front of an overwhelming force commanded again by George McClellan, Lee hid behind Maryland's segment of the Blue Ridge and surrounded thousands of Union soldiers in Harpers Ferry, where Lee had cornered John Brown three years before. Through singular misfortune, a copy of Lee's troop distribution fell into McClellan's hands on September 13, and after some characteristic hesitation the big Union army started after its dispersed opponent.

South Mountain, a long ridge that runs roughly north and south across the entire width of Maryland, stood between McClellan and the understrength rear guard of Lee's army. Three passes offered McClellan access:

Turner's Gap, to the north, Fox's Gap, a mile south, and Crampton's Gap, a few miles south of there. A few brigades of infantry defended Turner's and Fox's, but on the evening of September 13 only Confederate cavalry stood in the way of the enemy before Crampton's Gap.

Near Burkittsville, at the base of Crampton's Gap, Colonel Munford pushed his mounted troops (he commanded the entire brigade now) over the mountain that evening, meanwhile holding off a solid force of Yankee cavalry with some sharpshooters assigned from the 2nd Virginia Cavalry. Those sharpshooters detected a regiment of Northern horsemen driving toward them, but instead of retreating they saddled up for a charge of their own, scattering their pursuers with sheer audacity rather than weight of numbers. The Virginians lost only two men, one of whom had been killed; the other, Lieutenant Thomas Tibbs, took a bullet in the arm.[23]

With dusk the sprawling blue behemoth went to sleep. In the morning the beast awakened slowly, stretching lazily before moving forward to try the mountain passes in earnest. Surprised to see the enemy following so closely and so soon, General Lee sent some of Longstreet's infantry tramping back to South Mountain from Hagerstown, fifteen miles away as the crow flies. Maryland roads did not follow the flight patterns of crows, however, and especially when it came to the slopes of South Mountain.

Under another temporary brigade commander, the 18th Virginia spent most of the daylight hours of September 14 shuffling the dusty roads between neat, rolling farmland that turned suddenly and steeply uphill. With the sun still beating upon their backs, the survivors of the Appomattox Grays strained up the mountainside, only to be pulled back downhill and started uphill again in another direction. Perhaps ten dozen men remained with the regiment, and only seven officers, when the brigade deployed under telling shellfire on the heights north of the National Road. The sun was dropping out of sight behind them when hundreds of Yankees surged up from the far side of the mountain, swept around their left, and drove them back over the crest. The Virginians resisted stoutly, losing nearly a third of their own in a few minutes' fighting, but in the darkness they yielded the mountaintop.[24]

The victors failed to pursue, and once again Confederates counted their losses by flickering campfires. Edward Harvey was one of the seven company officers who fought with the regiment that day, and again he counted four neighbors whom Yankee fire had found. Three wounded men had managed to keep with the regiment, and they had been sent ahead in wagons, but one youth of eighteen lay dead upon the mountain. Elijah Dickerson, whom Lieutenant Harvey referred to by his nickname, "Bailey," had enlisted with the ill-fated recruits of March to replace his brother Henry, who had died of typhoid the previous summer; his death left his widowed mother entirely alone in her Pamplin home, where she, her two boys, and three slaves had once scraped out a living making clay pipes and growing a little tobacco.[25]

Though cut down to some eighty men, the 18th Virginia remained on the front line. Before midnight the fragments of companies gathered at the foot of the mountain and started toward Antietam Creek, where Lee intended to curl into a defensive posture. Having marched all day and fought a battle, they proceeded to march all night as General Longstreet's staff officers rode behind the column, slapping sleepy stragglers with the flats of their swords.[26]

Lee spread his thinned ranks before the town of Sharpsburg, resting his right flank on the Antietam. There lay the survivors of the 18th Virginia, atop a hill east of town, with the local Lutheran cemetery handy at their backs. Not until September 17 did McClellan send his divisions against the outnumbered, defiant Confederates; while the ensuing battle raged in the woods, cornfields, and a sunken road to their left, the Appomattox Grays huddled beneath a painfully accurate barrage from long-range guns on the Union left, just across Antietam Creek. These guns belonged to Ambrose Burnside, whose troops had forced their way up South Mountain the previous Sunday—the same Burnside who had gobbled up the better part of the 46th Virginia at Roanoke Island—and in the afternoon Burnside's men crossed the creek.

The battlefield lay eerily quiet on the Confederate left and center as troops near the cemetery, including the remnants of the 18th Virginia, formed to meet Burnside's assault. Four swollen brigades of Yankees rolled slowly toward the heights, pushing back the depleted defenders. The 18th Virginia sallied forth to challenge the assault, but intense volleys leveled the color guard and almost half of the riflemen in the regiment went down dead or wounded. The Virginia brigade pulled back through town to reform for another encounter, but the Federal advance had reached the outskirts of Sharpsburg when A. P. Hill's division arrived from Harpers Ferry, slamming into Burnside's flank and shivering the Union attack. On the verge of victory, the blue columns began sliding back toward the creek, and Confederate battle flags rippled over the ridge until the sun set. That night Lieutenant Harvey entered four more names in his diary: two of his comrades were dead by midnight, and two others would die within a few weeks.

Those banners flew throughout the next day, as well, while rain pelted the survivors, but on the evening of September 18 Lee led his army across the Potomac, into what his enemies were now calling West Virginia. On the morning of the 19th, Lieutenant Harvey bid good-bye to his wounded from the two battles as they started for the Winchester hospitals in wagons.[27]

Though Lee had left Maryland with an army barely 30,000 strong, he lingered near the disputed border of West Virginia with his head-quarters at Winchester, defying McClellan to come across and get him. The Army of Northern Virginia regained strength rapidly in the early weeks of autumn as detached units returned and absentees resumed their places in the ranks. Thousands of deserters and stragglers had weakened Lee's army in the Old Line State, and one of those who took French leave had been Sam Sweeney, who disappeared the day after the fight at South Mountain. Where he went during the fighting at Antietam no one will ever know, but in early October he showed up at the headquarters of Lee's cavalry commander, James Ewell Brown Stuart. By the end of that month Sweeney had been tagged for a permanent spot at cavalry headquarters.[28]

During the second week in October, J. E. B. Stuart made one of his famous rides around the Union army, galloping up through Maryland, into Pennsylvania, and back across the Potomac in five days, scooping up horses and supplies while confounding and embarrassing the Yankees. Before and after that raid, Stuart pitched his tents in the yard of the Bower, a plantation overlooking Opequon Creek between Charles Town and Martinsburg, and every evening the general would call for entertainment. His extended headquarters family enjoyed the services of a little string band that Stuart gathered that fall, and Sam Sweeney's voice and hands provided the best of the music.

On the march Sweeney draped his banjo over his shoulder as his comrades might have slung their carbines, and in camp he sat before roaring fires to lead the songs. Sweeney had come home from Tennessee to defend his native state under arms, but his banjo may have done more to sustain the Southern cause than any cap-and-ball weapon. The headquarters cavaliers who gathered beneath the Bower's live oaks heard in Sweeney's twanging strings the rhythms of a plantation life perhaps more familiar to them than to the mass of grey-clad horsemen who camped around them, and the music offered staccato reminder if any of them wondered why they followed Stuart's plume. Two years after he had found his grave on the bank of the Appomattox, Joel Sweeney's spirit still lingered in the Virginia darkness, resurrected by the artful dance of fingers he had taught to play.

Plucking at an instrument his older brother had contrived to echo the pulse of a dying time, Sam Sweeney buoyed the resolve of men who gambled their lives to preserve the outdated foundations of that moribund era.[29]

The nostalgic interlude at the Bower ended with the waning days of October. Badgered by his superiors in Washington, George McClellan finally pried the Army of the Potomac out of its camps along that river and marched for the interior of Virginia in the final fortnight of his military career. Ahead of him his cavalry scanned the roads, and beyond those mounted troops rode J. E. B. Stuart's brigades, slowing and monitoring the Union advance. General Stuart paid the enemy such close heed that he could not spare a day to grieve with his wife over the death of their daughter, back in Lynchburg; the little girl died as her father clashed with Yankee cavalry near Upperville. The massive Federal army stopped only briefly as it changed commanders, Burnside taking over for McClellan, and by mid-November the long blue columns turned for Fredericksburg, on the lower Rappahannock. Stuart galloped into that town before them, and soon Lee's infantry came to block the river crossings. The Confederate cavalry fell back to Spotsylvania Court House to wait for the next confrontation, and as frost settled over the landscape Sam Sweeney warmed himself before another fire and tuned up his banjo.[30]

General Stuart was not the only Virginian burying children that fall. Typhoid took the second and last of Nathan Hancock's sons in October, and a few days later Betty Tweedy lost her remaining child to scarlet fever. That same month her father, John Sears, buried a young slave woman who may have had too close contact with his ailing grandson.[31]

Death had seemed to visit every family that year: private correspondence from home frequently deteriorated into the enumeration of all the neighbors, cousins, or closer kin who had died in the past few weeks. Strangely enough, letters from the front offered cheer and optimism. Remarking on the "desponding spirit" of his sister Fannie's last letter, Captain Charles Webb of the 2nd Virginia Cavalry observed that her solemn mood seemed "very common in our family." He focused instead on positive news like the relatively safe post that her husband, Captain George Abbitt, enjoyed in the fortifications below Richmond. Neither the Webbs nor the Abbitts had yet suffered any immediate losses in this war, and Fannie Abbitt may have been touched by postpartum depression, for barely a week prior to his letter she had given birth to her fifth child—the one conceived early in her husband's recruiting furlough. Furloughs appeared to provide a common vehicle for regeneration in Appomattox that year, for Captain

Webb's brother Clifton, a lieutenant in his own company, had enjoyed a convalescent leave the previous winter that yielded him a son, as well. He had been home that summer again, picking up chronically absent troopers, and now he wanted another furlough, but his brother vetoed that request.[32]

Clifton Webb expressed almost as much interest in his farmland as in his new son. He directed his sister to put his slaves to work clearing more land for corn production, for it was corn that he could expect to pay off best. Certainly his neighbors had found it so: on the same day that his former comrades stood to arms at Antietam, Joel Walker Flood Jr. collected the cash for nearly two tons of corn he supplied to the Confederate government through Quartermaster Woodson — the village lawyer, who had secured a post at Lynchburg. That same month, Thomas Bocock submitted a bill of $566.50 — substantially more than his monthly pay as Speaker of the Confederate House of Representatives — for produce that Woodson had collected at Wildway, and that represented only the portion needed by the army. A. A. LeGrand made well over $700 from the government that summer on hay and corn, and his widowed sister-in-law, Nancy LeGrand, delivered more than four tons of corn to Captain Woodson at $1.16 per bushel. Woodson's forage master — none other than Robert Boaz, the former manager of the Clover Hill Tavern under McDearmon's ownership — eventually carried away four tons of hay and corn from the elder George Abbitt, and he levied Thomas Flood for about half that much, paying well for it, although in the uncertain paper of the new realm. Wilson Hix, who still owned acreage at Bent Creek and was buying up farmland around Appomattox Station and Clover Hill, put much of that land into corn with the next planting, and at the harvest he realized nearly five times the price per pound that Quartermaster Woodson had offered Captain Flood six months before. Despite the broad profit margin on such staples, many Southerners tried to expand their inedible cash crops in demand on the speculative market, and thousands of planters devoted the bulk of their land to cotton, or tobacco, in hopes of an even greater return. To avoid a shortage of food, early in 1863 the General Assembly restricted tobacco farmers to 2,500 plants for every field hand they owned between the ages of sixteen and fifty-five.[33]

With the help of his son William, who frequently signed documents as high sheriff, Wilson Hix found at least the early war years quite profitable. In 1862 alone he took in upwards of $400 in bounties for arresting and delivering deserters; that spring he received further payments for summoning free black residents to work upon the fortifications around Richmond, and in the fall the circuit court called upon him to tithe county residents for slaves to continue those same earthworks. Besides these fees of office, he began speculating in corn, buying it from other farmers for five dollars a bushel for resale, and with his son he started dabbling in government contracts. The two of them sold the Quartermaster Department at least $10,000 worth of tanned hides and shoe leather between March of 1863 and February of 1864, and they offered to provide more until the closing days of the conflict, when the soles of Confederate shoes were wearing through from constant retreat.[34]

Virginia teemed with entrepreneurs who saw the war as an opportunity for profit, and many of them leaned toward the salt supply. General Stuart's own brother was engaged in salt production way down in Saltville, and although William A. Stuart did not take unfair advantage of the demand for his commodity there were plenty who did. On the first day of October in 1862, the legislature passed an act that gave Governor Letcher authority to prescribe the maximum price of salt, beyond which a seller would be subject to misdemeanor penalties as severe as a $2,000 fine. Speculation in all markets posed a significant threat to the Southern economy and to civilian morale, and early in October the central government entered a provision in the conscription law to discourage price-gouging by drafting those artisans and manufacturers who exceeded a profit margin of 75 percent. The Extortion Act came into use by November, though with such selective application that publisher Charles Button had to use the example of a conscripted boot maker in faraway Knoxville to cast a warning for greedy Lynchburg mechanics.[35]

That same October, the adjutant general in Richmond instructed the enrolling officers to call upon all male citizens up to the age of forty, so long as they did not fit the sundry eligibilities for exemption, while the House of Delegates passed a Virginia law authorizing the conscription of slaves between the ages of eighteen and fifty-five for up to sixty days, for the purpose of working on fortifications. Thus did the Appomattox Circuit Court direct Sheriff Hix to visit the county plantations and select a few dozen of the slaves in that category for further labor at Richmond; no county or city was to be deprived of more than one-fifth of the eligible slaves, and no more than 10,000 were to be taken statewide on any given call.[36]

More than likely it was Deputy William Hix, rather than the sheriff, who spent late October collecting the contingent of laborers. The largest landowners could obviously stand the loss of some of their people most easily, and the two Flood plantations provided a number of men. At Pleasant Retreat Eliza Flood still kept thirty-four slaves, four years after the death of her husband and the consolidation of their labor force. Over on the

Bent Creek Road, at his father's former estate that he now called Eldon, young Joel Flood owned thirty-eight slaves of all ages. The sheriff took one of his best hands—one Henry, whom David Robertson considered "a very likely young man" worth $2,500 on the auction block. Late that month, with his gang of commandeered slaves in tow, the deputy boarded a freight car and headed for Richmond, where he delivered his charges to the Engineer Bureau.

While Lee and Burnside maneuvered and fought fifty miles to the north, the Appomattox slaves dug away at a new line of forts around and below Richmond. Late November and December turned bitterly cold, and the same sickness that debilitated the opposing armies struck the impressed laborers. Henry developed a sore throat, and on December 15—two days after a cataclysmic but victorious battle at Fredericksburg—his army overseer sent him to the engineers' hospital, where the doctor on duty diagnosed him with bronchitis. There he lay for more than a week, until the surgeons decided that he should just go home. He could neither sit up by then, nor walk, but with only five days left on his term of impressment they knew he would be of no more service to the Confederacy. Railroad hands put him off the cars at Concord Depot the day after Christmas with full-blown pneumonia, and he lingered at Eldon less than a week before he died. A few days later, Captain Flood initiated correspondence with the government committee assigned to settle such losses, seeking satisfactory reimbursement for Henry's monetary value: more than eighteen months later the Confederate States of America allowed him $2,000 in its inflated currency for the young man who then lay moldering in an unmarked grave of the slave cemetery at Eldon.[37]

Captain Flood turned twenty-four in the week after Henry's death, and he was already the wealthiest man of his age in the county. With his father away in Lynchburg, the youth continued to oversee his grandmother's plantation, knowing that he stood to inherit much of that, too. Folks referred to him as "Major" Flood, harking back to the militia commission his social status had secured, and he never corrected the fiction that he had held that rank in the Confederate army. He would not wear the grey uniform again, though, for he remained an "exempt agriculturalist" and he would rely upon his many slaves to keep him at home with his wife. In March of 1863 eighteen-year-old Ella gave birth to their first child, a girl, in the downstairs bedroom at Eldon.

As the list of casualties grew, more citizens of all classes sought some means of remaining at or near home. James Shelly, the oldest son of an impoverished Appomattox shoemaker, had come to draft age in the summer of 1862, but rather than enlist in the provisional army he joined a local unit that served as provost guard in Lynchburg: it may have helped that his family lived near lawyer Woodson, who had been appointed quartermaster in that city. In the end that home-guard service did the boy no good, though, for as he stood for duty on the night of December 15 he dropped a pistol out of his pocket and it fired as it struck the ground, sending a fatal bullet the length of his body.[38]

A few miles west of Appomattox Court House by the stage road, another able-bodied young man sat out the war in a schoolhouse at Spout Spring. Chapman Hunter Chilton, an 1858 graduate of Hampden-Sydney College, had come to Appomattox in the summer of 1860 to teach school at a salary of $500 a year plus whatever tuition he could secure. At the close of the second term of 1862, Chilton still had two dozen scholars; by the first term of 1863 the parents of students at Union Academy, near Spout Spring, were paying four dollars a month for primary education, six dollars for those learning the finer points of English, and eight dollars per month if their children were being prepared for college with higher mathematics, Latin, and Greek. Indigent children were charged at the rate of six cents per day.[39]

Union Academy was the school for which Lewis Isbell and John Flood acted as trustees over the academy building at Clover Hill, where for a time the county orphans appear to have lived and learned under the guardianship of John West. The original trustees had petitioned the legislature to establish an academy for young men at Walker's Church early in 1838, but that location proved too remote and the stockholders decided to move the academy to the Concord Church neighborhood, on the stage road near the Campbell County line. Henry Bocock served as principal there before his appointment as court clerk, and the academy operated there year after year, with substantially higher tuition than Headmaster Chilton charged during the war. Parents of students at Union Female Academy, situated nearby, paid even more—whether their daughters studied English or the piano. The county contained well over a thousand school-age children by the beginning of 1863, but few of them learned their letters in the formal surroundings of such chartered academies: these were schools for boys who would go on to Washington College and Hampden-Sydney, or for girls whose families could afford to indulge a taste for finished manners. Unmarried women like Elvira Woodson and widows like Sarah Abbitt, whose husband had perished in the typhoid epidemic of 1857, still tutored the preponderance of the county's youth in one-room or front-parlor common schools for pennies an hour. These scattered classrooms therefore remained undisturbed by the conscription law, save that they may have increased in number as straitened housewives sought extra cash in the absence of their husbands.

Captain George Abbitt's wife organized such a school. Unlike other wives, Fannie Abbitt undertook the project from no financial desperation. She sought, mainly, to provide her own children with an adequate education. The captain inquired about her success, remarking that if he did nothing else he wanted his children exposed to an education and inculcated with "good breeding." He encouraged his wife to do her duty with the rod when it became necessary, although he observed that their children required "but little whipping[,] being rather timid."[40]

Some of those husbands, as well as some soldiers who were husbands to no one, came home that winter, for the same cold weather and respiratory complaints that had killed the slave Henry were laying the troops low. Officers appeared to enjoy the best luck asking for sick leave: Captain Abbitt came home on a convalescent furlough that November, just in time to witness the birth of the son conceived on his recruiting trip. Before Abbitt returned to duty, Second Lieutenant John D. L. F. Patteson took leave on a surgeon's certificate, spending Christmas with his family at Rose Bower, on the stage road. One of the first lieutenants, William G. Coleman, had also come home sick through November; that left William S. Hannah and John Williams to command the company in the Richmond defenses, and Williams would get ten days to visit his family in February. Lieutenant Hannah and his brother John, a sergeant in the company, operated a sawmill at home, with which they made a fair sum satisfying government contracts. The lieutenant found no opportunity to go home with so many officers absent, but when Samuel Coleman's substitute deserted Hannah saw a chance to send his brother back. The substitute disappeared on November 1, and three weeks later Hannah asked the regimental commander to detail John with a few privates to return to Appomattox for that man and any other absentees he could find. The detail netted neither the substitute nor any other deserters, but it permitted the junior Hannah brother to put the mill in good order.[41]

Furloughs came with some ease in James Robertson's company of the 20th Virginia Artillery Battalion, as well, for it also lay within one of the forts outside Richmond, where the enemy had not shown his face in months. Joseph Megginson came home on a hospital furlough in the company of Lorenzo Kelly, the Clover Hill carriage maker. Their afflictions proved serious, though, and neither lived to return to his company: Kelly died a week before Christmas, and Megginson three days into the new year. James Carson, who felt well enough himself, won his captain's sympathy with the plea that two of his children had succumbed to diphtheria and a third lay on the brink of death.

In the 18th Virginia, most men earned their furloughs through the wounds they received in battle. Lieutenants Thomas Gilliam and James Glover Harvey had both been wounded at Gaines's Mill the previous June, and Gilliam remained at home through the winter. Of the officers in the Appomattox Grays, only Third Lieutenant Edward Harvey managed a furlough on his plea alone. Betty Harvey greeted her husband at the door of their Cub Creek cabin in the middle of February, never noting that he arrived on Friday the thirteenth. For seventeen days he lingered in the neighborhood, playing with their children and offering stories of life at the front; doubtless he told her much about her brother, Joel Cawthorn, and they probably visited her father, Reverend John Cawthorn. Edward gave his wife nearly $200 in Confederate currency and instructed her how to make it last. He left her the little diary he had carried through seven battles, in which he had recorded the names of all his company's dead and wounded. They had three opportunities to attend the services at nearby Wesley Chapel, but at a quarter to ten on Monday morning, March 2, he kissed her good-bye and started back to the war via Evergreen Station.[42]

Infantrymen and artillerymen, especially heavy artillerymen, had a better chance of earning furloughs in the winter because mud so restricted their activities anyway. The cavalry enjoyed no such respite, for mounted troops could still move with relative ease, and their scouting services remained vital across the calendar. And if cavalrymen seldom participated in their army's epic struggles, they enjoyed no seasonal immunity from battle. Sergeant Robert Isbell, one of the Appomattox Rangers from the Stonewall District, wrote his sister in March that his horse had been shot from under him at the battle of Kelly's Ford on March 17; he mentioned that First Sergeant George Snapp had been wounded, as well as some others, but he had not yet learned that Snapp died the day after the fight. That same day, March 18, the *Lynchburg Virginian* carried a lengthy obituary for a Lynchburg lieutenant in another company of the 2nd Cavalry who had been killed in a scrap at Hartwood Church.

By the second April after Fort Sumter, the publisher of the *Virginian* cut his daily down to two sheets, for lack of paper, and a fortnight later he trimmed that remnant to tabloid size. Back to a broadsheet by early May, the newspaper reported the arrival of Stonewall Jackson's body on the Orange & Alexandria on May 13 and the mayor's assignment of six citizens (including former Clover Hill merchant John H. Flood) to escort the remains to Lexington.

Paper was not the only shortage that spring. In April a worried John Woodson telegraphed the chief quartermaster at Richmond that he had no corn at all in Lynchburg: he had been sending all he obtained to the army, and there was none left over to feed the horses at the city's government workshops and storehouses. The local surplus had dwindled to almost nothing, he reported—probably because of all the speculation in cotton and tobacco.[43]

Those soldiers fortunate enough to pass a few days with their families spent much of their sojourn trying to stockpile necessities before they returned to the army. They provided opportunists with a ready market when so many of them began bargaining for commodities that were already scarce, but by May most of them had returned to their posts. Some of their less conscientious comrades remained behind to care for their families, keeping an alert child or slave on watch for the sheriff and the provost detail.

Others endeavored to elude their regiments through means other than outright desertion. William McDearmon stayed home for most of the war, if not for the duration. He spent most of those years working for his father, whose holdings near Appomattox Station had grown (despite bankruptcy) to more than 450 acres with the house, store, and other enterprises near the station. Fire destroyed half of this new commercial empire sometime between the summers of 1862 and 1863, but Colonel McDearmon offset that loss with more lumber production. That was where he kept William employed, and the son used both that occupation and his father's Richmond connections to keep himself free from army officers who bore him increasing ill will. In April of 1863 he traveled to Richmond on some business and made the mistake of venturing out to the camp of the 46th Virginia, on the York River, to visit his brother Samuel. Since taking his brother's place in the company, Samuel had obtained an appointment as courier on General Wise's staff—after Colonel McDearmon specifically asked for that favor on the excuse of young Sam's lame foot. Only upon William's appearance did Wise learn the story of the informal substitution, which he had never authorized and did not approve: it had allowed a fit soldier to stay home, he argued, and had given the regiment a hobbled youth in return. William presented a letter from Captain Abbitt sanctioning the exchange, but Wise tucked the letter in his vest pocket and told the surprised young man to return to his company. Turning to Samuel, the general said he might go home. The younger brother rode away, while William went straight to Captain Abbitt for a leave of absence; when that was refused, he went home anyway.

Once he heard his son's story, Colonel McDearmon addressed both the secretary of war and the chief of the Bureau of War, complaining that William had been discharged after hiring a substitute. He failed to mention his own involvement, or that the substitute was the principal's own disabled brother. Captain Abbitt explained that no discharge had ever been issued, and that he had expected William to return to duty once Samuel came to military age himself—which he would on the following July 22. General Wise replied that substitutes had to be permanent, rather than for a year's time, since that would deprive the army of trained men and replace them with raw recruits; he further denounced this particular exchange because young Samuel could not march, while William could.

"Samuel is a most excellent courier, yet a minor and disabled," Wise informed James Seddon. "William is an able bodied infantry soldier who has never seen service, has never been substituted or discharged, and needs better discipline than his father seems inclined to apply to him."

Colonel McDearmon had taken advantage of the wartime need for lumber by expanding the milling operation that remained nominally under his wife's ownership, and therein lay the key to William's release. When the first argument failed to bring William back home, his father turned to a contract with the superintendent of the Southside Railroad, H. D. Bird, agreeing to supply him with wood for the engines and crossties for the rail lines. Given the importance of keeping the Southside running, such a function would merit War Department permission to leave the army, but the old politician then had to convince the authorities that his son was the person who had obtained the contract, and the only one who could fulfill it. Assuming a tone of contented retirement, therefore, the forty-six-year-old Colonel McDearmon wrote to Secretary of War James Seddon and urged him to assign Private McDearmon away from his company. Seddon obliged. Young McDearmon had the audacity to send in for his army pay for the months he was gone—and collected it—but he never saw his comrades under arms again. That was just as well, for two of his lieutenants were involved in their own contracts to provide lumber from Appomattox mills—although both of them managed their operations through partners, without leaving their posts. One of those competing officers, William G. Coleman, tried for months to bring William McDearmon back to duty on the argument that the young man's contractual obligations could be met by someone else—such as his father, perhaps.

"McDearmon was enlisted in my company March the 18th 1862 and has not done the first day's duty in the company," explained Lieutenant Coleman in a letter to Secretary Seddon, early in 1864. "As he is a young able bodied man without any incumbrance I would respectfully ask that he should be returned to his company and some person that is not able to stand the field service be put in his place." William McDearmon finally eluded the wrath of his officers by transferring to the 2nd Virginia Cavalry; it made little difference to the War Department, since he never served with that regiment, either.[44]

Officers who wished to leave the service managed their escapes more easily. All one had to do was submit a resignation citing ill health, business concerns, or no reason at all, and it was likely to be accepted. The former officer might then find himself subject to conscription, but the resourceful could frequently find a way around that, as Joel Flood knew so well.

Major John B. Moseley commanded his regiment in the battle of Chancellorsville, where—in what otherwise proved to be a stunning Confederate victory—the 21st Virginia lost its colors to a New Jersey regiment. Moseley never submitted a report of the battle; he may have been suffering undue embarrassment from the indignity of the captured flag when, less than four weeks later, he submitted an "immediate and unconditional" resignation to the secretary of war, without further comment. A fortnight later he came home to the family plantation in southern Appomattox County. Sarah Evelyn Gilliam no longer waited for him, but his father had died the previous January and the estate needed tending—which also may have inspired the major's resignation. His father had left a score of slaves on the farm, and they offered all the protection Moseley needed against conscription. He would not again be called to service, but he had already attained the highest rank that any Appomattox citizen ever achieved in the Confederate army.[45]

Lieutenant Clifton Webb, who had expended so much energy looking for time away from the 2nd Virginia Cavalry since the beginning of the war, came home late in April of 1863 on a two-week furlough to find a horse. The chance to visit his wife and new son failed to satisfy his homesickness, though, and before he returned to duty he submitted his resignation to his brother Charles, who commanded the Appomattox Rangers. Though he was only thirty, and thus subject to the draft, Webb may have hoped to rely upon his mother's numerous field hands as his own exemption from further service under the fifteen-slave law.[46]

Officers with more moderate circumstances saw no advantage in resignation, for once out of uniform they would soon be herded back into the ranks with rifles in their hands, earning far less of the Confederacy's devalued currency than they did with swords on their hips. Edward Harvey and Peter Fore, modest farmers serving as third lieutenants in the 18th Virginia, owned only three slaves apiece and could not hope to remain long at home. Second Lieutenant Thomas Gilliam, the former postmaster at Walker's Church and owner of a small store, claimed only two slaves at the outset of the war, and even if he had wished to resign he lacked the resources or connections to secure a safe government appointment or an agricultural deferment.[47]

These subalterns and their fellows therefore followed the army with no hope of release. Longstreet's corps moved into southeastern Virginia and northeastern North Carolina late that winter to disrupt complacent Union occupation forces in coastal cities, but in May the 18th Virginia marched back to the Army of Northern Virginia with Richard Garnett's brigade. By early June that brigade and that army were rolling northward again, toward Maryland. On June 25 the Appomattox Grays forded the Potomac River once more at Williamsport, and two days later Garnett's brigade accompanied Pickett's division into Chambersburg, Pennsylvania.

This was rolling farmland not unlike Appomattox County. The barns were sturdier, often made completely of stone, and some of the crops were different, but for nearly a week the veterans of the 18th Virginia lounged outside the tidy German town. This countryside had known little of the war (although raiding Confederates would burn the town the next summer), and Appomattox farmers enjoyed a view of unspoiled pastoral beauty. They savored the long repose, as well, for this division had marched more than most Confederates since the beginning of the year: no one complained when the rest of the corps moved eastward on the morning of July 1, leaving Pickett's three brigades behind as rear guard.[48]

Cavalry arrived to take over for Pickett the next day, and the three brigades started for Gettysburg, twenty-five miles away, where most of Lee's army had encountered leading divisions of the Army of the Potomac. The Virginians tramped dusty roads all afternoon and into the darkness, listening to the distant thunder of battle whenever they stopped. They unrolled their blankets late and slept little, pushing on again early in the morning with James Kemper's brigade in the lead and Garnett's behind him. At midmorning the town appeared before the vanguard, and the division passed Lee's headquarters, veering right to shuffle past a Lutheran seminary, beyond which lay a long, low, wooded ridge. After three hours of rest in place, the division marched one last mile in the same formation, taking cover in the shadow of that ridge. Forming into line of battle, the men lay down where the Yankees could not see them; ahead, near the brow of the ridge, stood thickly ranked Southern artillery under Colonel Edward Porter Alexander, the First Manassas signal officer who counted himself a distant kinsman of Wilmer McLean. The guns, running out of sight in either direction, all pointed toward a corresponding ridge a mile away, where Union guns and infantry lay waiting. Between, a light breeze brushed golden wheat fields divided only by the double fences of the Emmitsburg Road. That distant crest lay almost barren of trees, however, save for a conspicuous copse at the center.[49]

That copse of trees offered the Confederates a natural target. For two days Lee had pounded the Yankees, driving them through Gettysburg on July 1 and onto the hills south of town. On the afternoon of July 2 and into the twilight he had hammered both ends of the Union line, hoping to cave in a flank and send the Yankees into flight. If he could thrash the Federals on their own territory, the Northern voter might have something different to say about continuing this war against the South, but the blue divisions outnumbered him and held a shorter line, on better ground. On the third day, therefore, Lee decided to throw his valiant infantry headlong into the belly of the enemy—bayonets gleaming and banners flying.

Early in the afternoon the long array of guns erupted. For nearly two hours the ground trembled as Porter Alexander attempted to wreck the Union artillery on Cemetery Ridge. Federal gunners responded, but the artillery of both armies overshot their marks and the infantry behind them suffered for it: Union shells killed or crippled a score of Garnett's men even in their protective swale. Alexander's long rounds fell among the Union reserve troops, though, leaving their front-line infantry relatively untouched.[50]

Toward three o'clock the guns on Cemetery Ridge dropped into gradual silence as battery commanders looked to their ammunition chests in anticipation of the inevitable infantry assault. Over on Seminary Ridge, Alexander interpreted the silence as evidence that the enemy artillery had been smashed. He consulted with General Longstreet, who concluded somewhat reluctantly that the time had come to make the attack General Lee expected of him.

At Longstreet's word, four division commanders notified twelve brigadiers to bring up their men. From their wooded swale came nearly five dozen regiments representing six Confederate states. On the left, Johnston Pettigrew gathered the North Carolina brigade that had started this battle in its quest for shoes, backing it with another fourteen regiments from Virginia, Tennessee, Alabama, and Mississippi. Behind Pettigrew rose ten more regiments of North Carolinians from William Pender's division; Pender had fallen the day before, and a Maryland Confederate commanded his brigades. On the right, three Florida regiments and an Alabama brigade from yet another division prepared to support the advance.

Between them all stood George Pickett's three brigades: fifteen Virginia regiments that had seen almost no fighting since Antietam, although the bloody summer of 1862 had reduced them to an average strength of fewer than 300 men apiece. Their path would bring them into the vortex of the fight this day. They would suffer the highest casualties, and this charge would forever bear their general's name.[51]

Garnett's brigade took the first line, on the left; Kemper formed his brigade on Garnett's right, and Lewis Armistead's five regiments followed Garnett. Garnett and Kemper rode horses, but Armistead led his men on foot.

Lieutenant Colonel Henry Carrington ordered the 18th Virginia into line at or near the left of Garnett's front. Company H, the Appomattox Grays, mustered fewer than forty men under arms that afternoon. They formed in two platoons, each in two ranks; Captain William Johnson took position on the right of the front rank, with First Sergeant William Elam right behind him. First Lieutenant James Glover Harvey posted himself behind the first platoon, on the left, while Second Lieutenant Thomas Gilliam occupied a similar position behind the second platoon. The tactical manual called for the remaining company sergeants to take their places on either side of these platoon leaders; so, probably, did those Confederate anomalies, the third lieutenants. In Company H these were the oldest officers: thirty-eight-year-old Edward Harvey and forty-two-year-old Peter Fore.

Jolting forward at route step, the mile-wide front crested a rise and came into full view of the long Union line. From directly ahead and from Little Round Top, over a mile to the right, Union artillery opened on the broad grey lines with the red battle flags. Garnett's brigade took some of the shellfire from Little Round Top in enfilade—the projectiles crashing lengthwise along the ranks and knocking down ten men at a time when they exploded. Their eyes glued on the copse of trees, the Virginians took no note of their fallen comrades save to close up and fill the gaps.[52]

The Pennsylvania landscape offered a fortuitous swale just short of the Emmittsburg Road, where Pickett's division reformed itself and waited for Pettigrew's line to catch up on the left. Then the flags swept forward again, crossing the road diagonally and climbing the post-and-rail fences before starting up the long, low slope toward Cemetery Ridge. Yankee artillery continued to tear at the lines, switching from shell to deadly, shotgunlike blasts of canister when the front ranks came into range. Tactics nearly a century old insisted that the advancing brigades should approach close enough to fire a volley and then rush in with the bayonet, but those tactics had been developed around smoothbore muskets with an effective range of a hundred yards. The men behind the stone walls of Cemetery Ridge carried rifles, and Garnett's brigade was nearly three times that far away when the blue line rose up and tattered his ranks with one volley, then reloaded for a second.[53]

As they were habitually instructed, these Yankees fired low, and the Appomattox Grays absorbed the full fury of that first volley. Captain Johnson took a bullet in the groin; First Sergeant Elam, Sergeant George Pollard, and at least four privates went down with leg wounds. The New Yorkers whom they faced fired again, at shorter range, and the Confederates returned fire before rushing forward. The copse of trees loomed just to the front.

James Harvey, the first lieutenant and the man who had recruited most of his comrades, fell dead on the field, and two of his men were killed with him. The other Lieutenant Harvey, James's uncle Edward, fell grievously wounded near the stone wall. A bullet smashed Sergeant Samuel Hubbard's right hand, and another struck Daniel Ferguson in the face; both fled to the rear. Three Dickersons suffered wounds but managed to escape. Near the enemy line, Corporal Samuel Farrar was shot through the shoulder and Henry Clay Jennings through the arm.

Their remaining comrades poured over the wall, but Pettigrew's men failed to come up on their left. General Armistead shifted his brigade into that gap, waving his men forward with his hat atop the point of his sword, but a Union rifleman dropped him at the wheel of a Federal gun. Somewhere behind the 18th Virginia, General Garnett finally fell from his horse, riddled. Reduced by the prolonged shellfire, then shredded by the repeated volleys of canister and musketry, his brigade lacked the strength to carry the ridge. Undaunted Virginians pressed on into the growing mobs of blue uniforms, but when they looked back they saw no more red battle flags save those gliding away in retreat. Pickett's Charge had failed, and the survivors finally threw down their arms.

All three of Pickett's brigadiers had gone down, and every regimental commander. What was left of Garnett's brigade returned in scattered fragments, mixed with the refugees of other brigades, and a major collected the refugees. Two-thirds of the brigade had been lost, and the 18th Virginia had suffered worst of all. Even after the remnants of that regiment had been reunited, it could not field a line the size of a company. The Appomattox Grays had lost twenty-eight men, eighteen of whom remained in the hands of the enemy; the company consisted now of two junior lieutenants leading a dejected squad of riflemen. Cavalier gallantry had dashed itself against modern armament, as it had on Marston Moor, and with the same result. Courage and tradition could no longer be depended upon to prevail against military and industrial might, as so many Virginians had hoped. The dawn of a new day lurked just below the horizon.[54]

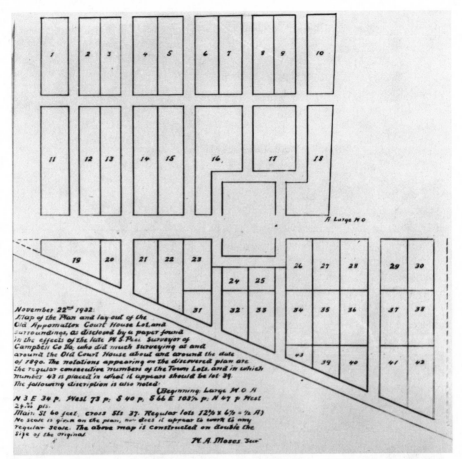

Original 1845 lot layout of Appomattox Court House. The Clover Hill Tavern straddled lots 16 and 17; the house where Lee surrendered was later built on lot 21 (Appomattox Court House National Historical Park).

Thomas S. Bocock, Appomattox County's first county attorney. He was a candidate for Speaker of the House of Representatives during the marathon contest of 1859–60, and he was the only man to serve in that capacity in the Confederate Congress (Appomattox Court House National Historical Park).

Richard Alexander Sweeney, who died on a musical tour in 1860 (Appomattox Court House National Historical Park).

Joel Walker Sweeney. Born within sight of what would become Appomattox Court House, he organized a minstrel show that included several family members, and he was credited with inventing the five-string banjo. He died at Appomattox in the autumn before the Civil War began; his grave lay only yards from the spot where Robert E. Lee awaited U. S. Grant's reply to his offer of surrender (Appomattox Court House National Historical Park).

Sampson D. Sweeney. The last of the famous brothers, Sam died early in 1864, while serving as J. E. B. Stuart's renowned headquarters banjo-picker (Appomattox Court House National Historical Park).

Sam Sweeney entertaining J. E. B. Stuart's headquarters staff, ca. 1862 (Appomattox Court House National Historical Park).

Charles H. Sweeney, ca. 1865. A cousin of Joel, Richard, and Sam (Appomattox Court House National Historical Park).

Charles H. Sweeney (at left), Mattie Sweeney (in white apron), and their children, ca. 1900. The main portion of their cabin still stands on the slope opposite Appomattox Court House (Appomattox Court House National Historical Park).

The only known photograph of Wilson Hix, onetime sheriff of Appomattox County and owner of the Clover Hill Tavern at the time of Lee's surrender (Appomattox Court House National Historical Park).

Lucy H. Hix, Wilson Hix's second wife (Appomattox Court House National Historical Park).

Wilson Hix's daughter, Emma, with her husband, Henry J. Cogan, and their child, ca. 1868. Cogan arrived at Appomattox Court House as an officer with the postwar provost detail (Appomattox Court House National Historical Park).

(top left)
Edward G. Hix, ca. 1890 (Appomattox Court House National Historical Park).

(top right)
Captain George W. Abbitt, Co. B, 46th Virginia, ca. 1862. Abbitt, who commanded his regiment at the surrender, later served several years as clerk of Appomattox County (Appomattox Court House National Historical Park).

(left)
Second Lieutenant William Glover Coleman, Co. B, 46th Virginia, ca. 1862. While acting as commander of his company, Coleman strenuously objected that Private William J. McDearmon had been detailed behind the lines to supply lumber for the Southside Railroad. The McDearmon family sawmill competed for such contracts with Coleman himself, who attempted to operate his business while serving at the front (Appomattox Court House National Historical Park).

Sergeant Daniel W. Gills, Co. H, 2nd Virginia Cavalry. In his capacity as county sheriff, Wilson Hix unsuccessfully attempted to have Gills—his deputy and later his son-in-law—discharged from the army (Appomattox Court House National Historical Park).

Ellen Bryant. Bryant, who lived north of
Appomattox Court House, claimed that her
father served as overseer on Joel Flood's
plantation. In 1866 she married Daniel
Cole, a Pennsylvanian with the county
provost detail (Appomattox Court House
National Historical Park).

High Bridge over the Appomattox River, east of Farmville. Cost overruns in construction
of the piers for this bridge helped bankrupt Samuel McDearmon, the original developer of
Appomattox Court House. The bridge became strategically crucial during Lee's retreat:
the last four spans, in the distance, were burned by Confederates on April 7, 1865 (Massachusetts Commandery of the Loyal Legion of the United States, U.S. Army Military
History Institute, Carlisle Barracks, Pa.).

Major General John B. Gordon, commander of the Second Corps, Army of Northern Virginia. Gordon, who ultimately led the Confederate surrender parade, had resisted Federal demands for a formal surrender ceremony before U.S. troops (Appomattox Court House National Historical Park).

Brigadier General Joshua L. Chamberlain, commander of a brigade in the Fifth Corps, Army of the Potomac. A genuine war hero who appears to have retroactively inflated his role even further, he later claimed that U. S. Grant personally named him to command Union forces in the surrender ceremony (*Companions of the Military Order of the Loyal Legion of the United States*, New York: L. R. Hammersley Co., 1901).

Jenyns C. Battersby's sketch of the last round fired by Confederate artillery from the Peers house. Battersby, the commander of the 1st New York Cavalry, did not arrive on the scene until after the gun had been withdrawn; his sketch shows it aimed to the northwest, toward the Tibbs house. The sketch first appeared in the *Harper's Weekly* of November 4, 1865; this copy was reproduced in Charles Carleton Coffin, *Freedom Triumphant* (New York: Harper & Brothers, 1891).

The restored home of Appomattox County clerk George Peers, from the yard of which the last shot was ostensibly fired. The stockade fence to the right of the house, a modern replica of one that appeared in an 1892 photograph, created a minor controversy of its own when it was suggested that a similar fence had existed during the fighting at Appomattox. The only contemporary renderings of the Peers house—the Battersby sketch and George Frankenstein's painting—show no such fence (photo by Harold E. Howard, 1999).

Captain Robert Moorman Sims, the Confederate staff officer who carried the flag of truce to General Custer, ca. 1905 (Appomattox Court House National Historical Park).

Wilmer McLean, ca. 1860 (Appomattox Court House National Historical Park).

Timothy O'Sullivan's 1865 series: the McLean house, formerly the "new" Raine tavern, with Wilmer McLean's two younger children and two servant girls on the porch (National Archives).

Timothy O'Sullivan's 1865 series: Wilmer McLean, Mrs. McLean, her two older daughters, little Lula McLean, and a servant girl on the porch of the McLean house (National Archives).

Timothy O'Sullivan's 1865 series: Appomattox County courthouse, guarded by the provost detail from the 188th Pennsylvania. Wilmer McLean stands at left, in the light jacket and vest; George Peers stands on the courthouse steps, in the grey suit; Captain James Geiser is at the center of the upper porch, with his sword before him (Library of Congress).

Timothy O'Sullivan's 1865 series: Clover
Hill Tavern, with George Peers standing
before the fence with his children. The
smallest child is Charles Peers, born in
January 1864; the girls are Lelia, age seven,
and Mary, age nine. The boy in the hat may
be a neighbor child or a son born after the
census of 1860 was taken, and who must
have died before the census of 1870
(Library of Congress).

Eustace Collett sketch of the McLean house, with the old Raine tavern standing at left, ca. 1865 (Appomattox Court House National Historical Park).

George Frankenstein painting of (left to right) the courthouse, the old Raine tavern, the Pryor Wright house, the McLean wellhouse, the McLean house, and the McLean outbuildings (Appomattox Court House National Historical Park).

George Frankenstein painting of the Peers house, from the northeast. As in the Battersby sketch, the outbuildings are east of the house, which has only one chimney on the south gable, and there is no stockade fence (Appomattox Court House National Historical Park).

George Frankenstein painting of Appomattox Court House as seen from behind the original Sweeney homestead, across the North Branch (Appomattox Court House National Historical Park).

Adam Plecker's 1892 view of the village from the stage road, at the intersection of Sears Lane: the two-story house at left center, long identified as the "Union Academy dwelling house," was occupied by Thomas Landrum's family at the time of the surrender; Francis Meeks bought it shortly after the war and lived there until his death in 1870 (Appomattox Court House National Historical Park).

Adam Plecker's photograph of the McLean parlor, where Lee signed the articles of surrender. This is the only known interior view of the house; it was taken only months before the building was dismantled (Appomattox Court House National Historical Park).

The courthouse as seen from the east, reputedly during the 1880s. William Rosser's blacksmith shop stands at right, with his home behind the white gate (Appomattox Court House National Historical Park).

SACRED DAY AT APPOMATTOX, APRIL 9, 1915.

Wreath-laying ceremony at the Confederate cemetery on the fiftieth anniversary of Lee's surrender, April 9, 1915. A few Confederate veterans stand in this image, including Joel Walker Flood Jr., just to the left of the woman in white (Appomattox Court House National Historical Park).

The dilapidated Clover Hill Tavern, ca. 1914
(Appomattox Court House National Historical Park).

The village in 1914, as seen from the stage road near the McLean house gate. Francis
Meeks's store stands at left, and the old Raine tavern (Ragland's store) at right; the
courthouse ruins are obscured by the trees at center (Appomattox Court House National
Historical Park).

A 1937 aerial view of the old village. The remains of the courthouse stand in the ellipse; the Clover Hill Tavern is at right; Meeks's store and the old saddle shop/barroom are just to the right of the road above the ellipse, and the new jail is just to the left of the road below it. The white house at the bottom is the home of Bessie Ferguson, daughter of William Rosser, who built the original portion of the house in the 1870s (Appomattox Court House National Historical Park).

The village from the east, 1939. From left: Meeks's store, with lean-to shed; saddler's shop (later a barroom and successively the law office of H. T. Parrish and Charles Sackett); barns that went with the home of Francis Meeks (the "Union Academy dwelling house"); the tavern guest house; the Clover Hill Tavern, with porch removed (Appomattox Court House National Historical Park).

The Bocock-Isbell house, June 1940 (Appomattox Court House National Historical Park).

A Massachusetts tourist stopping in front of Crawford Jones's law office in September of 1940; the Peers house stands in the background (Appomattox Court House National Historical Park).

Restoration work begins on Crawford Jones's law office (long misidentified as the Kelly house), April 22, 1941 (Appomattox Court House National Historical Park).

Archaeological work at the McLean house site, April 20, 1941; across the road stand Meeks's store and the Clover Hill Tavern kitchen (Appomattox Court House National Historical Park).

The reconstructed McLean house (photo by the author, 1997).

Douglas Southall Freeman addressing the crowd at the McLean house dedication ceremony, April 16, 1950 (Appomattox Court House National Historical Park).

The Clover Hill Tavern with a new porch and fence (photo by the author, 1997).

The restored Meeks's store (photo by the author, 1997).

The restored Bocock-Isbell house (photo by the author, 1997).

The village from the west, near Adam Plecker's vantage point of 1892
(photo by the author, 1997).

Red Fields, the home of George Abbitt, whose sons both served as officers in the 46th Virginia; he was the father-in-law of Dr. Samuel Coleman, who lived a mile from the village (photo by the author, 1996).

The home of Nancy LeGrand, on the LeGrand Road. It was her son-in-law who built the Peers house, and it was in front of her house that Captain Sims brought the flag of truce out to General Custer (photo by the author, 1996).

The remaining portion of John Sears's house, on the banks of Plain Run
(photo by the author, 1997).

Charles Sweeney's restored cabin (photo by the author, 1996).

The Willis Inge house, just prior to its demolition (photo by Ron Wilson, 1979).

The ruins of Pleasant Retreat, built in 1810. This was the home of Dr. Joel Walker Flood Sr., who died in 1858; his widow died here on April 10, 1864, and the house (or its office, nearer the stage road) purportedly served as James Longstreet's headquarters from April 9 through April 12, 1865 (photo by the author, 1996).

Rose Bower, the home of Lieutenant John D. L. F. Patteson. This former tavern stands where the Army of Northern Virginia turned south to Appomattox Court House. Lee's last council of war was held in this vicinity, about six miles northeast of the village (photo by the author, 1998).

Abbitt's store at Vera, Virginia, three miles northeast of Appomattox Court House. New Hope Baptist Church lay just across the road from this postwar structure, and here Longstreet's troops dug the last breastworks of the Army of Northern Virginia. Here, too, the road to Wildway—Thomas S. Bocock's home—turns from the stage road (photo by the author, 1998).

The first Raine tavern, which was the first new building erected at Appomattox Court House. In the 1870s Nathaniel Ragland moved it to this location, two lots east of its original site in front of the McLean house, and opened it as a store. This photo was taken in the 1930s; the building was severely damaged by a storm and was torn down by the Virginia Department of Transportation in 1940 (Library of Congress).

Samuel McDearmon's Georgian manse. This house overlooked the ravine where the North Branch of the Appomattox River originates, and Union officers used its hipped roof for a signal station at the conclusion of hostilities. Jacob Tibbs bought the house from McDearmon's trustees in 1856; his son, Lieutenant Thomas Tibbs, passed near the house in the final advance of the Army of Northern Virginia on the morning of April 9, 1865. This photo was taken about 1960, and the house was dismantled a few years later (Library of Congress).

THE SIEGE

Betty Harvey spent the rest of July and August trying to determine what had become of her husband. Four days after he was wounded she wrote him her customary weekly letter, sending it by way of Richmond with no idea where he was, or that he had even been in a battle. Then the news of Gettysburg drifted into the Virginia countryside, and Appomattox County's Southside neighborhoods fell into a frenzy of anxiety, for the decimated Appomattox Grays hailed almost entirely from that district: the casualties had included four Harveys, three Dickersons, and two each from the Ferguson, Fore, Hubbard, and Jennings clans. Eventually the young mother learned that Edward Harvey had been wounded and taken prisoner, along with her brother, Joel Cawthorn. She heard that her husband's nephew, James Harvey, was dead and that Andrew Paulett, the young carpenter whom her father had married to Lucy McCune just before he enlisted, had also been killed. As late as August 26 she wrote to Edward in care of his Union captors, at the Gettysburg hospital. The attendants could not find Lieutenant Harvey, and when they checked their records they discovered that he had died on August 6.

"The last one I ever wrote to him," Betty Harvey noted alongside the date of her Gettysburg letter, "and he was dead all that time." With that endorsement she put away her late husband's diary and prepared a widow's wardrobe. The dead lieutenant had left her with two small children to care for, and a 500-acre farm to attract another husband, but more than five years would pass before the memory of Edward Harvey had faded sufficiently to allow her to marry a widowed neighbor, choosing again a man fifteen years her senior. Lucy Paulett would not wait so long.[1]

At Rose Bower, five miles northeast of the courthouse, Sarah Patteson had not been especially worried about her husband. John D. L. F. Patteson was a second lieutenant in George Abbitt's Company B, of the 46th Virginia, which had spent most of the past year in Richmond or on the old Peninsula battlegrounds, and away from the warmest of the war. Only two members of Captain Abbitt's company had died so far during all of 1863: a Pamplin man had succumbed to one of the frequent camp fevers, and the other had drowned in the Pamunkey River while on guard duty near Cook's Mill. The drowning victim, E. W. Durham, had been one of those paroled prisoners from Roanoke Island, and once paroled he had gone home. He was exchanged the following August, and was supposed to return to his company immediately, but only the appearance of a provost detail had interfered with his intention to spend the rest of the war in Appomattox County; early in December of 1862 they came to drag him back, and he may have been trying to escape again when the river claimed him.

Lieutenant Patteson had come home as recently as July to retrieve another deserter, Richard Oliver, whom Sheriff Hix had lodged at the county jail, but late in August the brigade commander allowed the lieutenant another fifteen days to go home and "provide" for his family. The corn crop was almost ready for harvest, and perhaps Lieutenant Patteson worried about getting a good price on the surplus, for he owned nearly a score of slaves who could manage any of the necessary labor. Whatever his agricultural concerns, on the last Tuesday in August he arrived at his home, where the roads to Buckingham Court House and New Store diverged. As his captain had done a year and a half before, Lieutenant Patteson offered his wife his first attention, thus providing for his family by assuring its increase. When he returned to Richmond in the second week of September, Sarah was carrying their seventh child.[2]

As Lieutenant Patteson applied for his furlough, young Samuel McDearmon began to wish that he were back in the army. Perhaps it was the proximity of his father's home to the railroad depot, where local residents greeted, or said good-bye to, so many uniformed heroes. His father once remarked that the boy was infected with a military ardor for the cause, and there seems to have been some truth in it. He had reached the age of conscription but would have been exempt from most field service because of his crippled foot. He could ride a horse, though, and barely a month after his eighteenth birthday he made his way to Lee's army and joined the 2nd Cavalry.

Other Appomattox citizens rallied to the colors that summer under less inspired motivation, however. The enrolling officers grew especially persistent after the casualties at Gettysburg and the capture of the Vicksburg garrison, and numerous prominent citizens who had thought themselves safely exempt began looking for acceptable forms of military service. Clifton Webb had resigned from the 2nd Cavalry in June under the assumed protection of an agricultural exemption, but early in August he reenlisted as a private soldier, choosing the relative security of the company commanded by his brother-in-law, George Abbitt; the 46th Virginia had not suffered a combat casualty in a year. Captain Abbitt himself wished to resign during the second half of 1863, but he dared not do so for fear that he would be conscripted immediately. Lieutenant Patteson, who had begun the war owning enough slaves to claim exemption, remained on duty in the same company despite sufficient concern about his family's situation that he kept seeking excuses to go home; he might have resigned, too, were it not for the likelihood that the exemption requirements would be further restricted.

Even Thomas Cheatham, the 1860 census marshal and briefly a sergeant in Captain Jones's local defense battery, had found it necessary to enlist as a means of avoiding conscription. Cheatham was forty years old now, and had reportedly been suffering from varicose veins at least since his days in Jones's battery, but in the aftermath of Gettysburg he deemed it prudent to join his surviving neighbors in the depleted Appomattox Grays. He never carried a musket in the company, but soon persuaded someone to detail him to a civilian job at a railroad station.

The senior Samuel McDearmon also appears to have sensed the pressure of conscription, although he hovered just over the present age limit of forty-five. A few weeks after his son enlisted in the cavalry, the father sought immunity through an official appointment as the local collector of Confederate taxes.[3]

Lieutenant Thomas Tibbs, the wounded veteran of Crampton's Gap, had lingered at home all that summer. His arm had not healed well, and he had been dropped from the rolls of his company; he had finally determined to go on to college when the enrolling officers decided that he was now well enough to return to the army. Ordered off to Richmond with the prospect of being thrust into a strange regiment as a rifleman, he asked his father to invoke the influence of Thomas Bocock. The Speaker of the House interrupted a vacation at Wildway and rode to the capital to spring Tibbs from the conscript camp on the promise that he would enlist in a unit of his choice. Bocock handed the young man twenty dollars to pay his way home, and a fortnight later Tibbs carried through on his promise. He wanted to join a company from home, but with no prospects of a commission in Captain Abbitt's company he enlisted in a Lynchburg company of the 34th Virginia—which, like Abbitt's regiment, belonged to Henry Wise's brigade. A sympathetic field officer appointed Tibbs as the clerk of a court martial, where he could rest his aching arm that much longer. Lieutenant Patteson and the two erstwhile lieutenants, Webb and Tibbs, followed Wise's brigade to Charleston that autumn, where they remained safe through the winter.

With the sponsorship of his brother-in-law (the same Thomas Bocock), Boyd Faulkner had also found a relatively safe assignment. After the dissolution of Captain Jones's local defense battery, he had enlisted as a private in the Rockbridge Artillery, but before long Speaker Bocock wrote another of his casual letters to the secretary of war and a week later young Faulkner received a captain's commission and assumed the duties of a quartermaster. For all the exertions of the Conscription Bureau, though, his old commander, Crawford Jones, was never reduced to the indignity of field service. Nor did he have to leave the county to find the same danger that some of his neighbors encountered in the army. Sometime during 1863, the youngest of the village lawyers and the "fast boy" who carried Sarah Gilliam home from the Christmas party at Pleasant Retreat perished from one of the local plagues.[4]

John Hannah, a sergeant in the 46th Virginia, also died at home toward the end of September. Both his younger and his older brothers had served as lieutenants in his company; the younger one had died only six months after the company went to war, and the two remaining brothers had since been simultaneously soldiering and operating a sawmill. John was at home tending to the mill machinery when he fell ill, leaving no qualified supervisor to run the business. William McDearmon continued in competition with the Hannah mill from the security of his special detail, but William S. Hannah tried to manage his operation in absentia, while remaining on active duty. Like his fellow subaltern, William Glover Coleman, Hannah asked for the occasional furlough to attend to his government lumber contracts, but for the most part he remained with the company.[5]

E. W. Durham, the drowned deserter from the Liberty Guards, represented a host of soldiers who had become deserters by simply staying home when they had a chance to go there. By the fall of 1863 the Virginia legislature felt the need to target those absentees without weakening the front lines for provost details, passing a law requiring all "conservators of the peace"—which was to say sheriffs and justices—to arrest deserters wherever they found them, and giving them authority to raise posses for the purpose. Fines for neglecting such duties would run from $30 to $500.[6]

Sheriff Hix needed no such encouragement. He had been throwing deserters in jail right from the start, and it was largely because of such patrons that the circuit court voted to raise his per diem rate for keeping prisoners to $1.25. Even as the news of Gettysburg filtered into the village, Hix was boarding Richard Oliver, who was perhaps the last of the Roanoke prisoners to respond to exchange; Oliver sat in the old jail for twenty-three days before Lieutenant Patteson came back to pick him up. As 1863 wore on, Hix found the hunting enhanced as potential conscripts declined to come in when called and as conscription officials attempted to discourage such resistance. Late in August John McKinney, the county enrolling officer, sent Hix after four men who had not answered his notices, including one who had deserted from the 46th Virginia fifteen months before: in October Hix apprehended two next-door neighbors from the Walker's Church neighborhood, and he brought the other two in before Christmas. They appear to have taken no great pains to hide themselves, and the sheriff simply waited until their paths crossed, or called up a posse to visit their front doors one night. Hix's own son and any number of other exempted men would have been happy to serve their country in such a capacity, since it reduced the chances that their own class of exemptions would be imposed upon by Congress.

That autumn Hix was also faced with another impressment order for slaves. Union incursions from West Virginia during the summer had caused some doubts about the security of interior cities, and Confederate engineers had grown sufficiently solicitous of Lynchburg to ring the place with little forts. That required hundreds of slaves to dig the trenches and chop the logs for revetments, and Hix collected seventy-four slaves for the work; he also collected another $109.50 in fees and costs for his trouble.[7]

With court business all but suspended, Appomattox lawyers earned most of their fees these days by chasing the government for money it owed citizens who had answered its various appeals. Samuel Wheeler sent a man named Robert to work on the fortifications in front of Richmond, and Wheeler was supposed to have been paid $16 a month for two months of Robert's labor, but he had to engage Lewis Isbell to get the money. Sarah Woodson, a woman nearing eighty who owned several slaves, had sent one named "Big Anderson" to Richmond under one of the county court's periodic impressment orders, but he came back with the measles and died; like young Joel Flood before her, she found that the wheels of the Confederate government turned exceedingly slowly, and the war had barely six months left in it before she received even the 1862 value of her slave in the inflated currency of 1864. Those who lost sons in Confederate service encountered the same trouble. Pryor B. Wright, whose son Caswell had died early in the conflict as a member of the 2nd Virginia Cavalry, had named Crawford Jones as his administrator in order to obtain the pay due his boy. Francis Meeks employed both Thomas H. Flood and John W. Woodson to determine how much the army owed his dead son, Lafayette, and to have it pay that pittance to him; he waited until sixteen months after the boy perished for the devaluated sum of $30.40.[8]

Lafayette Meeks had been dead two years now, and his father had apparently overcome his grief by diving headlong into the real estate game at Appomattox Court House. He had bought the two long lots behind the store, including the spot where Lafayette was buried, as well as a nearby acre that Samuel McDearmon had included in his original town lots but had never been able to sell, and in October of 1863 he approached William H. Trent about his saddler's shop, between the store and the Clover Hill Tavern.

Trent had bought the shop and its partial lot when John H. Flood was trying to unload his village investments, just before John Brown's raid; Flood may have intended to convert the structure into another law office. In the days of the stagecoaches and long-distance horseback travel, saddlery had been a popular occupation, and in 1850 three such tradesmen had lodged at the Clover Hill Tavern alone. The railroad had severely limited horse-drawn transportation, however, and by 1860 the entire county hosted but one saddler. Trent's shop had smelled no leather for some time, save the boot leather of men looking for a drink, for the little building had been transformed into a barroom. Thomas Landrum, Crawford Jones's erstwhile second lieutenant, had been operating the groggery there for some time; Landrum was lodging his family in the frame house behind the store and barroom, on the Union Academy lots over which John Flood and Lewis Isbell acted as trustees. Squire Trent evidently wished to be rid of the property, for which he had paid Flood $200 in 1859. Mr. Meeks seemed uninterested in the building, or even in any of the lot except the portion alongside his store, but he paid Trent $150 in Confederate currency for the entire parcel. At the same instant, he transferred the barroom and all the land under it and on the tavern side of it to Wilson Hix, reserving a few square yards as a buffer to his store. Hix paid Meeks the same $150, so the carpenter-cum-entrepreneur realized the additional yard space for nothing.[9]

With the approach of winter came more furloughs, and as usual the officers of the Appomattox company in the 46th Virginia took advantage of their brigadier's accommodating political nature. Somehow Lieutenant Patteson won yet another visit home from November into December, barely ten weeks after his last leave and his third visit in five months; Captain Abbitt came home on convalescent furlough in December. Lieutenant Coleman asked for a chance to attend to his sawmill, where his free black laborers worked without appropriate supervision, and that request was denied at first because it would leave only a second lieutenant, William S. Hannah, in charge of the company. Eventually Coleman persuaded General Wise that Hannah was competent to command, and he was granted a short stay at home. Once Coleman returned, Hannah himself went home under a similar necessity.[10]

Another officer came home to Clover Hill for good that December. Charles Raine, who had grown up in the house now owned by Wilmer McLean, had probably not seen Appomattox Court House since his brother's burial at the family cemetery there, in 1860. Since then he had lived in Lynchburg, where he had married and fathered a son of his own. At the outset of the war he had helped to raise a battery of light artillery, with which he fought in some of the earliest engagements, and by the war's second year he commanded that battery. His four guns traveled with the Stonewall Division, and Raine won accolades at nearly every action from the Valley campaign to Gettysburg, where for a time he took command of his battalion.

Late in November, still smarting over his failure to run Lee's army down after Gettysburg, George Meade moved the Army of the Potomac against Lee in one last effort to finish him off before winter, but Lee was not about to be finished off. He dug his army in behind imposing new works along Mine Run, between Culpeper and the old Chancellorsville battlefield, and dared Meade to attack. After what amounted to some tentative prodding, Meade pulled back and went into winter quarters.

That tentative prodding included a little artillery duel in the vicinity of a chapel called Zoar Church. Charles Raine, just back from sick leave in Lynchburg, brought his battery up to discourage the Yankees, but as he was directing his gunners' fire a Union solid shot struck him and killed him instantly.

"The country lost a most gallant officer and valuable citizen," wrote his division commander. As soon as the artillerymen could carry what was left of their captain's body to the rear it was loaded onto the Orange & Alexandria line for the journey to Lynchburg, from which the remains traveled one last time back to Appomattox Station. Like his brother before him, Captain Raine made the final journey to Clover Hill in a wagon, stopping short of the village. Mourned by his young widow and their puzzled child, he joined his parents, his brother, his sister, and an assortment of nieces and nephews. He had not lived to see thirty, and he would never know the fate of his nation — or that its fate was met in the house where he had grown to manhood. He died supposing that the Old South lived yet, and might survive: one day the son he left behind would raise a towering monument on the father's grave, as though to complete the illusion that it had.[11]

Men at the front might have held to the conviction that they would somehow prevail, despite the deterioration of their army and the constriction of both territory and supplies — perhaps they had to cherish such a belief, in order to go on — but the women at home grew less hopeful. Elvira Woodson recounted a sad Christmas in a letter to an old friend, although her brother Drury had come home; her friend replied with what seemed to be greater sympathy for the soldiers in the field. Observing that they appeared to be deserting in large numbers, she wondered how they could carry on the war much longer.[12]

Certainly Appomattox County had its deserters, especially among the prisoners who had proven so reluctant to return to duty after they were exchanged, or sick and wounded men who took permanent advantage of convalescent furloughs, and a few had actually fled their posts to return home: Robert Worley had served only eight weeks before bolting back to his family, and Willis Inge's oldest son would desert as soon as his regiment arrived in Richmond from a winter campaign in North Carolina. These absentees drained the army's strength, but at the end of 1863 fewer than a score of the county's soldiers were absent without leave; at this date the real attrition came from those who had died, resigned, or been discharged, disabled, or captured. By the opening of 1864 at least 136 Appomattox men were already hors de combat, and with the deserters they represented a full third of those who had taken up arms.

Sixty-six of the Appomattox volunteers were already dead, and they were dying more frequently all the time. In January Morgan Powell, who had joined his two brothers in the 20th Virginia Heavy Artillery, embarked upon a furlough from the relative security of Battery Number 9, north of Richmond, only to be shot to death at home by a nephew to whom he had taken a switch. Reuben Staples, one of five sons of Powhatan Staples who served in that same heavy artillery company, came home with consumption and expired on January 17.[13]

The death that struck the most somber chord around Clover Hill that season, and at least in the cavalry of the Army of Northern Virginia, came less than two weeks into the new year. Sam Sweeney, who had kept his brother's music alive for J. E. B. Stuart and the South, fell ill after Christmas with smallpox. Quarantined at the pest hospital at Orange Court

House, he died on January 13, oblivious at last to his banjo. His body found a grave with the other victims of the little epidemic, but the attendants gave him no special services and his burial site was eventually lost. Only the death of General Stuart himself, four months hence, would dampen the cavalier spirit more.

Charlie Sweeney had been sick at home since the Gettysburg campaign, but in January he went back to a new assignment with General Stuart's horse artillery. He arrived late in the month to find that his older brother Bob, the left-handed fiddler, had been summoned to Stuart's headquarters as the last of the cavalry's musical Sweeneys.[14]

Not quite as quickly as these veterans died, others stepped forward to take their places. The recruits came primarily from the young men who had just come of age, or who had not quite come of age. When Captain Abbitt returned to his company on January 7 he brought along John R. Patteson, nephew of Lieutenant Patteson, and John H. Gordon—both of whom had just turned, or were about to turn, eighteen. James P. Webb, a relative of Mrs. Abbitt, had enlisted in the company when he was only sixteen, and had been discharged for his youth, but now he was old enough and he, too, followed the captain back to war.

Roland Ferguson had four teenage sons at the outbreak of the war. Two had already enlisted, and when the third turned eighteen, early in 1864, he joined them.

Charles Plunkett, whose older brother had died wearing the first sergeant's stripes in Abbitt's company, was only seventeen that January; although inspired with enough patriotism to enlist, this heir to John Plunkett's mercantile estate exercised enough discretion to choose the 20th Virginia Heavy Artillery, of which his townsman James E. Robertson was now the major. Amasa Isbell joined Plunkett in the relative comfort and safety of Robertson's battalion; the only duty these Appomattox artillerists saw outside of Battery 9 that winter came soon after Plunkett and Isbell arrived, when fifty men from Company A were assigned to guard 400 Yankee prisoners on their way from crowded Richmond warehouse-prisons to a brand-new stockade prison at Andersonville, Georgia.[15]

Even Joel Flood saw another chance to reap some battlefield glory that winter. He had apparently inquired whether James Kemper had any openings on his staff, while that general was recuperating from the wound he had suffered in Pickett's Charge: Kemper wrote the secretary of war at the end of January asking for Flood as an official aide-de-camp in place of a lieutenant killed at Gettysburg.

"Joel W. Flood has served under me," Kemper wrote, remembering Second Manassas, "is experienced, capable and of tried valor." The secretary duly appointed Flood a first lieutenant on February 17—a step down from his earlier commission, but a staff position would amount to a promotion in social terms—and after mulling it for nearly three weeks Flood accepted.

One of the ingredients in his decision may have been an act of the Confederate Congress passed on March 1 extending the grasp of the Conscription Bureau. Henceforth the age limits for military service would be seventeen to fifty, and all white male residents of those ages were instantly considered soldiers of the republic. Those who had previously been discharged, or who had hired substitutes, were once again fair game. Certain of the specific professional exemptions were continued, albeit with increased eligibility requirements, and the agricultural exemption was limited to those plantations that employed fifteen or more field hands, exclusive of other slaves. That restriction pinched Captain Flood rather closely, for of the thirty-eight blacks he owned in 1863 barely fifteen could have been counted as adult field hands.

Five weeks after Flood accepted the commission, his status changed drastically. On April 10 his grandmother, Eliza Bolling Flood, died at Pleasant Retreat, leaving Joel that entire plantation. Besides the big brick house and a couple of thousand acres of land, Pleasant Retreat supplied the new squire with thirty-four additional slaves. The farm carried with it a responsibility that may have caused the young man to regret accepting the commission, but he had earned no great reputation in his former command, and with his country at such an extremity he could hardly bear to decline field service again as soon as a new exemption offered itself. He found a solution to his dilemma by early May, however, when the still-ailing General Kemper was deprived of his combat brigade and ordered to organize the Virginia Reserves, with his headquarters at Lynchburg.

"I was appointed to that position for active service in the field," wrote Flood, complaining of Kemper's new administrative assignment and hinting that he was suffering from the dreaded respiratory plague of that age. "The state of my health and other causes unfit me for the new position that devolves upon me, the duties of which being of a clerical character would confine me very much to an office, and my condition is such that I cannot stand such confinement. I prefer to take my chance under the law and serve my country in a more active capacity where I can be more useful."[16]

As he may have suspected, the conscription law would go no further in depriving slave labor of its white supervision, and the more active capacity in which he intended to serve his country was as a wealthy planter.

If the tailor ever finished his new staff uniform, it went back into a closet at Eldon. Lieutenant Flood reverted to the persona of Captain Flood once more, to become Major Flood again with the passage of a year or two. Under the more stringent legislation only one white man was permitted to remain on each plantation, though, and one of Flood's overseers was compelled to enlist at the age of forty-five. He went to his grave two months later, leaving a wife and several children.

The reserves that Kemper was ordered to mobilize were the regiments and battalions composed of those residents at the tail ends of the military age limits. Besides locking those eighteen- to forty-five-year-old men already in the army to service for the rest of the war, the new conscription law directed boys of seventeen and men between forty-six and fifty to enroll in reserve companies for service within the state. A sizable number of men within the field army's age limits worked their way into each state's reserve regiments, either because of administrative exemptions or physical infirmities, and a few volunteers both under and over the age restrictions of the "reserve class" found their way into that limited service.

Those who fell within the prescribed ages were given until May 1 to enlist in reserve companies, while the Conscription Bureau would assign a colonel to command each regiment when ten companies sprang into existence. Throughout April, grandfathers and grandsons came out of the Virginia countryside to accept this alternative to the provisional army.[17]

Before they stopped coming forward, the state had raised four full regiments and thirteen battalions. In the Piedmont, each county produced just about enough residents of those ages to fill one company. Nearly a hundred of them appeared at Appomattox Court House on April 20, to be enrolled by a lieutenant from Richmond who directed them to elect their own officers. A slight majority of them fell within the specified age groups, but a full third of those who gathered at the courthouse that day would have been fair game for the fighting army were it not for some disability or dispensation. One of the recruits was nineteen, and at least half a dozen of them were in their thirties—including Charles Wingfield, who had been discharged from Captain Kyle's artillery company for a hernia and kidney disease, and Leroy Rosser, who had been rejected from the same company because of a bad heart. Judging by the county censuses, more than a score were between forty and forty-five, however, and had managed to avoid service thus far because they were unfit, had unusually large families, or had been able to persuade the enrolling officers that they were older than forty-five: in an era without birth certificates, that required only the production of a family Bible or the affidavit of a willing elder. Rosser himself had somehow aged fourteen years between 1860 and 1864, but even he could not convince anyone in authority that he was over fifty.[18]

One volunteer well beyond the age limit offered his services. John W. Johns, one of the original county commissioners and a militia officer from the War of 1812, rode in from his farm on the Oakville Road and signed his name to the roll. Such was his reputation in the county that the reservists elected him their captain, despite his seventy-nine years. Samuel McDearmon enlisted as well, but he declined to appear for service on the excuse of his duties as tax collector, and he remained a private on the roster for all of his former status as colonel of the militia. Wyatt Abbitt, the current colonel of the county militia, used that position to avoid any other service whatever, although he would be only forty-five that summer and there was no one left to serve in his paper regiment; like many who owned the timberland and capital to support a sawmill, he continued to fill government lumber contracts, collecting more than $19,000 in one ten-month period.[19]

Another third of the reserve company consisted of men in their late forties, and one—John Fore—was fifty. That April muster at Clover Hill also included a handful of sixteen-year-old boys who were hoping, perhaps, for a little adventure, and four of them soon found themselves with warrants as sergeants or corporals. A disproportionate number of the teenagers were elected to offices, in fact. Of the five officers besides Captain Johns, two of the second lieutenants were seventeen. The first sergeant and all but one of the eight noncommissioned officers had not yet reached eighteen, either. Samuel Sears, who had been living at Walker's Church with his grandparents since he was orphaned in the typhoid epidemic of 1857, became a second lieutenant within eight weeks of his seventeenth birthday. His sister Fannie's brother-in-law, Edward Hix, was named a sergeant at sixteen. The older men evidently shunned such appointments to avoid additional obligations.

Amherst County had already organized a similar company, and Buckingham County raised one shortly afterward. Once the requisite number of companies had formed, the Conscription Bureau designated it the 3rd Virginia Reserves and commissioned a Farmville veteran as its colonel. Richard A. Booker, a former captain in the 18th Virginia, had been shot through the chest at Second Manassas but had still had to hire a substitute to take his place before the War Department would accept his resignation—even though he had passed the upper age for field service.[20]

As May opened, the reservists remained at home with no greater prospect of being called to duty than the shadow companies of militia. The officers, especially the boys, basked in the glory of their nominal offices, and their subordinates perhaps reflected that they had at least offered their services, but all of them still looked upon the veteran legions of the provisional army as their real protectors. That sense of isolated security would evaporate within a matter of days.

The swamps of South Carolina harbored a variety of fevers that respected no military ranks, and in the grips of one of them Captain George Abbitt had dropped to 130 pounds during the winter of 1864. Two lengthy furloughs at home had failed to fatten his frame, and his men had begun to chide him as his uniform billowed about him. His health had become a central theme in his letters to his beloved Fannie, and he was finishing one of those letters on May 4 when a staff officer interrupted him to say that the regiment had been ordered back to Virginia.

"I don't know now wheather to say the news are good," he told Fannie. While his native state might prove more salubrious, and it would bring him closer to home, the Virginia theater had earned a reputation for deadliness. The 46th Virginia had not lost a man to hostile fire in over two years—and Abbitt's company never had; eighty Appomattox men remained active on the rolls of the Liberty Guards, aside from the perpetually absent. It was with mixed emotions, therefore, that the senior captain boarded his regiment on a northbound train the next morning.[21]

With the prominent exception of those in the 18th Virginia, the soldiers of Appomattox had not seen a lot of fighting by the spring of 1864. Even the local company of the 2nd Cavalry had buried only three victims of Yankee bullets thus far, despite constant activity and rigorous campaigns.

The Appomattox Invincibles, now known as Company A of the 20th Virginia Heavy Artillery Battalion, had lived the more common experience of the county's soldiers. After their inglorious performance in the western mountains, and nearly two years of unremarkable garrison duty, these men had found it convenient to forget their ambitious nickname. More than eightscore Appomattox men had joined that company under James E. Robertson: in three years only a dozen of them had gone under the sod, including one who was murdered at home, a couple of consumptives who should never have been accepted, and James Evans, who had come home to bury a dead comrade only to be kicked to death by a horse during the funeral.

Since the middle of 1862 Robertson's men had languished within the fortifications of Battery 9, alongside the Brook Turnpike north of Richmond. During that interval Robertson had been promoted to major and Samuel Overton had taken over the company, but it had seen no action at all except for one Union cavalry raid: Judson Kilpatrick's troopers had threatened the outer defenses during an ill-fated dash at the capital on March 1, 1864, and these heavy artillerymen had taken up muskets to help repel him; the Appomattox phalanx had come back with one sixteen-year-old veteran hobbling from a leg wound and another man daubing at a facial laceration. Until the final curtain, this would be the only blood shed by these city-bound soldiers.

Had it not been for the heavy details for prison guards, Captain Overton's men would never have seen anything beyond the perimeter of their forts. An inspector who nosed around the camps north of the city that spring concluded that, although heavy artillery was intended to double as infantry during an assault, the command that encompassed Robertson's battalion was not well trained in that arm. Nor was it much better at its primary function, he noted — and he especially criticized a detachment of Overton's men. This colonel reported that the noncommissioned officers who bore responsibility for aiming their pieces remained largely ignorant of gunnery principles, adding that the entire force had grown demoralized after so many months of inactivity. He finally suggested that it would be better to convert the lot of them into infantry and send them to the front, but that, too, would have to wait until the last extremity.[22]

Richmond itself was about to become "the front" again, for all the efforts of Robert E. Lee to keep the Army of the Potomac at arm's length. With spring that year Ulysses Grant assumed overall control of the United States Army, and within six weeks of taking that command he initiated a concerted and coordinated series of assaults against every corner of the Confederacy. Besides William Sherman's campaign against Atlanta and other movements in the West, the multiple prongs of Grant's offensive would pierce Virginia from five general directions.

While Grant pushed the Army of the Potomac against Lee on May 4, he simultaneously ferried six more infantry divisions up the James River under Benjamin Butler, a major general who had already engendered the unlimited hatred of the South. On May 5 Butler's Army of the James landed at Bermuda Hundred, a peninsula between the James and the Appomattox Rivers, essentially flanking Lee on his right. Meanwhile, another army of Federals started up the Shenandoah Valley — "up" the valley being southwesterly, in Virginia parlance — to flank Lee on the left. At the same time, George Crook led an infantry division out of West Virginia toward Dublin Depot on the Virginia & Tennessee while he sent William

Averell toward Saltville with a hefty brigade of cavalry; Stephen Burbridge was also supposed to move a Kentucky brigade against extreme southwestern Virginia. By the second week of May, heavy fighting had erupted on all fronts.

At this juncture Butler posed the most dangerous threat. With some 30,000 men at his disposal, he wielded the largest force outside the Army of the Potomac, and when he disembarked it at Bermuda Hundred he lay within a ten-mile march of the vital rail center at Petersburg—and less than twenty miles from the back door of Richmond. To defend both of these cities the Confederacy could field perhaps 5,000 dependable troops, besides the heavy artillerists at Fort Darling, below Richmond, and a few untrained battalions of government clerks, artisans, and operatives.

By rights, Butler should have been able to waltz inland a few miles and snip the railroad and the telegraph lines, turning a division to stall any pursuit from Petersburg while he swooped down upon Richmond with the rest of his army. By May 7 it all should have been over, but by May 7 Butler had hardly moved. On that date most of the Army of the James lay along the neck of Bermuda Hundred, flailing at a line of entrenchments running from river to river while a single Union brigade tiptoed gingerly toward Petersburg. A few hundred Confederates greeted that brigade at Port Walthall Junction, five miles north of the city, and discouraged it from further progress. The next day several Union brigades offered the same tentative movement, but with a brigade of reinforcements the Confederates again held them in check. On May 9 Butler tried this same point again with the better half of his immediate force, but the outnumbered Confederates convinced the Yankees that they still held the upper hand. That evening the 46th Virginia arrived in Petersburg, having abandoned its baggage on the other side of a gap that Butler's cavalry had made in the rail line. The Army of the James turned its attention northward to Richmond just then, though, and Wise's brigade found time to reassemble in leisure.[23]

Butler's divisions retired to their lines at Bermuda Hundred as though stepping aside to allow the Confederates right of way on the Richmond-Petersburg Turnpike. Pierre Beauregard, who commanded this department as far as the James River, took full advantage of that unintentional courtesy and hurried northward from Petersburg with another division of his troops from the Carolinas: with that division marched the depleted 18th Virginia. Wise's brigade stayed behind, in Petersburg.

Not until May 12 did Butler try again, this time creeping north toward Richmond. After three days of preliminary skirmishing and maneuvering, four of his divisions lined up before Richmond's defenders near Drewry's Bluff while the generals wondered how they should go about the capture of Richmond. Beauregard took little time to wonder, assuming the initiative with a dawn attack on May 16. Swinging hard with his left in dense fog, Beauregard scattered a brigade on the Union right, and was bending that flank back against the turnpike—the enemy's escape route—when he directed his own right-hand division to join the assault. With their comrades, the surviving Appomattox Grays clambered over the muddy parapets of their fresh entrenchments at midmorning and lunged straight down the Richmond & Petersburg Railroad tracks. The enemy bolted, but Samuel Farrar, who had been a teacher and militia captain in the early days of Appomattox County, fell dead alongside the tracks in one of the Federals' parting volleys, leaving a wife and three children in the Rock Church neighborhood. His first lieutenant, Thomas Gilliam, went down with a wound that would kill him less than two weeks later.[24]

Butler's troops started spilling back toward Bermuda Hundred, and Beauregard expected to chase them only a short distance before they ran head-on into a division that was supposed to be moving up from Port Walthall Junction. Beauregard had left Major General William Whiting there with two brigades, including Henry Wise's. The equivalent of a single small brigade opposed Whiting's advance, but that general refused to move and the Yankees continued unmolested toward their works on Bermuda Hundred. Beauregard fumed over the lost opportunity, as did Wise, but in the 46th Virginia Lieutenant John Patteson had cause to be thankful for the delay: it may have afforded him enough more life to learn that his wife had borne him another son at Rose Bower that very day.

Before dawn the next morning Whiting's troops moved out—under another general—but by then Butler had sealed off the base of his peninsula. The Confederates dug in opposite, but for days fighting flurried up and down the front. Wise's brigade took the right of what would become known as the Howlett line, absorbing 150 casualties over three days in the new trenches. An especially nasty scrap erupted on May 20, causing nearly two dozen casualties in the 46th Virginia. Perhaps Lieutenant Patteson and his namesake nephew, John, were celebrating the news of the new child, for they were struck down together: young John was killed on the spot, while his uncle died the next day from a wound in his left side. Instantly, Appomattox County was provided with its third new widow that week, as well as seven more fatherless children.[25]

While the troops that had come from the Carolinas stymied Butler, Confederates in the lower Shenandoah Valley enjoyed even better luck.

On May 15 John C. Breckinridge, who had recently sat as vice president of the United States, so thoroughly pounded Franz Sigel's Union division at New Market that Sigel fled back the way he had come. Down in the southwestern part of the state, Burbridge's raid from Kentucky started late and fizzled early, but on May 10 Crook had managed to sweep his understrength opponents aside and burn both Dublin Depot and the New River railroad bridge before withdrawing back over the mountains; meanwhile Averell had come within range of Wytheville, though he avoided Saltville and did little damage. Even those defeats proved relatively harmless, for Crook and Averell might have turned down the valley, had they arrived uncontested, and come upon Breckinridge from behind as he faced Sigel.

The Army of Northern Virginia kept fighting as the other opposing forces reeled back to their camps. Lee had struck Grant broadside in the Wilderness, west of Fredericksburg, on May 5, hammering at him for two days. Unlike the previous May, he was unable to cow his enemy, and rather than retreating back across the Rapidan Grant moved southeast, to Spotsylvania Court House, on May 8. Stuart's cavalry confronted the Union vanguard there that day, and there died First Sergeant William H. Glover of the 2nd Virginia Cavalry, who had once clerked in his brother's brick store alongside the Clover Hill Tavern. The brother, Samuel, still rode with the company as a private; he also retained the store, although the trade there must have fallen off considerably.

As Grant and Lee sidestepped in a convex arc toward Richmond, Philip Sheridan led the bulk of the Union cavalry inside that arc for the same objective. Stuart left Spotsylvania Court House to confront him, and a Yankee shot him in the stomach as the cavalry chief took an active part in the engagement at Yellow Tavern, just outside the capital; Stuart died the next day, robbing Bob Sweeney of his most appreciative audience.

Sheridan proceeded a little farther toward Richmond but soon reined his horsemen away from the city, aiming for the old Peninsula battleground. Grant headed that way himself, after eleven long days at Spotsylvania Court House and a few more days' delay at the North Anna River, and on May 27 Sheridan's cavalry crossed the Pamunkey River ahead of the great blue throng, skirmishing with Confederate cavalry and screening the crossing of the army. The 2nd Virginia Cavalry tangled with Sheridan's troopers again the next day at Haw's Shop, barely a dozen miles from downtown Richmond, where Michigan cavalry under a young brigadier named George Armstrong Custer made a dismounted charge that drove the Southerners from the field. The retreating Appomattox Rangers carried away Corporal George Carter, who had suffered the same stomach wound as General Stuart, and he lasted only a few hours longer. They left behind two prisoners: one of Captain Flood's early recruits and Peter Pankey, one of the conscripts from the late winter, who would die in a Maryland prison camp eight weeks hence.[26]

With the Union army so close to the capital and in such healthy numbers, neither Lee nor Beauregard could well afford to detach troops to protect the interior. The raids in the Shenandoah and along the Virginia & Tennessee had demonstrated that certain strategic points in the interior might need some protection, and that seemed the perfect assignment for the new regiments of Virginia Reserves. On May 16 the War Department directed General Kemper to finish the organization of the reserves and immediately call them up for service, giving him authority to marshal the aid of local enrolling officers to identify the men within the appropriate age brackets. That was the day Joel Flood chose to submit his resignation as an aide on Kemper's staff.

Perhaps surprised to find their services demanded at all, and certainly so quickly after their initial muster, most of the Appomattox County company reported to Lynchburg, where they and several other Southside companies were turned around and headed back to High Bridge, just beyond Farmville. The more impressive railroad bridges invited the most daring enemy activity, and evoked the greatest departmental solicitation: the destruction of the bridge over the New River gorge, for instance, had cut the rest of Virginia off from the supplies of salt, firewood, and mineral ore in the southwest, and the lack of materials and fuel had silenced all the Lynchburg furnaces and foundries since May 13. There were few greater engineering feats in the Confederacy than High Bridge, and its demolition would have probably isolated Lee's army permanently from the resources of the mountains. While the real armies jockeyed for position around Richmond, the boys and the older men of Appomattox and Buckingham Counties dug away at earthworks on either end of this monument to Colonel Samuel D. McDearmon's bankruptcy; Private Samuel D. McDearmon did not deign to join them.[27]

Soldiers and slaves were turning over Virginia's red soil everywhere that spring. At the mouth of the Appomattox River Butler and Beauregard continued to cultivate the left bank, while Confederate engineers had churned up a string of fortifications on the right bank below Petersburg, in case the Federals developed any ambitions in that quarter. Across the James, Grant and Lee settled into substantial breastworks northeast of Richmond for another fortnight's fighting, some of it especially brutal; one more Appomattox cavalryman died contesting the advance to Cold Harbor, and while the infantry grappled there Wade Hampton took the cavalry and chased after Sheridan, who had swung away to the north and west on another raid. Hampton caught up with Sheridan—and Custer, again—at Trevillian Station, where another Appomattox boy fell mortally wounded. In a month, twice as many of the Appomattox Rangers had lost their lives in battle as during the previous three years.

Captain Charles Webb had escaped all the spring fighting. Early in April the good doctor had been assigned to staff duty at cavalry corps headquarters, and instead of directing his men in action with the enemy he had been busy directing ammunition forward to his men as they engaged the enemy without him. The luck of that assignment turned against him, though, and in mid-June he came down with typhoid. By the end of the month he was dead.[28]

Captain Webb's brother-in-law, Captain George W. Abbitt, had begun to feel ill again shortly after the 46th Virginia reached Petersburg, and he took ten days in a hospital there at the beginning of June; he returned to duty briefly, but on the same day that Webb was carried to the Richmond hospital to die, the surgeons sent Abbitt to the general hospital at Farmville.[29]

During the interim between Abbitt's hospital stays, Grant slipped his entire army over the James and attacked Petersburg from the east and south. The sudden movement and the feat of bridging so broad a river with pontoons surprised General Lee completely. Beauregard guessed the truth days before the Yankees began crossing, but Lee doubted the Creole's judgment and refused to move his own army until the enemy had actually descended on Petersburg.

Wise's four regiments had remained on the Howlett line into early June, neutralizing Butler and participating in the occasional sally against the Federals' works; another of the original Liberty Guards died in such an attempt at the beginning of the month. Soon thereafter the brigade pulled back toward Port Walthall Junction, and Wise was assigned to an expanded military district that included Petersburg. On June 9 a Union cavalry brigade crossed the Appomattox from Bermuda Hundred and galloped around to the south of Petersburg, assailing the city from the Jerusalem Plank Road. An impromptu militia company and some Virginia cavalry stalled this raid long enough for Wise to bring down the 46th Virginia and a motley collection of reserves, regulars, and convalescents to drive the Yankees away, but thereafter Wise kept his own regiments near the city, with the 46th Virginia within the city limits.[30]

This brigade formed the backbone of the Petersburg garrison, which

Beauregard estimated at 2,200 muskets when Grant sent his army toward him. Below Petersburg engineers and slave labor (some of it from Appomattox County) had erected a string of artillery lunettes and rudimentary infantry works known as the Dimmock line, but those fortifications required a certain number of soldiers to offer any resistance. Beauregard pestered General Lee for reinforcements, but Lee still thought the main Yankee army lay before him and the best he would do was offer to return Robert Hoke's division, which Beauregard had loaned him after bottling up Butler.

The first of Grant's infantry struck Petersburg from the east, appearing late on the morning of June 15. Beauregard began howling for reinforcements, warning that he could not divert enough troops to hold Petersburg and still contain Butler at Bermuda Hundred. Wise filed the 46th Virginia into the Dimmock line nearest the Appomattox, leaving the 26th on its right and to the right of that the 34th Virginia—with which Thomas A. Tibbs, onetime first lieutenant of the Appomattox Rangers, now carried a rifle.

Another former lieutenant in the 2nd Cavalry, Clifton Webb, had just resumed his place in the ranks of the 46th after a few days in the hospital. His brother-in-law, the feverish Captain Abbitt, stood alongside him behind Captain Dimmock's undermanned parapet.[31]

For some reason the Federals hesitated, but they were gathering strength all the time while Wise saw no new troops coming up behind him. Finally, at seven o'clock that evening, the long blue lines surged forward. Greeting the Yankees on either side of Battery 5, the three Virginia regiments held out half an hour against three divisions, but soon a brigade from Massachusetts, Pennsylvania, and New Jersey drove the 46th Virginia out of its breastworks north of the battery; Captain Abbitt's company put up as good a fight as any in the regiment, losing two of the regiment's ten men killed that day, including Lieutenant John Williams; on the far side of Battery 5, Corporal Tibbs may have been the first Appomattox man to see black soldiers in action, as a division of U.S. Colored Troops moved against the right of Wise's line: one brigade of that division equaled the effective strength of Wise's entire command, and it swept the Dimmock line clear of Confederates for half a mile.[32]

Had an aggressive general led those Yankees, Petersburg would have fallen that night, but Beauregard pulled Wise back closer to the city and started a new line of entrenchments. Hoke's lead brigades began to arrive, literally at a trot, and Beauregard put them to work on the new fortifications. During the night he called Bushrod Johnson's division down from

Bermuda Hundred, leaving only a thin string of pickets to bluff Butler for a few hours longer, and by the time Johnson's troops buttressed his line Beauregard had about 10,000 men: he faced five times that many, in three separate Union corps.

For most of June 16 the Union host lay quiet as its three independent corps commanders shuffled their troops and consulted with one another. Not until five o'clock did they attack, but the outnumbered Confederates held most of their ground until nightfall. By then Lee himself was on the way with George Pickett's division, but still he doubted that Grant could have crossed the James. Assuming that it was only Butler's troops who were pounding at Petersburg, he discounted the threat from Bermuda Hundred, as well, but Pickett found Butler advancing from there and drove him back, fighting until near midnight. The Army of the Potomac renewed the assault on Petersburg before dawn on June 17, but by midafternoon of that day Lee had not been convinced that Grant's whole force lay before the city and he declined to bring the last of his own troops from the left bank of the James. Wise's regiments stayed on the front line yet again, absorbing another round of heavy casualties: Captain Abbitt saw a dozen more of his men shot that day, and although none of them died most of them were lost forever to the company. Mariah Wright's son Gilliam, a corporal in the field artillery, had his leg broken by a bullet just below the hip, from which he expired after twenty painful days.

Not until the morning of June 18 did Lee come to believe that the danger lay before Petersburg, rather than Richmond. At last he ordered his own army to cross the James at Chaffin's Bluff, keeping Butler sealed in Bermuda Hundred so the reinforcements could pass unmolested into Petersburg. The battle-thinned 18th Virginia had recently rejoined its old brigade in Pickett's division, so the Appomattox Grays stood among the troops holding Butler on his peninsula; Samuel Dickerson, another of the conscripts taken from Appomattox County late in February, was shot dead that day while Lee's other veterans passed behind him on the way to the beleaguered city.[33]

Lee's tardy arrival finally stabilized the Petersburg front. His reluctance to move resulted, in part, from having detached the Second Corps from his army, which left him especially vulnerable to deceptive maneuvering. That corps, led now by Jubal Early, was climbing off railroad cars in Lynchburg even as Beauregard struggled to save Petersburg, forty leagues away.

Early had been sent to answer another challenge in the Shenandoah Valley. Major General David Hunter had taken over Franz Sigel's defeated army, turning it around both geographically and psychologically. Between June 4 and June 12 he had driven south on the Valley Turnpike, routing a little Confederate army at Piedmont before taking possession of both Staunton and Lexington, where he burned the Virginia Military Institute and the home of the former governor, John Letcher. Along the way he picked up George Crook and William Averell, with 10,000 of the men they had led into southwestern Virginia the previous month. At that point Lee agreed to let Early go with some of his most tried veterans.

From Lexington Hunter moved over the Blue Ridge toward Lynchburg. He directed Averell to send ahead a party of 200 horsemen to ride around the city and cut the railroad, and Averell dispatched that many West Virginians and Pennsylvanians under a couple of lieutenants. Ranging forward alone, these 200 struck the Orange & Alexandria near Amherst Court House on June 13, tearing up the tracks before reining southeast for the James River. The raiders crossed below Lynchburg, skirting the northwest corner of Appomattox County. They turned up that evening at Concord Depot, on the western edge of the county, where they ripped up a few hundred yards of the Southside Railroad tracks and burned a couple of waiting trains. Then they disappeared again, heading back for the main body. Except for passing prisoners, these troopers were the first Yankees to lay eyes on Appomattox County in more than three years of warfare.[34]

Hunter appeared southeast of Lynchburg on the afternoon of June 17. Averell attacked the outpost on Diamond Hill, five miles from town, and with Crook's help he forced the defenders out of their works. Just back from the Richmond theater himself, General Breckinridge collected the remnants of the Valley commands, including some straggling companies of Virginia Reserves, on the outskirts of the city. Early's lead regiments arrived that evening, to the beating of drums and the cheers of soldiers and citizens.

Hunter heard the commotion and suspected the cause, but the next morning he started skirmishing with the Confederate pickets, looking for a way around the intimidating redoubts that Southside slaves had constructed on either side of the main roads. As he reached to his right and left, Confederates rushed forward to cut his army in half, but Hunter pulled his wings back in time to avoid that catastrophe. By early afternoon his cavalry commanders at either end of the broad arc he held around Lynchburg reported seeing large numbers of Confederates, and finally Hunter concluded that he was in trouble. He waited until dark, keeping his pickets close to their Southern counterparts until midnight while the rest of his column stole away on the road to Salem. General Early only learned of the retreat at dawn, and his infantry could not march fast enough to catch even Hunter's rear guard.[35]

Harassed by Confederate cavalry, Hunter withdrew into the mountains of West Virginia. Lynchburg had been saved with only the aggravation of some mischief to the railroad, and after Early had chased Hunter out of the Valley he undertook a plan that he and Robert E. Lee had discussed privately a few days before: since he could not return to Petersburg without inviting Hunter to come back, and since his corps was too valuable to leave idle at the foot of the mountains, Early took the only other option available to him and headed north, on the offensive. Three weeks later he would post his pickets on the outskirts of Washington City.[36]

No sooner had the threat from the west been blunted than another developed from the east. Two divisions of cavalry galloped away from the Army of the Potomac on June 22, heading straight for the Southside Railroad. Before pursuing Confederates could do anything about it, the Yankees destroyed Ford's Station, burning two more complete trains and a sawmill for that line; the next day they headed for Burkeville Junction, and it looked as though they intended to burn High Bridge, which was defended only by the poorly armed—and even more poorly trained—3rd Virginia Reserves. After demolishing the depot at the junction, though, the Federal column turned down the Richmond & Danville tracks, burning every station on the way and tearing up miles of track.

Not until the strategic Staunton River bridge could anyone stop the mounted horde. The Virginia captain who commanded that post collected 938 citizens, reservists, convalescents, and passing soldiers to defend the bridge, and when the Union cavalry appeared before him on June 25 he poured more than half his force into works he had just built on the left bank of the river. This motley battalion put up so fierce a fight that forty-two dead Yankee cavalrymen lay before them afterward, and as the Southerners blazed away at the attackers from in front, regular Confederate cavalry assailed them from the rear. The firing continued into the night, but the blue columns withdrew under cover of darkness. Harried all the way back to Petersburg, they left behind some 900 of their original 6,000 men, but they had interrupted rail service and had done considerable damage to the Southside line in particular. Railroad cars, locomotives, and sawmill machinery did not come easily in the South this summer of 1864.[37]

John Cawthorn, rector of Bethany Baptist Church, south of Evergreen, opened a letter from his son Joel late in July. It came by way of the Union prison camp at Point Lookout, Maryland: Joel had been in enemy hands for more than a year now. A good many local boys still languished there with him on the first anniversary of Pickett's Charge, but they all fared well, he said, and his own health matched that of any of them. His uncle, Sam Thornhill, who had moved from Appomattox to Missouri before the war, sent him money for extra food whenever he needed it, but Joel craved news from home.

"Let me hear from my Dear Brother," he asked. His brother Charles had enlisted in the same company, the Appomattox Grays, exactly one month after Joel was captured.

John Cawthorn found that he had to comfort his family as often as his flock, for the war had laid a great burden on them. When his older son was captured at Gettysburg his eldest daughter's husband, Edward Harvey, had been killed; Samuel Jennings, the husband of the next oldest daughter, still served with Cawthorn's younger son in that battered company, while Harriet Cawthorn's beau, Robert Cheatham, had lost the use of his arm at Second Manassas.[38]

Young Drury Woodson, who had followed Cawthorn in the clerical profession, also discovered that a minister's duties often took a somber turn during such times. Doctrine frequently mattered less than proximity, and since Drury Woodson stood close in blood as well as geography it was probably to his door that Mary Woodson sent her oldest son when she needed someone to bury her husband. John Woodson had come down with typhoid late in the spring—his last paperwork as the Lynchburg quartermaster was dated June 1—and he suffered for a month at home before the disease proved too much for his forty-year-old system. On the first of July he closed his eyes for the last time, leaving his wife the little law office at Clover Hill, one of the numerous little Patteson farms a couple of miles north of the village, five children between the ages of four and thirteen, and the published appreciation of the justices of the county court. With little more resources than that, Mrs. Woodson prepared to hold onto the property her husband had accumulated, raise their children, and survive a quarter century of dignified widowhood.[39]

Only hours after John Woodson was lowered into his grave, Hubbard Martin climbed down from the Lynchburg train at Appomattox Station. According to his captain, Martin was "a good and faithful soldier." Captain Abbitt wrote that assessment more than three decades after Private Martin's last absence without leave, and like any veteran he may have forgotten the negative side of his neighbor's service, but Martin had been one of the first to volunteer in the Liberty Guards and he had fallen prisoner at Roanoke Island. His name had graced a round-robin letter from the Roanoke prisoners to President Davis the following April, asking for speedier exchange, but Martin failed to return immediately when that exchange was finally accomplished. He went back to duty in the fall of 1862, followed the regiment to South Carolina, and remained with it when the crisis came at Petersburg. Martin's rifle braced the Howlett line, and he raced to Petersburg with his comrades to repel the Yankee cavalry on June 9. He stood in the ranks when the Federal juggernaut struck on June 15, and two days later he helped hold back most of the Army of the Potomac. At midafternoon on June 17 he was one of the few in his company who could say that he had been in all the regiment's battles, but on that day a bullet plowed a furrow through his scalp, knocking him senseless, and by that evening Martin was on his way to Chimborazo Hospital, on the bluffs overlooking the James River.

After a couple of weeks the surgeons sent him home on a forty-day furlough. His family lived less than a mile from Nebraska, and not much farther away lay the humble abode of John Mitchell, whose daughter Mary had evidently caught Hubbard Martin's attention in years past; she may have been the cause of his reluctance to leave home in the summer of 1862. Neither of them had ever been married, although she was twenty-four and he thirty-four, and almost as soon as Hubbard stepped down at the depot, he and Mary sought out Reverend Woodson. They were married on July 11, and the wounded veteran so enjoyed his new situation that he lingered at home once again when his furlough ran out. Perhaps he feared that he might be killed before he had a chance to continue his line, for he only went back to his regiment after Mary had conceived.[40]

Thanks to convalescent furloughs and disability discharges, it was a busy summer for Reverend Woodson, with more pleasant duties than burying his own kin. A week after the young minister read the service to the Martins, Charlie Sweeney approached him with a teenage girl whom he wanted to marry. Home again from the army, Charlie set up house-keeping in the little family cabin near the old home place, opposite Clover Hill, where he and Mattie would spend the next forty-five years. Three weeks later another furloughed soldier came to Woodson with one of the Via girls from the Stonewall District.[41]

Hubbard Martin's scalp wound had proven fortunate in more ways than one. Not only did it afford him an opportunity to consummate his designs on John Mitchell's daughter, but it may have saved his life. On the night of June 17 Henry Wise's brigade had fallen back, along with the rest of Beauregard's little army, about a mile from the line on which Hubbard

Martin had been wounded. There everyone dug in again, creating a new labyrinth of trenches in an arc nearer to Petersburg, and the two armies settled into a siege. Grant kept extending his lines to the west, trying to encircle Lee and cut off his supply lines, but through June and July he allowed a regiment composed largely of Pennsylvania coal miners to dig a tunnel beneath a nearby Confederate fort. In the final days of July the miners finished a couple of wide chambers beneath the fort, filled them with kegs of powder, and waited for permission to blow the redan to pieces. That fort sat a couple of hundred yards to the left of the trenches occupied by the 46th Virginia.

The explosion came early on the morning of July 30. It began with an ominous rumbling that quickly erupted in smoke, dust, and flame, sending some 300 Virginia artillerymen and South Carolina infantrymen skyward along with their guns and great chunks of clay that had once been their fort. Confederates up and down the line either fled or stared, stunned, while a Union brigade streamed into the crater caused by the blast.

The Yankees stopped to help dig survivors from the debris. That proved their undoing, for had they instead swept up and down the trenches and pushed ahead to the heights beyond they might have captured Petersburg that day. As it was, the dazed Confederates were able to mount a feeble resistance and rush reinforcements to the scene. The fight lasted all day: five Federal divisions ultimately threw themselves into the crater or at the ragged ends of the interrupted Confederate works, but they either bogged down in the morass of loose clay and disorganized commands in the crater or faltered under a furious blaze of gunfire and artillery from the surviving works.

Just south of the crater, Henry Wise's men offered some of the most stubborn resistance. A company of the 34th Virginia that had originally served as heavy artillery—Thomas Tibbs's company—manned a gun near the crater that had been abandoned by its crew, and that single Napoleon sprayed shell and canister into the flank of the blue lines that began pouring into the chasm.

The 46th Virginia lay alongside the shattered South Carolina brigade that had garrisoned the fort, enduring artillery fire most of the day and repelling a brigade of the Union Ninth Corps that made a tardy assault directly in front of the regiment. A shard from one shell struck Joel Ferguson in the hip, severing his spine, and the young recruit screamed so that his brother William ("Buck," as most Appomattox men named William seemed to be called) enlisted Richard Childress to carry him to the rear. They worked their way down the traverses leading to the Jerusalem Plank

Road, sweat pouring from them as the mercury climbed over a hundred degrees, but Childress, another three-month veteran who was only sixteen years old, dropped from the heat. Buck Ferguson roused Childress enough to send him back down the trench for help. As the brothers waited, Joel cried ceaselessly for water, prompting Buck to crawl out of the trench and run for the regiment's well. That well lay within range of the Yankees in the crater, and as the older brother dipped for water a bullet shattered his skull, killing him instantly. Someone else carried Joel to the field hospital, where surgeons shook their heads and turned to patients who stood a chance of survival. He died two days later.[42]

In the end the Federals fled the crater, leaving behind some 4,000 dead, wounded, and prisoners, and Confederate pickets soon stood once again on works rebuilt along the edge of that bloody excavation. The line there stood for another eight months. Hubbard Martin resumed his place in the ranks that fall, after the harvest; perhaps recalling Hubbard's failure to return after he was exchanged, and the deaths of the Ferguson brothers during Hubbard's absence, Captain Abbitt filed charges for a court martial that might have concluded in a firing squad. As a wounded veteran who had never shirked in battle, though, Martin was not the sort officers were likely to have shot, and his punishment consisted principally of the loss of his pay. Given the value of Confederate money by the time his trial ended, that amounted to no punishment at all.[43]

As Confederate fortunes flagged on the battlefield, so did confidence in its money, each bill of which bore the caveat that it was redeemable only after the Confederacy and the United States had concluded a peace treaty; specie payments had been suspended since the outbreak of hostilities. The treasury answered the need for money by merely printing more bills, sparking the inevitable inflation, and by the late autumn of 1863 many Southerners found Confederate treasury notes unwelcome payment for a wide variety of debts. Captain Abbitt's mother-in-law, Nancy Webb, boarded with Fannie through 1863, and when she and Fannie discussed extending the arrangement for another year the mother complained of the high cost, at four dollars per month. As diplomatically as a wise son-in-law might, the captain observed that Mrs. Webb should consider the value of the money she paid; he hinted broadly at other members of the family who refused to accept that same money in payment for the mortgage on his farm.[44]

A congressional effort to rehabilitate the Confederate dollar failed miserably early in 1864. The act of February 17 authorized the circulation of a new series of notes: to reduce the impact of inflation, a tax of 33 percent was imposed on the old notes used for the payment of public debts after April 1—or after July 1, for bills in denominations of $5; $100 bills carried additional taxes, unless used to buy new Confederate bonds. Congress hoped that this would encourage the public to buy bonds, trade the old bills for new ones, and reduce prices on goods for sale. Among those who maintained faith in the Confederacy, that worked: from his new home at Clover Hill, Wilmer McLean bought his first $500 bond on April 21, and over the course of the summer he set aside another $1,000 for two more.[45]

More Virginians, however, appeared to view the reissue as nothing less than repudiation of at least one-third the value of the national currency, and who was to say whether that would be the extent of it? One Oakville man who had bought his farm from Benjamin Walker came home from the camp of the 20th Heavy Artillery in July and tried to pay off the balance of his mortgage, only to find that Colonel Walker wanted nothing to do with the old money; on the advice of Thomas Bocock, just back from the Congress that had caused this trouble, the nervous mortgagee stopped at the courthouse and filed an affidavit documenting his effort to pay. The treasury act of February turned the South to a barter economy in which the paper dollar became the subordinate tender—the currency of last resort. By the spring of 1864 Captain Abbitt could express satisfaction that his wife's uncle, Martin Webb, had paid her for Mrs. Webb's board with a sheep, but he complained that his own brother, Dr. William H. Abbitt, refused to give her another one for four bushels of corn.

"Buck loves his sheep it seems dearly," Captain Abbitt wrote, just before the Petersburg campaign. "I was under the impression that he was willing to give the sheep in pay for four bushels of corn he had already recd., but I suppose I misunderstood him."[46]

To give the new money a semblance of value, the Confederacy levied substantial taxes on its citizens, but those taxes would obviously be payable in government notes. In Appomattox County it was Samuel McDearmon to whom land owners paid their national taxes, and for some they proved considerable. For all his political success, Thomas Bocock had not accumulated fabulous wealth as a planter, yet his war tax amounted to $411.82 in the autumn of 1864. In real terms that amounted to relatively little, though, for just into the new year Bocock accepted $5,000 in Confederate money from Dr. Samuel Coleman for five barrels of corn.

Tax officials demanded a heftier rate of exchange for payment in kind. At the end of August that year, Wilson Hix allowed James Moss only a penny a pound on cured hay and sheaf oats for tax-in-kind payments, and only $2.50 a bushel for wheat. Even with Confederate money floating around so freely, Moss still deemed it less expensive to pay his tax with two tons of oats, three tons of hay, fifteen bushels of wheat, and fifteen pounds of wool thrown in, suggesting that he found the season's yield satisfactory.[47]

Dr. Coleman, meanwhile, had evidently not been tending to agricultural concerns at his little farm west of Appomattox Court House. It could not have been a matter of throwing his energies into the more profitable enterprise of tobacco production, for with only one female slave to his name he could not legally have grown more than 10,000 plants. It seems unlikely that a young, newly established doctor could have made much money at his profession during the war, but perhaps he speculated in the goods his neighbors longed for, because he seemed solvent enough to hire a substitute when he wanted out of the army and he had managed to remain out even after his substitute deserted; like Wilson Hix, he may have been speculating in corn for the government market. At least there was no other reason for a man with 254 acres of arable land to want for corn, for the war had had little occasion to interrupt the county economy: the two cavalry raids at Concord Depot and Burkeville Junction had been the only enemy incursions to even attract the attention of Appomattox citizens. Dr. Coleman's only excuse may have been a lack of available labor, for military levies had removed the majority of prime white farm hands, which in turn increased the competition for renting surplus slaves from the larger plantations.[48]

While food remained fairly plentiful at home, the troops before Richmond and Petersburg encountered periodic shortages. With the siege, most of them lost the opportunity to supplement their bland army rations with a little foraging in the countryside, for even when they did have a chance to range free of the trenches they found the nearby neighborhoods picked clean. As Grant reached farther west, pinching off the Weldon Railroad, little famines erupted within Lee's army. After the end of August only the Southside Railroad connected Petersburg's defenders with the Southern interior, and Grant urged the Army of the Potomac toward that. At the same time, he dispatched Phil Sheridan into the Shenandoah Valley to assure that, even if the Southside line remained intact, it would have that much less provender to transport to Lee's army.

By early fall, George Abbitt had begun craving something to stimulate his malnourished frame.

"I would like very much to get a box from home soon with a little brandy," he hinted to Fannie on October 8, after mentioning that some of his men had obtained some delicacies that way. The brandy came, only to be begged from him sip by sip, but other packages brought applesauce and sorghum molasses for sweetening his drab diet of hardtack and salted meat. Next he asked for apples, spare ribs, and some pork, filling his letters with requests he had never had to make before. By the colder season of late November, those requests included clothing. He asked for some shirts ("if they are pretty") and confided that he was nearly out of his drawers.

"My coat won't last me the winter," he added. "I am already getting ashamed of it."[49] Besides the poor rations, deteriorating supply system, and the growing filth and boredom of a permanent camp, the trenches offered perpetual danger. The main lines lay relatively close here, and some of the picket outposts reached within yards of the enemy's. Not a man in Captain Abbitt's company had been killed by the enemy for the first three years of the war, while ten died in (or as a result of) the furious fighting of May, June, and July, but from the first of August until the spring of 1865 Abbitt lost five more of his best men even though the 46th Virginia participated in no significant actions during that time. All of them were killed by sharpshooters, who put a bitter edge on the dull life before Petersburg.

Hegeccous Davenport, a forty-nine-year-old bachelor from Spout Spring, dropped dead from a single bullet on October 30. On November 24 a Yankee marksman detected Thomas Conner crawling back from duty on the picket line and drilled him through the lungs; a member of another company bolted out and brought him in, against orders, and Conner lived to reach the Petersburg general hospital, but everyone knew there was no hope for him and he asked Captain Abbitt to send his body home when he died. The day after Christmas William Worsham, a teenage veteran of the entire war, was killed on the line. Commenting on this incidental slaughter of his comrades, farmer Charles Arrington wrote his wife that "I believe I can sharpshoot with Lyncoln's best at any time."

It was the cold that Arrington dreaded more than the enemy, for it became so dangerous passing back and forth to the picket pits that he had to find his way out in the dark and stay there until the following night, without the warmth of a fire. Men with inadequate diets and threadbare clothing found the winter's cold more biting than they otherwise might have, and from early January they suffered from periodic heavy snowfalls that soaked their dilapidated brogans and turned the trenches to mud.

"I don't think I can stand it," he said of the winter chill. Perhaps the cold did prove too much for him on picket one day in mid-January: he may have stood up to stamp his feet, or thrashed about in his shallow pit too vigorously, and a sharpshooter ended his misery.[50]

By then the assorted perils and privations had begun to drain the Army of Northern Virginia. Men drifted away as never before, and the proximity of Union pickets made it all the easier. The Yankees offered rewards for deserters who came in with their arms and equipment, for the Confederacy would find it nearly as difficult to replace the material goods as to raise new recruits, and any Southern soldiers who did desert within certain dates could avoid prison and simply submit to shipment north of the Potomac. Periodically these offers came wafting through Confederate camps, delivered by the wind on thin slips of paper.

Progressively more soldiers took advantage of such offers as the season grew colder. In the last ten days of November A. P. Hill's corps lost sixty men through desertion to the enemy, including one North Carolina officer. A hundred men from Pickett's division sat in the guardhouse that month, charged with desertion or attempting to desert, and on the night of November 24 alone four men from Captain Abbitt's company slipped across the lines, asking for asylum. Brothers Calaway and Wyatt Mann, their cousin Thomas Mann, and Samuel Webb, all native sons of Appomattox County, took the oath of allegiance in Washington three days later and remained in the city; four months afterward, Webb even went so far as to enlist as a substitute in a Union Maryland regiment, under another name. These were hardly reluctant conscripts the company was losing, but willing volunteers from 1862 and early 1863; Abbitt shared his dismay with his wife.

"I hope those are the last of my company that are so lost to conscience as to forsake all, country & Friends, and go forever into disgrace," he told her. They were not: James Giles, who had enlisted with the company at the very outset, at the age of sixteen, went over to the Yankees on December 4. Henry Johnson, an early volunteer and a widower with children at home, departed two days before Christmas and asked the Union authorities for transportation to Springfield, Illinois.[51]

Robert E. Lee blamed these losses on scanty provisions and continuous duty in the trenches. George Pickett attributed the sudden rise in desertion to leniency at the political level, for every man in his division sentenced to death for desertion since the middle of September had been reprieved. Lee conceded that the law needed "rigid execution," but President Davis chastised the generals for offering criticism of his executive clemency.

Still, Lee and Pickett made a good point. While Lee's army melted away, Union generals were handing out cash rewards, furloughs, and promotions to those of their pickets who succeeded in shooting their own deserters. Hubbard Martin, the Appomattox bridegroom who had taken so long an unauthorized honeymoon the previous summer, seemed little impressed that December when his court martial fined him a portion of the near-meaningless Confederate currency that was so long overdue him anyway. He left Captain Abbitt's company again in February, without benefit of furlough, as his wife came close to the end of her term.[52]

A similar rash of desertions struck the Appomattox Reserves, who had been ordered from High Bridge to the Staunton River bridge during the second week of November. On the same night that the Manns and Samuel Webb decamped from the 46th Virginia in front of Petersburg, one of the teenage reservists left for home, as well. When five divisions of Yankees left the Army of the Potomac early in December on a foray down the Weldon Railroad, the 3rd Reserves and other railroad guards hurried off in a sleet storm to pose what opposition they could, but the Federals returned after wreaking much havoc and the Appomattox Reserves turned around and started back to that vital bridge on the Danville line. The march evidently proved too much for five of them, who deserted as soon as the company reached the old post; four of them fled in one night, including Thomas Webb, the forty-nine-year-old "comick dancer" of the antebellum minstrel circuit. By the end of December, only forty-one men remained with the company of the original hundred.[53]

Fourteen of the missing were absent without leave, one died shortly after the return from North Carolina, and old Captain Johns had been discharged. The rest had been detailed or indefinitely furloughed to some critical occupation or "private necessity." A shoemaker, a section hand, a blacksmith, and a wheelwright had been detailed to their trades, but now farming had become an essential occupation and three men were assigned to that "duty." Those detailed for personal crises all seemed to have left large broods of children at home.

At home there still remained many men of fighting age who enjoyed good health, and as the Conscription Bureau reached farther afield to reinforce the front lines these men scrambled for some skill or technicality on which to appeal for exemption. George Martin, a thirty-year-old Appomattox farmer, had the good fortune to know the tanning process although he never considered himself a tanner. It was also his luck to know Samuel McDearmon, who had not lost the habit of making a dollar wherever he could, and William Daniel Hix, whom the voters had finally elected sheriff in place of his father. Hix, whose office exempted him from conscription, had been selling tanned leather to the government at a generous profit since the days when Confederate money still meant something, and he continued to solicit contracts from the Quartermaster Department, with perhaps a different medium of exchange. Late in 1864 McDearmon and Hix circulated a petition to General Kemper asking him to exempt Martin, "a practical tanner who can do many hides," and eventually Martin was assigned to the 53rd Virginia with a furlough long enough to deliver leather under an army contract. Old Wilson Hix, meanwhile, passed around a petition to detail Edward Evans, another tanner, away from the army. Hix's son William, who lived at Appomattox Station now, near McDearmon, obtained the contract in his name while Martin and Evans (facing the trenches if they failed to produce to Hix's satisfaction) immersed themselves in the foul-smelling tanning solutions. Meanwhile, other citizens in the Clover Hill neighborhood accommodated William Howard with a petition requesting his exemption on the strength of his efficiency as a clothier.[54]

Chapman Chilton, the teacher at Union Academy in Spout Spring, may have wondered as 1865 opened whether his exemption would last much longer. The latest conscription law allowed teachers to remain at their desks only so long as twenty scholars endured their instruction, and when Chilton opened the school again on February 27 only eleven marched through the door. Three weeks later three more showed up, and eventually he enticed another eight; he may have found it expedient to offer reduced tuition, or accept the fast-depreciating Southern scrip, to attract the required score.

Soldiers in the ranks sneered at such stay-at-homes and their flagging support for those who did fight. Late in January a South Carolina soldier posted near Pickett's division chastised his fellow citizens in a letter to his sister.

"I understand the people are allmost whipped at home," said this man. "[A]m sorry to hear it. I think So Car ought to be the last state to give up." He suggested that the people should decide, once and for all, whether to "be ruled by Abraham" or "fight it out."

"If they are going to fight it out," he warned, "every man able to stand on his feet ought to go, & take their Negroes with them, and fight with the determination never to succumb. If not they will rue the day they voted for secession."[55]

Plenty of men able to stand lingered at home, despite such determined sentiments from a lad who would follow the flag to the bitter end. Evidently every patriot had been gleaned from Appomattox, for so zealously did the surviving civilians avoid service that the army received only three recruits from that county in the last seven months of the war. Jesse Harvey gave up his exemption as steward of the poorhouse to enlist late in the fall.

Either James Stratton, a Spout Spring farmboy, or Charles Wesley Cardwell, of Concord Depot, was the last volunteer from Appomattox County. Stratton, who had just turned eighteen, joined the Appomattox Rangers in March. Cardwell had recently celebrated his seventeenth birthday when he took the cars to Richmond that same month and enlisted with his neighbors in the 20th Heavy Artillery at Drewry's Bluff.[56]

While so few came forward to fight, those who manned the trenches lost hope and absconded with increasing frequency. Wise's brigade suffered a disproportionate number of desertions, perhaps because most of the men lay within a few days' walk, or a few hours' ride, of their homes. Captain Abbitt's own brother-in-law, Clifton Webb, a former officer, took French leave in February; the captain asked his wife what she had heard of him and urged her to tell him of General Lee's amnesty proclamation, which had just been issued and stood until early March.

Lee pestered the War Department about the epidemic of desertions, which he attributed as much now to inadequate rations as to discipline.

"I have no doubt that there is suffering for want of food," he informed Secretary Seddon. "The ration is too small for men who have to undergo so much exposure and labor as ours." At one point, when a January rain washed out part of the Danville rail line on which so many provisions arrived, Lee appealed to Southside farmers for all the bread, meat, meal, and molasses they could spare. So scarce did food become in the 46th Virginia that one winter afternoon Captain Abbitt saw Robert Wooldridge frying what appeared to be a squirrel. Inquiry proved that it was a rat.

Lee's amnesty proclamation did no visible good, and may have encouraged even more to desert in the expectation that they could return under another amnesty. On February 23 Bushrod Johnson reported that thirty-five men had deserted from his division the night before, and that ten of them had come from Wise's brigade. In the ten days ending February 25 Lee's army lost 1,094 deserters, an astounding 217 of whom came from Johnson's division: relatively few were going home on unauthorized furloughs, either, for 178 of Johnson's deserters trotted directly into enemy lines.[57]

The army could not long sustain more than a hundred desertions a night from its combat units. At the end of January Lee counted just under 70,000 men under his immediate command, including every officer and man present for duty from north of Richmond to the Virginia Reserves on the Danville and Southside Railroads. Ten days later there were 7,000 fewer of them, and by the first of March he was down to about 57,000, of whom only 46,000 could have taken the field.

Captain Abbitt still suffered frequently from the fever that had assailed him in South Carolina, and it came on him again as the winter of 1865 ground toward its conclusion. The surgeon wanted to send him to the hospital, but the lank Abbitt clung to duty, stalking the trenches in the new coat his wife had sent him and turning morose at the accumulated misery of an apparently endless endeavor. Unlike the men who abandoned him, he seemed willing to persevere, but he complained that everyone and everything about him seemed "gloomy, sad & desponding."

"Is it owing to the weakening condition of my own mind," he wondered, "or is it really so?"[58]

THE FLIGHT

Having wrung every white citizen from the South who could be attracted, persuaded, cajoled, shamed, or forced into the army, the Confederate Congress finally authorized the unthinkable: the government that had been established in protection of the right to enslave black people turned, in the final extremity, to those very black people for its salvation. On March 17, 1865, two Richmond slaves who had been scheduled to hang that day for burglarizing a home offered themselves as the first recruits for a black Confederate battalion, thus winning executive clemency. George and Oliver—they had no other names—were taken to an empty building on the corner of Cary and Twenty-first Streets, where they shouldered broom handles to begin learning the fundamentals of close-order drill. Within ten days nearly three dozen other slaves had joined them, earning their own freedom in return for the promise of helping to preserve slavery.

By the final week of March the opposing trenches stretched some forty miles, from above Richmond down to the James, across Bermuda Hundred, over the Appomattox River, below Petersburg, and out to Burgess's Mill, on Hatcher's Run. On paper, the Army of Northern Virginia had enough men that if they stood with their arms outstretched and their fingertips touching they would just about reach from one end of their fortified line to the other. On the opposite side, Ulysses Grant could field two men to Lee's one. The situation would only worsen, for the long blue line kept jumping a couple of miles to the west every few weeks, and eventually it would have to cut the Southside Railroad, which served as Petersburg's last direct connection to the rest of the South. Up north, journalists had only to look at a map to understand this, and the *New York Herald* predicted that

Lee's army would soon evacuate Richmond. Immediately inside the siege lines, though, editors perhaps lacked enough perspective, and a Richmond counterpart laughed at the idea.[1]

Soldiers suffered from no such delusions. Robert E. Lee knew something had to be done, and soon. He took the initiative early on the morning of March 25, sending John B. Gordon into the predawn darkness east of Petersburg with the remnants of Stonewall Jackson's old corps. Gordon burst into Fort Stedman, grabbed 500 prisoners, and ripped a thousand-yard gap in the Union perimeter. As the sky began to lighten, however, they saw ahead of them a second line of works nearly as strong as the first, and it soon became clear that Gordon's corps would be annihilated if he tried to carry those entrenchments now that the Yankees were alerted. By the time Lee authorized Gordon to pull back, Union artillery and infantry up and down the line had trained a crossfire over the line of retreat, and those who attacked Fort Stedman at dawn sought safety in it by breakfast. A division of new Pennsylvania regiments — each one as big as a Confederate brigade — slammed into Gordon's weary infantrymen and drove most of them back toward Petersburg; hundreds of Southerners surrendered inside and around Stedman, further weakening an army that could little afford their loss. Lee's last offensive had not lasted four hours.[2]

The *Richmond Examiner* boasted of the 500 Federals who marched into the city under guard that Saturday evening, but the word on the street told the real story: Lee was thinking about breaking out and leaving both the capital and Petersburg to the enemy, but he was too weak even to do that, let alone defeat his besiegers in the field. Any sane man could tell that it would only be a matter of weeks before the last rail lines fell, and the army would have to run away, starve altogether, or surrender. The limp Confederate dollar reflected the clarity of the calamity as the price of gold skyrocketed: it closed downtown at $151.50 an ounce that Monday, sending government notes into their final inflationary plunge.[3]

As he had been doing since the previous May, Ulysses Grant began the spring campaign by sliding several of his divisions to his left, trying to crumble or slip around Lee's right flank. Now he sent two corps of infantry toward Hatcher's Run, partly to make another attempt on that flank and partly to cover a raid by Sheridan's cavalry on the Southside tracks. To meet that threat, Lee sent a few brigades from George Pickett's division and some from Bushrod Johnson's division, of Richard Anderson's corps.

Henry Wise's brigade lurched into the low, swampy terrain ahead of the westernmost Confederate trenches, running head-on into a little two-regiment brigade commanded by Joshua Chamberlain, a former Bowdoin professor and now a brigadier general. With the first volley, what would come to be known as the Appomattox campaign had begun.

Chamberlain's big regiments were both fairly new—neither had been in uniform much more than six dreary, uneventful months—and they fell back quickly before the fury of Wise's veterans, firing as they went. Union artillery and infantry reinforcements came up, and after an hour or two Wise's regiments were driven back to their starting point. Three Appomattox boys fell dead that day, and the senior captain in the regiment had charged right into enemy hands, leaving George Abbitt to command the 46th for however much longer it might survive.

Rain inundated both camps that night and liquefied the roads, stalling operations for a day. On March 31 Pickett took a couple of Johnson's brigades and moved a few miles west to an intersection called Five Forks, where Sheridan appeared headed, but for Johnson's use he left behind Eppa Hunton's brigade, which included the 18th Virginia and the depleted old company known as the Appomattox Grays. Despite the rain Johnson pushed out again to the south, striking what he supposed to be the Union left flank on the White Oak Road, and this time he led with Hunton's brigade. These Virginians drove the enemy for a mile or more, but then they encountered heavy going (two more Appomattox men suffered their death wounds in the downpour that afternoon), so Johnson shook out Wise's brigade again and moved it up alongside Hunton's. Here the Union advantage of numbers told, for more fresh Federals came up to greet the fought-out Confederates and forced them back to the White Oak Road again.[4]

The next morning the enemy was gone. April broke quietly along Hatcher's Run: too quietly, and at four o'clock in the afternoon firing erupted a few miles down the White Oak Road, at Five Forks. There Pickett's infantry and most of the army's cavalry were surprised from behind; the infantry fled from the field—"every man for himself," as one man recorded in his diary that evening, and Union cavalry gathered up hundreds of prisoners from the throng streaming northward; among those who threw down their arms and marched into captivity was Joseph Abbitt, an autumn conscript and erstwhile storekeeper of Appomattox Court House.

An entire Union infantry corps, supported by another three divisions of cavalry, now had control of the flat, maneuverable landscape to Johnson's right and rear; before dark he put his men on their feet and started them on a night march for the railroad, behind them. They reached the tracks a couple of hours after midnight and lay there through the morning of April 2, all the while listening to artillery booming from the direction of Petersburg. Just before noon Johnson heard that Sheridan's cavalry had reached the railroad a few miles to the west, and that Grant had broken through the lines at Petersburg, to the east. Leading fourteen regiments that happened to include all of Appomattox County's surviving infantrymen, Johnson turned north and west, wheeling about into fighting stance once that evening to support the cavalry that covered his retreat, among which rode the Appomattox Rangers.[5]

Once aware that Lee had been flanked at Five Forks, Grant had begun pounding the Petersburg defenses in preparation for an all-out assault the morning of April 2. That morning had not grown old when Robert E. Lee concluded that this would be his army's last day in Petersburg. He told the secretary of war that he would hold out until night, if he could, and he advised the government to escape via the Richmond & Danville Railroad. Meanwhile, he drew his troops in from around Petersburg and crossed them over the Appomattox, sending them in the direction of Amelia Court House, where he intended the army to rendezvous.

The commanding general's eldest son, Major General George Washington Custis Lee, received orders that night to cross the James River with the two brigades under his command. One of those, Stapleton Crutchfield's brigade, consisted of four battalions of Virginia heavy artillerymen, including the 19th and 20th, in which so many Appomattox men marched. They left their big guns behind forever, and these men who had never endured a forced march or fired a shot in anger during three years of war shouldered muskets and took up the road to Amelia Court House, more than two days away on the roads they had to travel. As they shuffled westward on feet soon to blossom with blisters they encountered Lieutenant General Richard Ewell, the one-legged commander of Richmond's defenses, who had brought with him from the capital Joseph Kershaw's little infantry division, a small brigade of cavalry, and a few miscellaneous detachments.[6]

A month previously, inspectors had counted nearly 57,000 men with the Army of Northern Virginia, of whom about 46,000 were ready for field service: even at that strength, there had been more men absent than present. Since that time a few reinforcements had come in, Tom Rosser's cavalry division among them, but Lee had lost thousands of men at Fort Stedman and Five Forks. At least a couple of thousand had deserted since the last returns had been tabulated. Still, it was fully as large an army that converged on Amelia Court House as Lee had led into Maryland in 1862, and he had saved himself from almost certain destruction there.[7]

Few of those who had followed Lee into Maryland in that long-ago September were with him now. They had been buried there, or at Gettysburg, or somewhere along the bloody trail from the Wilderness to Petersburg; they huddled in military prisons on Lake Michigan, or Lake Erie, or at Point Lookout; they hobbled about their homes on crutches; they skulked about their farms like fugitives, watching for the sheriff's posse or the provost marshal. In their places marched teenagers who had grown quickly to manhood in a few months of brutal service, along with grey-haired patriarchs, pampered garrison soldiers like Crutchfield's artillerymen, a few hundred sailors armed as infantrymen, and battalions of Virginia Reserves. There still remained the wiry, wily veteran with the long stride and resolute mouth who had thus far managed to avoid a bullet—or who had survived one—but now he formed the backbone of this army rather than the muscle of it.

Lee had expected not only to rendezvous and reorganize at Amelia Court House, but to distribute supplies there. The town sat alongside the Richmond & Danville line, and Lee anticipated finding a small mountain of ration boxes at the depot. His son, Custis, had also sent 20,000 rations in wagons ahead of his own makeshift division, after doling out a couple of days' food. Both generals Lee would be disappointed. Confederate authorities who knew the army would rendezvous at Amelia failed to direct any food there, which drove the senior Lee to the last major error of his three-year tenure with this army. Instead of allowing his leading divisions some sleep on the afternoon of April 4 and then pushing them on without dinner, he decided to linger through the day, sending foraging parties into the countryside to commandeer food while he awaited the laggard elements of his army. Meanwhile, he dispatched a rider southward with an appeal for the commissary department to deliver 200,000 rations at Burkeville Junction. Perhaps he hoped to see the wagon train Custis had sent in advance, as well, with enough rations to give at least half the army one good meal. The next morning a detachment of Yankee cavalry put an end to that hope, though, with a dash on the division wagon train at Paineville— ominously, northwest of Amelia.[8]

Ahead of the army trundled a host of refugees, many of them Pickett's lost and demoralized riflemen. Benjamin Sims, a Louisa County conscript from the 17th Virginia, had followed the stampede from Five Forks straight to the banks of the boiling Appomattox, which had washed out some of its bridges and surged too swollen with recent rains for any hope of fording. He and a Lynchburg friend saw only a few of their comrades and concluded to go home. They followed the river upstream for two days, traversing the path of Lee's retreat ahead of their army until they encountered a bridge over the Appomattox. On the night of April 3 they slept in a barn near Powhatan Court House, turning west the next morning on the stage road to Lynchburg. Averaging twenty miles a day, they tramped the old highway past the courthouses of Cumberland and Buckingham Counties, stopping now and then to beg food from residents; an old woman near the Buckingham line gave them all the bread they could carry with them. In the afternoon of April 6 the pair passed Rose Bower (home of the grieving Widow Patteson), the plantations of Joseph Abbitt and Thomas Flood, and Pleasant Retreat, sitting off to their right with its six massive rooms dark and empty. As evening drew about them they descended the slope past the little Conner and Sweeney houses, stepped across the now-docile headwaters of the north branch, and climbed the last hill into Appomattox Court House. It happened to be court day, for whatever business the justices found worthy of their attentions in such turbulent times, and the town hosted numerous transients in and out of uniform who had already brought news of the military disaster. The governor—spindly, sixty-eight-year-old "Extra Billy" Smith himself—had stood on the porch of the Clover Hill Tavern that very afternoon to calm the crowd and offer encouragement to carry on the fight. If Sims and his friend caught even secondhand driblets of the speech, it had none of the intended effect; they slept in the village that night, and continued on to Lynchburg in the morning.[9]

A captain of Pickett's division, recently paroled from a Northern prison, learned the details of his old command's disaster while stopping in Lynchburg. He and a companion determined to start overland toward Danville in hopes of intersecting with the army, but the roads out of town crawled with soldiers in disorganized flight from the Yankees. They met at least one officer among the crowd, who prattled wildly about the fury of Sheridan's cavalry.

These stragglers, if that somewhat generous term could be applied to those in flight ahead of their fellows, may have carried an exaggerated version of the disaster, for the last they had seen of their army had been the destruction of one of its most famous divisions. The preponderance of Lee's army lay dutifully in camp about Amelia Court House all day Wednesday, April 5, still dangerous despite blisters and empty haversacks. But for the Napoleonic dictum that armies travel on their stomachs, Lee might have understood how crucial it was to keep his troops moving, for their safety lay in securing Burkeville Junction, less than twenty miles to the southwest. There the Southside Railroad crossed the Richmond & Danville: the

Confederate cabinet had gone to Danville, to be followed eventually by Governor Smith and the state government, and there Lee hoped to make another stand, perhaps on the banks of the Staunton River where a ragtag little brigade of reserves and convalescents had thrashed a Yankee cavalry division the year before. Or if he chose not to fight there he could attempt to join Joseph Johnston's forces in North Carolina, where they might enjoy enough combined strength for a stand-up fight in the field.

The sojourn at Amelia cost Lee possession of the junction, however, and effectively sealed the doom of his army. Union cavalry trotted between Lee and Burkeville Junction at Jetersville late on the afternoon of April 4, and in the darkness came the first of the Fifth Corps infantry, under the same General Chamberlain who had faced Wise's brigade on March 29 and 31. By the morning of April 5 there were enough blue uniforms at Jetersville to hold Lee in check until the rest of the Union army could come up to finish him; it was from this force that the cavalry burst ahead to attack Lee's wagon train and burn his son's rations. This presence forced the Confederate army onto winding, confusing back roads, where the hope of resupply hovered somewhere between very little and none at all.[10]

Kershaw's infantry division and Custis Lee's collection of reserves and converted artillerymen had lost the better part of a day looking for a passable bridge over the Appomattox. These troops, the last of Richmond's defenders, did not catch up with the main body until the morning of April 5. General Lee waited until that afternoon to press on, sending James Longstreet's oversized command off first. Richard Anderson followed, commanding the remnants of Pickett's division now as well as Bushrod Johnson's remaining brigades. After a few hours of sleep Richard Ewell's two divisions of garrison troops started next, stepping off in company with the equally footsore naval battalion. For his rear guard Lee assigned John Gordon's corps of ten veteran brigades.

A cavalry scrap before Jetersville told Lee what he already ought to have guessed — that the enemy had full control of the Richmond & Danville Railroad, thus denying him the Southside as well. At this point he could afford neither the time nor the casualties that an assault would consume, so he directed the head of his column northward on a side road, veering west again on a country track toward Amelia Springs. The general made his bed for the evening in a building at the sulphur springs resort there while his army passed by throughout the night. The darkness and confusion slowed their advance, but now Lee had to gain the time he had lost looking for provisions. If by sheer energy and determination a couple of dependable divisions could reach Farmville ahead of the pursuit, he might yet pick up the Southside Railroad and continue his race to the west, or south, to Johnston's army.[11]

Union cavalry pestered the column throughout the night, leapfrogging along side roads to launch successive ambushes. Men stumbled sleepily through the darkness, banging into each other, tripping over discarded equipment and slipping in the mud after a morning rainstorm soaked the roads and their clothing. Only the first two corps, Longstreet's and Anderson's, had passed the springs when Lee arose the next morning; the accordion effect of the column worsened toward the rear, and those who marched farthest back spent most of the night waiting for the men ahead of them to move. They wasted their night's sleep standing in the ranks, and Ewell straggled up at eight o'clock, only seven miles from his evening stopping place; Gordon's infantry slogged along impatiently behind him.[12]

The Army of Northern Virginia spanned about fifteen miles that dreary morning, all the way from Longstreet's foremost elements, which were approaching Rice's Depot on the railroad, to Gordon's rear guard, still on the other side of Amelia Springs. As the weary wanderers crept forward, long blue columns paralleled their march on muddy roads to the north and south, and another followed on the same road, not far behind Gordon's last soldier. Only through the courtesy of a Union division commander, who overslept that morning and failed to move in time, did the entire Confederate column escape on the road to Deatonville and Sailor's Creek. As it was, Gordon had not yet disappeared from view of the springs when that tardy division of the Union Second Corps appeared on the main road—under a new general, now. The leading Union brigade spread out to open fire upon Gordon's train, and he had to deploy a few regiments in reply. From that point onward Gordon's foremost divisions crept forward as quickly as those ahead of them would allow while the last one, under Bryan Grimes, backpedaled the entire distance, fending off the persistent Federals. Lee might have determined the progress of his army by the sound of the fighting at its tail. Even if they had not been trailing so closely on his heels, the Yankees might have found the path of Lee's retreat by the trails of discarded tents, baggage, and camp equipment on either side of the road, or by the smoldering remains of abandoned wagons.[13]

Between the extremities of Lee's army that April morning lay a broad, marshy valley cut by two branches of a stream that mapmakers alternately labeled Sailor's, or Sayler's, Creek. Higher ground looked down upon the creek as though from the brim of a bowl. Longstreet's corps had passed through there that morning, diving down into the valley past James Hillsman's little house and crossing the longer branch of the stream on a country bridge before climbing back up to the tableland that typified the region. By then General Lee had ridden ahead from the springs and caught up with the head of the army, and when Longstreet reached Rice's Depot Lee directed him to build breastworks facing back to Burkeville Junction. At that point the commanding general had no cause to suppose that they faced much danger from any other direction, save for the annoyance of cavalry forays.[14]

Had he lagged about four miles back, the general would have seen where the greatest danger lay that day. As William Mahone's division—the last of Longstreet's column—descended into the creek valley, it might as well have vanished so far as the head of General Anderson's column was concerned. Those exhausted foot soldiers, who had been on the march for nearly twenty-four hours (and most of them without food all that time), had allowed a gap to develop between their corps and Longstreet's; the country was thickly wooded in spots, the lurching baggage and supply wagons that shouldered along beside the troops impeded the line of sight as well as the line of march, and the road curved here and there, so their dangerous distance from each other grew undetected.

About an hour before noon, this gap began to cause trouble. Custis Lee, riding at the head of Ewell's motley corps, reined his horse to the bank of an insignificant little stream known to locals as Sandy Creek, and there he heard a commotion a couple of miles ahead, toward the front of Anderson's two-division corps. Sheridan's leapfrogging cavalry had struck again, hitting the wagon train in the middle of Anderson's corps from the southeastern road in a four-way intersection known as Holt's Corner. Parts of Pickett's and Johnson's divisions fanned out on either side of the crossroad while the trains continued to rumble along behind them. At first this infantry brushed the cavalry off, but this time the Yankee horsemen did not ride far. Solicitous of the wagon train, General Ewell directed it onto another road that turned northwest from Holt's Corner, where the cavalry had last struck. That entailed quite a bit of backing up and wheeling around for some teamsters who had already passed the turn, and for a time the entire corps stopped cold, wagons and all. A portion of the train continued on behind Anderson, on the direct road to Rice's Depot. Meanwhile, more mounted Federals opened fire on the rest of the wagon train behind Ewell, and he threw out a strong line of skirmishers from Custis Lee's heavy artillery brigade to protect the procession.[15]

These Yankees, a mere brigade of Michigan cavalry, had no intention of attacking the train at that moment. They played a couple of pieces of artillery upon the wagons, essentially using them for target practice, but Ewell's defensive movement offered precisely what they wanted: they were hoping to keep him from moving forward to join Anderson while other troopers harried that column.

George Crook, whose cavalry division had struck that first blow at Holt's Corner, guided his brigades through the woods to the south and west, feeling for a soft spot. His horses splashed across the upper reaches of Sailor's Creek, swung back toward the Rice's Depot Road, and galloped into the gap ahead of Anderson's portion of the train, slashing at the undefended wagons. Pickett withdrew his four brigades from their line of battle at Holt's Corner and hurried them to meet this latest surprise. With their repeating, breech-loading carbines Crook's Federals dismounted to confront him, but at first Pickett's veterans hurled the Yankees back.[16]

As Henry Wise told the story about five years later, when those he criticized were still alive to dispute his claims, Johnson ordered him to shear off two regiments to help a South Carolina brigade hold Holt's Corner. Thus, when Wise received an appeal to go to Pickett's aid he had only two more regiments with which to respond: the 34th Virginia and the 46th, now under Captain George Abbitt. Wise found the enemy just across Sailor's Creek; he moved ahead of Pickett's division, as did Johnson's remaining brigades (whom Wise forgot to credit for their assistance), and this reinforced battle line pushed Crook's 3,000 troopers up out of the valley and onto the plain. Then came George Custer with three more brigades in blue jackets. Bursting with excitement at the chase, these 3,000-or-so Federals brought the odds on this part of the field squarely to the Union advantage, both in numbers of men and ferocity of firepower. They began tattering Wise's left flank with their repeating carbines, and the two Confederate divisions stretched themselves into a short, solid line of battle, standing perpendicular to the road.[17]

The greater part of the wagon train, meanwhile, lumbered in a wide arc around this fight, veering within a couple of miles of the Appomattox River. When the last of the wagons rolled abreast of his two divisions, General Ewell brought them back into ranks and moved them ahead on the road to Rice's Depot, to help Anderson with the force that blocked his way. The head of Gordon's corps followed as far as Holt's Corner, where it turned right with the last of the wagons. Whether Gordon could not see the last of Ewell's corps on the main road, or whether he stuck with the wagons in accordance with Robert E. Lee's instructions, he left the rear of Ewell's corps uncovered. Ewell had evidently not consulted with him about their respective routes, nor had he cautioned his trailing division commander, Joseph Kershaw, to watch his own back. Behind Gordon marched the Union Second Corps, trotting at a double-quick now that the prey lay within sight; even closer behind, on the other road leading to Holt's Corner, marched the Sixth Corps.[18]

The last Confederate had not long passed Holt's Corner when the Michigan cavalry brigade that had been harassing the wagon train started slashing at Kershaw, forcing him to hurry his men down the road past the Hillsman house. Fitzhugh Lee, the commander of all the remaining Confederate horse, had been caught behind his troops by the cavalry blocking Anderson's front. He lingered for some time, waiting for Anderson — or Anderson and Ewell together — to burst through and continue on to Rice's Depot; it seemed to him that they had plenty of infantry (and artillerymen acting as infantry) to throw the swarms of Union troopers out of the way, if only they would get on with it.

Ewell and Anderson discussed that very plan, but with their diminished numbers, shortage of artillery, and the condition of their men Ewell may have doubted the chances of success. He favored breaking off the fight and cutting cross-country to the west, where they might find another road. That appealed to Fitz Lee, too, for it would have put the infantry in the same thickly wooded terrain as the main wagon train, where the geography would have stymied Union cavalry. Anderson eventually carried his argument for putting up a fight, convincing Ewell of the odds because he had seen the ground in front, whereas Ewell had not. Ewell told him to prepare his two divisions for an assault while he brought Custis Lee and Kershaw up to add more power to the punch.[19]

Above the Hillsman house, Holt's Corner lay undefended now. Three divisions of the Sixth Corps poured into the intersection from the southeast, where Crook's cavalry had first appeared, while the Second Corps spilled into the crossroads from the Deatonville Road. Horatio Wright's Sixth Corps turned left, down the main road to Rice's Depot, in the wake of Kershaw's division; Andrew Humphreys swung the Second Corps to the right, going after Gordon and the longest length of the wagon train.

Ewell's troops had all crossed Sailor's Creek now and stood on the hill beyond. As Union infantry formed ranks on the opposite slope, near the Hillsman house, Custis Lee and Kershaw swung their troops around into line of battle without waiting for orders. Sixth Corps artillery went into battery near the Hillsman house, throwing shells into the grey ranks before Lee, at least, had finished his dispositions. He waved his men to the ground; some of them found swales that offered substantial protection, but others suffered the full force of the barrage. Ewell's artillery had all followed the wagons, so the brigades on the banks of Sailor's Creek could mount no reply.

Kershaw's division turned about and took the eastern side of the road, while Lee formed on the left. Lee put Colonel Crutchfield's untried artillery brigade on his own right, against the road, with the Virginia Reserves, the local defense troops, and his only regular infantry on his left; he pulled the 19th and 20th battalions out of Crutchfield's artillery brigade and braced the extreme left of his line with them. Behind this line formed the naval battalion. For the moment they simply lay there, waiting for the Union infantry to make a move.[20]

Colonel Crutchfield, like Dick Ewell, had once served under Stonewall Jackson. Also like Ewell, he had already given a leg for the Confederacy, but both of them had strapped on wooden replacements and climbed back into the saddle to continue the fight.

Here, back to back within a mile of each other, stood all the remaining foot soldiers of Appomattox County, plus a few dismounted cavalrymen who had once ridden with Fitz Lee. All the county's heavy artillerymen huddled against the shelling with Crutchfield's brigade, rifles in their hands, while the infantry braced Anderson's front: with Pickett, the Appomattox Grays still mustered a few men in the 18th Virginia, of Eppa Hunton's brigade, and a number of Appomattox men had transferred to the 38th Virginia, of George Steuart's brigade; the largest contingent of Appomattox infantrymen remained in the 46th Virginia, under General Wise.

When Ewell reached his troops again he could see that he would have more than enough work on his own front, and he immediately rode back to Anderson with the news. Anderson offered to try to break through the cavalry alone if Ewell could hold off the infantry in the rear, and Ewell sat back to watch him try. Pickett's men loosed a few good volleys at Custer's division, causing that audacious cavalryman some concern, but two brigades of another division arrived just in time to stall the Confederate assault. A courier rode back to tell Anderson that the attack had failed, and he found the general alongside Ewell, who immediately turned back to his side of the battle while Anderson galloped to his own front.

Anderson could do little with what he found. Pickett's division—the veterans of the Peninsula, Manassas, Antietam, and Gettysburg—had disintegrated, leaving more than a dozen pieces of Anderson's artillery on the field. Johnson's division likewise retreated, although at least Wise's brigade maintained a semblance of order. Union cavalry burst over the rudimentary breastworks the two divisions had scratched together, chasing the fugitives.

Ewell hoped for time enough to get his men back up and point them into the woods for the cross-country escape he had first envisioned, but he never reached his line of battle overlooking the creek. The woods suddenly grew thick with Yankee cavalry, and as Ewell rode back toward Sailor's Creek a detachment appeared on his left, inside what should have been his own lines. He glanced to his right, where the main Union line still lay firing in his direction, and the road ahead of him buzzed with their bullets as well as the perpendicular trajectory of shells coming from the Sixth Corps artillery. Ewell knew a hopeless situation when he saw one, and he surrendered to the first Federal officer who rode near.[21]

Ewell never witnessed the destruction of his last command. Kershaw and Custis Lee fought that fight while he consulted with General Anderson, and it yielded the day's greatest glory as well as the darkest tragedy.

The Union artillery blasted away for half an hour, unmolested, at the deadly range of half a mile. Two Federal infantry divisions lay before those guns, ready to advance, and a third marched to their support. Finally the infantry strode forward the few hundred yards to the soggy bottom-land along Sailor's Creek, jumped into water about waist-deep, and waded across. Kershaw and Lee both opened up, but the blue ranks rolled steadily onward. Stapleton Crutchfield formed his artillery brigade under fire — the first time in four years of war, for the vast majority of his men — and raised his sword for a counterattack. These untested garrison troops ought to have broken at the first good volley, and they had done well to stand the shelling as long as they had, but now they surprised everyone on both sides of the battlefront by sweeping down the hill and driving the tempered veterans of the Army of the Potomac back up the slope toward the Hillsman house.

"I was never more astonished," wrote the commander of the Sixth Corps three weeks later. "These troops were surrounded—the First and Third Divisions of this corps were on either flank, my artillery and a fresh division in their front, and some three divisions of Major General Sheridan's cavalry in their rear."[22]

Colonel Crutchfield was killed, along with dozens of his men. A five-company Georgia battalion alone lost thirty men killed or mortally wounded, while a Virginia battalion alongside it lost about a hundred killed and wounded. The Yankees came back, though, over the creek again and up the slope, wrapping around Lee's left and reaching for Kershaw's right. The Michigan cavalrymen who had delayed Ewell's march now pitched in alongside their infantry, hitting Kershaw's line directly on the right flank and collapsing it. Kershaw advised Custis Lee that his division was falling back, exposing Lee's own flank to the hailstorm of bullets that now came his way. The naval battalion stepped into the breach and put up a short, vicious fight, but Union artillery took a deadly toll and the enemy infantry had all but encircled Lee's division. With that the younger General Lee surrendered, and that part of the battlefield fell quiet except for the wailing of the wounded and the orders barked to prisoners.[23]

Just over a hundred Appomattox men had taken part in the battle, knowing that they stood within a two-day march of their firesides. On different parts of the field, ninety-two of them threw down their rifles and surrendered. Of the twenty-seven men who followed Pickett with the Appomattox Grays, the Federal victors gathered in all but one: all three of the company's remaining officers gave up their swords, and First Sergeant Isham Gilliam surrendered with a terrible wound in one arm that would cost him his life barely a week later. Five of the Grays taken that day had been captured at Gettysburg and had only recently come back to the ranks. Elizabeth Harvey's brother, Joel Cawthorn, went between the bayonets again, and five neighbors from the Harvey clan joined him.

No Appomattox men escaped from the artillery brigade unless they scurried into the woods early in the fight, and if any of them did they never returned to their posts. Three remained with the 19th Heavy Artillery Battalion and forty-nine with the 20th—every one of whom fell into enemy hands. Major Robertson became a prisoner with his men, five of whom were wounded in their first and only real battle; Captain Samuel Overton, of Bent Creek, had taken a bullet in the leg. Charles Wesley Cardwell, the seventeen-year-old Confederate who had not yet been a soldier for a month, fell in with his comrades, already footsore and hungry, for the long trek back to Burkeville Junction and Point Lookout prison. Those bound for Point Lookout would all survive, but some of those taken at Sailor's Creek ended up at a new prison in Newport News, where—with the war essentially over—black Union guards killed more prisoners per capita than in any other Federal compound; three of the Appomattox County prisoners who had come so close to home would die from intestinal complaints at Newport News, or on the way home from there.

The wreckage of Anderson's corps had fled north and west again, Pickett's men taking to their heels for the second time in a week. The surrender of Ewell's corps lured Sheridan's cavalry in the other direction, allowing a substantial number of Johnson's troops—and a lesser number of Pickett's—to escape. Henry Wise's brigade carried away most of the surviving Appomattox soldiers. Charles Faulkner, son of the minister to France, brother-in-law of Speaker Bocock, and, at seventeen, an aide-de-camp to General Wise, bolted into the brush with a handful of other staff officers. First Lieutenant Thomas Tibbs managed to stay with his regiment. Captain Abbitt brought off 8 members of his company, marshaling fewer than 130 officers and men in his entire regiment.

Even the Appomattox Rangers lost a few men at Sailor's Creek. A couple of hundred dismounted men from the 2nd Virginia Cavalry followed the train as a special battalion under the command of a major: these stragglers tried to help, and three Appomattox men among them joined the prisoners when it was all over. James Stratton, the last recruit to ever join the Rangers, made it off the field despite a minor wound.[24]

All this time General Gordon had been hurrying the remnants of the wagon train around his alternate route and trying to keep the Union Second Corps away from them. Sailor's Creek ran a trifle deeper here, and the swamp that surrounded it stretched a little wider. The two branches of the creek converged just downstream from Gordon's road, which crossed both branches on two consecutive bridges. Each wagon sank a little lower into the soggy roadbed before and between the twin bridges, and the weakened spans soon threatened to collapse under the weight of artillery and ordnance. Drivers began turning off the road to ford the creek, which ran about three feet deep (and which one exhausted signalman mistook for the Appomattox itself). Teamsters and stragglers alike panicked when word sprang up the line from the rear that pursuing Federals had come into sight. By the time the news reached the double bridges, it was as though the enemy had broken through and were galloping around the last bend with sabers flashing.

"Yankees!" came the cry, and dozens of teamsters jumped from their seats to cut their teams from the traces. Those disabled wagons simply added to the confusion, jamming the center of Gordon's escape route.

There was no need to panic on this side of the battlefield, at least yet. When the wagons bogged down, Gordon slowed the pace of his troops, finally stringing Bryan Grimes's division out in line of battle to fend off the harbingers of the Union force behind him. General Humphreys reciprocated with a division of his own, and the Second Corps of the Army of the Potomac tried to crack the Second Corps of the Army of Northern Virginia. Soldiers in blue and grey suffered about equally from fatigue and hunger, for the Federal army had outmarched its own supply wagons, and the opposing battle lines flailed away at each other with little effect; the Confederates fell back stubbornly, and the Yankees crept forward in step with them. As the day grew late Humphreys broke off a division to circle around Gordon and cut in front of him, but Confederates near the creek saw the flanking force and began lobbing shells into it. At that Gordon called for help, and when none came he supposed that he had better save his infantry; he directed all but a rear guard to divide around the road-block and slog across the stream, leaving behind some 300 wagons. Just at dark the Yankees detected his withdrawal and dashed at Grimes's division, taking a few guns and several hundred prisoners, but the main body of Gordon's corps escaped.[25]

When the war was young, the affair at Sailor's Creek would have been considered a bloodbath of enormous proportions; a couple of thousand men had been killed and wounded, and some 7,000 Confederates now lay in Union hands, including a lieutenant general, two major generals, and five brigadiers. Bushrod Johnson's division, the biggest with the army just a month before, came out of the battle with about a third of the men who had begun the march from Richmond. George Pickett's entire division now numbered fewer than a thousand souls. Eight hundred of General Kershaw's men eluded the Yankee cavalry that had scattered them, and only 300 officers and men from Custis Lee's impromptu division had managed to break away and find the main column.

Concerned about the lagging half of his army, Robert E. Lee rode back from Rice's Station toward the scene of his son's stand, taking William Mahone's division with him. They reached a bluff overlooking the valley, and there Lee saw a few organized troops pushing the refuse of Anderson's and Ewell's commands ahead of them like flotsam before a flood. He asked Mahone to form his division in a battle line on either side of the road. In the gloaming, as they waited for an attack that never came, Mahone's tired veterans watched a pitiful parade of teamsters who had abandoned their wagons, officers who had lost their men, and infantrymen who had thrown away their rifles. At about ten o'clock, after the last of the fugitive mob had passed between the wings of his division and gained a fair distance, Mahone called his men into line behind a screen of cavalry and sent them on, still sleepless, into the darkness.[26]

The towering railroad bridge that had spelled the end of Samuel McDearmon's little Piedmont empire now assumed enormous strategic importance. The destruction of that bridge while Lee's army lay east of it would not only deprive that harried force of any supplies from Lynchburg, but would close off the nearest crossing of the unfordable Appomattox River—if whoever brought down the railroad span also destroyed a nearby wagon bridge. Toward that end, Major General Edward Ord had dispatched a couple of regiments of infantry and his own headquarters escort of eighty Massachusetts horsemen to burn the bridge. Ord, commander of the Army of the James from Bermuda Hundred, ordered his raiders out from Burkeville Junction before he learned that Lee was turning his army that way, and once Sheridan told him that the Confederates were headed for Farmville he sent a courier ahead to warn his bridge burners.[27]

Fitz Lee's troopers, ranging ahead of the army under Tom Rosser, had already joined James Longstreet at Rice's Depot when they caught wind of the little Union column near High Bridge. With his own division and Fitz Lee's, Rosser confronted the intruders just below the bridge. The Confederates heavily outnumbered their opponents, who could field barely 800 horse and foot together, but the fourscore Massachusetts cavalrymen put up a vicious fight, losing eight of their eleven officers before the survivors all surrendered. The brigadier whom Ord had sent to lead the expedition fell dead in a saber duel with General James Dearing, who was mortally wounded himself a few moments later, but once the Massachusetts men surrendered so did the two regiments of infantry. The bridge remained safe, waiting for the thousands of men who, at that moment, were trying to extricate themselves from the morass along Sailor's Creek. At the southern end of the bridge lay the broad earthworks the 3rd Virginia Reserves and Southside slaves had built to defend the span the year before. Eight mismatched cannon peered through its various embrasures, but without gunners to man them.[28]

Those who escaped from the cataclysm at Sailor's Creek stumbled through the darkness by fits and starts on the road to Farmville, inching forward only to stop and wait, standing belt-buckle-to-bedroll for minutes at a time until the troops ahead moved on. So many wagons had Lee lost now that he moved what was left of his trains ahead of his army, the exhausted and underfed teams miring in the mud and slowing everything to a crawl. For most of the men in grey this was the second night march in a row—with a battle between those sleepless nights, for many of them; the only Confederates who slept soundly that night were already prisoners.

Just as the destruction of High Bridge before his arrival would have trapped Lee south of the Appomattox, its demolition after his passage would prevent immediate pursuit north of the river and buy him a little more time. Hoping for that respite, he pushed his army hard that night. The first of his main column—the fleetest of Gordon's refugees—reached the approaches to High Bridge after ten o'clock and lay down for a short nap. The infantry used the railroad bridge, walking the planked ties outside the rails, while engineers shored up a smaller bridge that spanned the river on the wagon road so the artillery and wagons could cross in the darkness. Some units marched right over while others fell out for a couple of hours' sleep. Mahone's division trailed the organized divisions of the army, coming within sight of the bridge around midnight and again dividing onto either side of the road as a rear guard. Stragglers, principally from Johnson's division, limped along between them into the wee hours of the morning.[29]

General Johnson spoke to Lee, who told him to reassemble his division on the heights north of High Bridge; General Wise later claimed that Lee appointed him to that duty, although Lee never corrected Johnson's claim, made only four days later. Whoever drew the assignment, it proved impossible in the darkness, with most of Johnson's shaken troops still south of the bridge.[30]

For all the haste, loss, and destruction that had characterized the retreat, the army had maintained a measure of its old esprit until the evening of April 6, but with the close of that day the most loyal Confederates could not deny the evidence of despair that lay in the wake of their fellows. For several days disabled wagons, dead horses and mules, and scattered equipment had signaled demoralization in the eyes of their enemies, but Southern stalwarts had viewed that as trimming down for the next stand. It seemed different, now, with a quarter of the army killed or captured, hundreds of men tramping along without rifles, and the remaining divisions consolidated into two corps. General Lee noted during the night's retreat that significant numbers of infantrymen threw away their rifles to hasten their flight. On that dismal Thursday a wounded North Carolina captain of nearly four years' service, who had ridden ambulances and walked all the way from Five Forks, took ominous note of the official papers and books that littered the roadside; if clerks and staff officers were throwing away headquarters paperwork, that savored more of panic than efficiency. The next morning, after bidding adieu to the wife and sister-in-law of a Signal Corps major who had traveled with the wagon train for a few hours, the captain learned that most of his diminished brigade had been scattered or captured in the rout of Johnson's division. One officer observed early on April 7 that the army seemed "spirit broken." Others who kept diaries recorded with undisguised disappointment, discouragement, or anger that their own baggage had been lost in the wagons along Sailor's Creek.[31]

That wounded captain belonged to Matthew Ransom's brigade of five Tarheel regiments. On Friday morning Ransom's brigade arrived on a hilltop overlooking the Appomattox just north of Farmville, where all five regiments could muster no more than eighty men. With them stood five

Alabama regiments, each of them about fifty strong. These two brigades, rallying with Henry Wise's and one other, composed Bushrod Johnson's entire division. Standing in ranks alongside the road with their flags displayed, they attracted scores of lost and footsore riflemen from the promiscuous procession.[32]

The last of the column crossed High Bridge just before dawn, with Mahone's division trotting after them. A handful of pickets remained with the mongrel battery, along with a company of engineers who set fire to the railroad bridge and tried to burn the wagon bridge below, but before they could complete the second part of their instructions these saboteurs were driven off, at sunrise, by heralds of the Union Second Corps; a regiment of Maine men dashed ahead and beat out the flames on the wagon bridge. Only a few of the nearly two dozen spans of High Bridge burned before Yankee pioneers raced out and chopped out a section, cutting the blaze short.[33]

Long-awaited rations lay at the depot in Farmville, and Longstreet's men reached them first, early in the morning. The railroad dipped back south of the Appomattox again to reach the town, but Lee felt relatively safe there after ordering High Bridge and the wagon bridge burned. As Longstreet's leading brigades filled their haversacks, however, Union infantry spilled across the salvaged wagon bridge and strode after the tail of Mahone's division. Lacking a wagon train to impede them, these Federals soon caught up with their prey: Mahone's lagging picket line snapped a few rifles at them and came bolting in to report heavy blue columns headed their way. A squadron of cavalry trotted rearward for a look, coming back at a gallop to confirm that the enemy had moved north of the Appomattox in force, and was coming down upon them quickly.

Back at Farmville, where General Lee had spent a few hours resting, that news hit hard. Sheridan had already sent two divisions of cavalry to Prince Edward Court House, whence he would order them to Prospect Station, again cutting off the direct wagon and railroad route to Lynchburg: by now Lee probably knew that he had lost that portion of the race, but the appearance of infantry north of the river threatened to seal off his only other escape route. Immediately he ordered the wagons filled with those rations that had been unloaded and sent the rest steaming back toward Lynchburg, before those roving Yankee horsemen intercepted them. He turned Longstreet's divisions around toward the river again, and as he and Longstreet passed the provost guard he cautioned them to move their prisoners northward quickly: the two little battalions of guards were herding at least five times their number in prisoners, some of whom had come all the way from Petersburg.[34]

The provost guard was about to receive even more unwilling guests. Francis Barlow's division of the Union Second Corps, which had saved the wagon bridge, led the pursuit north of the river, followed at intervals by two more divisions of that corps. Barlow caught up with the Confederate rear guard again and brought it to bay, but this time things did not turn out so well. The brigadier he sent out to feel the enemy's skirmishers took a bullet through his dashing handlebar moustache (the last Yankee general killed in this war), and in the ensuing confusion a good chunk of his skirmish line found itself obliged to surrender.

Edward Porter Alexander, who as a captain had used Wilmer McLean's furniture as a telescope rest at Manassas, now wore a general's wreathed stars as Longstreet's chief of artillery. To him fell the responsibility for burning the railroad and wagon bridges nearest Farmville, where Sheridan and Ord's corps would normally have crossed; the engineer regiments were not handy, and even if they had been Lee was not pleased with their failure at the other wagon bridge. Alexander proved a much more efficient incendiary, withholding the match until the enemy came in sight, and the last Confederates scampered across while the flames licked one end of the span.[35]

Behind them the Confederates left ten dozen or more charred wagons, for which there were no longer enough horses and mules. With consolidated teams and baggage culled yet again, the trains had gone on ahead of the infantry. Just over half the 1,400 baggage wagons and ambulances that had started from Petersburg still lumbered along roads heading north and west. The rest stood abandoned along the roadside—at Farmville, at Sailor's Creek, and all the way back to Amelia County.[36]

Henceforth Longstreet's corps took the rear of the column. At Cumberland Church, three miles north of Farmville, he put his corps in position on rising ground, blocking his army's escape route with Mahone's division on one side and Charles Field's on the other. In no time at all the infantry had raised a substantial breastwork while their artillery found advantageous positions. Gordon, meanwhile, hurried the trains ahead of him as well as he could.

Andrew Humphreys pushed his Second Corps head-on into Longstreet and threw out skirmishers, but then dawdled through the drizzly afternoon while Southern guns shelled him from half a mile or more. Less than thirty months before, this same General Humphreys had led a division up another long, open slope against this same James Longstreet, whose corps had lain entrenched behind the infamous stone wall of Fredericksburg, and Humphreys had seen his troops torn to shreds in minutes with nothing to show for it but their wounds and widows; he was not about to storm this fortified hill now. He felt around for a vulnerable flank, but at both ends Longstreet outflanked him, so he waited for reinforcements and sent back for a diversionary action against whatever Confederates remained near Farmville.

Humphreys suggested that the Sixth Corps might be able to create that distraction, or perhaps Sheridan and Ord. He supposed the bridges were still intact, and that part of the Confederate column lagged near Farmville, but neither was true. By sheer coincidence, though, George Crook had waded his cavalry over the river (which ran too deep for infantry here); one of his mounted brigades encountered Gordon's corps and the wagon train on a side road off the Buckingham Plank Road. That brigade lit into Gordon's column, where it found more trouble than it had bargained for. Tom Rosser swooped down with his all-Virginia cavalry division and one of Thomas Munford's brigades of four more Virginia regiments—including the 2nd Virginia, with the Appomattox Rangers—and in short order the Pennsylvanians who had charged the train were galloping back to their own lines, minus their embarrassed general, two of his staff, and a fair number of their fellows.[37]

When he heard the commotion of cavalry a mile west and south, Humphreys supposed the Sixth Corps had struck the requested blow. Taking that cue, he flung a division out on his right, hoping to lap beyond the Confederate left. Three veteran Union regiments swept out from the extreme right, rolling up within brickbat range of the fresh breastwork, but Mahone swung an Alabama brigade against their own flank and sent them flying, capturing scores of them as well as taking the battle flag of the proud old 5th New Hampshire. The Yankees were just a little too eager today—or too early.

"Lord!" remarked a Virginian in Mahone's division. "We don't want any more prisoners at this stage."[38]

Gordon herded the wagon train over the worst roads yet, pushing into Buckingham County toward a crossroads called Sheppards. Longstreet's divisions settled in as though for the night around Cumberland Church, wet and cold, to block the Second and Sixth Corps from tearing into the somnambulant column. Sheridan's cavalry, including the chastised Crook, rode west for Prospect Station, on the Southside Railroad, for Lee had clearly given up the direct Danville route in favor of roads curving nearer to Lynchburg. The Fifth Corps and Ord's Army of the James also tramped west on the rail line, and they all trod the shorter road to Lee's next chance to collect those elusive rations, at Appomattox Station.[39]

Only part of Longstreet's corps had drawn regular rations that day. Elsewhere in the army there marched men who clung to treasured little stores of meal, meat, or hardtack, but most of the private hoards had given out. Some begged at nearby farmhouses, while many satisfied themselves with parched corn and others simply went hungry. All those who pressed on through the darkness stumbled in a fog of fatigue, with nothing more than a nap over the previous two nights.

At the very head of the fleeing army rolled the supernumerary artillery batteries entrusted to Reuben Lindsay Walker, the chief of artillery for the now-defunct Third Corps. General Walker had taken a northern route, rejoining the army at Cumberland Church just ahead of the first infantry. From there he led the way, and with him went the remains of Richard Anderson's corps artillery. Walker pulled the guns to the side of the road relatively early that evening, just short of the Appomattox County line. Gordon's column kept going until well after midnight.[40]

Back at Cumberland Church, a Federal officer brought a message for General Lee under a flag of truce. It came from Grant, at Farmville, who suggested as delicately as possible that the game was up. If Lee failed to surrender, Grant hinted, the rest of the blood shed in this campaign would be on his hands. With the clattering progress of his hungry, exhausted troops echoing around him, Lee replied that he doubted the extent of his predicament, but—as though for the sake of argument—he asked what terms Grant might offer if it came to that extremity. No answer came that night.

Longstreet did not even withdraw his corps from Cumberland Church until midnight, sneaking north on the Buckingham Plank Road and turning west on a road that paralleled Gordon's march a couple of miles to the north. Although that carried him over a longer route, he lacked so cumbersome a wagon train, and with the plank road under their feet his men made better time than they might have in such rain. Those who had stolen a few winks at the breastworks around the church had had their last sleep that night, however, and in the glow of dawn the leading regiments passed through a settlement known as Curdsville. Pushed so hard, his men began straggling in such numbers that Longstreet composed a general order to the four division commanders left in his corps, reminding them of the standard marching procedure.

"Hereafter on all marches the troops of this command will march in the manner laid down in the Tactics," he warned. "On all halts each division will mass on the one in front of it, form its line, and stack arms. Straggling will be prevented by the exercise of every exertion." As Mahone, Field, Henry Heth, and Cadmus Wilcox read their copies, some of them may have guessed that this would be their last march, but Longstreet's divisions remained the strongest and best organized in this shrinking army.[41]

On the other road, Lindsay Walker's artillerymen threw off damp blankets an hour after midnight. With much creaking of leather and wood, rattling of trace chains, and cursing of cannoneers, the guns jolted back into motion. At about the time Longstreet passed Curdsville, Gordon's vanguard passed through Sheppards, two miles south, where two roads intersected near a single house built by a man named Sheppard. Humphreys and the Second Corps trailed Gordon, while Wright followed Longstreet with the Sixth Corps.

The two columns converged again on the Richmond Stage Road. There, where two local roads ran into the stage road, sat a private home, a couple of outbuildings, and a store that had apparently been opened for business just the year before by Richard Gilliam, a young man whose occupation as an overseer may have saved him from military service. In honor of his little enterprise, this junction had been given the name of New Store; Appomattox County lay about eight miles farther on, at the bank of Holladay's Creek.

Around noontime, Union cavalry made its appearance at Pamplin Station, on the railroad. This lay just inside Appomattox County. At the depot where rail cars had claimed some of the Southside line's earliest accident victims stood four trains, all laden with the supplies Lee had sent back from Farmville.[42]

THE MEETING

Over the past four years more than 700 Appomattox men had taken up arms, either literally or metaphorically. More than a hundred had fled Richmond with their companies on the fiery night of April 2; perhaps a score of those—all that remained of the 700—crossed the county line with the army on April 8. Captain Abbitt stepped into his native shire at the head of his regiment, and a little squad of his neighbors followed him under Lieutenant Hannah. A few troopers still carried sabers with the Appomattox Rangers. Lieutenant Thomas Tibbs, formerly an officer with the Rangers, now marched with the biggest regiment in Wise's brigade. Forty-year-old William Hubbard, who had been captured in Pickett's Charge but was now freshly exchanged after nineteen months at Fort Delaware, plodded among the shattered remnants of Pickett's division as the sole survivor of the Appomattox Grays.[1]

Thousands of men stumbled along without arms, now. A dozen pounds of rifle and the strap of a loaded cartridge box dug deeply into the shoulders at this stage of fatigue, and in the darkness roadside vegetation consumed tons of such burdens. Then there were the artillerymen whose guns had been captured, abandoned, or broken down; some of them had been organized into infantry battalions, and some had not. This retreat included teamsters and the ambulance corps, telegraph operators, musicians black and white, sutlers, signalmen, sailors, marines, and some of their officers. Clerks, employees, and couriers by the dozen walked and rode, with or without sidearms, some of them still civilians although they clung to the flag as devotedly as any of those in uniform. Ragged platoons of Virginia Reserves, most of whom were also lacking any uniform but the occasional

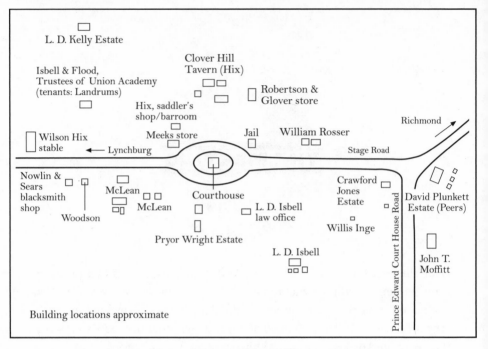

Map 5. Appomattox Court House, 1865

overcoat, kept with the column. Chaplains, surgeons, and quartermasters from disintegrated regiments gravitated toward each other, riding in little clusters; with Pickett's blasted division there traveled a man who characterized himself as a "missionary," who evidently preached to the troops without commission — and probably with more conviction than some of his official counterparts; another such volunteer minister endured the retreat with the staff of General Wise. A few dozen slaves carried fifes or drums, drove wagons, or followed loyally behind their masters, in token representation of the swarms of body servants who once accompanied this army.

Unmolested by the enemy, the fugitives suffered only from hunger and fatigue this Saturday. Here and there a measure of cautious confidence infected a Confederate who dared to suppose that safety lay within reach: the sun shone clear and bright, and no sound of distant gunfire worried these persistent pilgrims, although George Meade trailed closely with some 30,000 infantry from the Army of the Potomac. Another 30,000 Yankees and more sped westward south of the Appomattox under Sheridan and Ord, with other thousands lagging a day or so behind. From the vanguard of his column to the last straggler, Robert E. Lee could not have raised 30,000 men of all arms and ranks. His vaunted infantry num-

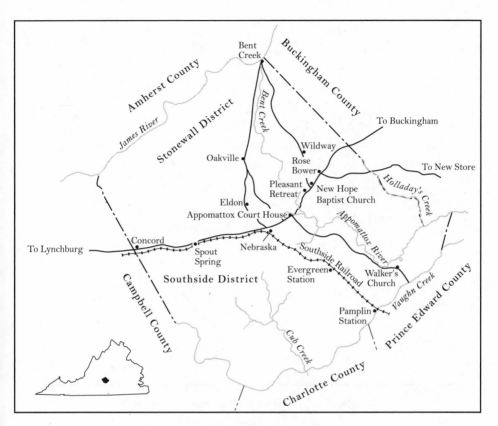

Map 6. Appomattox County, 1865

bered barely 22,000 that day: deducting more than 2,000 officers, hundreds of enlisted staff and noncombatants, and several thousand who wandered bare-handed or without any organized company, Lee would have been hard-pressed to put 10,000 rifles in line for a last stand.[2]

Dazed and demoralized fugitives lost or threw away entire arsenals of arms and equipment to expedite their retreat, and even then they fell behind by the score, to be picked up by the Yankees who dogged their footsteps. Singly and in squads, hundreds of other soldiers had detached themselves from the army, or had lost the column when they stopped to sleep, and their vagabond flight swept wide to the north of the main army. Appomattox farmers found themselves beset by beggars in dingy uniforms, bellies empty and hands outstretched. Old Andrew White, a Scottish immigrant who had made his fortune at Bent Creek, welcomed four famished wayfarers, whom he fed and boarded on well-appreciated featherbeds; these four were followed by more the next day, while at least one of the others stopped, ill, at Samuel Walker's plantation a few miles upriver.

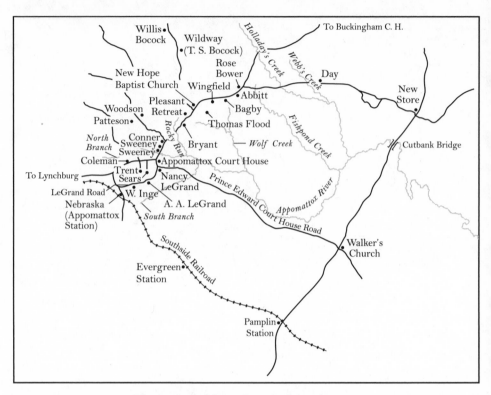

Map 7. Area of Operations April 8 and 9, 1865

"Find him a genuine Virginian," said the ailing soldier, "hospitable and kind."

A straggling corporal from the Washington Artillery of Louisiana, in flight among strangers since Sailor's Creek, crossed the Appomattox on Cut Bank Bridge. Following a route to Appomattox Court House suggested by a local doctor, he asked for a meal at the home of Spencer Gilliam, near Walker's Church, where he received a "splendid dinner." The presence of a "pretty girl in curls" at the table helped to flavor his food: she may have been any of Gilliam's four daughters, including Sarah Evelyn Gilliam, who had proven so fickle a fiancée to Captain John Moseley three years earlier.[3]

The Louisiana corporal took the longer road not only to seek food but to avoid the crowded column and the deep mud it churned. The pace improved for the main army after New Store, though. The stage road withstood the march much better than the latest roads this army had trod, and the glut of artillery leading the retreat rolled along at better than a mile and a half an hour. That pace kept the guns abreast of the Yankee cavalry that was racing toward Appomattox Station south of the river.

That river would soon cease to separate the combatants. The leading batteries of Lindsay Walker's column descended the slope toward the north branch of the Appomattox sometime after noon that Saturday. The rooftops of Appomattox Court House gleamed in the afternoon sun before them; the Sweeney apple orchard bordered their march here, and the grave of Joel Sweeney lay, all but unnoticed, on the hillside behind his family's dilapidated former home. The artillerymen splashed across the stream—barely a brook, here—and climbed 500 yards into the village. These were the first soldiers on campaign that the villagers had ever seen, and some residents peeked from behind curtains at them while others fled at their approach. The guns and caissons creaked right through the town, past the courthouse, the tavern, and Mr. McLean's house, winding ever westward up the rise by the Raine cemetery and out of sight. The first of them rumbled past Samuel Coleman's modest house not long before Union cavalry appeared near his father-in-law's home, Red Fields, on the other side of the depot. Alerted to the enemy's approach and fearing a battle in his dooryard, Dr. Coleman decided to escort his wife and daughter to the Abbitt plantation. Their only slave, a forty-year-old woman called Hannah Reynolds, remained at the house.[4]

Lee's orders had called for another rendezvous on the railroad, and General Walker's artillery had reached the slow bend in the stage road nearest the depot by midafternoon. A mile to the south sat three more trainloads of supplies from Lynchburg, just waiting for someone to pick them up. Unfortunately for hungry Confederates, the men who would claim those supplies were wearing blue cavalry jackets, and at that moment they were riding a roundabout route from Walker's Church that would bring them to the depot from the southeast.

Under the impression that he had won the race, General Walker turned his batteries off the road to rest; the head of his column had reached beyond the Bent Creek Road, while the tail stretched all the way back to Clover Hill, mixed in with baggage and supply wagons. According to Walker's instructions, they would resume the road to Lynchburg at seven o'clock that evening, but for now they would rest: these men had been on their feet for most of the previous thirty-two hours, and some had had no sleep at all during that time.

One gunner from a Norfolk battery had been struggling along with a wound, and somewhere along the road that afternoon he spotted a shack where he suspected there might be a well. He knocked at the door, finding inside the most astonishing family he had ever seen, living in absolute filth. The father and oldest son suffered from a deformity of the wrists that turned the palms of their hands sharply inward; the mother was obviously retarded—"idiotic," as this soldier described it—and one daughter had been born without arms, but with flipperlike hands protruding from her shoulders. A younger child limped with a clubfoot. The oldest daughter, who apparently carried no visible deformity or disability, had two children of what the artilleryman considered "more than doubtful parentage" clinging to her, although she seemed no older than eighteen herself. Forgetting his thirst, he called some of his comrades to witness the pathetic scene.[5]

These were not the only unfortunates encountered by soldiers that day. Around the same time, a few miles to the southeast, an Ohio cavalryman riding with George Custer sought refreshment at a plantation house, but instead of sustenance he found a crazed young man chained to the floor of a slave cabin, clad only in a rough shirt. The servants identified him as their owner's only son, who had lost his reason a few years before; he had the habit of tearing off his clothes, but his insanity had leaned toward violence, as well, and he had come close to killing a field hand once, when he snapped a lighter chain.[6]

At 3:00 P.M. General Lee turned off the stage road near Webb's Creek, a mile east of Holladay's Creek (the Appomattox County line), where he intended the trailing corps of his army to encamp. As soon as he stopped he dictated orders for Longstreet to encourage his troops a few miles farther. Ignorant of the local nomenclature, the commanding general referred to Webb's Creek simply as "one of the head waters of the Appomattox": he told Longstreet that this was the first water his column would find, advising him to keep moving until he could camp there. There the men could cook the rations they had brought from the Farmville depot, he suggested, and they might steal a few hours' sleep. Gordon, Lee said, had reached "a small branch," Fishpond Creek, two and a half miles beyond Webb's Creek, but Gordon's corps was still pushing on and his vanguard was already approaching Appomattox Court House.

"The Gen is now just south of the creek on which he wishes you to encamp," he informed his old war horse, "& desires to see you, if you can come."[7]

Longstreet's divisions ranged nearly to New Store, seven miles back, where the rear guard clashed with pursuing Union infantry around 4:00 P.M. That affair ended quickly, and the Yankees turned to the store itself, which they broke open and rifled. The Second Corps, leading the pursuit, settled in around New Store for a few hours before lurching four or five miles farther on; officers and men alike felt the panic in their prey.

"We are routing the enemy horse, foot, & dragoon," one Pennsylvanian wrote his mother that day.

While those looters at New Store feasted, the Confederates plodded westward. As the sweating brigades reached the creeks their columns melted into the surrounding forests and fields, from which hundreds of campfires soon twinkled.

At the front of Gordon's infantry column, Bushrod Johnson's refugees stopped "about a mile" short of Appomattox Court House, spilling into pastures and woods along the rise opposite Clover Hill. The provost guards and their hundreds of prisoners bivouacked nearby. Between the two surviving corps of the army marched a multitude of disarmed, disconnected troops, whose numbers had swollen that day with another crop of stragglers. The problem seemed worse in Gordon's corps, where one captain complained that field officers and generals seemed oblivious to it, riding "in dogged indifference" at the heads of their dissolving commands, rather than at the rear, where they might have stopped it. As a result, this captain observed, some brigades arrived in Appomattox County as mere skeletons. The dregs of Pickett's division and the divisions of Henry Heth and Cadmus Wilcox began falling out around New Hope Church and the road junction that led to Wildway. Supply wagons and caissons began pulling off into the fields and going into park. As successive brigades saw the troops ahead of them veering to the side they, too, took to the fields. The last of Gordon's units bivouacked around Charles Wingfield's little tenancy and the homestead of Luke Bagby, a discharged Appomattox Ranger; Gordon established his own headquarters somewhere in the vicinity of Pleasant Retreat. E. P. Alexander unrolled his blankets that night on Joseph Abbitt's property. The sun set as these men in dingy grey eased their tormented joints to the ground and kindled little fires for warming their first rations in a day or two. Still farther back, along the creekbanks beyond Rose Bower, Mahone's troops wolfed the last of their meals and rolled into their blankets for a few hours' sleep. Behind them, at the tail of the army, lay Charles Field's division, the largest left in either of the two Confederate corps.

Some in this army had still received no rations, eating a few fistfuls of parched corn instead of hard bread and beef, and hunger had begun to compromise the scruples of even the officers. A lieutenant of the 1st Virginia Infantry Battalion, serving with the provost guard, filched some turnips at a nearby farm. As flickering flames began to speckle the landscape, the distant-but-discouraging grumbling of cannon echoed over the treetops, announcing the presence of Yankees somewhere ahead.

"Everything looks gloomy," said one of George Pickett's remaining colonels.[8]

The artillery these men heard belonged to Lindsay Walker. George Custer's cavalry division had trotted across the railroad from Walker's Church, passing George Abbitt's huddled family at Red Fields, and around four o'clock in the afternoon the skirmishers of Custer's first brigade sighted wafts of smoke at the depot, where the trains sat waiting for Lee's army. Troopers spurred their horses ahead to catch the engines idling, waving the crews down to the ground while Custer steered a few regiments beyond the station to secure it.

Hearing a commotion of gunshots and whistles at the depot, Walker suspected the cause and began wheeling his guns into line. With no infantry support save a couple of companies of transmogrified artillerymen, he drew dozens of muzzles in a broad arc centered on the depot, nearly a mile away. Custer, who later reported that he faced two divisions of infantry here, did not act as though he saw any now: he spread three mounted regiments before the serried guns and moved them slowly forward through fields and forest to skirmish with Walker's handful of riflemen.[9]

The horsemen edged tentatively forward, exchanging shots with the Confederate skirmishers in the brush ahead. Over the past decade much of the timber near the station had been cut for the railroad, either to satisfy the need for ties and boiler fuel or to open land for buildings like Benjamin Roberts's modest cabin, before which Walker's impromptu skirmishers lurked. The second-growth vegetation on this battlefield hampered both Union cavalry and Confederate artillery, but the horsemen urged their mounts grimly forward. Facing several hundred Yankees with repeating carbines, the few dozen ersatz Southern infantrymen fell back before the glare of a drooping sun until a couple of their batteries loosed a hail of canister over their heads; the volley sailed over the Union brigade, as well, but the troopers flinched at the blast and began looking for cover. As more of Custer's regiments arrived he threw them in on the right, where in the approaching dusk they might have cut the stage road between Walker's artillery and the rest of the army, but shellfire and still more canister drove them back. One Vermont lieutenant, a recent Dartmouth College graduate with a short but gallant record, went dashing toward the guns on this last evening of the war only to be knocked from the saddle by a shell fragment that tore away half his right hand and bored through his arm near the shoulder.

Everywhere in Walker's column Confederate officers rallied little bands of stragglers to face the cavalry. Eventually, though, enough Union horse came galloping into the station to give them the advantage. Thomas Devin's division came up on Custer's right, and a couple of hours after dusk they began worrying the Confederate gunners away from their pieces. Walker pulled back to a more compact perimeter while some of his command turned their horses toward Lynchburg, abandoning guns, wagons, and long-awaited campfires to the yelping Yankees.[10]

Part of a mounted New York regiment reached the stage road east of Walker's massed guns and turned right, galloping toward the village behind Lieutenant Colonel Augustus Root. With bugles blaring they veered past hundreds of wagons, ambulances, and caissons parked beside the road or trapped in an endless jam. Teamsters and stragglers scattered, sprinting headlong before the New Yorkers, who emptied their revolvers at anyone in the roadway. At least one Louisiana gun crew tried to disperse the horsemen with canister but could not fire without killing frantic Confederates. Instead, the gunners themselves fled into the woods, abandoning their piece. As Root's reckless troopers crested the rise just west of Appomattox Court House they surprised General Pendleton, the chief of artillery for the Army of Northern Virginia. Forgetting his fifty-five years, Pendleton leaped his horse over one of Farmer Tibbs's rail fences and sped out of sight into the darkness.[11]

The Confederates camped north of the courthouse were settling in for a meal and some sleep just then, or lightening their loads for a hastier departure in the morning. The Virginia lieutenant of the provost guard was just returning to his prisoners and his campfire to parch some corn and enjoy the turnips he had "flanked" from a nearby garden. A captain from North Carolina, still suffering from a glancing head wound, spent the evening overhauling the baggage in the ambulance he shared with other convalescents. Another North Carolinian who had driven his regiment's medical wagon over a hundred miles of miserable roads watched the wagon and most of its precious medicine burned, along with scores of other vehicles parked alongside it.

Eugene Henry Levy, a gunner with the Donaldsonville Artillery of Louisiana, bathed his face and feet in the North Branch and then splashed across the ford, scaling the slope to the Clover Hill Tavern. There he bargained with a "buxom negro cook," who agreed to transform his ration of flour into bread, but she had not even made the dough when Levy heard Root's cavalry burst into the village. When they had passed Levy tried to escape via the front porch, but one New York cavalryman had lagged behind and leveled a carbine at him. That marked the end of three and a half years of war for Levy, who started toward Appomattox Station ahead of his captor; the Yankees put him behind the reins of one of the stalled wagons for a time, but there was no untangling the snarl of conveyances that night and finally they prodded him ahead on foot. Levy spent the night in the field opposite the front door of Red Fields, with hundreds of other prisoners from Walker's artillery and the baggage train.[12]

Moments after Levy surrendered, Colonel Root's dash ended abruptly before William Rosser's blacksmith shop. There the first resistance greeted him, and a roving Confederate rifleman dropped the ambitious colonel dead in the road alongside a massive oak tree. That feat inspired other scattered soldiers to take arms against such impudence, and the cavalrymen swarmed back out of the village, herding a few unfortunates like the Louisiana artilleryman.[13]

The cavalry foray had come to an end, but a line of organized infantry rose from its blankets anyway. Bushrod Johnson's division lay nearest the village, resting about campfires on the hillside across the Appomattox, and on instructions from Gordon these troops fanned out to the front under one of Johnson's brigadiers, William Wallace. Wallace's own brigade had been reduced to regimental strength, and General Lee had evidently decided to consolidate some of his commands: he relieved Richard Anderson, whose corps had disappeared at Sailor's Creek, and sent him home; he appears to have similarly dismissed Bushrod Johnson and George Pickett, though more for battlefield inefficiency than for lack of troops. The actual order for their relief never surfaced, and both Johnson and Pickett wrote their reports with the air that they had never received it. Both remained with the army until the surrender, and General Longstreet continued to address Pickett as commander of his division: three weeks later Pickett still fancied his home as "Headquarters, Pickett's Division," but both his and Johnson's military careers ended before the dawn of April 9.

Wallace roused Johnson's sleepy division and marched it into the village, forming a short line of battle, but the enemy made no further appearance. An hour before midnight these few hundred survivors of the debacle at Sailor's Creek lay down beside their rifles for a little more sleep. Not three miles away to the southwest, Yankee cavalrymen set about devouring three entire carloads of bacon, courtesy of the quartermaster at Lynchburg.[14]

General Mahone, who was in delicate health, sought shelter that evening. He chose a log cabin alongside the stage road, somewhere near the rear of the army. This rude structure, probably the same one visited by the wounded Norfolk artilleryman earlier in the day, was occupied by "a family of deformed people" whose handicaps appalled the general and whose squalid surroundings seemed to reflect the dilapidated condition of the Confederacy. Shuddering at the image of his wretched hosts, Mahone curled up on a bed too small even for his diminutive frame and tried to sleep.[15]

By now most of the enlisted men in this exhausted army lay wrapped in their blankets, as well. Firelight still flickered at Lee's headquarters campsite, though, toward the rear of the sprawled army, as the commanding general consulted with his remaining lieutenants. He concluded that Longstreet would retain the rear guard, holding off the Union Second and Sixth Corps, while Gordon and Fitzhugh Lee would push on at one o'clock in the morning toward the depot, Campbell Court House, and eventually Danville, where President Davis and the rest of the government sat waiting; the excess artillery and the wagon train would turn for Lynchburg, from which it might be saved by rail. If it was only Sheridan's cavalry that lay between Appomattox Court House and the railroad station, they would brush it aside and proceed, but if blue infantry had come up the game was over: Lee would have to respond to Grant's appeals for surrender. Another such missive had arrived that evening, implying an offer to release the entire army on parole, but Lee had answered it with an invitation to begin general peace talks.

Grant and Lee each commanded all the armies of their respective governments, but neither wore authority to initiate so sweeping a dialogue. Even if they had, Grant held too strong a military hand to exchange it for the uncertainty of political negotiations, and he declined. Lee had not yet determined the extent of Grant's advantage, however, for none of Lindsay Walker's fugitives had seen anything ahead but cavalry. Lee issued his orders, and Fitz Lee brought the last of his cavalry up from the rear while John Gordon cast about for a solid division to lead the drive.[16]

While the Confederate generals made their plans, Yankee infantry plodded wearily westward under bright moonlight on roads parallel to the railroad. The Fifth Corps had been following Sheridan's cavalry since Five Forks, but General Ord wedged his Army of the James in behind the cavalry at Prospect Station and impeded the progress of the Fifth Corps the rest of the day, causing long delays and depriving exhausted foot soldiers of any time for real rest. Everyone marched from two dozen to thirty miles between dawn and sometime after midnight, and if the countrymen of Appomattox were not cowed by the Yankees' numbers they must at least have been intimidated by the division of U.S. Colored Troops that marched with them; this portion of the Twenty-fifth Corps followed the white troops of the Twenty-fourth, bringing the Piedmont planters the specter of their worst fears.

The fleetest of the Fifth Corps began falling out along the roadside near midnight, still a few miles from Appomattox Court House. Ord's troops had turned toward the depot, stopping short of that place, as well. The last regiments in each column were still coming in at 2:00 A.M., some twenty-three hours after they had taken to the road. For another hour, at the other end of the line, lagging brigades of the Union Second Corps eased closer to the tail of Lee's army, turning in a couple of miles short of Webb's Creek.[17]

By then, Lee's columns were rolling westward. At midnight most of Longstreet's corps resumed the road, and Gordon was bringing his last divisions into the village by 3:00 A.M., hurrying them along the soupy shoulders of a road jammed with parked artillery and assorted wagons. As the first hint of light broke the darkness over Appomattox Court House, the entire advance corps of the Army of Northern Virginia stood within shouting distance of Wilmer McLean's veranda.

To spearhead his assault, General Gordon finally chose four little brigades from Alabama, Georgia, and North Carolina under Bryan Grimes, asking Grimes how many men he had lost at Sailor's Creek and how many rifles he could muster. In the wee hours of April 9 he moved Grimes through the village and ordered him into line of battle facing the ridge west of town. To bolster his ranks, Gordon first gave him the remnants of Johnson's division, under William Wallace—including Wise's brigade, in which Thomas Tibbs still carried a sword. When Grimes complained that even this combined force would not be able to clear the enemy from the stage road, Gordon gave him his other two divisions, as well. The other six brigades, including a few dozen survivors of the once-mighty Stonewall Brigade, shuffled up the stage road before dawn to take their places to the left of Grimes. That still yielded a front with barely 2,500 muskets, Gordon calculated—perhaps a bit conservatively.[18]

General Wallace, named for a Scottish chieftan who fought the better-equipped English at great odds, may have reflected on those lopsided Highland struggles as his four little brigades marched into line. His own brigade mustered barely 300 rifles; fewer still of Young Moody's brigade had returned to the colors after Sailor's Creek, and not 100 of Matthew Ransom's. Wise's four regiments could hardly have boasted 200 men, even with the reinforcement of a few survivors from Stapleton Crutchfield's converted heavy artillery brigade: the chaplain of the 26th Virginia counted only 20 members of that regiment in line that morning, although 95 of its officers and men would accept paroles three days later. More of Bushrod Johnson's erstwhile division milled about in the unarmed mob that huddled between the two halves of the army than carried muskets into this last fight.[19]

Wise's brigade went in on the extreme right of the Confederate infantry. For Lieutenant Tibbs, crossing his father's own fields and glancing at the hipped roof of the very house he had left to go to war, the rhetoric of defending one's hearth may have seemed especially apt. Three thin divisions of cavalry, about 2,400 strong and mostly Virginians, spread into the woods to the north of what had been Samuel McDearmon's hilltop manor, with the 2nd Virginia Cavalry among them. The grave of their young comrade of the early days, Lafayette Meeks, lay within sound of their hoofbeats.[20]

On the other end of the line, Longstreet roused his divisions around midnight and pushed them far enough forward to take advantage of a breakthrough if Gordon could manage one. He stopped just south of New Hope Church, where one road turned off to Wildway and another toward Flood's Mill, and as the units arrived Longstreet aligned them behind fresh breastworks looming across the stage road. Mahone's men and Field's division quickstepped from the tag-end of the line of march, reaching the main body by midmorning. Not far behind them came the harbingers of the Union Second Corps, which had spent the night the other side of Webb's Creek. The Sixth Corps had taken the road early from New Store and spent the morning on the heels of the Second.[21]

On Gordon's front, dawn revealed a single brigade of Union cavalry and a section of artillery guarding the intersection of the Oakville Road, by which Lee's army might again sidestep its pursuers if the stage road itself could not be opened. Armed with an assortment of breech-loading and repeating carbines, the cavalrymen shivered without fires behind a fence-rail breastwork; the brace of rifled guns and a line of dismounted skirmishers lay within half a mile of the village, near the lane leading to John Sears's farm.

Grimes swung Johnson's division toward the Yankees' left flank in the military equivalent of a right-hand roundhouse punch, aided by North Carolina cavalry, while advancing his own division directly at their front. That combination sent the Union cavalry brigade stumbling backward in spite of its superior firepower, and jubilant Confederates gathered in the pair of three-inch rifles, complete with teams and equipment. Momentarily victorious, the foot soldiers wheeled to their left, putting the stage road safely behind them. Grimes advanced one brigade west of the intersection to watch for further threats from that direction, but he faced most of his own division and all three of the others to the south and informed Gordon that the way to Lynchburg (for what was left of the wagon train) and Campbell Court House (for the army) was open. Fitz Lee's cavalry spurred ahead north of the stage road, pressing the outnumbered but well-armed enemy steadily backward. They encountered another brigade of Federal horsemen near Dr. Coleman's house and sent them packing as well, overrunning one more gun.[22]

Confederate fortunes looked a little brighter as the sun started to climb, but the tide began to turn near 8:00 A.M., when the Southern horsemen charged headlong into a third Union cavalry brigade, only a mile from the Bent Creek Road. Two Pennsylvania regiments countercharged, killing the color-bearer of the 14th Virginia Cavalry and blunting the momentum of the Confederate drive. These Pennsylvanians dismounted, and three-quarters of them spread out on the ground with their repeating Spencers while the others led all the horses to the rear. The Confederates came at them again at full gallop, breaking through them, too, and capturing fifty of their horses, but the Spencers multiplied the effectiveness of the prone Federals sevenfold and the Southern charge eventually withered.

A mile behind the Virginia cavalry, Grimes's watchful brigade of Confederate infantry had moved over the ridge past the Oakville Road, but just then a column of Union infantry arrived on the field and started filing into line on the right of their beleaguered cavalry. That infantry belonged to the Army of the James, under Ord. These men had been up and marching hard since 3:00 A.M. on only three hours of sleep, after covering thirty miles the day before. One brigade came pounding up from the station at the double-quick as the last of the Federal cavalry, including the Pennsylvanians, withdrew from the field. These Yankee foot soldiers formed a three-regiment front—each regiment the size of a Confederate brigade—and started toward Clover Hill. A long swale running parallel to their line of march momentarily shielded their progress from Grimes's infantry and artillery, but Confederate cavalry lingering near Dr. Coleman's house slipped around the left of this brigade, snapping up half of an Ohio regiment as prisoners and throwing the survivors back in confusion. The fugitives flocked into another brigade of their own division, though, and quickly reorganized for a second attempt while the other brigade veered into Dr. Coleman's fields to extend the front. A third brigade in dusty blue uniforms was already trotting up from the station, with several more behind it.[23]

Its size doubling and then tripling, this infantry column advanced again through scrub oak and brambles so thick that officers had to send their horses to the rear. Dark formations, each comprising hundreds of men, emerged from the woods west of Dr. Coleman's and into the fields south of the road, where Confederate artillery began to play upon them with case shot and canister as soon as they crested their protective ridge, mortally wounding the slave Hannah Reynolds on the eve of emancipation. Slowly this ominous procession rolled forward, picking up strength like a hurricane over the open sea, as a second division and parts of a third arrived and fell in alongside. Ultimately the Confederates at the road junction faced a mile-long line of Yankees, among whom stood several regiments of U.S. Colored Troops.

Meanwhile, two divisions of Charles Griffin's Fifth Corps were swinging up the LeGrand Road. At Willis Inge's farm they turned north, toward the old Trent place and John Sears's house. A heavy skirmish line preceded them, flushing Gordon's skirmishers from those farmyards and driving them back on the village. The surging blue tide stopped only once, to fix bayonets for one grand, final assault. At the same time George Custer led part of his cavalry division even farther out the LeGrand Road, beyond Gordon's left, toward the home of Reverend LeGrand's widow and the Prince Edward Court House Road.[24]

With such pressure in front, on his right flank, and threatening his left, Gordon began pulling his divisions backward over the same ground they had traveled. He called back for help from Longstreet, who had at least twice as many infantry still under arms but who already faced two corps at New Hope Church. Despite his own problems, Longstreet immediately ordered Wilcox's division to Gordon's assistance and, once he was satisfied with his entrenchments across the stage road, he peeled off Mahone's five brigades, sending them toward the North Branch at a run. He kept only Field's division, the remainder of Heth's, and Pickett's derelict 800, among whom stood four or five dozen armed men. He directed his artillery chief, General Alexander, to accompany the reinforcements and select a suitable line of battle for Gordon to fall back upon.

Alexander rode to the top of the hill overlooking the Appomattox and Clover Hill, beyond which Gordon's men were backing stubbornly away from overwhelming numbers. The "military" crest of the hill, from which the defenders' fire would prove most destructive, lay below the topographical crest, so Alexander chose to position his troops between the Conner farm and the Sweeneys' apple orchard. He studded the hill with artillery and with artillerymen armed as infantry; when the captured guns came in from Gordon's front he gave them to some Virginians whose battery had been left behind, and they gleefully discarded their muskets to serve the new pieces.[25]

Lee had positioned himself not far behind the Conner farm, between the extremities of the army. From there he could see the rooftops of the village and the approaching billows of smoke that told the tale of Gordon's steady retreat. Even before the backs of his infantry appeared on his side of Clover Hill, the old general recognized that all doors had been closed to him, and when he heard of Gordon's need for help he knew it was time to talk to General Grant. After calling Longstreet and Mahone up for a brief interview, he left Longstreet in command and rode north to New Hope Church with two staff officers and a mounted sergeant. They passed through the lines with a flag of truce and asked to see Grant. Somewhere along the way Lee realized that he had forgotten to notify Gordon of his intentions, and he sent word to Longstreet to dispatch a flag of truce into the village. Longstreet sent Captain Robert M. Sims, whom he had recently attached to his own staff.

Instead of meeting Grant, Lee received Grant's answer to his last proposal about peace negotiations, declining such a meeting. Lee directed Lieutenant Colonel Charles Marshall, his military secretary, to write a request for a new meeting on the subject of surrender, and Marshall carried that back to his Union counterpart. He was told that Grant was riding around to the Army of the James, at the far end of Lee's army, and that it would probably take less time for a message to reach him if it went the other way. An ailing George Meade, commander of the Army of the Potomac, was traveling in an ambulance behind the Second Corps, and Lee sent to him for a suspension of hostilities. Meade, aware that Grant had refused to see Lee and perhaps fearing a deliberate ploy for delay, said he could authorize no truce.[26]

Back at the courthouse, Captain Sims found Gordon losing his grip on the village. The ridge that Grimes had won so easily that morning now lay strewn with dead Confederates and their abandoned artillery, before which stood the entire Army of the James. From the south came the infantry of the Fifth Corps, with its skirmish line arching all the way from the Widow Wright's house to the western edge of the village. Confederate infantry backed through the village; some North Carolinians on the retreating skirmish line took shelter behind John Raine's great, neglected stable and other nearby outbuildings, where they rammed home some of the last bullets ever fired by the Army of Northern Virginia.[27]

After telling Gordon of Lee's desire for a truce, Sims galloped down the Prince Edward Court House Road, where Custer's cavalry harried Gordon's left. Madly waving a white towel over his head, he crossed Plain Run and burst through a thin cordon of Confederate engineers acting as infantry supports for an isolated little battery. Near the LeGrand Road he entered Union lines and was introduced to George Custer, whom he said haughtily refused to recognize any truce that did not entail immediate and unconditional surrender. Sims returned to Gordon "in almost a straight line," his phrasing suggesting that Gordon now stood near the intersection of the stage road and the Prince Edward Court House Road. Custer soon followed, Sims recalled, and demanded that Gordon surrender, but the wiry Georgian declined. Custer then asked for Gordon's immediate superior.

Longstreet commanded in Lee's absence. He stood alongside the road above the Sweeney orchard, where Alexander was forming his battle line. With a Confederate escort, Custer rode up and made the same demand to Longstreet that he had to Gordon, threatening annihilation if he did not surrender immediately. Longstreet gave him the same obstinate refusal, and when the swaggering young cavalryman persisted Longstreet lost his temper and scolded him for his impudence, inviting him to go ahead and attack if he dared. Custer turned back toward the village, where Gordon and Phil Sheridan were concluding a similar conversation, but ultimately Sheridan agreed to a temporary suspension of hostilities.[28]

Another officer carried a flag westward from Gordon's position, out the stage road, but the handful of 14th North Carolina sharpshooters behind and around the Raine stable either missed it or failed to heed it. The flag had already passed into Union lines beyond them when they let fly at approaching Federals with one last scattered volley. Their fire dropped a cavalryman who was advancing with the Fifth Corps skirmishers, prompting a score of indignant Pennsylvanians to rush among the buildings at the edge of town and flush them out. Most of the Southern marksmen fled back through the village, but a dozen or two Tarheels — the last battlefield prisoners the Army of the Potomac would ever take — threw down their empty rifles and marched off under guard.[29]

One more brief rattle of musketry erupted across Plain Run when one of Custer's cavalrymen galloped at the engineer troops guarding the guns along the Prince Edward Court House Road. This Yankee brazenly demanded the surrender of that contingent, but he drew a flurry of fire for his trouble. Gordon immediately sent a messenger toward the sound of that firing with news of the truce. Then the entire battlefield fell silent. The last division of the Fifth Corps, which was about to sweep across Plain

Run and join the tide cresting Clover Hill, instead stopped short on the Sears farm, and some of its soldiers climbed on the roof to see what was happening over there. A mile to the north, a Signal Corps lieutenant led three privates out from Union lines to the Tibbs house, where they, too, climbed to the rooftop to keep an eye on the trapped army.[30]

The potential for trouble remained at the rear, though, where the Union Second Corps was spreading out for its attack on Longstreet's breast-works below New Hope Church. Runaway slaves, perhaps from the nearby Flood plantation, reported that Southern skirmishers were throwing away their weapons and wandering back to the main body, but that hopeful clue failed to calm Meade's aggressive mood. He still resisted a truce, though he had read Lee's note to Grant asking to discuss surrender before sending it on. Longstreet was faced with fighting a battle here, against great odds, while the rest of the army observed its own truce. Meade had been laid low with what he called a "malarious catarrh"; he also suffered acutely from the constant, close supervision of General Grant, which often left Meade feeling like a supernumerary at his own headquarters: Grant had seemed particularly jovial that morning as he departed, and Meade may have been anxious to avoid disturbing the lieutenant general's good humor. Perhaps even more influential in his consideration of Lee's request was the secret that the commander of the Army of the Potomac also harbored deep resentment over Phil Sheridan's tendency to arrogate for himself the glory gained by the entire army, and Meade must have rankled at the thought of Lee surrendering without his portion of the army taking any hand in the final fighting.

At last a Federal officer who had been allowed through Confederate lines brought Meade proof that Union forces across the Appomattox had consented to the truce. Though that consent had initially been granted by Sheridan, and the messenger himself was a member of Sheridan's staff, Meade managed to avoid acknowledging that unpleasant detail. Instead he told Lee that he was aware of a cease-fire "between your command and General Ord." On the basis of that news, Meade said he would agree to withhold his attack until 2:00 P.M. [31]

Up at the Conner farm, Mahone's troops had begun hacking at Alexander's new line of works facing the North Branch. Presently General Mahone himself told them to stop digging, remarking that it would not be necessary. Puzzled veterans laid their tools aside and glanced at each other, wondering what could have happened, and the buzz of rumors radiated from the spot where their general had spoken. Speculation about surrender muttered its way through the ranks, punctuated with curses and then sobbing as the image crystallized amid the determined throng.[32]

As his message to Grant flew from both ends of his contracting army, General Lee returned from New Hope Church and rode down into the valley of the Appomattox, turning off the road into the Sweeney orchard. Coming down from his now-superfluous battle line, Alexander directed some nearby soldiers to arrange a seat under an apple tree, sending them a short distance away when they were finished to offer their chief some privacy. There Lee awaited Grant's reply, near enough to Joel Sweeney's grave that if the stilled fingers had come back to life he might have heard them strum one last serenade for the age that was about to die.[33]

Lee's request ran into Grant just before noon. Grant estimated that he received it some four miles west of Walker's Church, and thus six miles short of Appomattox Court House. He wrote back that he would be coming in from the Farmville Road, returning the message by one of his aides, Lieutenant Colonel Orville Babcock. Babcock and a lieutenant who accompanied him evidently spurred their horses to a full gallop, reaching the village about forty-five minutes ahead of Grant. Babcock crossed into Confederate lines and descended into the basin of the Appomattox, where he found Lee still sitting under the apple tree, and there he delivered Grant's message. Presently Lee signaled to Colonel Marshall, and orderlies brought the horses. Leather creaked as Lee, Babcock, Marshall, the lieutenant, and a Lynchburg private named Joshua O. Johns pulled themselves into their saddles and started up the rise.[34]

As Marshall told the story, he rode ahead at Lee's behest to find a suitable building for the two generals to meet. Probably he rode straight for the courthouse — where local people congregate in any Southern town — passing George Peers's house, Crawford Jones's empty little law office, and the county jail. He lit upon Wilmer McLean, who had availed himself of the truce to venture outside, and Marshall asked if he knew of a place.

"He took me into a house that was all dilapidated and that had no furniture in it," Marshall remembered, and he rejected it. That house may have been the brick home of Pryor Wright, just south of the courthouse, which his widow had vacated upon his death more than a decade before. Or it could have been the old Raine tavern, still standing at the road's edge in front of McLean's home: the tavern had probably seen no tenants in a few years, either. As a better option McLean offered his own comfortable residence, and when Marshall saw it he sent the orderly for the other officers. They left all four horses with Private Johns, in the yard. Their boots drummed up McLean's wide porch steps and they entered the front door, which opened on a central hallway that separated two big rooms. Just inside, a door opened to the left into the parlor, and there they chose to wait. Babcock asked the lieutenant to wait outside and signal Grant when he came along.[35]

Grant and his entourage arrived about half an hour later, guided by one of Sheridan's staff officers, who had apparently taken them on a wrong turn. He encountered Sheridan and Ord, whom he invited to join him. Pounding up the steps with much of his personal staff following, he found Lee, Marshall, and Babcock in the parlor. He chatted with Lee for a time about the old army and the war with Mexico before they discussed the terms of surrender. Grant had suggested that the Confederates need only lay down their arms, officers excepted, and they might all be allowed to go home after the formality of signing paroles. Lee indicated that such terms were acceptable, and Grant began putting them in writing. Lee read them, made one stylistic correction, and Grant directed one of his staff to start copying the draft in ink. Lee mentioned that many of his soldiers had brought their own horses to war, and Grant assured him that any man who claimed a mount would be allowed to take it home. At some point in their conversation Lee also mentioned that he was without forage for his teams or rations for his men; of forage Grant could offer none, but from the captured trains at Appomattox Station he could easily supply the 25,000 rations Lee estimated he would need. Grant introduced Lee to the other generals, and the room began to fill with junior officers from the staffs of Ord and Sheridan. Once the copies of Grant's terms and Lee's capitulation had been finished and signed, Lee departed with Marshall and the orderly.[36]

Some of the generals at the McLean house now descended upon the owner with offers of cash for his furniture, which they wanted for souvenirs. They emptied out the parlor, buying some and taking the rest, until nothing remained on the floor but the carpet and little Lula McLean's rag doll. A captain on Sheridan's staff scooped up the doll.

While the relic hunters scurried about the interior of the house, most of the generals watched Lee ride away, and later some of them remarked upon his dignified demeanor. That dignity crumbled as the general passed out of the village and down the slope to his army, and witnesses on the other side of the Appomattox noted the obvious sadness of his posture and expression. His troops had all been withdrawn into the valley, where they stood ready to welcome their commander in his hour of defeat. Not long after the three grey uniforms disappeared from the view of those at the McLean house, the lingering Union officers heard a dull, rising roar as hundreds and then thousands of weary voices strained to greet the man coming down from Clover Hill. It began with the artillerymen, whom General Alexander had formed along the roadside; he had instructed them to take their hats off and stand in silence as Lee rode by, but someone let loose with a cheer and no one could stop the rest of them from picking it up. His expression unchanged, Lee pulled off his own hat in silent acknowledgment, while his troops waved theirs at him. During his absence his staff had made camp on the hilltop opposite the Conner farm, about a hundred yards from the road, and as he climbed toward his headquarters flag Mahone's troops burst from their ranks behind the unfinished breastworks and swarmed around him, tears streaming down their dirty faces. Their voices carried across the amphitheater of the Appomattox. When he dismounted, those closest to the eye of the swirling throng reached their hands out for his, and he shook some of them. Then he waited for them to fall silent and told them briefly what had happened. He said he had made the best terms he could, and they would be able to go to their homes.

With that Lee withdrew to his tent, accompanied only by a few personal friends. The soldiers returned to their battle line, from which their officers began marching them to gloomy campsites along the stage road, all the way from the river to Pleasant Retreat.[37]

Lee had not long retired to his tent before the Union soldiers heard the results of the conference at the McLean house. The news reached the cavalry and the Fifth Corps first, since Grant turned west on the stage road when he left McLean's house. These soldiers had seen the handwriting on the wall that morning, when the shrunken hulk of Stonewall Jackson's old corps had stumbled so hastily backward before them, and word of the surrender offered enough anticlimax to temper their reaction. Cheers soared and fell, hats flew, and bands struck up the usual diet of national airs, but few of those who could see the defeated army in the basin of the Appomattox recorded any prolonged, frenzied celebrations among their fellows.[38]

Yankees at the other end of the Confederate lines showed no such restraint. Out of sight of their vanquished opponents, pity failed them. Unaware of the impossibility of Lee's immediate tactical plight, they drew from his capitulation greater surprise and gratification.

One of Meade's staff officers brought the message up the stage road, through Confederate lines. He lifted his cap to announce the surrender, and the single sentence raised a flock of other caps into the air like a swooping flight of starlings. Meade's chief of staff called for three cheers, and for three more to General Meade himself, and then he looked into Meade's ambulance and suggested that he ride back down the road to carry the good news to the rest of the Second and Sixth Corps; with the Fifth Corps on Sheridan's side of the enemy, those six divisions between New Hope Church and New Store represented all that was left of the army Meade had led from Gettysburg. At first Meade balked, complaining of his illness, but finally he climbed out of the ambulance and into the saddle. Whipping his cap from his head to wave in lieu of a banner, he dug spurs into his horse's sides and bolted up the stage road, shouting the news.

"Boys," one soldier heard him say, "your work is done. Lee has surrendered. You can go home."[39]

Bedlam followed the grizzled messenger. A brigadier in the Second Corps told his wife that his officers and men went "perfectly wild," throwing their hats and even their shoes high into the air.

"The Army was perfectly crazy," observed the commander of a battery of Regulars, when Meade passed on to the Sixth Corps. Hats and caps momentarily darkened the sky, and other batteries started firing salutes. Men who had been lying on blankets eating their dinners began tossing each other in those same blankets.[40]

Meade rode so recklessly that many failed to recognize him. One soldier mistook the exuberant army commander for General Grant, which only heightened the excitement. An orderly sergeant from Pennsylvania merely noted that "an officer came tearing from the front as if his life depended on it, waving his hat," but when that officer shouted that Lee had surrendered his entire army, the air filled with knapsacks, haversacks, and canteens.[41]

Not quite all the army had surrendered, however. Undetected by the signal station on top of the Tibbs house, hundreds of Confederates had chosen flight to the prospect of prison, and a good many more were thinking about it.

The only organized effort to escape began before the flags of truce went out. At his uncle's final council Fitz Lee had proposed getting the cavalry away as soon as surrender seemed inevitable, and he had perceived that inevitability as soon as those swarms of blue uniforms appeared on the ridge near Dr. Coleman's house. One of the three divisions, under General Lee's second son, retired to Appomattox Court House to share the fate of the army, but Tom Rosser and Thomas T. Munford broke free with their divisions. Accompanied by Fitz Lee and his staff, Rosser's eight regiments disappeared into the woods to the west, making straight for Lynchburg. Munford led his three brigades up the Oakville Road and then overland,

across the Bent Creek Road to the stage road, coming out on the Lynchburg side of Appomattox Station. His sudden appearance there, at the rear
of the Union army, sparked an alarm among the Yankees, who lashed out at
his troops from the vicinity of Elizabeth Robertson's home. Mrs. Robertson, widow of village entrepreneur David Robertson and mother of Major
James Robertson, lived in the house with her own widowed daughter and
three grandchildren.[42]

At first one Federal brigade piled into Munford, but a second soon arrived and the blue lines pulled back to align for a charge. Before the bugles
sounded, though, a horseman brought word of the truce. Instead of hurl-
ing eight full regiments forward, therefore, the Union commander sent out
a lone officer with a flag of truce. Munford came forward with some staff
officers, perhaps including his quartermaster, Captain William H. Trent.
They met three or four Union generals, who told them of the truce and the
anticipated surrender. They chatted amiably for a few moments, and Munford passed around a canteen of peach brandy that Trent had retrieved on
a visit to his home the evening before. When the canteen was empty, Munford and his men returned to their lines. His drinking partners considered
themselves bound by the truce and declined to move. Munford, who did
not feel compelled to abide by it, turned his men for Lynchburg, where
they had been mustered in four years previously.[43]

Rosser's and Munford's divisions melted away as they rode, for discouraged troopers fell out at every crossroads; a corporal from the Washington Artillery, lost in the woods since the stampede of the previous night,
encountered whole squads of cavalry coming back along the Bent Creek
Road to surrender, brandishing white kerchiefs on the ramrods of their
carbines. Those who did continue on to Lynchburg overtook the survivors
of Lindsay Walker's artillery train: at Concord Depot Fitz and Henry Lee
met their cousin, Bob, the commanding general's youngest son. By the
hundreds, unattached gunners wandered instinctively with their fellows.
Some of the batteries still moved along intact, if sorely reduced by desertion and captures, but Walker's column continued to disintegrate as
demoralized cavalrymen passed and told them that Lee was going to surrender—or already had. Some of the crewmen and cavalrymen took this
as their cue to turn for home, including at least one battalion commander,
but others refused to believe it or doubted that Lee's surrender meant
the end of their struggle. One officer rode ahead to impress replacement
mounts for the troops and teams from farms along the way, and before
dusk of April 9 a skeleton contingent of Richard Anderson's corps artillery
marched over the James River and into Lynchburg, dragging twenty-eight

guns and a handful of caissons. Their valorous exertions went for nothing, for the commander at Lynchburg knew the end had come and he ordered the battalions all disbanded. The habit of depriving the enemy of arms and matériel persisted, so before they departed the batterymen destroyed all their gun carriages.[44]

Hundreds of other Confederates who could point to no technical exemption from the truce or the surrender agreement decided to take to their heels, as well. Though the white flags called for all troops to remain where they were when the firing stopped, men who foresaw military prison overlooked the lapse of honor in their flight. Nor were enlisted men the sole violators. Lieutenant Colonel David Gregg McIntosh, commander of a battalion of artillery under E. P. Alexander, left his men to their fate and simply rode away cross-country with Brigadier General Martin Gary of the cavalry, hiding in the woods until evening before venturing out on the roads. General Longstreet's adjutant, Osmun Latrobe, escaped with these officers, but along the way someone convinced him that slipping away under a flag of truce would be considered dishonorable: Latrobe returned to Longstreet's headquarters by evening.

John Paris, chaplain of the 54th North Carolina in Gordon's corps, had overheard other officers discussing a plan to "take to the bushes," and he thought that might be the course for a loyal Confederate. He discussed it with the captain who commanded his brigade, though, and concluded that duty called for him to stick with his men and accept the consequences. Even Fitz Lee, who had consulted with the commanding general beforehand about getting away with the cavalry, worried that he may have compromised his uncle's honor.[45]

It was perhaps partly to discourage their men from slipping off that various generals took to the stump that evening to apprise them of the generous terms Grant had offered, but the greater part of the speeches sought to relieve those soldiers of the last ditch from any blame for the army's demise. That, at least, was the sentiment that most men remembered and recorded, both in Gordon's camps overlooking the Appomattox and in Longstreet's bivouac on the Flood farm.

Already preparing a postwar brief in defense of a nation and an army crushed only by overwhelming numbers, the future senator and governor John B. Gordon formed his diminutive divisions in a hollow square and told them that they had faced a mighty host of 50,000 Yankees with only 8,000 infantry, 2,000 cavalry, and "no" artillery—forgetting the five dozen guns and the overabundance of crews that the two infantry corps had shared. Some in his audience expressed surprise that they had been so few, for Gordon had neglected to mention some 12,000 more infantrymen who had stood by without weapons, or in armed disorganization, while their 8,000 comrades carried the battle.

One of Gordon's division commanders—big, burly James Walker—did not forget those who had failed to participate in the final fight just beyond the village.

"This morning," a Norfolk artilleryman heard Walker bellow, "I led into battle seven hundred good and true men. This afternoon, my muster rolls showed me fifteen hundred. Where were you all when the stern voice of battle pointed out to every man his place and post of honor?" In his frustration Walker belabored the suspect 800 mercilessly, though they had borne the same miseries as their comrades until the brink of defeat.[46]

Back on the Flood farm, the men of Mahone's division listened to more personal and positive remarks from lesser commanders. Field officers in Mahone's old brigade, in particular, exchanged affectionate farewells with the Mississippians under Nathaniel Harris. Expecting that they would part on the morrow, the veterans gathered under a pale moon that rose early and nearly full to hear an assortment of regimental commanders and General Harris compliment their fellow Confederates on their fortitude and gallantry. Unlike the fuming General Walker, Harris included everyone within earshot when he reminded them that they all could take home with them the satisfaction of having fought to the bitter end.[47]

Nothing better illustrated that bitter end than the free passage of Federal soldiers through the middle of the Army of Northern Virginia. Pickets prevented random mingling between the armies that night—the imagined sharing of haversacks notwithstanding—but Sheridan's cavalry was supposed to march away in the morning and his supply train still lagged behind the Sixth Corps, near New Store. Special arrangements allowed it to come down the stage road through the Confederate camps, and a Michigan quartermaster considered himself lucky to draw the assignment of leading that train, since it afforded him an opportunity to see the entire captive army. Some of the enemy scowled at him as he invaded their last refuge, but on his way out to find the wagons he passed the Confederate provost guard and hundreds of Union prisoners, many of whom had been captured just that morning. It was still light enough for them to detect the red neckerchief that identified him as one of Custer's staff, and they greeted him with a startling shout. By the time he came back through with Sheridan's supplies, those prisoners had all been turned over to Federal authorities, who marched them off to the depot on their way to a parole camp.[48]

Left behind with the Fifth Corps and his own Twenty-fourth Corps to

monitor the surrender process, General John Gibbon directed his orderlies to establish his headquarters tent in Wilmer McLean's yard that evening. His staff members ensconced themselves within the courthouse en-
closure. Their baggage wagons arrived near dark, and for the first time in
almost a week they slept beneath tents.[49]

The rations Grant had promised had to come only from the depot,
where they sat in boxes wearing the brand of the Confederate States government, but they did not reach Appomattox Court House that night.
Most Confederates, including probably General Lee, went to sleep hungry, but so did the victors: the pace of the retreat and the miserable roads
had left nearly everyone's commissary wagons far behind. Yet the lack of
food occupied the soldiers of neither army very much.

"We have no rations," recorded a Maine diarist whose tent stood just
down the hill from Lewis Isbell's house, "but fee[l] thankful and happy."

If those encamped north of the village dwelt upon their growling stomachs, few of them even mentioned it. As these men hunched about campfires or rolled themselves in ragged blankets, their reflections turned to
lost comrades, the uncertainty of the future, and the task of accepting the
end of all they had struggled for. Gazing at his division's rifles stacked un-
guarded in a field, a young North Carolinian became one of the first on
his side of the picket line to understand that the events of that spring day
had tolled the death of the Confederacy.

As though replacing romance with reality on the strength of that reflection, clouds soon moved in to cover the moon and darken the camps.
Before midnight a cold rain began to soak the sleeping thousands.[50]

THE PARADE

Rain fell through the night, drenching tents and any who slept without them. Morning met a lowering sky, and periodic cloudbursts emptied upon the helpless multitude throughout the day. Waking sodden, cold, and hungry, soldiers cast about for fuel to warm themselves and dry what was, for most on the Confederate side, the only set of clothing left to them. Gunners from a Norfolk battery found dry wood in the walls of an old and presumably unoccupied log cabin near their camp, and during the course of the day the entire cabin went into their fire, one log at a time. Even that proved insufficient, and some dry fence rails followed the cabin before the day ended.[1]

Early on the morning after the surrender Sheridan's cavalry departed Appomattox, where his horses could obtain no forage: the noisy brigades splashed into the village, around the courthouse, and veered south between the Peers house and Jones's vacant law office. From Pleasant Retreat to the Appomattox, all the ambulances, wagons, artillery pieces, caissons, and mounted troops left in the Army of Northern Virginia pulled onto the muddy stage road and started for Clover Hill, where the overseers of the surrender intended to collect them before the unfed teams starved to death. The artillerymen sought new camps near their doomed guns, from the ravine cut by Rocky Run to Sweeney's orchard. The army's ambulances all creaked up near the village, where that night Yankee drivers would take them away and leave the sick to find shelter under the trees.[2]

Most of those who had surrendered expected now to obtain their paroles after abandoning their weapons. William Mahone's entire division and at least part of Field's division marched from their camps and stacked their arms in a nearby field that morning, turning back with the expectation that they had met their half of the agreement. Mahone added a touch of formality to the exercise, offering another speech along the lines of Gordon's.[3]

It was on this day that the waking citizens of Richmond and Washington learned of the surrender. The news came into Washington by telegraph at 9:00 P.M. on April 9, but the hour did not stop artillery officers in the forts around the capital from firing thunderous salutes as the news reached them, as late as 4:30 A.M.

"Washington is ablaze with excitement," wrote one soldier to a mother who would never have to read that her son had been killed in battle. "From this epoch dates the downfall of the rebellion. It utterly destroys the last vestige of resistance to the authority of the government."[4]

Such sentiments might have seemed premature, since other Confederate armies survived in North Carolina, the Deep South, and the Trans-Mississippi, but this soldier seemed to recognize what civilians in the North, and many in the South, did not: that Robert E. Lee and the Army of Northern Virginia had come to symbolize all Southern resistance. Those other armies had all suffered significant and repeated defeats, while Lee had won impressive victories and, until a week previously, had held his ground against the encroaching enemy. Through a trying winter that saw the Army of Tennessee essentially destroyed and its patchwork replacement driven across two states, Lee had maintained his lines before Petersburg and Richmond, his troops serving both literally and figuratively as the bodyguard for the Confederate government. Now Richmond was gone, Lee's army was gone, and, so far as most Union soldiers thought, so was the Confederacy.

"The war is now over," one soldier wrote his brother this April 10, while a captain who described the surrender to his father a few days later added, "of course, this ends the war." Even many of those last and most loyal Confederates seemed to agree, like the North Carolinian meditating upon the stacked arms the night before.

"The opinion seems to prevail that the war is ended," admitted one second lieutenant—the senior remaining officer in Stapleton Crutchfield's artillery brigade—"but I can't think so. There is life in the old land yet." A chaplain who asked his diary if the Confederacy were ruined seemed to answer his own question, although he shared the young lieutenant's hopeful doubt.[5]

Union soldiers who managed a visit with or across the picket line found a sense of relief, if not glee, among their former combatants.

"The most of the Rebs seem to be glad that Lee has surrendered," wrote a Maine sergeant, and after strolling amid their encampment a captain from his regiment judged that for a majority of the Confederates "the surrender is more welcomed than regretted." A Pennsylvania chaplain in the Fifth Corps wrote on April 13 that "most of the prisoners seemed about as well pleased as our own men though some of them looked rather sullen." A young colonel from Rhode Island who spoke with a number of Lee's men found the same spirit, as did a soldier who saw large numbers of homeward-bound Confederates in the days after the surrender.[6]

For all those appraisals, some of those in grey remained loyal to the Lost Cause and defiant even in defeat. One Virginia chaplain heard taunts cast across the picket line and so far forgot his role as to join in the shouting. A Pennsylvanian who chatted with Confederates at their own campfires on April 12 found many of them bitter: the officers stood firmest in their resolve, he observed, and some denied that the struggle was over yet.[7]

For another month and more there would be those who refused to recognize defeat: as late as May 16 an Alabama Confederate who had just received his parole wrote of his autumn plans "if" the war ended. Confederate Virginia's commonwealth secretary, George Munford of Lynchburg, stood among the last who counseled further resistance. On April 28 he proposed moving his entire family to Texas, since Virginia seemed utterly conquered, and one month after the surrender he lamented the apparent acceptance of his fellow Virginians.

"The people seem to have become like Spaniels," he complained, "willing to lick the hand that smites them." [8]

Recalcitrant as Munford appeared in his letters, he conceded that nearly everyone else he encountered appeared ready to submit to federal authority. Most of the senior officers of Lee's army exhibited that same determination to Union officers whose business brought them into their lines, especially in light of General Grant's generous surrender terms. Grant's patron in the U.S. Congress, Elihu Washburne, rode out to see his most famous constituent's handiwork right after the surrender, and he interviewed a number of Southern generals in their camps. He came away extremely optimistic of the prospects for reunion.[9]

General Grant sought to further those prospects on the morning of April 10. With several staff officers he left his camp a mile west of the courthouse, traversed the previous day's battlefield, and rode through the village toward Lee's picket line. When the guard posted on the bank of the North Branch brought him up short, Grant explained that he wished to speak with General Lee again. A messenger splashed across the ford and after a little delay Lee came riding down the hill from his headquarters.

The two commanders talked at some length, and Grant introduced the idea that Lee could hasten peace if he were to advise the rest of the Confederate forces to lay down their arms. That argument recalled Lee's own offer of April 8, which Grant had declined, but this time it was Lee who objected, on the grounds that he would first have to consult with President Davis. Grant did not press the issue, and their conversation drifted to other details of the surrender, such as the status of the hundreds of Union prisoners Lee had handed over and the printing of parole certificates for the departing Confederates. Their discussion lasted about half an hour, and as it broke up several men on Grant's staff obtained Lee's permission to venture over the river and visit some of their Old Army friends among his generals.[10]

April 10 saw much visiting between the two armies, at least among the officers. To avoid unpleasant encounters Lee had posted guards to prohibit promiscuous wandering, and he asked Grant to do the same. The resulting pickets proved so strict that soldiers in either camp wondered whether their roles had not been reversed: a man in the 17th Maine, back near New Hope Church, complained that he felt like a prisoner himself, while one of Cadmus Wilcox's North Carolinians remarked that the utter absence of Yankees made it hard to believe that it was his army that had been captured. The Fifth Corps seemed to be the weak spot in the cordon, for it was there that the first wanderers were detected on the evening of April 9; corps headquarters immediately prohibited the traffic, and those orders had to be repeated to Fifth Corps division commanders on the morning of April 10. At first only general officers were permitted to pass, but after the meeting between Grant and Lee a few staff officers were allowed to accompany each general.[11]

At about 10:30 A.M. General Meade decided to ride through the Confederate camp to visit General Grant, or so he told his aide, Theodore Lyman. Meade took his son and Colonel Lyman down the stage road, finding the opposing lines of pickets at the Flood estate standing their posts casually and chatting amiably with their nominal enemies. Lyman rode ahead for a guide and found none other than General Field, who rode back and brought the others on himself. Meade remarked that it was a pity the former combatants could not circulate more casually, to which Field replied that it was the temper of the Confederates that threatened to bring trouble, at least while they could still reach their rifles.

They passed long stacks of rifles and battle flags standing in Joel Flood's sodden fields, and Lyman noticed that no cooking utensils hovered over the campfires of this disorganized encampment, for the promised rations had not yet been delivered. Meade opted to stop in and visit his old friend, Robert E. Lee—or, as Field told the story, Meade had come specifically to visit Lee, rather than Grant. When they arrived at Lee's headquarters the general was out, but as the trio of Federals returned to the stage road they met him, just riding back from his interview with Grant: he was wearing a plain blue overcoat and a tall grey hat to ward off the rain. Meade pulled off his cap in greeting, but Lee did not recognize him until Meade introduced himself.

"But what are you doing with all that grey in your beard?" asked Lee.

"You have to answer for most of it," replied Meade, with uncharacteristic humor.

The party shook hands all around, and the two generals retired under the tent fly while the staff officers stood around the headquarters fire in the rain. Hinting at the exhaustion that had crippled the command system as well as the individual troops, Charles Marshall confided to Meade's aide that he had gone three full days and nights without sleep during the retreat, and that at one point he had caught himself talking absolute nonsense.

As the blue and grey uniforms circled about Lee's fire, their caped shoulders hunched against the raw, damp air, there strode toward them a soldier whose face had been deeply carved by sixty decades. His white hair was swept straight back, he wore a pair of silver spectacles on the bridge of a thin nose, and instead of an overcoat he had wrapped old grey blankets about himself like a Mexican bandit. This unlikely creature proved to be Brigadier General Henry Wise, formerly governor of Virginia and commander of a brigade that had included many soldiers from the county in which he then stood. Wise and General Meade had married sisters in ancient times, and Meade had asked to see him. Before their visit ended Longstreet came to pay his respects, as well, and when the Union officers returned to their own lines Meade sent his son back to Wise's camp with an ambulance to go home in and an abundance of provisions.

Perhaps Meade never intended to see Grant that day; if he did, he may have learned from Lee that Grant expected to leave Appomattox forthwith. Possibly he rode on to the village and found that Grant had already left. Colonel Lyman, who recorded their journey in his diary, suggested that they proceeded to Appomattox Court House.[12]

The village saw more business during that week than it ever had, or ever would again. Fireplaces at the Clover Hill Tavern blazed to cut the chill of that drizzly April 10 as Confederate generals filled Wilson Hix's chairs: a Union colonel found Longstreet, Gordon, Pickett, Henry Heth, and several other brigade and division commanders filling the tavern late that morning. Longstreet, Gordon, and General Pendleton adjourned across the road to meet their Union counterparts on a commission charged with refining the details of the surrender: despite its roaring fires the tavern had proven too spartan, so John Gibbon, the senior Union officer on that commission, had reserved the parlor in McLean's house. Grant had also stopped at McLean's to take care of some paperwork before starting back to City Point and Washington. Longstreet, a close friend of Grant's in the old days, saw him there as he made his way to the meeting: the commission's business waited while the two passed a pleasant hour over cigars.[13]

When they set to work, the six commissioners quickly determined that the Confederate troops would stack their arms and equipment in a designated spot, turn over all horses not claimed as private property, and march for home under the command of their officers. In a final paragraph they excluded from the surrender terms any cavalry that escaped before the capitulation, thus legitimizing the flight of Fitz Lee, Rosser, and Munford. Later they added a stipulation that authorized each paroled prisoner a parole certificate identifying him as one of those eligible for the terms of Lee's surrender, including the right not to be disturbed by federal authorities. That would delay things a bit while the blank certificates were printed, but it would protect Lee's soldiers from being arrested when they encountered Union troops on their way home.[14]

Even before the six generals had signed the articles, Confederate cavalry glided up the slope to the intersection of the stage road and the Prince Edward Court House Road to begin laying down their sabers and outdated carbines. A brigade of Union cavalry stood by to guard the captured arms until Grant's ordnance chief could pick them up and transport them to Burkeville. When they had disarmed themselves, these cavalrymen — mostly from Munford's division, but with a few hundred of Rooney Lee's men and those who had refused to follow Rosser — rode back into the valley of the Appomattox to await the first printed parole blanks.[15]

By late morning food was finally rolling into Appomattox Court House from the depot. Union and Confederate soldiers alike drew one day's rations for the first time in two or three days, and caffeine-deprived Confederates beamed when they discovered that the provisions, which had come from their own captured supplies at the station, included coffee and sugar. Campfires blazed anew, and hot food improved the general mood in the cold, damp bivouac of both armies.[16]

Before he left Appomattox Court House, around noon that day, Grant ordered most of the Army of the Potomac to follow him. He directed the

Second and Sixth Corps to turn back for Petersburg in the morning, while he instructed Gibbon to finish up the surrender proceedings and march to Lynchburg with the Twenty-fourth Corps and part of the cavalry. The Fifth Corps would remain behind with Gibbon, for the present, and all would endure the rain and cold together at the end of a long, uncertain supply line.[17]

Charles Marshall, Lee's secretary, spent part of April 10 composing a farewell address to the army for his general. As Marshall recalled it years later, Lee had to shut him up in an ambulance, with a guard outside, to give him enough leisure to write six compound sentences that reflected the general's regard for his men. Lee edited the pencil copy, striking a sentence that seemed to encourage more sectional animosity, and when Marshall had transcribed a final draft he gave it to a clerk to begin copying. That clerk, a teenager named Norman Bell, detailed from the Norfolk Light Artillery, started scratching off copies for all the corps and division commanders.[18]

The artillery train moved again in the afternoon, inching closer to the courthouse. The rest of that day the weather bound the forlorn Confederates to their tents, if they were fortunate enough to have any. Many did not, especially among the artillerymen whose battery wagons had been captured or burned, and after an entire day of raw, intermittent rain some of them grew desperate. Alongside their parked pieces a few gunners from Norfolk—comrades of the clerk, Bell—found a small but suitable house that seemed to have been abandoned by its owners. Their refuge may have been the old Sweeney home, just up the hill from the ford; the family that grew up there had all either died or married into other nearby households. The gun crew would have taken the place for themselves, but Rooney Lee and his staff had appropriated it for their own use ahead of them, so the Norfolk boys crawled underneath.[19]

Darkness inspired a little more fireworks in the Union camps. Some of the artillery in the rearmost divisions fired a few salutes, now that Grant was not around to put a stop to it; the captive Confederates could faintly hear the discharges echoing beneath the rainclouds. Batteries nearer to Appomattox Court House thought enough of their prisoners' feelings to refrain from so boisterous a demonstration, but some ingenious infantrymen improvised a more subtle and pretty display by loading their muskets with light charges and firing Confederate artillery fuses into the air. The Fifth Corps artillery chief observed that the fuses burned through the air like Roman candles.

"The effect together with the camp fires was really beautiful," he thought. It was the only celestial beauty any in Lee's army saw that night, though, as they rolled themselves in wet blankets to sleep on the cold ground.[20]

As the evening grew later, some of the officers and enlisted staff of Bryan Grimes's division noticed that General Lee remained awake beneath the tent fly that served as his last headquarters. With some temerity (for Lee was a man of moods and occasional temper) they approached within easy earshot to offer a moonlight serenade—though lacking most of the light of the full moon, which lay behind thick clouds. The mixed chorus ranged from private soldiers to at least one brigadier general, and a few North Carolina bandsmen accompanied them. No record of their choral program survives, but with the expectations that their army would disperse on the morrow they could only have indulged in sentimental, nostalgic melodies: perhaps "Lorena," or "Aura Lea." Patriotic tunes like "The Bonnie Blue Flag" and "The Southern Soldier Boy" would have seemed too ironic on the eve of a surrender ceremony, and on such a night no one could have borne the sadness of "The Vacant Chair." The band concluded with an instrumental called "Parting is Pain." When the last note of that mournful air drifted away Lee emerged, as was the custom, to thank his entertainers. Those in attendance recalled the general showing what, for him, would have been deep emotion; well he might, to see so poignant a display of his troops' affection on this, his last night as their commander. For one Alabama private who stood among the singers, shaking the hand of Robert E. Lee provided a memory he could carry into old age, to sweeten this entire dismal episode. For the rest, the hillside soiree seemed to bring to a moving conclusion the great adventure of their youth, which in its turn had ended all that they had known before.[21]

It may have been his last report to Jefferson Davis that kept Lee up late again that night, and he continued it in the morning. Everyone supposed that the surrender would be concluded on Tuesday, but collecting the captured property took longer than anyone supposed. The first bundles of parole certificates arrived, and the commanders of the fragmented cavalry regiments signed them for those who had not bolted toward Lynchburg. Rooney Lee's entire division needed only 298 certificates for officers and men, and the colonel left in charge of Rosser's eight Virginia regiments signed 137 paroles, including his own. In all, the division that Tom Munford had led away eventually surrendered 1,108 men of all ranks, leaving perhaps a thousand of J. E. B. Stuart's once-invincible beau sabreurs who actually got away. The cavalrymen all left on Tuesday, nearly all of them riding out on their own horses (or horses they claimed to be their own) under a light, steady rain.[22]

Heavy fog hung over the North Branch that morning, shrouding the mile-long array of artillery that now hugged the side of the stage road from the slope east of the village to the hill by the Conner house.[23] The camps of Gordon's infantry filled the fields on either side, and at the top of the hill across from the Conner farm Lee's orderlies struck the headquarters tents. The headquarters flag came down for good, and some of the staff took souvenirs from it; nineteen-year-old Norman Bell stashed one of the stars in his coat pocket. Lee and his staff finished their last meal at Appomattox while an escort of Massachusetts cavalrymen waited to see him safely on his way to Richmond, but a crowd of visiting generals delayed his departure, submitting their final campaign reports and seeking a few last words. One headquarters wagon stood by with their tents, bedding, and mess equipment, while Bell sat holding the reins of a single ambulance. At last they mounted, rode down to the stage road, and turned north, toward Rose Bower, Buckingham Court House, and home.[24]

Next it was the artillery's turn to surrender. The men took their paroles and departed in small groups, many of them unharnessing horses from the teams, but most of the guns remained where they were alongside the road. With no small arms to surrender, the paroled artillerymen could hardly march before the enemy and lay down their weapons, so they simply wandered away. E. P. Alexander lined up thirty-nine guns and ten caissons, representing all the artillery left to Longstreet's corps, including a few surviving guns of the defunct Third Corps. Armistead Long amassed only twenty-two guns and three caissons from the Second Corps and what remained of Anderson's Fourth Corps. John Turner's division of the Twenty-fourth Corps accepted this dilapidated arsenal, but the ordnance details spent most of the day trying to remove them in mud that only grew deeper with each passing hour of rain. From other locations outside Lee's final perimeter — mostly on the roads to Lynchburg — Union officers collected twenty-two more cannon. A few miles away, at Red Oak Baptist Church, soldiers from the Twenty-fourth Corps unearthed thirty-two additional gun tubes that had been dismounted and buried, as though in graves, by Lindsay Walker's harried artillery train.[25]

General Gibbon's quartermasters had to clear the roads of 640 wagons and ambulances, as well, and about 2,000 rawboned horses and mules that went with them; that was all that remained of some 1,400 vehicles that had fled Richmond and Petersburg with the army. The Yankees loaned back to various Confederate generals 73 wagons, 31 ambulances, and a few pack mules to take themselves and their baggage home, but that still left them with a five-mile train drawn by staggering teams for which no feed could be found but grass. Ulysses Grant, who was known for his great love of and sympathy for horses, thought about the starving animals as he made his way east; from Burke's Station he instructed Gibbon to send the artillery and as many small arms as he could by rail, and to burn the caissons, leaving the wagons for local citizens to pick up for their own use.[26]

It was not only the livestock that lacked sustenance: soldiers on both sides were turning surly with increasing hunger. Most had endured short rations for days before the surrender, and none had been supplied to either army until April 10. That delivery had consisted of only a single day's allotment of beef, hardtack, coffee, and sugar, with some units missing out on part of the distribution. James Eldred Phillips, a lieutenant in Mahone's 12th Virginia, conceded on April 11 that his men had grown "very hungry" in their camp on the Flood plantation. Phillips encountered Francis and Mariah Meeks, whom he seemed to have known previously; he noted that they lived on the farm where he surrendered, in apparent reference to the Flood property. The couple may have occupied a house half a mile south of Pleasant Retreat that was owned by Joel Flood, and near the bivouac of Mahone's division; in his conversation with them Phillips evidently alluded to the empty haversacks in his company. A sergeant in the same regiment ate his last piece of hardtack that Tuesday, complaining that he was "getting hungrier and hungrier." An officer in their brigade had nothing to eat but a few shreds of beef that day, while a North Carolinian nearby had not been given any bread or hardtack since his last Confederate ration of April 8. In a region that subsisted so enthusiastically on pork, ham, and bacon, the beef would not have been all that satisfying even in abundance, and no Southerner mentioned any abundance of food that day.[27]

On the other side, hungry Yankees took matters into their own hands. A Maine soldier whose regiment moved into the village Tuesday afternoon watched five of his companions return from foraging in the neighborhood with supplies of ham, cornmeal, and molasses; on another foray they restocked their supply of cornmeal and molasses, adding some wheat flour as well. He failed to mention whether these field delicacies had been purloined or paid for, though it would have been uncharacteristic for prowling Federals to leave money for anything they took from Virginia families.[28]

Union cavalry bore the worst reputation for such thievery, but Grant's soldiers, horse and foot, had enjoyed profitable foraging throughout this campaign, and while they showed unusual respect for their surrendered counterparts they reserved little for the civilian population. A Massachusetts surgeon observed that his regiment's foragers had "real fun" the entire way, bringing all manner of choice fowl and additional provisions back to camp. Unoccupied homes were stripped of anything edible, according to the good doctor, and a man in his regiment corroborated the claim.[29] This region of Virginia had been unmolested during the war; except for a few fleeting moments on June 13 last, Appomattox County had not felt the boot of an armed Union soldier until the preceding Saturday, so the smokehouses and chicken yards remained full when the first troops arrived.

"Our marches in the last few days we travelled over a country where never before any Union troops in arms ever marched," wrote a Pennsylvanian who had come by way of New Store, "and we got a good bit of smoked pork and other eatables."

"I had some Splendid Short cakes," admitted a Fifth Corps soldier who camped near Plain Run. "[T]he people Still said they had nothing to live on in the South[.] if You hear any person say so tell them that it is a damn lie[,] because every house we come to had plenty of everything[.] they use a power of corn meal[,] but I tell you after we passed through there was mighty little left unless they hid it[,] which a great many did." [30]

With the village suddenly surrounded by ten times the population of the entire county, and miserable roads hampering the army's supply trains, private larders were bound to run empty quickly. When Sheridan's cavalry and the Fifth Corps rolled back on his farm to find campsites, Willis Inge watched blue uniforms stalk into his barn and lead away five steers, a heifer, seventeen sheep, and fifteen hogs, as well as taking numerous chickens and turkeys, corn, and cured bacon, all right before the eyes of three Union generals. The Yankees also appropriated three horses and some seasoned lumber, Inge claimed, besides burning several miles of oak fence rails in their campfires; he estimated his total loss at nearly $2,000 in U.S. currency.

William Trent lost a similar amount of stores and livestock, with the addition of a mule. York Wright, a half-emancipated slave belonging to John Sears who worked in his owner's blacksmith shop on the edge of the village, insisted that it must have been Union soldiers who spirited away his small personal supply of flour, bacon, and chickens. Louisa Morgan, who later testified that she lived near Clover Hill, filed a substantial claim against the U.S. government for the theft or confiscation of every variety of agricultural product, from vinegar, salt, and tobacco, to hogs, hens, and horses. Farms around the village lost heavily, but people who lived near the railroad stations suffered nearly as badly at the hands of the cavalry, who showed no mercy to Southern womanhood. Mary Dickerson, a widow living near Evergreen Station, had lost both her sons in the first year and a half of the war; she calculated that Union soldiers deprived her of more than a quarter of a ton of bacon, large quantities of corn and molasses, and all of her horses, oats, and fodder, to the tune of almost a thousand dollars. Federals relieved her neighbor Samuel Baldwin of horses, cattle, and small amounts of bacon and meal. Frances M. Dickerson, another widow in that vicinity, also lost valuable livestock and supplies to the passing blue columns. None of these civilians ever realized any compensation for the plundered property, and although most of them probably exaggerated their claims the losses doubtless left many of them pinched for months to come.[31]

Most of the citizens gave willingly and generously to the Confederates, although the sheer volume of destitute men either cleaned out the charitable or curbed their hospitality. Lieutenant Phillips, for instance, had to go without food for two entire days before Mrs. Meeks gave him some bread and meat. Phillips was among the last Confederates to leave Appomattox, and when he started homeward in the wake of thousands who had enjoyed the largess of the inhabitants he could not find a mouthful to eat.[32]

Scanty provisions militated against much more delay in distributing the paroles and getting both vanquished and victors away from Appomattox. General Gibbon wished to start the Twenty-fourth Corps on the road to Lynchburg, so he ordered a Fifth Corps division into the village to relieve Turner's troops, who were collecting Confederate property. Charles Griffin, commander of the Fifth Corps, chose his first division, under Joseph Bartlett, and early in the afternoon Bartlett's three brigades marched into the road near the courthouse. Later they formed ranks in the drizzle and waited, they supposed, for the rest of the Confederate army to come through and lay down their arms before them, but the Southrons seemed not to be following the same program.[33]

Longstreet's divisions had stacked their rifles and flags in Captain Flood's fields as early as the morning of April 10, hours before the surrender commission had even concluded its agreement, and they felt that they had thereby earned their paroles. At about 6:00 P.M. on April 11 the remaining infantry, under Gordon, marched out of its camps 6,000 strong, turned into another of those ubiquitous fields, and straightened their lines. General Gordon rode out in front of them and gave the last stalwarts of his corps the requisite speech, full of compliments, encouragement, and sentimentality; then they stacked what arms and flags were left to them and faced toward the road, marching back to the camps while a band—perhaps the same one that had serenaded Lee—blared away at "Dixie." Bartlett's expectant division saw nothing of this; neither, apparently, did anyone in the Union army. Congressman Elihu Washburne, who had arrived that day from Prospect Station, was about the only U.S. official to witness the scene. His presence was only accidental, for he had been visiting former members of Congress and the senior generals among the Confederates.[34]

Over in the village, the Union generals were not amused. They may have gotten the news from the Honorable Mr. Washburne, who lodged that night with General Gibbon in the McLean dooryard. Bartlett's division marched back to its camp on the slope south of the courthouse. Gibbon sent word into the Confederate camp that this was not going to do at all, and the four remaining members of the surrender commission appear to have reconvened. The Union officers, Gibbon and Griffin, insisted on a formal parade of the Confederate infantry between opposing ranks of U.S. forces as a symbolic submission to federal authority. Longstreet and Gordon objected that this sort of humiliation was not required by their previous agreement, which bore no reference to the presence of Union troops at the laying down of arms. Gossip that must have filtered down from General Griffin suggested that Gordon fought harder than Longstreet to avoid the ceremony, but then Longstreet intended to miss the event and Gordon was going to have to lead the prisoners' march. In the end they could only comply, for Gibbon held the rest of the parole certificates, but the Confederates went away with the satisfaction that at least they would not be subjected to the indignity of literally grounding their rifles; they could stack them as though for bivouac, and simply march away.[35]

With that the commissioners adjourned forever, and more bundles of parole slips passed into the Confederates camps.[36] The fraternal atmosphere returned, and perhaps to protect that spirit the generals put their disagreement out of their minds for all time, leaving those who found the evidence of it to wonder what it had all been about.

The American Civil War offered the material for a million myths and legends, and the conclusion of hostilities provided more than any other passage in the conflict. Some of the most attractive (and consequently more enduring) of those final fables originated with the most compelling raconteur among the victors. In the dim, distant light of old age, Joshua Chamberlain would remember that he had commanded the troops that accepted the formal surrender of Lee's army. He would also recall having been especially chosen for that honor, and by none other than Ulysses

Grant himself. General Chamberlain proved as magnificent a soldier as he was a literary stylist, but while he was courageous and coolheaded he also tended to wrap life's little dramas in ribbons of romantic imagery in which he, himself, was somehow entwined. A passage from a letter to his sister written from Appomattox Court House offers a taste of how the young brigadier saw himself.

"I have had the advance every day there was any fighting—have been in five battles—two of them being under my own direction and brilliantly successful—twice wounded myself—my horse shot—in the front line when the flag of truce came through from Lee—had the last shot & the last man killed, in this campaign; & yesterday was designated to receive the surrender of the arms of Lee's Army of Northern Virginia." [37] Chamberlain conceded that this recitation seemed like boasting, and it did. This letter marked the first time he claimed to have commanded the Union side of the surrender parade, and over the next four decades he so convinced himself of the truth of it that early in the next century he declared it publicly. By then the people who would have known better were all dead, and Chamberlain went to his grave with his beloved recollection unchallenged, but his posthumous memoir revealed that the eloquent professor-turned-soldier had employed his own imagination to elevate his place in the proceedings.

As Chamberlain told the tale, after being personally selected to command the troops that would receive the surrender, he was apprised of the details of his duties: he dated those instructions from the night of April 9, in one version, and April 10, in another. The day after the ceremony he informed his sister that he had received the surrender with his brigade, distinctly implying that that brigade had been the only Union organization present. In the account that appeared after his death he admitted that the other two brigades of Joseph Bartlett's division were there, as well, but he maintained that he had asked the corps commander's permission to borrow them, so they could share in the honor. That gave him the entire division.

"I thought this troubled General Bartlett a little," wrote Chamberlain around 1913, two decades after Bartlett's death, "but he was a manly and soldierly man and made no comment. He contented himself by mounting his whole staff and with the division flag riding around our lines and conversing as he found opportunity with the Confederate officers." If Bartlett, his entire division, his staff, and his division flag were on the scene, then it was Bartlett who commanded the troops; if he made no comment, it was because his position had not been usurped. Chamberlain occupied a subordinate role, commanding the longest section of the line. His brigade filed into place along the northernmost portion of the road, and he took position on the extreme right of his line, where he would be the first to greet the Confederates when they came.[38]

In darkness Bartlett spread his division along both sides of more than a quarter mile of the stage road, from Chamberlain, down the slope north of George Peers's house, to Wilmer McLean's fenced yard. The horizon had barely begun to grey with the shrouded sun of April 12 when his fourteen regiments dressed ranks, dropped the butts of their rifles between their feet, and waited once more for the men across the river. In their camps from the Sweeneys' orchard to Pleasant Retreat nearly 20,000 Southern soldiers rolled out of blankets still soaked from incessant rains. Cold and grimy, they stumbled into formations, marched to the fields they had visited the evening before, and retrieved their rifles and colors from the stacks. If no man recovered his own weapon it mattered not at all: the Yankees would never know the difference.[39]

The sun had begun to brighten the clouds over the LeGrand Road when the head of the Army of Northern Virginia appeared in the stage road. Leading the march was the Second Corps, commanded by General Gordon, whom one of Griffin's staff officers recognized as the principal opponent of this ceremony.

"They realize, I hope, that they are really surrendering to us," that officer remarked to himself.[40]

John B. Gordon could use the language of his ancestors to the same dramatic effect that Joshua Chamberlain could, and between the two of them they composed a touching picture of their meeting that day. Each told it in flattering terms of the other, and neither mentioned that Gordon had been forced to do this all over again. In their reconstructed version of events Gordon rode at the front of his troops, his head drooping in dejection and embarrassment, and Chamberlain brought him out of it in an instant by bugling his men to attention and bringing their weapons to a shoulder. Chamberlain said that he intended to offer the motion as a gesture of respect, and Gordon said that this was how he perceived it, wheeling his horse to return a sweeping salute with the tip of his sword. In their remembered mimodrama they celebrated the welcome reunion of separated brethren, and set the tone for a divided nation.[41]

It may even have happened that way, but Gordon made no mention of it until he saw Chamberlain's published account, nearly four decades later. Chamberlain left most of the romantic details out of the story until then, although neither he nor Gordon were men to leave romantic details lying idle for so long. On the day after the surrender, Chamberlain wrote home simply that his brigade received the Confederates "with the honors due to troops, at a shoulder & in silence. They came to a shoulder on passing my flag & preserved perfect order." Order may have been as much on the general's mind as honor, for he specifically noted that his superiors wished no scenes to humiliate the defeated army. Bringing the troops to "shoulder arms," at attention with the rifle tucked against the right side of the body, was the common means of bringing silence to the ranks; had Chamberlain intended a formal salute, he would have ordered his men to present arms, with their rifles held before them.[42]

The first mud-caked division climbed the last rise, made its way toward the courthouse, and stopped. Field and company officers barked orders, and the column of fours spun to the left, facing the blue cordon that stood before the late Crawford Jones's law office, the broad lawn of Squire Isbell's house, and the McLean house. With much rattling and clanking they fixed what bayonets they had and stacked their rifles together like shiny shocks of corn, draping their cartridge boxes over the rusty bayonets. Against these interlocked muskets mournful color-bearers leaned their tattered banners — and in some cases the bare flagpoles. Dozens of units had lost, divided, or hidden their flags, and some regiments surrendered barely enough rifles to arm a platoon. This time there were no speeches; the disarmed division stepped back into place, faced right again, and marched away.[43]

Some who had already received their paroles headed homeward from there, dropping out to continue down the stage road, but most of the column turned back to the camps across the river while Union quartermasters collected the stacked weapons and colors. When the road was clear, the next division marched up to perform its prescribed part. No one on either side appears to have kept a record of the order in which the divisions came, but a chaplain in the 54th North Carolina mentioned that the order of march had been established by brigade and division: Confederates did not number their brigades and divisions, but the order of battle in the Second Corps always listed the divisions commanded by Grimes, James Walker, and Clement Evans first, second, and third. Henry Wise's brigade appears to have been among the earliest — presumably still attached (with the rest of Bushrod Johnson's troops) to Grimes's division. A heavy artillery officer who now marched as an infantryman with Wise noted that he started to the courthouse "soon after sunrise." The old Stonewall Division, with barely 1,200 survivors under General Walker, stepped off precisely at sunrise but did not reach the surrender ground until 8:30 A.M. Evans probably came last of the three, for a Virginian in his division who started for home right from the ceremony did not make Prospect Station until dark.[44]

Longstreet's corps followed, but without Longstreet. Field's 5,000 filled the road, delivered their arms, and marched the three miles back to Pleasant Retreat to wait for paroles. By contrast, George Pickett's entire division—the red-bannered horde that had swarmed toward Cemetery Ridge with a good many doomed Appomattox men—left only fifty-three muskets in the road.[45]

Not all of those in the Confederate camp marched to the courthouse. Hundreds dropped their muskets where they were, or threw them into the woods. The colonel of the 38th Virginia, of Pickett's division, could count barely ninety officers and men in his regiment that morning; a few of them may have carried some of the fifty-three muskets, but he appears not to have bothered making the trip to the village to see that they were turned over. The sick remained in camp, awaiting ambulances borrowed back from their enemies. A few hundred straggling artillerymen needed only their paroles to begin their homeward journeys. Instead of following the Second Corps across the river, two Virginia battalions of the provost guard reported at 7:45 A.M. to the quarters of their own commander, where they stacked arms, collected their paroles, and started for home.[46]

As the generals brought their commands into the village they relinquished control to subordinate officers, and several of those generals gravitated toward the McLean house. Congressman Washburne stood there, watching the proceedings, and some of them joined him. Gordon, E. P. Alexander, and Cadmus Wilcox met on McLean's piazza with plans of riding out of town together. Washburne said he saw the Union commander, General Gibbon, hand Wilcox a $50 greenback to take him home; Wilcox and Gibbon were both natives of North Carolina and had attended West Point in classes only a year apart. Washburne also saw Henry Wise, still looking extremely bedraggled in an old grey overcoat.[47]

The troops that had belonged to the Third Corps marched in last, and Mahone's division appears to have come in at the tail of the entire army.[48] Next to Field's, this was the biggest division Lee had had on hand for the last ditch—more than 3,000 strong. These were the men who had thrown back four Federal divisions at the battle of the Crater, a little over eight months before, and had punished the Union Second Corps only five days since, saving their army for another forty hours. When they set aside their arms it would all be over: the Army of Northern Virginia would exist no longer, and the Confederacy would spin a short, tight spiral into eternity.

Perhaps as Mahone's veterans pulled the belts of their cartridge boxes over their heads they felt the sadness that accompanies extinction. Wandering off disarmed into an uncertain future, they could not realize that the army they dissolved that day would continue to live so long as any one of them survived to say that he had fought with Lee. Among the still-stout ranks of William Forney's Alabama brigade there stood a lad hardly seventeen years old who would outlast all who had marched across the Appomattox with him: in an age when jet aircraft soared overhead he would be the last man walking who had taken part in this day's events, in blue or grey; he would be the last Confederate soldier on earth, and only when he crossed over to join his comrades would this army die.[49]

Indistinguishable now from the many thousands who had passed before Bartlett's division over more than six hours, this fated private turned back for the Flood plantation with his fellows. They strode back down the hill past silent spectators from Michigan, Maine, and Massachusetts, splashing across the North Branch and up the opposite slope, past the now-uprooted tree under which Lee had waited for the end, past the little house where Joel Sweeney had strung his first banjo, past the spot where General Alexander had placed them in their last line, and then they passed out of sight of the double blue line near the village. If any of those tired sentries turned to watch this dolorous procession winding through the thinning camps on the hillside, especially the veterans among them, they may have had the thought that occurred to George Meade's aide when he and his chief encountered the same scene, two days before. Leaving Lee's headquarters after their visit, Theodore Lyman had felt a touch of anguish as his horse ambled through what he called "the sad remnants of an army that has its place in history."

"It would have looked a mighty host," Lyman wrote of the scene a few days later, "if all its soldiers that now sleep between Gettysburg and Lynchburg could have stood there in the lines, beside the living."[50]

THE TRIAL

Congressman Washburne had ridden only six miles from Appomattox Court House when he encountered Major General Fitzhugh Lee on the Prince Edward Court House Road, returning from his intended escape to share the fate of his uncle's army. The younger General Lee's troopers had trailed away by the dozens as he made his way to Lynchburg, leaving him in the end an escort of five staff officers; at least this was the report he made to his uncle, while telling the Yankees that he had dispersed his men upon hearing official news of the surrender. He soon concluded that he could achieve nothing by his flight save to embarrass his uncle and compromise the good will engendered by Grant's magnanimous terms. He turned back to Farmville, chasing after Grant's army one last time and overtaking General Meade in that town on the night of April 11. Meade directed him back to Appomattox Court House. The risk of trouble only increased as Lee turned into the wake of the departing army, running into groups of Union stragglers and an occasional ominous band of armed, self-emancipated slaves, but he reached Clover Hill safely a few hours after the last Confederate division had lain down its arms.[1]

In the ten miles between Walker's Church and the county seat Lee's party had ridden against a thickening stream of disarmed infantrymen in grey, working their way homeward to Petersburg, the Carolinas, or the Deep South. They would have passed generals Gordon, Wilcox, Alexander, and a few more wearing the wreathed stars on their collars. Thousands of other veterans, Richmond-bound, headed north from the village toward Buckingham Court House, back along the churned morass of the road to New Store, or out the Oakville and Bent Creek Roads, to the James River or the western counties; one man from across the Alleghenies encountered several neighbors of a different persuasion among the West Virginia regiments of the Twenty-fourth Corps. They clung together instinctively those first few miles, with the decimated commands dividing at every intersection until the once-mighty army had disintegrated into the same scattered fragments and individuals who had originally come together under the colors to give it birth. Some few, Tennesseans or Virginians of the uppermost Shenandoah Valley, took the road to Lynchburg or Campbell Court House. Having parted from Robert E. Lee for the last time, General Longstreet aimed for the latter place on the first leg of an ill-fated odyssey to Texas.[2]

Not all of the Confederates got away on the day of the surrender. Unfinished parole lists kept thousands overnight, and most of them went to bed hungry. Except for those who had managed to beg something from inhabitants like Mrs. Meeks, the surrendered soldiers had gone without food since the single day's ration of Monday, and to worsen their misery another heavy rain began pelting their blankets at dawn on Thursday. All but a few of the remaining Southerners took to the roads in that morning torrent. Those whose path did not lead them through the camp of the Union army found no food at all until they reached the next populated settlement, and even there they fared poorly.

The Yankee commissaries west of Farmville had little to give, either: the Fifth Corps troops that had overseen the surrender drew no food the next day save some fresh beef from local barnyards, and one company invited brigade-level discipline when it set up a chant for hardtack.[3] A Virginia sergeant who left at the break of day bought or begged some cornmeal at a mill crowded with soldiers, but it was not until he reached Pamplin Station that afternoon that he encountered anyone willing to turn it into dough and bake it for him. That accommodating cook came in the shape of a young and exceptionally personable woman who smote the dejected sergeant immediately.

"She made me feel that the world had not really come to an end," wrote the sergeant that evening.[4]

Directed to scour the abandoned Confederate camp for arms and equipment that had not been turned in, General Chamberlain sent over his original regiment, the 20th Maine, along with the 1st Maine Sharpshooters. These gleaners found nearly 500 rifles abandoned between the North Branch and Pleasant Retreat, as well as a brass fieldpiece, a score of artillery caissons, and dozens of serviceable wagons.[5]

This additional property represented only what the soldiers had dropped where they camped, rather than offer it in formal surrender. More diligent dissenters may have taken their rifles far enough into the woods that they were never found by Union soldiers. Still others carried their weapons all the way out of Appomattox County, on the hopeful and desperate journey to join Joe Johnston's army in North Carolina.

Two Georgia brothers who bolted away at news of the surrender took the most roundabout rout to Johnston, trudging north on April 9 past House Speaker Thomas Bocock's plantation on their way to the James River. Crossing into Amherst County on the ferry the next day, they stopped at a humble, isolated cabin occupied by a woman who had not heard of the surrender. When they told her of it she screamed her thanks to the heavens, which perplexed the loyal pair. They expressed dismay at her happiness, but she replied that their news only meant that her husband would be coming home. Perhaps a bit more discouraged, the two continued on their way to another army hovering on the verge of surrender.[6]

A few of Lee's soldiers loitered at Appomattox Court House, where some remained for eternity. Ivy Ritchie, a sergeant in the 14th North Carolina, had been killed when Bryan Grimes sent his infantry toward the little battery by the Oakville Road at dawn that fateful Sunday. Comrades had buried him hastily, but the regimental chaplain went back to Longstreet's camps to find the victim's brother, who did a better job of it.[7]

Captain Miles C. Macon, of the Fayette Artillery, had also fallen in the final battle, apparently amid such confusion that the survivors of his battery had abandoned him. It was left to young Edward Hix and some of his neighbors to bury the body.[8]

One of that handful of men who had advanced with the 26th Virginia that morning had been brought back with a wound that would kill him during the night. Seven Virginia cavalrymen had been killed in the fight for the Oakville Road, and two Marylanders in Munford's last clash near Mrs. Robertson's house. Nearly two dozen dead Confederates lay in shallow graves between the village and the station, and citizens opened their homes to some of the wounded.[9]

Then there were the sick. Any army of that day traveled with a significant percentage of men too ill to fight, or in some cases to march, and when the Union army offered to lend back enough captured ambulances to transport Lee's sick there were still a few too weak or feverish to travel. Out near New Hope Church, Drury Woodson took in one soldier when the army dispersed: the man suffered from typhoid fever, which eventually settled in his lungs to bring on pneumonia. Their afflicted guest was a Quaker from central North Carolina, conscripted into the army against his pacifistic principles. He lingered for more than eight weeks before he died, nursed by Woodson's daughter, Elvira. Miss Woodson, without her usual occupation as a schoolteacher, also tended to a Montgomery County boy who had served through the entire war only to endure the summer of 1865 in his final illness.[10] These two and other scattered victims were lowered into temporary graves near where they died.

Miss Woodson was not the only unemployed Appomattox schoolteacher that spring. Chapman Chilton, the schoolmaster at Union Academy, closed up that little institution in the uncertainty following the surrender. On the first of April he had added eight new students to his tuition list, making a total of twenty-two scholars who had signed up since the session began on February 27. Mr. Chilton evidently considered the government dissolved, and the term therefore ended, with Lee's surrender. He abandoned the academy, he said, to "various occupants such as Rats & Mice, Squirrels & Owls." He did not bring his ferule down to open another session for eleven months.[11]

By the time the Fifth Corps marched away from the courthouse, early in the afternoon of April 15, few in the ranks or looking on seemed to dispute that the Southern rebellion had come to an end. That belief spread quickly from Appomattox: when Joseph Johnston and General Sherman agreed to a truce, half of Johnston's cavalry suspected imminent surrender and fled for home; in South Carolina citizens assumed that the capture of Lee's army doomed Johnston's, too, and commenced their mourning for the Lost Cause. That acceptance of defeat left the question of government. Many in the South hoped that their own state governments would be allowed to reconvene, or that new legislatures might be promptly elected. Since the federal government had maintained all along that secession was unconstitutional, and that the slave states had never really left the union, logic would also have dictated that those states deserved representation in Congress. The spirit of conciliation that prevailed at the McLean house, both during the conference of April 9 and the ceremony of April 12, seemed to portend a relatively painless reunion, and when Elihu Washburne reached Richmond he telegraphed President Lincoln his promising observations among Confederate generals. Knowing the bitter spirit harbored by Radical Republicans in Congress, he specifically cautioned the president against calling an extra session of that body.

Washburne's telegram clicked off the Richmond transmitter at noon of April 15. Even as he composed the message Lincoln lay dead at the hands of John Wilkes Booth.[12]

The news of Lincoln's assassination reached Richmond by wire on the afternoon of April 15. Union generals who received the telegram opted not to release the information, to avoid either triggering a riot of Union troops or signaling any Confederate rising that might have been planned to coincide with that disruption of the federal government. The story leaked out the next day, when a personal friend of Lincoln's vented his outrage in the presence of some Confederate officers in the Richmond provost marshal's office. By evening the story was being circulated throughout the city, and soon it was spreading all over Virginia.[13] Instantaneously the spirit of the Union victors turned bitter and vengeful.

"A few days ago," one brigadier wrote his wife the evening of April 15, "I was counseling moderation, conciliation, and magnanimity toward the Rebels both in and out of the army. I now feel like a demon. I feel a remorse within my heart, that I ever treated a Rebel magnanimously." This man, who had marched away from Appomattox well satisfied with defeating the Confederate army, now took an oath to "wage war against the southern slaveholding population."

An enlisted man at Burkeville who had still only heard rumors of the murder by April 18 spun himself into a frenzy over it.

"I say that we ought to Hang every Damn Rebel in the Southern Confederacy," this man told his parents. "I go in for killing every one and Burn every traitor up North by a stake. I think instead of taken Gen Lese Army Prisoners it would have bin better to have hoisted A Black flag and Butchered every one."

Even conservative Union soldiers expressed deep regret over the assassination. Though less emotional than the president's more devoted followers, they feared that it would impede the process of reunification.

"What a loss to the country is Lincoln," wrote a New York captain. "The South has lost its friend in power & in his place has got one of its most bitter enemies. I have been no advocate of A. L. while living but since our late successes he has shown a true Christian charity & kindness of disposition to the people of the South." [14]

Astute Southerners shared that sympathizer's view. A general with Sherman's army observed that "the better class" of North Carolinians denounced the assassination, supposing Andrew Johnson would be more rigid and demanding with the conquered provinces than Lincoln would have been. Writing the same day as that Union general, a Virginian just out of the cavalry had already detected a tightening of the reins that had gone so slack after the surrender.

"They were getting very liberal," that veteran cautioned his wife, whom he hoped Union authorities would allow to join him, "but Old Abe's death puts an end to it all." [15]

Soon enough Southerners would see what they believed to be the vindictive side of their conquerors, but that sentiment failed to take root among the occupation forces for all of the universal grief over Lincoln's death. By the time Appomattox Court House heard of the assassination, there were no occupation troops to wreak vengeance, for the division that had been sent to Lynchburg returned on April 16 and the next morning John Gibbon started his entire corps on the road back to Farmville. On the day he left, Gibbon reported all quiet at Lynchburg and at the scene of the surrender, where mired wagons, equipment, and stray horses and mules cluttered the landscape. He took with him only the captured guns and wagons for which he had adequate teams; his chief quartermaster authorized Sheriff William Hix to distribute the balance to "deserving destitute inhabitants of the vicinity."

Sheriff Hix's father had survived for decades as a local politician and backwoods entrepreneur, while his uncle had been Speaker of the House for the Confederate Congress: the young sheriff had grown wise in the combined paths of economic and political success. Perhaps he could not resist the sudden influence this authority gave him: draft animals in particular had grown especially scarce in the wake of Confederate impressment, and anyone found with horses or mules with the C.S. brand would have to surrender them if they did not hold authorization from Hix. Within days he began gathering not only strays but animals that local farmers had appropriated, turning them over to the wealthier planters rather than the "deserving destitute": among those he accommodated was John M. Harris, a seventy-year-old farmer who had owned forty-six slaves before the war. When small farmers banded together to protect their random booty, Hix deputized about a score of former soldiers, armed them, and wrested those animals back by force; one man who interfered with the recovery of a horse was reportedly shot by Hix's henchmen. With no Union troops anywhere in the region, the sheriff and his posse generally prevailed in such disputes, growing bold enough to even range into Amherst and Campbell Counties to collect reported livestock.[16]

The back roads Lee had followed from Farmville to Appomattox offered a treasure in salvageable material in the days following his army's passage, and the departing Federals left nearly as much bounty themselves. One planter whose land they camped upon found "great numbers of wagons & gear, spades, picks, shovels, . . . trace chains & a great many useful things, besides many broken down horses and mules." In the waning days of April the livestock all disappeared into barns and pastures, along with all the serviceable tools, wagons, and equipment. Enough useless wreckage remained in the wake of the last scavengers that a horseman passing from Buckingham County to Lynchburg on April 29 was still able to describe "one eternal scene of desolation & destruction" along thirteen miles of his route, "on both sides of the road as far as the eye could reach." Wagon hulks, charred and chopped cannon carriages, and enough artillery ammunition "for two great battles" littered the ditches and adjoining fields, where most of it would remain until it had rotted and rusted back into the earth. The decaying carcasses of no fewer than 500 horses and mules raised a stench so powerful that it seemed to repel even the buzzards. Those animals that had survived the march—and those that had not, before they collapsed—had eaten every blade of grass in sight, while the soldiers of both armies had burned every fence rail for miles to warm themselves through the raw days and nights of their sojourn. The traveler found that the armies had left a wasteland in their wake.

"What they will do for [a] living is past my comprehension," he said of the Appomattox farmers.[17]

The question of subsistence hung all the more worrisome with the shortage of available labor. Aside from the normal attrition, at least 115 Appomattox soldiers had perished over the past four years, and dozens more had been permanently disabled by wounds, but the real problem arose from the uncertain status of the black half of the county's population. The slave trade persisted on a reduced scale even after Lee's surrender: in late April or early May Thomas Bocock bought sixteen women and children from Thomas H. Flood for the bargain price of less than two dozen bushels of corn and seventy-four bushels of wheat, but Flood appears to have been shedding himself of slaves who offered no useful services; Bocock may have accepted them as an act of charity, and a near neighbor of his soon took five of them in. Male slaves, meanwhile, had abandoned their work if not their plantations. They considered themselves independent of their former masters from the moment the Union army first arrived, and once they learned of the military edict declaring them free they refused to work for anything less than "liberal compensation." That did not bode well for the upcoming harvest, for even those planters who had been as well off as the Floods and Bococks could fall back on no more wealth now than the crops growing in their fields.[18]

A desire to monitor relations between Southerners and their former slaves appears to have prompted the War Department to send troops back up the ravaged line of the Southside Railroad. Some few recalcitrant Confederates avoided capture in the interior, and lingering platoons of former soldiers reportedly roved the hinterlands, subsisting through random robbery, but it was more the social order than law and order that motivated this latest march into the mountains. In the last hours before the March adjournment, Congress had passed an act "to establish a bureau for the relief of freedmen and refugees," and now the new president decided to bring that bureau to life under the control of the War Department. On May 11, while the rest of what had been Phil Sheridan's cavalry marched northward for Washington, one brigade turned back for the Virginia Piedmont under Colonel Samuel M. B. Young. The next day the secretary of war named a commissioner for his new bureau and issued the orders that commissioner would need to operate effectively.

On May 13 Colonel Young's four regiments arrived in Appomattox, where a detachment arrested Sheriff Hix and seventeen of his posse, disarming and dispersing them; the main body continued on toward Lynchburg, where Young established his post. Lynchburg—which one agency official could still call "such a Rebel town" twenty months later—became the district headquarters for the Bureau of Refugees, Freedmen, and Abandoned Lands.[19]

Alluding to Sheriff Hix's depredations, among other problems, Young cautioned his superiors that there was "trouble brewing" in Appomattox, Amherst, and Campbell Counties. He dispatched one squadron to Amherst Court House and an entire regiment to Appomattox Court House. Within a few days those troops seem to have restored order, and most of them gravitated back to Lynchburg, but on May 20 Young received orders to send one captain, two lieutenants, and twenty-five men to each of the counties under his jurisdiction. Those orders included instructions to provide each of the detachments with only five days' rations, but they established a federal police force that would last for months.

That force soon caused a few problems itself. Less than a week later Young issued a general order threatening summary execution, without arrest or trial, to any soldier caught plundering or inciting freedmen to do so. Enlisted men would have to turn in their sidearms while off duty, and could not travel more than a mile from their camps without Young's own permission. He explained that so harsh an order was necessary "on account of the many depredations committed by some unprincipled and low lived men belonging to this command."[20]

Colonel Young sent one additional detachment of the 21st Pennsylvania Cavalry into the northern quadrant of Appomattox County to suppress marauders black and white. That patrol scoured the district during the last two weeks of May, making friends with the population and driving away any outlaws who may have preyed upon the inhabitants. One afternoon the captain in charge of the troop stopped at Eldon as he started up the Bent Creek Road, where Joel Flood and Ella offered him lunch and entertained him. The swarthy Captain Flood gave his Keystone counterpart a sketch of his family history, which purportedly ran straight back to Pocahontas, while Ella concluded the visit with a turn at the piano, accompanying her own rendition of classical airs in both French and Italian. Her fluency impressed the young cavalryman, whom she astounded with the revelation that she could speak five languages. He noted that the young couple had two children already; he might have expressed even more surprise had he been able to foretell that both of those children would someday stand on the fringes of national renown.[21]

Captain Flood appears to have welcomed his former enemy with genuine hospitality, expecting that all had been forgiven and that the blue uniform now represented a restoration of civil order and the protection of his considerable property. Soon after this luncheon the young squire found cause to question that assessment. On May 29 President Johnson issued his amnesty proclamation for former Confederates, restoring all their property rights save that in human chattel, but he specifically excepted fourteen categories of penitent insurgents, from erstwhile diplomats, governors, and generals to high-seas raiders and those guilty of mistreating prisoners of war. The clause that ensnared Joel Flood and most of the men in his family and social circle was the thirteenth, which excluded former Confederates with taxable property of more than $20,000. That provision not only jeopardized those patricians' ownership in their lands but encouraged those who wished to confiscate the vast plantations for distribution as homesteads among the freedmen. The new chief of the Freedmen's Bureau in Virginia, Orlando Brown, proved an especially enthusiastic advocate of that policy: his efforts that spring infected freed slaves with the belief that they would soon live upon their own land, which cast the planter class into deep gloom.

The pall hung even darker for the most famous resident of Appomattox County when a grand jury at Norfolk began indicting higher officials of the Confederacy.

"There is little left to us now, but honor," Thomas Bocock informed his sister-in-law that June. "Confiscation, Imprisonment all stare me in the face; and I trust very little to the clemency of our conquerors. They are bitter, intolerant, and exacting." The former Speaker of the House dared not even leave his plantation for fear of arrest, and he stood ready to abandon his birthplace and all he owned to escape to some foreign country.[22]

Foreign flight seemed preferable to quite a few Southerners, whether they had been excluded from the amnesty or not. Some cabinet officials took to the sea, and one governor considered it. A Virginia officer sailed for Venezuela, where he attempted to establish a colony of expatriate Southerners on the upper Amazon, and one enduring community of ex-Confederates did take root in Brazil. E. P. Alexander, the artillerist with the connection to Wilmer McLean, made a valiant effort for a commission in the Brazilian army. As late as August, when a Northern observer made his way to Appomattox Court House from Lynchburg, he encountered a paroled soldier who would have migrated to Brazil but for a lack of funds.[23]

The vast majority of Southerners, even among those excluded from amnesty, never considered leaving their homeland despite the social and economic uncertainties. President Johnson's proclamation offered the possibility of individual pardons for the excepted classes, and wealthy landowners applied for such clemency in droves, easily swallowing an oath of allegiance to the U.S. government in return for their property. Joel Flood and his father were among the first to ask for such a pardon. Henry Flood asserted that he had been too old and disabled for service in the Confederate army, and had never performed any; his son admitted to his year of limited duty early in the war but claimed that he had had no further military connection, omitting his brief appointment to General Kemper's staff. Both their petitions were granted within days, and their success inspired relatives like Henry Bocock and John Flood to submit their own requests. Undoubtedly to avoid drawing attention to himself, Thomas Bocock made no application for the present, but for most of his neighbors the first great threat to their way of life disappeared that summer.[24]

The next challenge to the plantation economy came with a military decree that established official freedom for the former slaves on whose labor it had been based. On June 16 the commander of the new Department of Virginia composed such an order, carrying Lincoln's most famous proclamation into effect at last. Like Thomas Bocock, those farmers whose former slaves remained with them suddenly faced reluctant workforces. Black men had already left their families in sufficient numbers statewide that the department commander sought to prohibit the trend in his original order, and the Lynchburg district chief cautioned the senior officer of the detachment against undertaking the care of women and children thus abandoned. Those who employed field hands had to either take in their families, too, or allow the men to travel between their homes and their work, and if any women and children were still set adrift without support the provost marshal was to house them in the poorhouse or any vacant dwelling he might find.[25]

The provost marshal at Appomattox held the responsibility of aiding the indigent and resolving labor troubles, but disputes over government mounts consumed much of his time. Sheriff Hix still came to his attention now and again: first he was accused of running twenty-five or thirty head down to North Carolina for resale, and then of authorizing a crony to take a mule from someone who had boarded it since the surrender. The leaves would fall three times after the armies left Appomattox before neighbors ceased to wrangle over livestock abandoned by Confederate and Union quartermasters. Archibald LeGrand and Dr. John McDearmon would spend the summer of 1866 arguing over a horse the doctor claimed on no better grounds than that he had no other, while LeGrand owned many. At about the same time, John Sears petitioned for the return of cattle he said had been left to him by Union general Samuel Crawford, who had made his headquarters at the Sears house. Sears had loaned several milk cows to neighbors, purportedly with the understanding that they would be returned on demand, and those neighbors refused to yield them; Wilson Hix declined to return one that had escaped into his pasture. Several freedmen complained, as late as thirty months after Lee's surrender, that their employers or other white men were keeping horses or mules they had salvaged from the starving herds. The local provost marshal tended to decide in favor of those who held possession of the animals, but cases brought before the Freedmen's Bureau usually concluded in favor of the poorer party. With tacit jurisdiction over abandoned property, the bureau adjudicated a number of cases between white antagonists, apparently applying the same economic logic to them as to the cases involving freedmen. The persistence of these disputes evidently reflected William Hix's favoritism: summarizing a case that dragged on until late August of 1867, a bureau investigator blamed the former sheriff.

"Hix's management of the public property left in his hands," reported that officer, "has given general dissatisfaction except to his friends."[26]

The Union soldiers who stayed on to maintain order won broad praise from prominent citizens for their "gentlemanly and humane" deportment, as one Lynchburger described it. They protected private property, instituted a pass system for transient freedmen that echoed eerily of the antebellum code, and treated the white citizens with surprising courtesy. By June of 1865 that benevolent occupation had endeared the conquerors to many of the conquered, and earned what one of President Johnson's friends called a "most remarkable" acquiescence to federal authority. Johnson's observer noted that in the Southside counties, where slaves had been most prevalent, the planters asked only that the freedmen be compelled to honor their labor contracts.

Two different detachments of Pennsylvania cavalry served as the provost guard for Appomattox Court House until late July, when a company of the 188th Pennsylvania Infantry marched from the depot to relieve the mounted troops. These men settled in for a longer stay, pitching tents in the courthouse yard. If some of the citizens of Clover Hill still rankled at the notion of military occupation, many of them managed to overcome their political objections enough to accept these friendly Yankees, and a few even embraced them: within two years three of these soldiers would marry local girls.

One of those who would take a village girl as his bride was the commander of the company, Captain James Geiser. He may have boarded at the home of Martin Webb, a wealthy planter who lived a mile out the Prince Edward Court House Road, or he may have met Webb's oldest daughter, Nannie, when she came to Francis Meeks's store. One way or the other, though, the young captain grew attentive of her that summer: when a freedman initiated a complaint against his former master over a horse with a U.S. brand, Captain Geiser solved the matter by taking the horse from both of them and giving it to Nannie Webb.[27]

One of Geiser's first communications from Appomattox Court House consisted of a request for half a dozen horses. His duties sometimes required him to send men on a twenty-mile march, he explained, and it was impossible for them to collect such contraband as military armament on foot; he had learned that large numbers of "government arms" lay around the county, probably in the form of Confederate rifles discarded on the retreat. His regimental commander forwarded the request, but rather than wait for an answer to his appeal Geiser may have found it easier to simply appropriate branded government stock from the more crowded local barns, at least for his own use: within a couple of months his superiors in Lynchburg were asking about a horse that an Appomattox farmer claimed Geiser had taken from him, while Geiser was trying to draw forage for a private horse on his own account. The young captain had not sojourned long at Clover Hill before several of the less prominent citizens besieged him with complicated petitions about the disposal of cattle and horses.[28]

It was Geiser to whom the poor had to appeal for rations. The district superintendent of the Freedmen's Bureau at Lynchburg, Captain Robert Lacey, reported to his Richmond chief that most of the people who had applied for rations on the excuse of poverty were "cheats and swindlers," and he advised abandoning the practice. The new commander of the military district at Lynchburg ordered his subordinates to refuse rations after August 1, but as the assistant provost marshal, Geiser appears to have winked sympathetically at some charitable distribution. He composed one report for the week of August 12 in which he noted that the freedmen were shirking their work and mentioned that he had given food to six black and six white recipients—most of them children. He never filled in the date on that sheet, though, and submitted instead a copy reiterating that the freedmen were shirking but that there had been "some improvement since the destitute rations have been dispensed with." Then he added an addendum in which he denied having issued any food among the citizens, claiming that he had handed out his entire store of 1,000 rations prior to that date. Not until the middle of September would he admit to giving away more government provisions.[29]

Reluctant labor threatened to waste excellent crops that summer. Wheat failed, perhaps from the ceaseless spring torrents, but by mid-August the provost marshal described the corn crop as "the finest and most abundant that has been raised for many years," and he observed large tobacco transactions daily. He hinted, however, that all this might be jeopardized if the former slaves refused to go back into the fields.

"The freedmen do not yet understand their condition," that officer lamented. "Many of them are lazy and disposed to ignore the responsibility of taking care of their women and children." If the males among the county's black population could not fathom their status, the provost marshal seems to have contributed to the misunderstanding. Although Union troops bore the responsibility for enforcing the new principle of freedom, Captain Geiser felt justified in "punishing" some who defied his orders to go into the fields. Punishment in that era usually took the form of a flogging, which Geiser apparently applied to the ringleaders of a local labor action: he accused them not only of refusing to work themselves but of offering to kill others who hired themselves out. In some cases Geiser sent his troops to the plantations to drive laborers into the corn at the point of the bayonet.

Despite the common belief among Virginians that free blacks would never work, it may have been as much economic wile as laziness that kept the hands out of their former masters' fields. Captain Geiser soon detected that many of the freedmen in Appomattox County still believed the federal government would give them land of their own to work, and for that reason they preferred not to sign contracts that would oblige them to other landowners. Presidential policy was about to scuttle their expectations, but some of the would-be homesteaders seem to have reasoned out their options and may have even understood the concept of aiding their potential competitors in production. Smaller farmers could salvage their crops by supplementing their hired labor with their own, but the land-rich had to scramble for hands. Thomas Bocock employed the survivors of his own slave community and recruited his neighbors' former bondsmen, offering a bonus in the abundant corn for those who helped him save that first peacetime harvest. In neighboring Buckingham County, another planter hired some freedmen at wages, rented portions of his tract to some of his own former slaves, and farmed the rest of the acreage on shares.[30]

The crop had no sooner been gathered than a shortage of livestock impeded the next planting. That shortage worsened as Captain Lacey commandeered more of the government animals that farmers had taken in, creating additional friction between himself and the provost authorities. That friction, arising from the conflicting responsibilities of the two offices, had the potential to filter down to the garrison at Appomattox Court House, where Captain Geiser's company provided personnel for both provost duty and the Freedmen's Bureau. In July Geiser responded to orders from Lynchburg by appointing a sergeant and three orderlies to duty with the bureau at his headquarters. Either because Geiser's own duties left him too little time or because he seemed unsympathetic to the freedmen, Captain Lacey soon named Geiser's own lieutenant to the position of assistant superintendent of the bureau in Appomattox County. Lieutenant Henry Cogan assumed his duties in August; while the assignment left him technically independent of his captain, the two officers continued working together in apparent harmony while they each courted village girls.

For all of the difficulties with the harvest, Union authorities hailed a revival in the Piedmont economy within four months after the last Confederate flag was furled.[31] The only economic rejuvenation in Appomattox, aside from the corn crop and promising speculation on the tobacco harvest, came from the soldiers posted at the courthouse and a thin but constant tourist trade. After the surrender Appomattox Court House drew an assortment of artists who came to capture images of the hamlet where the great war had ended. One of the more obscure, Eustace Collett, is remembered only for a sketch he drew of the McLean house—along with the ramshackle Raine tavern—from the yard of the house across the road. George Frankenstein, a native German from a family of artists, made Appomattox one stop in a tour of Virginia battlefields. He stood his easel in front of the

{ THE TRIAL }

Raine stable, on the roadside near George Peers's house, atop the hill by the Conner farm, and before New Hope Church, finishing one or two oil scenes in each location; Frankenstein's brush offered what would become the last surviving glimpses of the Sweeney homestead or Pryor Wright's brick village home.

A celebrated photographer also visited Clover Hill in 1865. Timothy O'Sullivan, an employee of Alexander Gardner, had recorded some of the most famous vignettes of the conflict, including an arranged image of a dead Confederate rifleman behind a stone breastwork at Gettysburg. Choosing early afternoon sun on what appears to have been a Sunday, O'Sullivan made at least six plates: two of Wilmer McLean's house, three in front of the courthouse, and one before the Clover Hill Tavern. He stopped first at McLean's, erecting his tripod behind the old Raine tavern and posing the owner and his wife in chairs on the porch; their eight-year-old daughter Lula and Mrs. McLean's two older daughters sat on the top step, along with a fourth girl. O'Sullivan took another shot from the northwest corner of the yard as McLean's only son, Lula, and the other girl gathered on the porch; a servant stood behind them. In the three courthouse studies the Pennsylvania infantrymen lined up along the courthouse fence and up both sides of the stone steps: in two of them Captain Geiser posed on the second-story porch with his naked sword while George Peers elbowed in among his men, standing his two young sons on the fence for one view. Other residents, all in their Sunday best, wandered into the courthouse yard before the last snap of the shutter, including a tall young man still wearing the Confederate uniform. Mr. McLean walked over for one pose, tucking his hands in his pockets and exposing a broad vest. Peers, the rest of the civilians, and the mysterious Confederate all adjourned to the tavern yard for one more collective portrait, while Peers stood in front of them all with his four little children.

Notations on O'Sullivan's work at Appomattox imply that he arrived in late April, but evidence in the prints suggests he did not come until the second half of the summer. Because of the condition of the railroad he would have been hard-pressed to reach the courthouse by April 16, and if he had he would have found General Gibbon's staff officers milling about. For a month after that there would have been no troops at all in the village, and until late July the courthouse would have been surrounded only by cavalry. The thinned canopies of the black locusts in both photographs testify that O'Sullivan's subjects gathered before the camera no earlier than mid-August, when those trees begin to shed their leaves; possibly he waited as late as the fourth week of September, to avoid the bumpy wagon ride around High Bridge. Whenever he did visit, shadows reveal that a couple of hours passed while the artist repositioned his apparatus. By midafternoon he had put his equipment away and turned back for the depot, where he took one last exposure before heading east with the only photographs anyone would ever see of Clover Hill as an active village; the community's heyday would be but a memory before another outdoor photographer uncovered his lens there.[32]

As O'Sullivan's images demonstrated, the Confederate uniform had not disappeared from Appomattox County in spite of military edicts prohibiting it. John Dennett, a Harvard-educated journalist who toured the county in the middle of August, encountered the grey jacket and trousers so frequently in the country east of Lynchburg that to him it seemed "the universal male dress." He interviewed one limping resident in that outfit at a tavern, apparently near Concord Depot, during the lunch he ate just before riding to Appomattox Court House. This veteran offered an assortment of opinions for the attentive traveler, from the comforting belief that his fellows would never again fight for independence to the unsettling conviction that the freed slaves would never work without the incentive of physical punishment. His delivery increased in both velocity and volume, uncovering smoldering resentment toward the government he had failed to overthrow, and finally Dennett mounted his horse for Clover Hill, where he arrived at the New Englander's interpretation of evening.

This Northerner found the famous village tiny even by Virginia standards. Other than the courthouse and the old jail—which he noted stood "in ruins"—he estimated that the town could boast only twenty or thirty buildings. Those buildings included the cavernous old Raine stable, behind which those last Tarheel skirmishers had hidden, barely four months before: Wilson Hix had bought the barn from the Raine estate in 1864, after Charles Raine was killed, for the benefit of his dwindling tavern trade, and Dennett led his horse into one of the stalls of that silently historic structure. He put up at Hix's tavern, commenting on the intense heat, the single sheet that covered the bed, and the vermin that inhabited it. The next day he visited Mr. Meeks's store, remarking upon the paucity and antiquity of his merchandise, but he noted that the store and the tavern hosted a perpetual cavalcade of loungers chewing tobacco and drinking apple brandy by the glass, languidly monitoring the movements of the soldiers across the road. As much as they complained to him of indolent freedmen, Dennett observed that the white denizens of the region exhibited little inclination for industry themselves.

Villagers had plenty of leisure for conversation, though, and some of them squired the sojourner around the sacred sites. Dennett heard an early version of one of the more widespread surrender myths when a resident pointed into the valley of the North Branch and described Lee and Grant holding their initial meeting there: a gaping hole nearby marked the site of the apple tree that had been uprooted and minced into relics. Local tour guides had evidently begun to confuse Colonel Babcock's introduction to Lee with the April 10 meeting between Lee and Grant, and soon the world would hear an alternate history of Lee surrendering beneath that apple tree. Dennett's hosts knew that the actual articles were signed indoors, however, and for that scene they directed him back to Wilmer McLean's house.

McLean welcomed the visitor, showing him the sitting room that had been cleaned out by souvenir hunters and the one memento the owner had managed to retain: a stain that had seeped into the window seat and wall plaster when one of Grant's nervous secretaries spilled an inkwell. McLean entertained the itinerant correspondent with his favorite personal irony: having watched the shooting war begin on his own plantation and end in his parlor. He had told the story to General Alexander, to Congressman Washburne, and apparently to all the dignitaries who had trod his porch the previous April. It had become his claim to immortality, but now, as Southerners struggled for economic recovery and Northerners cultivated more pleasant recollections, most of the country strove to forget the conflict that had made his name known. John Dennett retrieved his horse from the echoing stable and started back for Lynchburg while Wilmer McLean retreated into his celebrated house and resumed the postscript of his days.[33]

The soldiers obviously waited for this immigrant witness to depart before going on a bit of a drunk. A paymaster finally visited them at the courthouse, and for all Captain Geiser's admonitions to the contrary the residents could not resist making a few dollars on their apple brandy. The soldiers' revelry could not have escaped the notice of the loitering provincials at the tavern and store, who would have related it to Dennett. Geiser smote village society a vigorous blow when he forbid further sale or trading of liquor.

The captain referred to the spree in his weekly report, but he insisted that the freedmen were giving him more trouble than his troops. Rather than signing contracts for a year's employment with individual planters, as the Freedmen's Bureau advised, Appomattox blacks refused to commit to anything beyond the current crop. Some still believed the big plantations would be divided among them, while others may have hesitated out of fear that their more militant neighbors might harm them. In the first week of September one family was driven from its farm: surviving documents do not specify whether that family was white or black, or who may have intimidated them. Ownership of a farm would ordinarily have suggested white victims, but the greatest hostility at that juncture seems to have been harbored by the resisting elements of the black population for their more compliant fellows. No casualties resulted from the crime, but neither could Captain Geiser seem to solve it.

Another incident that same week did entail bloodshed. Two or more soldiers—presumably from Geiser's company—initiated a bizarre assault on a forty-five-year-old man who lived a few miles from the courthouse. Wilson Franklin, a former overseer and a veteran of the war's early months, had lived for years with a woman of indeterminate race: roving officials alternately categorized her as white and black, and children of both races inhabited their home, all bearing the same last name. Perhaps the Union soldiers recoiled at Franklin's interracial mingling, but whatever the cause of their displeasure with him, they tied him up and directed a black man to flog him. Not yet satisfied, one of them then shot him. The provost marshal at Lynchburg instructed Geiser to arrest the assailants, but the investigation into this attack appears to have foundered as quickly as the last.

A fortnight later occurred yet another crime that must have chilled the tone of tavern gossip. Willis Bocock's overseer fell into argument with one of Bocock's former slaves over a debt for shoemaking, and the black man filled his antagonist full of lead, fleeing to Lynchburg as his victim breathed his last. A few days later the suspect was brought back and lodged in the Buckingham County jail (for the new Appomattox jail had not yet been completed) while newspaper editors handled the killing as if it were the natural result of emancipation.[34]

While the military authorities struggled to preserve order, Appomattox voters attempted to restore their civil government, electing a new slate of county officers who took their seats on September 5. George Peers was named court clerk again, and Lewis Isbell resumed the office of county attorney, but two newcomers became judge and sheriff; at the age of twenty-eight, William Hix retired to private life.[35]

Hix turned to a small business and agriculture, the region's two main occupations, risking some cash to stake a cottage industry while he began farming land belonging to his wife's family out near Walker's Church. His diversified investments represented the steady commercial growth that

Captain Geiser reported, regularly and monotonously, to the Lynchburg office every week. A new bureaucratic official, the internal revenue assessor, began scouring the county that summer for industrial manufacturers he could tax for their production—and for merchants, liquor dealers, auctioneers, and doctors he could assess for licenses. By autumn this official had reached Appomattox, where an assortment of residents paid him exorbitant taxes on various types of brandy they had produced. Samuel McDearmon, having returned to his modest peacetime post of station agent, paid a license fee to continue managing his hotel at the depot. As in days of old, a couple of the more comfortable residents paid two dollars a year for the privilege of owning a piano, but not everyone seems to have been held to account: Martin Webb paid the piano tax, while Ella Flood's instrument seems to have avoided detection. With tobacco production picking up, several Appomattox entrepreneurs entered into the manufacture of pipes, particularly in the vicinity of Pamplin Station, and the tax man started squeezing them for six cents a pipe. It was here that the former sheriff went into business with a Cub Creek farmer, William M. Hannah; the pair bankrolled some cottage pipemakers at Pamplin's, where Hannah owned a village lot.

A New York man moved into Lewis Isbell's house at Clover Hill the winter after the war, joining Martin Webb in a small pipe manufactory there. In Appomattox as in the rest of the South in the months after the war, some of the capital for new enterprise came from the bottom of carpetbags, but this district attracted fewer transient investors than many, and their ventures tended to be smaller. The tax assessor encountered a few businesses operated by men who had not lived within the county at the outset of the war, but most of those (like Lewis D. Jones, who bought New Store) had come from neighboring Virginia counties.[36]

Court day that September bore all the excitement of prewar days, for an extra session of the state legislature had ordained October 10 for congressional and General Assembly elections. Under intensely hot and humid conditions prospective officeholders stood before the crowd to press their qualifications, and the flavor of the debate had changed little in four years. The issues mostly ranged closer to home—preserving a source of labor and reestablishing the old regime under the guise of the new order, essentially. With Union officers standing nearby, the speakers may have modified their rhetoric against the impositions of the federal government, but the candidates reflected the sectional differences of the 1850s. Former Whigs like Benjamin Walker and newspaper publisher Charles Button stood respectively for the House of Delegates and the state senate against erstwhile secessionists, including William M. Hannah. One candidate for the senate dropped out when the military authorities hinted he would not be allowed to take the seat if he won it. Benjamin Walker withdrew from the delegate race for the same reason, and his opponent from Prince Edward County won without opposition. Hannah and Button finally contended alone in the senate race, each as champion of his anachronistic cause, and Hannah prevailed by a margin of three to one.[37]

Restoration of the civil court system notwithstanding, the Freedmen's Bureau attempted to maintain control of the criminal justice system. The Supreme Court had not yet ruled such interference unconstitutional, and as September waned a circular arrived from the Richmond headquarters authorizing the assistant superintendent to sit in judgment of criminal trials involving both races when the potential punishment would not exceed a $100 fine or three months' imprisonment. Instead of attorneys, each county would appoint "agents" to represent the black and white populations. Higher crimes would go to a military tribunal, in Lynchburg if the offense took place in Appomattox. Nearly three weeks passed before Superintendent Lacey reported that no agents had been appointed for whites because no one seemed willing to perform such a demanding duty without compensation. Eventually he found an acceptable candidate, though, naming George Peers to represent litigants of his own color. The bureau finally must have offered some payment, at least for the freedmen's agent, because Samuel McDearmon accepted the position: McDearmon left no evidence of ever having engaged in anything that did not bear the prospect of profit.[38]

The intercession of the Freedmen's Bureau in the justice system reflected the delicate dance that agency performed between protecting the rights of the former slaves and introducing them to the concept of self-support. Each week Captain Geiser submitted increasingly pessimistic reports about the deteriorating "condition" of the freedmen and the trouble they caused him by refusing to work or to sign contracts for the coming year. He began issuing rations to the poorest again, with the expectation that he would have to distribute more all the time, and now all the recipients were black. When Geiser left Appomattox in mid-October, Henry Cogan added his duties as assistant provost marshal to those of assistant superintendent of the Freedmen's Bureau, and he continued both the dismal reports and the destitute rations.[39]

Back in Richmond the bureau's state commissioner, Colonel Brown, responded to such problems by circulating a reprimand to the superintendents for not pressuring the freedmen into employment contracts, and for failing to inculcate a sense of family responsibility and industry. Brown followed his circular with an order requiring black males to undertake contracts with any planters who could use their labor. Superintendent Lacey in turn ordered Lieutenant Cogan out into Appomattox County's magisterial districts to take a census among the black families and to convince them that they would have to provide their own homes that winter, earlier bureau promises notwithstanding.

White citizens in Lynchburg came up with another plan for reducing poverty among the black population—by reducing the black population. The Lynchburg Emigration Society spent the summer and fall of 1865 persuading local freedmen that their best hope lay in returning to Africa. The colony of Liberia, on the west coast, had already been established as a haven for former American slaves, and on November 4 a ship sailed from Baltimore bound for Monrovia, Liberia, with 174 passengers from the Piedmont.[40]

The transportation of fewer than fifteen dozen people from several counties offered no effective relief for the social and economic plight of the black people living between the James River and Vaughn Creek. The natural winnowing of death removed more of them from Appomattox than the lure of Africa, for now that the war was over black mortality once again surpassed that of the white community. George Peers recorded sixty-five deaths under "colored" in the county register in 1865, and only forty-seven among white citizens, including a few who had been killed in the final battles. The actual disparity may have been greater: not all deaths appear to have found a place in that register (the name of so prominent a resident as Eliza Bolling Flood was never entered), and the demise of poor black inhabitants was even more likely to escape notice. Still, free black people perished in far lower proportion to the general population than they had as slaves. In 1860, with 119 recorded slave deaths, their mortality had exceeded that of the white residents by 108 percent.

If death held the county with a lighter grip, the birthrate had declined even more precipitously. The last child born in 1861 would theoretically have been conceived before any soldiers left their homes, and that year the county saw 351 children born on both sides of the color line; in 1865 there were only 107 births, and the next year only 141. Five years after the war, Appomattox families were still producing far fewer children than they had in 1861. For all the local citizens who had died in their prime between Bull Run and Five Forks, the slump in births could not be blamed on any scarcity of prospective parents, for romance seemed to flourish in the months after the surrender, and offers of matrimony soared. No records survive for marriages in 1863 or 1865, but during the other war years weddings dropped off from the antebellum average of about twenty-seven to as few as thirteen. In 1866 the court clerk issued 125 licenses, of which no fewer than 102 were signed and witnessed. Part of that surge was accounted for by the ability of black couples to marry for the first time, and readers of the *Lynchburg Virginian* delighted in the story of one man who paid the one-dollar fee for a license in the autumn of 1865 and then came back asking for a refund, explaining that his intended wife's "husband" had come home. Still, white couples sought 87 of those 125 licenses in 1866, more than doubling the greatest previous total. Postwar grooms were older than their 1860 counterparts by an average of about eighteen months, reflecting the war's attrition of the younger generation, but their brides were younger than those of 1860 by the same year and a half: apparently soldiers had spent their years away developing a greater appreciation for the peace and comfort of a family, while younger girls had been growing to womanhood for four years with virtually no proposals to consider, as much as doubling the field of eligible women.[41]

So greatly did marriageable women outnumber prospective husbands that three of the few dozen Yankees at Appomattox Court House managed to lure girls away from their families over the next few months. First they marched away from Appomattox Court House, though, rejoining their regiment after four largely pleasant months of occupation duty. The regiment turned back for Petersburg the next month, mustering out of service on December 14. Within a few weeks of receiving their discharges Lieutenant Cogan and one of his corporals returned to Clover Hill to claim their brides. The corporal acted quickly, marrying Ellen Bryant on January 21 and carrying her back to Pennsylvania, but Lieutenant Cogan lingered in the village, arranging his own appointment as postmaster of Appomattox Court House as though he intended to stay. Cogan was a carriage maker by trade, and he may have gone to work for William Rosser alongside Lawson Kelly, taking up some of the tools his brother Lorenzo had left behind. Somehow he sustained himself until August of 1866, when he married Wilson Hix's twenty-one-year-old daughter, Emma. By then Captain Geiser had come back, too, for Nannie Webb; they loitered in Appomattox long enough to have two children, and eventually Geiser found himself conscripted to hold county office.[42]

Traveling between Richmond or Petersburg and the mountains had grown easier since Mr. Dennett made his pilgrimage from the capital in July. Dennett found the journey complicated and inconvenient, involving three different trains and two shuttles by wheeled vehicles; he had had to trundle under the damaged High Bridge in a wagon, at a cost of one greenback for himself and his trunk, and his train had seldom surpassed the speed of a trotter even on flat ground. Union engineers had begun rebuilding High Bridge soon after Lee surrendered but had been called off the project almost immediately, so when Dennett crossed the broad valley of the Appomattox there he found the four burned spans still missing. The red earthen fort built by the 3rd Virginia Reserves yet guarded the eastern approach to the bridge, and the timbers of the wagon bridge, down below, still bore the charred evidence of Confederate incendiaries.

Just as Dennett reached Lynchburg, the military authorities in Richmond turned the Southside line back over to the owners of the company. With the incentive of ownership restored, the company assailed the interruption at High Bridge first, patching in great wooden sections of trestle and reopening the structure in just under two months. Although the decrepit ties and rails still slowed traffic to a crawl, that completed the line as far as the James River gorge, six miles short of Lynchburg. Steam packets ferried passengers up the James for that last leg until, late that fall, the company turned its attention to the bridge at Robertson's mill.[43]

Retreating Confederates had put this structure to the torch with much greater success than those who tried to burn High Bridge. Repairs proved risky because of the height of the bridge, but unemployed men from all over the countryside came to work for rare cash. William S. Hannah, the former second lieutenant of Captain Abbitt's company, played a part in the project, perhaps as both a workman and as a supplier of lumber from his family's mill. Early on the afternoon of December 7, as a score of men scrambled to brace the two newest spans, gusty winds started swaying those sections until they broke loose and plunged into the river, fifty feet below. The plummeting framework took everyone with it, and two men died instantly. The others were all seriously hurt, including Hannah, who suffered a nasty fracture. Two Lynchburg doctors came to tend the injured, and William Christian traveled all the way from his farm on the other side of Appomattox Court House to help them. In covering the tragedy the *Lynchburg Virginian* offered an early example of what would become the Southern tradition of giving former Confederate officers an honorary promotion of one grade, referring to the Appomattox millwright as Captain Hannah; for Hannah, the onetime second lieutenant, the newspaper implied a double promotion.

Their injuries cost the laborers any further wages, for the railroad simply hired more men and resumed construction within a few days. The bridge was finished in another seven weeks, and the first direct train from Petersburg in nearly ten months rolled into Lynchburg on January 29.[44]

The resumption of rail service insured economic recovery for the little businesses springing up at Pamplin and Nebraska Stations, but it did little to aid prosperity at Appomattox Court House or the big plantations in the northern corner of the county, where the James River canal had played such an important role. The Southside made it more convenient for tourists to reach the scene of Lee's surrender, but, as the first anniversary of the event approached, few people retained enough interest for such a journey except for those straggling artists. Most of the incidental visitors who did stop were those who still used the stage road, and they would have been passing through anyway. To the casual wayfarer, and to residents reviewing their account books, Clover Hill hung suspended in an increasingly distant past.

There were, in and around the village, those who would have been content to freeze their society in time while the government at Washington tried to force them into the future. The legislature likewise resisted change, attempting to revive the old regime through statute: Virginia joined other states of the Old South, for instance, in passing a vagrancy law aimed at forcing black laborers back onto the plantations. The law applied to any who lacked work or who refused it at "the usual and common wages given to other laborers." Not only must the former slaves work, therefore, but without the right to demand better pay. The alternative was jail, where they would work for nothing. Such coercion may have inspired the rush to complete employment contracts that the *Lynchburg Virginian* noted in December.

These measures merely enraged Northern reformers, who recognized such legislation as the resurrection of slavery under the guise of liberty. When Congress convened in December, Radical Republicans rebelled against President Johnson's lenient policies. They rejected the House and Senate representatives elected by the Southern states: in so doing they eliminated the greatest opposition to their own Reconstruction agenda, which began in February with an extension of the Freedmen's Bureau's authority and culminated in June with passage of the Fourteenth Amendment. This last act simultaneously made citizens of the former slaves and stripped former Confederate officials of the right to hold office again until two-thirds of Congress relented. These new congressional impositions inspired such reactionary rhetoric in Virginia that the military commander closed down one Richmond newspaper in mid-February.[45]

The first taste of the Freedmen's Bureau's additional powers came to Clover Hill in the form of a teacher. Charles W. McMahon arrived at Appomattox Court House with the intention of teaching illiterate blacks to read, and he met with trouble at the outset. With no troops in sight to discourage them, a group of Klan-like vigilantes calling themselves "regulators" targeted the teacher as a particular threat to the docility of local freedmen. A man who identified himself as captain of those regulators caught McMahon alone and warned him to leave the village before he found himself dangling from a tree; McMahon ignored him, and one night early in March of 1866 a mob descended on the schoolhouse and attempted to destroy it, causing considerable damage but leaving it standing. Captain Lacey offered protection from Lynchburg, but McMahon proved himself a cool customer and asked Lacey to keep his soldiers away lest they aggravate more of the community.

The officers who monitored McMahon's situation assured their superiors in Richmond that "the leading citizens have taken ground for him against the rabble."

"The law abiding citizens have quelled the rioters and no more trouble is anticipated," Captain Lacey reported to Colonel Brown, a few days after the incident. "I regard the whole affair as completely settled so long as troops are in Va.," he concluded, nearly a fortnight later. Lacey's correspondence suggests that the identity of the "ringleader" was known, although he was never named and apparently never arrested.[46]

While the army officers in Lynchburg understood that the "leading citizens" had rallied around the freedmen's teacher, they might have wondered whether those same "law abiding citizens" had abetted the assault in any way. Education offered the surest avenue to social and economic improvement, and the wealthier residents surely perceived the education of blacks as a threat to their hope of preserving the plantation economy through socially and economically repressive legislation. Not long after the affair at the schoolhouse, federal officers in Lynchburg discovered that even the county officials of Appomattox had joined in the effort to enforce slave-era restrictions against black citizens.

The new Congress had authorized the Freedmen's Bureau to continue bringing anyone who interfered with freedmen's rights before military tribunals. By its decision in *Ex Parte Milligan* the Supreme Court ruled such trials unconstitutional in April of 1866, but for nearly a year the Lynchburg office reviewed the more serious cases in county courts to determine whether justice was being dispensed equitably. One of the first cases involved a white man named Akers, evidently from Lynchburg, who had been visiting his grandmother in Appomattox one day in 1865 while her former slaves conducted a wedding on her property. The celebration brought large numbers of freedmen and lasted long enough that a nervous constable finally arrived with an armed escort and arrested the guests for "unlawful assemblage." Akers stepped in on behalf of the blacks, threatening to shoot the constable, but the armed party nonetheless took many of them into custody and peremptorily whipped thirteen of them. Then, the following April, county attorney Lewis Isbell asked the grand jury to indict Akers for obstructing the constable in the performance of his duties, and those six Appomattox citizens obliged him.[47]

Bureau observers nevertheless determined that fairness predominated in most hearings and trials conducted between March of 1866 and February of 1867. That fairness surprised one bureau officer, especially in "such a Rebel town" as Lynchburg, and he attributed it to the implied threat from the troops occupying the city. Black defendants often confessed to the crimes with which they were charged, although one officer suspected that the confessions were "usually extorted"; transgressors were still occasionally sentenced to whippings, but the same officer believed that most of the freedmen preferred to take the maximum thirty-nine lashes rather than spend six months in jail. The bureau intervened in no Appomattox case, however, and after February of 1867 abandoned its review of court cases: the *Milligan* decision had been published a few weeks before, eliminating the threat of military trial that had given the Freedmen's Bureau its greatest influence over the civil authorities.[48]

Two young men who had gone to war in 1862 and did not return to Appomattox County until four or five years later found that little had changed, even after a year or two of emancipation: the black population remained in thrall, and the measure of a man's worth still hung on the devotion he had shown to the Confederacy. These two came home later than any other Appomattox veterans because they had undertaken further military obligations that detained them longer, and because that additional service had made it judicious for them to remain away.

John Cumby, a farm boy raised just over the line in Campbell County, had married young and already had two children by the outbreak of hostilities. He had not supported the Confederacy with much enthusiasm, enlisting only when the conscription law threatened to take him, and he had been captured twice, at Antietam and at Spotsylvania. The first time he was quickly paroled and returned to duty as soon as he was exchanged, but the second time the Yankees sent him to Point Lookout prison, in Maryland, where he had hardly arrived when he announced that he wanted to take the oath of allegiance. In fact, he was even willing to join the Union army, if he were not sent back to fight his own countrymen (who would have executed him had they recaptured him).

By that stage of the war a lot of his fellow prisoners felt the same way, and in June of 1864 Cumby enlisted in the 1st U.S. Volunteers—the first of six regiments that would be known as the Galvanized Yankees, composed entirely of erstwhile Confederates. By October he and the rest of his regiment had followed the Missouri River upstream to Fort Rice, in northern Dakota Territory, where they endured a bitter plains winter and frequent attacks by Hunkpapa Sioux led by an obscure chief named Sitting Bull. On May 19, 1865, Private Cumby joined a work detail outside the fort when the Sioux launched a little foray, and Cumby came away with a bullet through his right forearm.

After a few months at Fort Rice Cumby returned to Fort Leavenworth, where the army discharged him as an invalid. Sometime in 1866 he returned to his wife and children, moving them into a tiny house on the Appomattox side of the county line, where even with his near-useless arm he found himself a welcome worker on other men's farms. The slaves he remembered had been freed, but that nominal freedom had changed little yet except to bring slightly more value to Cumby's labor; state laws that effectively forced the freedmen back into the fields helped to reduce that value again, however, as had slavery. Had Cumby not realized a meager pension for the experiences he did not yet dare tell, his condition would not have been any different than it was in 1861.[49]

Samuel Webb kept his distance from his native county for considerably longer, and with good reason. While John Cumby had disappeared from his regiment under honorable circumstances, Webb had absconded in the middle of the night from Captain Abbitt's company, which included many of his more determined neighbors. Few of them could have known that he, too, had joined a Union regiment, and it would have been easy for him not to volunteer that detail, but the final betrayal must have provoked greater guilt than other deserters appear to have experienced. When Webb—or John Glover, as he was known by the Yankees—came back to his native county he felt himself an outcast, and his life passed in quiet penance. He spent more than seven fruitless years trying for a pension from the federal government, misrepresenting himself as a reluctant Confederate conscript who had deserted at the first opportunity: ironically, it was his former company commander, county clerk George W. Abbitt, who witnessed this claim, but even a generous pension bureau that had already approved so many fraudulent and exaggerated applications would offer no help to so tardy and questionable a patriot. A quarter of a century after Webb's defection Captain Abbitt's nephew came through his neighborhood to collect the census, and Webb identified himself as a Union veteran. Suffering from rheumatism and a skin disease, he lived with the widow of another Union soldier who, since they were not married, collected her own pension. In one last demonstration of shame, Webb gave the young enumerator his alias, John Glover, but the boy knew his story and recorded both names.[50] The people of Appomattox might forgive, but they did not forget.

THE RESURRECTION

One year after Lee's surrender another sweet burst of spring provoked remembrance among the women of Appomattox Court House. The troubling uncertainty of national collapse and economic turmoil had ebbed, and they made their way to church or the village store with minds less muddled by plans for mere survival. In their passage along the stage road they may have searched the ditches for flowers, finding instead the raw graves of unclaimed Confederates bathed again in cold April showers. Sadness touched their sensitive souls—sorrow for young men who lay apparently forgotten, for the Lost Cause to which they gave their lives, and perhaps for the way of life that had disappeared from the earth with them. With these blended sentiments more than two dozen wives and daughters gathered in the courtroom on May 18 to form the Ladies Memorial Association of Appomattox. They elected the wife of a newly arrived minister as president and named Jennie Peers treasurer, while Ella Flood agreed to take the minutes. The president read a moving letter from the mother of Captain Macon, of Richmond, thanking Edward Hix and the others who buried her son, and with the inevitable flourish of handkerchiefs the ladies proposed to gather all the Confederate dead of Appomattox into a single cemetery.

Theirs was but one of many such societies that coalesced across the South that spring of 1866, fueled by similar emotions. Most of the other organizations sought to decorate the graves of Confederate veterans, but the Clover Hill committee had first to offer their Confederates graves worthy of decoration, and they enlisted some of their men in the project: at the next meeting, a week later, Joel Flood said he would donate any money the group needed. The women approached Fountain Wright for a piece of land on the main road, apparently near his father's brick house in the village, but he demurred. Joel Flood then offered some land north of the village, and Betty Tweedy asked her father, John Sears, to give them a plot of ground; Sears gave them a fraction of an acre at the end of his farm lane, just west of where it intersected with the stage road. The association chose the Sears piece and then requested Francis Meeks, whose own son occupied the only formal soldier's grave in the village, to clear the lot. Despite his sixty-three years, Meeks hacked away at the brush and briars during a few days in the first half of August. Sarah F. Abbitt, daughter of Nancy LeGrand and widow of the doctor who had built George Peers's house, arranged for lumber to build the coffins, getting some of it for nothing. They hired carpenters to build the coffins. By then the Floods had departed on a lengthy vacation abroad, so to pay for these incidental expenses the women invited a former Confederate officer from Richmond to address the community with a benefit lecture on the subject of "Johnny Reb," and Wilmer McLean—Major McLean, to these ladies—agreed to entertain their guest.

After more than six months of preparation, the women mobilized the village men for the least pleasant portion of their endeavor on the last day of November, sending them up the stage road with shovels. Jennie Peers prevailed upon her husband, George, and her brother, Charles Sackett; Sally Abbitt recruited her late husband's cousin, George A. Abbitt, and her brother, Thomas LeGrand; Martha and Carrie Hix called on their brother, Edward. Wilmer McLean went along, and John McKinney, and the bankrupt former sheriff, William Paris. The village harness maker, Thomas Smith, fell in with them. So did Bob Sweeney, who had replaced his cousin as J. E. B. Stuart's headquarters banjo player, and Captain Robert Kyle, who had led ten dozen Appomattox men to Richmond in 1862. John Sears joined them, too, although he was pushing seventy.

These volunteers spent the afternoon and evening of November 30 digging eighteen graves in a single row. The next morning they undertook the work they had wisely postponed since summer, unearthing the disintegrating bodies of Captain Macon and seventeen of his comrades and carting them all to their new resting place on the brow of the hill. Sealing their grisly cargo in the simple coffins, they dropped them into the neat graves, arranging eight headboards bearing names and units with varying degrees of accuracy: the passage of nearly twenty months had erased whatever evidence had been left to identify the others. County attorney Isbell, whose politics had helped propel the conflict that killed these men, honored the departed with a few patriotic remarks that might have caused him trouble if Union officers had overheard. Reverend George W. Leyburn, whose wife presided over the women's group, offered the obsequies that had not attended these soldiers' first funerals. With that, the workmen replaced their hats and took up their shovels.

Thereafter, the ladies of Appomattox had the graves they needed to decorate each May. Livestock interfered with the cemetery at first, so they lobbied for a plank fence around it, but with the completion of that fence they had also concluded their purpose. For a few years the officers continued to hold annual meetings in the spring, but with nothing to report or correct they soon stored their minute book away.[1]

With the war more than a year behind them, village residents (white village residents, at least) began to recognize in their days a semblance of the peace and hopefulness their community had known when the Sweeneys' banjos last rang behind the tavern. Crops promised to be better than even the year before. Students were going back to school; Union Academy had reopened under Mr. Chilton. The sudden rush for marriage licenses—two and three a week, instead of one or two a month—testified most effectively to the infectious optimism, and for some it represented an additional readiness to lay the past to rest. The past had clearly haunted Betty Tweedy, who had buried her husband in Texas eleven years before and had struggled homeward only to watch both her children carried away by scarlet fever. Now, four years after that last tragedy, at the age of thirty-eight, she married a widower and began again.[2]

Peace also promised a new beginning for Sarah Landrum, one of the many daughters of Archibald LeGrand. She had been the bride of a youth who died during the war, and a year after the fighting stopped the still-young widow married Lawson Kelly. Her first husband had been a relative of Thomas Landrum, who had come to town at the beginning of the war to open the bar in the old saddler's shop. Thomas Landrum had avoided field service with a commission in Crawford Jones's local defense battery, but in the final days the army had finally collared him; he appeared before Lee's provost marshal after the surrender, representing himself as a "conscript guard" and claiming a horse he had haltered. He brought the horse back to the rented home he and Marsha Landrum shared with their four children—the house in the field opposite Wilmer McLean's—but they did not remain there long. Shortly after the surrender Landrum took a job with the railroad, finding a new life for his family in Prince Edward County.[3]

Lawson Kelly was but one of many veterans who regained enough confidence and economic prospects to go courting in the summer of 1866. Thomas Harvey, who had been wounded during the Seven Days, captured during Pickett's Charge, and then exchanged only to be captured a few weeks later at Sailor's Creek, came home from a Yankee prison in June of 1865. Soon thereafter he began devoting his attention to Elvira Woodson, whose prejudice against marriage seemed to wane with the progress of peace, and by the next summer the neighborhood knew them as a couple; in August he chided her for talking in her sleep when he heard rebounding gossip that they would be getting married soon. He wanted to get married in October, he admitted, but since he had told no one about it he assumed that she had been the source. As it happened, they were married in October, and spent more than sixty years together.[4]

Jennings Conner, himself captured twice during the war, also married that autumn. Like most of the Irish who lived northeast of the village, he chose from within that ethnic enclave. He and Missouri Sweeney, the last of the musical siblings, took their vows on October 3; to disguise the decade between them, Missouri shaved a number of years from her age and Jennings added a couple of years to his. Six weeks later Jennings Conner's niece married Daniel P. Ferguson, yet another local boy just out of a Union prison.[5]

Nor did this sanguine atmosphere find expression only at the altar. Francis Meeks, who might have been expected to begin liquidating his property at his age, instead continued accumulating the village lots behind his store. When Thomas Landrum left the house in the field for greener pastures, Meeks bought the building and both lots that it sat upon from the Union Academy trustees. He and his wife moved into the house, and he kept his eye open for still more land.[6]

With a similarly buoyant heart Charles McMahon, the Freedmen's Bureau teacher, continued his mission in the village through the rest of the year, despite the early threats against his life. His classes had attracted an increasing number of students. The schoolhouse still showed the effects of the March raid, but he waited until December to have it repaired. The roof may still have diverted the rain, but it must have offered little protection against the wind and chill. The final days of 1866 turned bitterly cold, with a snowstorm beginning the night of Sunday, December 30. By New Year's Eve the ground had turned white, and the poorer residents of Appomattox huddled in desperation about the ineffective fireplaces of their cabins; early that week McMahon appealed for money to rehabilitate his school or, better yet, to build a new one. Bureau officials first offered him only $150 to fix it up, but early in 1867 they finally approved his preference for building an entirely new school in the ambitious dimensions of thirty-two by forty-two feet, at an estimated cost of $300.[7]

Lieutenant Louis Stevenson, the assistant superintendent who authorized McMahon's building, lacked the teacher's hopeful view of the prospects for the future. In a report to Superintendent Lacey written a few weeks after he authorized McMahon's new school, Stevenson judged that nothing had changed in the relations between black citizens and white, nor did he expect to witness any.

"So long as the black man plods along in his old slavish manner," Stevenson supposed, "so long will the feeling be friendly towards him on the part of the whites, & I think no change can be looked for during the present generation."[8] To someone for whom social justice meant as much as national unity, four years of carnage and suffering might as well not have happened.

Many in Congress felt the same way. Radical Republicans determined to force change by eliminating as many former Confederates from the political process as possible, in hopes of making room for more moderate ideologies in Southern state and local government. Just before its customary adjournment in March of 1867, Congress passed its own Reconstruction bill over President Johnson's veto, sweeping aside his more sympathetic policies and laying down its own terms on which the conquered provinces could regain their former places within the union. To monitor the president who had become their enemy, the congressmen immediately called themselves back into extra session through a special provision in their bill.

The Reconstruction Act imposed some of the strictures of the Fourteenth Amendment even in those states that had not yet adopted it, barring anyone from service in state and local government who had held office before the war and then had violated the oath of office by serving the Confederacy. To assure that such turncoats were expunged from government, Congress also gave the military commanders of the various states the authority to register voters and schedule elections. That proscription would soon put George Peers and Lewis Isbell out of their jobs. Peers, who had worked for the county all his adult life, might have wondered what else he could do for a living, but the question waited for a few months while federal officers prepared for new elections.[9]

The delay in implementing this disqualification allowed Squire Isbell to prosecute Spencer Patterson, the black shoemaker, for the murder of Willis Bocock's overseer the previous autumn. Late in April the former Bocock slave was found guilty of manslaughter and sentenced to ten years in the penitentiary. Just six weeks later, as though the murder case had alerted the county to the need, the court accepted a new jail from its builders; the brick edifice had gone up in the southeastern corner of the courthouse lot, across the stage road from the ruins of its predecessor.

Like most legislation, the disqualification clause did not always achieve the result that its proponents had hoped for. Under its provisions, political privileges would be denied to the likes of Lynchburg city councillor John H. Flood, the former Clover Hill merchant, militia major, and active Whig. Flood appears to have harbored true union sentiments: although he was only thirty when the war began, he had come no closer to the Confederate army than when he served as part of the honor guard for Stonewall Jackson's casket. To avoid conscription during the final weeks of the conflict he sought a position as tax collector for his district at Lynchburg, and—because he had also held minor office before the war—that brief tenure would prevent him from taking part in the new government. Meanwhile, last-ditch Confederates like "Buck" Trent, Captain George W. Abbitt, and Flood cousin Robert B. Poore were still eligible, since they had not sworn an oath for any elective or appointed offices before taking up arms against the United States.[10]

Lieutenant Stevenson ordered the newly appointed Appomattox County registrar, John J. Purvis, to begin registering new voters at the courthouse on June 24, and to close the registration process on July 10, after a five-day stop at Union Academy. Purvis, a Lynchburg merchant, held the required registration sessions, allowing anyone who seemed of age and claimed residency to enter his name on the checklist. After he completed the registration process, Stevenson instructed him to have the county clerk provide him with a list of men who had held office before the war, so he could prepare a list of rejected voters.

While scores of prominent white citizens were going to be denied the right to vote, hundreds of former slaves were lining up to register, and Charles McMahon began coaching his students on the importance of that right. He effectively established the county's chapter of the Union League when he invited them to evening meetings at the new schoolhouse, the lights of which attracted the attention of white citizens living nearby. The last thing white Virginians wanted to see was black voters, and a confrontation seemed unavoidable. Anthony North, who had been tax assessor during the war and owned a farm near Oakville, warned McMahon that he intended to disperse the next gathering. If the occupants refused to let him and his companions in, North said, he would break the door down. The next meeting would have been held on Saturday night, July 27, and on Friday Lieutenant Stevenson sent three messages to Appomattox Court House, addressing one to North (whose name he misunderstood), one to McMahon, and one to Sheriff Johnson. He warned North that his threat was known, and that he would be arrested at the first act of violence. At the same time he cautioned McMahon not to resist if their assailants forced their way in, but to adjourn immediately and report the disruption. He also notified the sheriff as the first line of defense against the mob, since the limited number of troops in Lynchburg prevented the posting of any regular guard.

Either detection discouraged North and his followers or the bureau failed to record the result of his visit. If he intended to interrupt the registration of voters, however, federal officers foiled his mission. Six days after North's threatened foray, Stevenson ordered Purvis to hold a second round of registration sessions, beginning with a day at the courthouse on August 13 and ending with another at Union Academy on August 17. These brief meetings were meant largely to allow the rejected voters a chance to appeal if they felt they had been unjustly removed. Purvis displeased the Freedmen's Bureau somehow during the second session, and on the closing day Stevenson notified him that the major general commanding the department had revoked his appointment. In his place came James Geiser, out of the army now but back in the thick of the fray at Appomattox.[11]

George Peers's personal knowledge of the courthouse records proved too valuable to forego, even during the transition to an electorate that excluded him. In the end Dr. Robert Patteson consented to take the nominal position of county clerk, while Peers performed all the county's business under the new and informal position of deputy clerk. Once again, little had changed.[12]

James Geiser may have been appointed to assure federal officials that loyal eyes oversaw the October election of delegates to a constitutional convention. The disenfranchisement of so many ex-Confederates had left black citizens with a sound majority in the county—862 voters to 732 registered whites, on the eve of the election—but Appomattox County's district included Prince Edward County, where black voters outnumbered white by two to one, leaving little chance that any conservative delegate would go to Richmond.[13]

Tension heightened with the approach of those elections that fall, especially as the Union League meetings grew and spread. White citizens may have suspected black attendants of planning mischief at those private conclaves, while league members certainly anticipated trouble from militant whites, and both factions began arming themselves. Captain Geiser had evidently never conducted the search for government arms for which he had requested horses, more than two years before, and Lieutenant Stevenson learned that hundreds of such weapons still lay in the hands of citizens.

He told the constable to collect them and turn them over to the sheriff. This the constable somehow managed to do, presumably by conducting searches of private homes, and eventually he collected about 500 rifles that had probably all entered the county in the hands of weary Confederates.

Election day brought predictable results, with the tallies confirming that the county was divided by color. The two Republican candidates—one white, one black, and both from Prince Edward County—polled 839 and 840 votes respectively. That suggested a 97 percent turnout of black voters, although a scattering of white unionists may have supported the Radical cause. The Democrats attracted votes totaling no more than 67 percent of the white electorate, reflecting abstentions in either discouragement or protest.

When it was all over, Stevenson asked his commander at Lynchburg what to do with the 500 rifles. He stored them, finally, in the new brick jail off the southeast corner of the courthouse. If there had been any prospects for a second battle of Appomattox, they ended there.[14]

The political lull allowed an interlude for religious reflection. A lot of souls had been shaken by the war, and when it was over the old churches North and South witnessed a migration of denominational loyalty as those whose faith had been stirred sought spiritual comfort. Appomattox Court House had always been considered a Baptist community, with services offered in the courthouse to save the trek out to New Hope or Liberty churches, but late in November of 1867 appeared the first proposal for a formal congregation within the village, and it came from the Presbyterians. Nearly a score of residents petitioned for the church, not including any of the Presbyterian McDearmons from the depot or Evergreen. Soon the village faithful were meeting in their own building on part of the acre that had been Samuel McDearmon's first Union Academy venture, where the poorhouse had stood. John Rosser, himself a communicant of Liberty Baptist Church, sold them three-quarters of that acre, across the Prince Edward Court House Road from his house and just south of the Moffitt place. With a full second story and a hipped roof it looked more like a school than a church, but it was the only one Appomattox Court House would ever know.

Reverend Leyburn inspired the movement, having cultivated a following over the past couple of years' residency. Lewis Isbell signed the petition to the West Hanover Presbytery, as did his fellow village lawyer Robert Poore. Dr. Patteson also joined them, and Thomas Johns, along with several members of his family.

Three names new to the village appeared at the top of the document.

These petitioners were the wife and older children of Nathaniel Ragland, a Richmond dry goods merchant whose signature did not appear with theirs. Mrs. Ragland had been Martha Trent, daughter of Thomas Trent and sister of William H. Trent; during the latter part of the war she had lived at the old Trent place while her husband remained in the capital. She was there when the Union army came through (she remembered the Yankee soldiers as rude, threatening, and thieving), and now she appears to have returned to Appomattox ahead of her husband.

Mrs. Ragland must have expected to stay within reach of the village if she presented herself as a prospective parishioner, and her husband may already have been on the way. Soon he would open a store in the old Raine tavern on the edge of the stage road; Wilmer McLean still owned the run-down building, but McLean had been strapped for money of late and would have been glad of the chance to rent it to someone. He may even have vacated the brick house and rented that to Ragland, who would have been hard-pressed to find room for his wife and six children on the second story of the tavern: Mrs. Ragland remembered her husband buying the McLean property in 1868, and it was about then that McLean and his family disappeared forever from Appomattox Court House.[15]

Ragland did not buy the house in 1868 — a Baltimore business partner of McLean's would take it from him at public auction in 1869, finally selling it to Ragland in 1872 — but the family probably moved in that year as tenants. On October 5, 1869, her seventeenth birthday, Sallie Ragland married James Featherston in the same parlor where Lee had surrendered, with Reverend Leyburn officiating.[16]

Ragland's business put him into competition with the emporium of Francis Meeks, directly across the road. Three years before, a passing observer had wondered how even Meeks could make a living in so isolated a village, but Ragland seemed to prosper.

In that respect Ragland differed from the plantation owners whose patronage he depended upon. The principal cash crop of Appomattox County was tobacco, and by the end of 1868 ambitious planters had produced so much tobacco that their agents could hardly sell it. Wartime production had dropped so low that the first good crops sold well, but on New Year's Day in 1869 the Richmond firm of Spotts & Gibson sent Thomas Bocock an apologetic epistle, offering discouraging predictions on the prices the next crop would bring, not to mention the tobacco that already filled their warehouse. The 1865 crop had only amounted to 7,536 hogsheads statewide, they explained, and in 1866 it had only risen to 27,000; the 1867 crop had totaled nearly 44,000, though, and the 1868 harvest filled more than

47,000 hogsheads. The 1869 yield was expected to run between 50,000 and 55,000: with the added pressure of more production to the west and overseas, prices were plummeting. That sort of news hit hard in a region where so much of the land had already been devoted to the pungent plant.[17]

Larger landowners began selling the more remote pieces of their sprawling estates to satisfy immediate debts. The newly liberated slave population offered a ready market for house lots, but they had little cash with which to buy. Those who owned existing cabins fared better by renting them to freedmen and their families, who began filling up the empty buildings in the village, too. John Robertson, a shoemaker with a wife and three children, squeezed his family into Crawford Jones's empty law office sometime in the late 1860s, adding a fourth child in November of 1869. Across the Prince Edward Court House Road from Robertson, in a hovel between John Moffitt's and George Peers's houses, lived another black family; a third occupied Willis Inge's little cabin. Wilson Hix would not have missed the chance to lodge some paying tenants in the old slave cabins behind the tavern. Francis Meeks bought a half-interest in the vacant house belonging to Lorenzo Kelly's estate, just beyond the little-used lane residents used to call Back Street, and rented it out to a family. Of the twenty-six households that composed the heart of the village by the summer of 1870, fourteen were predominantly black. Two of the white families each housed a black servant girl; two otherwise-black families appeared to be headed by a white male and a white female, respectively.

Some interior districts practiced a degree of integration unthinkable five years before, or fifty years hence. Next door to Wilson Franklin's unusual household lived a black farm laborer and his white wife, who had formalized their union in the summer of 1869, as she was about to give birth to their daughter. Teeming with illiterate residents, their isolated neighborhood seemed to permit social divergences that would have scandalized the townsfolk.[18]

While black and white citizens managed to live in an integrated community with relative harmony, and in rare instances in mixed families, their political associations remained exceedingly strained. The constitutional convention, dominated by Radical Republicans, produced a draft that incorporated the exclusion of former Confederates from voting, among other clauses obnoxious to white Virginians. A vote on adoption of that constitution might have revived the conflicts of 1867, but the conservative Republican commander of the military department withheld a referendum on the question. Soon after his inauguration on March 4, 1869, President Ulysses Grant ordered the constitution put before the people.

The issue of permanently disenfranchising former Confederates went on the ballot as a separate question, though.

The vote was scheduled for early July. The same referendum would serve to elect a new governor and legislature. Charles McMahon, the freedmen's teacher, filed for the House of Delegates from Appomattox County as a Republican, expecting to ease into that office on the strength of the black majority. Robert B. Poore, Joel Flood's cousin and first lieutenant in the Appomattox Rangers, ran against McMahon as a Democrat. At twenty-seven, Poore had not been old enough before the war to serve in any office that required an oath of allegiance, leaving him among the few prominent county residents eligible to run.

Save for McMahon, Appomattox County boasted few white men of Republican sympathies. That party had to import its speakers, and early in June a radical carpetbagger from New York swung through to rouse support. His rhetoric failed to win the county for McMahon, though it did soon secure a seat in Congress for the orator himself.

Dividing the constitutional question shook the political alignments. Black voters had learned to view the new constitution as their salvation, and may not have comprehended the impact of separating the clause on Confederate disenfranchisement, while white voters could now accept the document. In Appomattox County black voters with personal loyalty to the Flood family (or who feared becoming unemployed "vagrants") seem to have given Poore the edge he needed, and he beat McMahon 929 to 738. The new constitution passed Appomattox County by a similar margin, without disenfranchisement, and voters followed suit statewide. The next year Congress accepted the state back into the fold, ex-Confederates and all: for Virginia, Reconstruction was over.[19]

While farmers watched their crops sold for less than the cost of production, more Appomattox residents turned to manufacturing, usually in the form of small shops like those of the pipemakers. Charles Diuguid built a new blacksmith shop on his lot just outside the village boundary, in the shadow of the Raine stable; William Rosser expanded his little carriage shop, adding employees; William Layne, another saddler, moved into John Moffitt's house; John Rosser established his own blacksmith shop alongside the Presbyterian church. The county's industrial output quintupled between 1860 and 1870, but that failed to compensate for the blow tobacco prices had struck. With the election of officials from the old school, village residents found county commissioners willing to recognize that the agricultural depression had devalued their property, and assessments tumbled.

Joseph Dixon, the absentee landlord from New York, owned eleven lots and parts of two others, consisting of the Bocock house, every lot around it (including a small law office behind the new jail), and the lots surrounding Pryor Wright's brick house: in 1869 Dixon had been taxed for land and buildings worth $3,300, but in 1870 his assessment dropped to $1,750. Aside from the tiny lot that it stood upon, Robertson & Glover's big brick store, though no longer a store, had been valued at $1,250; that fell to $800. Another nonresident owned the old McLean house—now the Raglands' home—and nearly everything else in the triangle southwest of the courthouse, for which he had been assessed $3,060 in 1869; his valuation plummeted to $1,250. The assessment of Crawford Jones's old law office was cut by 25 percent, and Mary Woodson's assessment on her late husband's office was reduced by 40. For the tavern and all its attendant buildings, including the saddlery-cum-bar, the tax assessor abated Wilson Hix less than 18 percent, but he eased Francis Meeks's total tax burden by more than 26.[20]

Mr. Meeks did not live to enjoy his abatement. One day in January of 1870 he developed a nosebleed that would not stop, and within a few hours he had bled to death. Mrs. Meeks attempted to carry on with his little emporium: Lucinda Bryant had taken the postmaster's appointment from Henry Cogan, operating the post office from a corner in the store, and the two women kept house together for another year or two. By 1872 Thomas Johns bought the store and the lots behind it—even the land where Lafayette Meeks lay buried—while Mrs. Meeks rented out her house and moved away forever.

With that, Nathaniel Ragland became the only merchant in the village. His trade soared: he bought his home and the surrounding lots from McLean's erstwhile partner, secured the post office contract for his own store, and settled in for a long tenure.[21]

Economic troubles seem to attract lawyers, and Clover Hill hosted several again by the early 1870s. When William Rosser built a big new house near the site of the original jail, Henry D. Flood rented Rosser's old cabin as space for a new law office in the village, but he retained his own practice in Lynchburg; for the office at Appomattox Court House he installed his nephew, Robert Poore. Poore divided his time between private practice and public duty, both as a delegate and as the county attorney. Henry T. Parrish, a Farmville lawyer, a graduate of Virginia Military Institute, and a friend of Thomas Bocock, came to Appomattox Court House as a judge for that magisterial district. Parrish had served briefly as colonel of the 16th Virginia, but he had "retired" for ill health before that regiment saw any fighting and spent the rest of the war in office assignments. His Appomattox judgeship provided only partial employment, so he also opened a law office—initially in the old saddlery and bar, between the tavern and Meeks's store. Then, when Lewis Isbell left the village after some unspecified indiscretion, Parrish moved into his old home and used the law office behind the jail, renting everything from Dixon.[22]

Charles Sackett, a young attorney who lived with his sister and brother-in-law, George Peers, represented the county as commissioner in chancery by 1869. It was he who administered the suit that deprived Wilmer McLean of his house, and he drew the regular duty of disposing of property that had been forfeited to the county through nonpayment of taxes. By 1871 the office lot of Crawford Jones had fallen into the county's hands that way, in lieu of tax payments on both that piece and Jones's 400-acre estate on Fishpond Creek. In 1871 Sackett offered the village lot to its current tenant, John Robertson, but through either poor research or deliberate design he exchanged the deed description of the Jones office lot with the more expensive parcel belonging to the estate of Lorenzo Kelly, charging Robertson $350 for property assessed at $150. Sackett threw in a small gore of land that the road layout had cut off in front of the office; he gave the struggling shoemaker five years to raise the money, and somehow Robertson did.[23]

While the village grew and the buildings changed hands, the man who had begun it all passed quietly from the scene. Samuel McDearmon, who had lived as a nominal pauper for nearly two decades while his wife assumed formal ownership of their property, died of a stroke at his home near the depot on May 15, 1871. According to his wife's recollection, he was fifty-seven years old. Now that he was dead she had no reason to fear his creditors from the Clover Hill speculation, and she reported to the county clerk that he had been involved in the family sawmill business. So involved had he been, in fact, that he produced $2,000 worth of lumber in 1870, and that had not been his only enterprise: in partnership with an Evergreen miller, he had ground nearly the same value in wheat flour that year, and three times that much in cornmeal. While McDearmon had spent his time attending to the hotel at the depot and his duties as station agent, his sons acted as managers of the lumber business, which had supported their families as well as their father and mother. The proximity of the railroad broadened their markets, as it did for George Abbitt and William G. Coleman, whose mills lay nearby. Even Richard Austin, who had abandoned his little foundry for a lumber mill in the northern quadrant of the county, enjoyed the benefit of close river transportation.[24] Appomattox Court House, meanwhile, could offer only the deteriorating stage and plank roads of an earlier era.

Samuel McDearmon's younger brother, John, had inherited their father's farm, hiring managers to operate it while he worked as a country doctor. Even under the acute devaluation of 1870 he owned an enviable estate by the standards of Appomattox County, to which he added the income from his medical practice. As the national centennial approached, Dr. McDearmon lived a modest but comfortable life, but he was nearly fifty-nine years old and he had never been married. That spring he took notice of the young daughter of his current manager, Martha Ada Baker, who was only twenty, and on April 25, 1876, they were married by Reverend Leyburn's successor in the Presbyterian pulpit. Barely three weeks later, McDearmon, his bride, and her mother were awakened by a knock at the front door. Dr. McDearmon held a lamp as he opened the door, finding two black men on his porch. They said that a third man lay sick in the yard, but as he strode out to look they attacked him, knocking the lamp from his hand and clubbing him to the ground. As he tried to rise, one of them shot him in the abdomen. The pair pushed their way into the house, demanding money of the women, who gave them twelve dollars. They committed no more mischief save, strangely enough, to steal McDearmon's wedding clothes, and then they departed, leaving their victim writhing on the ground.

Dr. McDearmon lived five days. Peritonitis killed him on May 23, by which time one of his assailants had been arrested. The newspapers remained unusually quiet about the crime, neither excoriating the murderers nor covering the case after their capture. No one remarked on the irony that both of Samuel McDearmon's brothers had died at the hands of armed men, and no one seems to have suspected any complicity on the part of the young bride, whose four-week marriage availed her a sizable inheritance.[25]

By then Wilson Hix was dead, too. Portly and worn out in his eightieth year, he died just before the tenth anniversary of Lee's surrender, leaving his sons to squabble over his estate. After five years of chancery, Edward finally took the tavern. William had established himself at Walker's Church, where he gathered his various enterprises under the auspices of "Wm. Danl. Hix & Co." With the same proprietorial tendencies that had typified his tenure as sheriff, he began calling that community "Hixburg," printing it on his stationery, and after a while the name stuck.[26]

Virginia was beginning to recover a semblance of its antebellum flavor by the middle of that decade. A poll tax had sharply reduced black voter turnout, and power had shifted back to the patricians who had dominated in the days of slavery. Things looked brighter for Appomattox County, too: tobacco prices had finally recovered, and crops of all kinds promised a good yield for 1875, but the best economic news came from the new towns that were springing up near the railroad—Nebraska, Evergreen, and Pamplin Station.

A visitor to Appomattox Court House the summer after Wilson Hix died found a quaint, picturesque village that throve only on legal and political conflict. The courthouse still rang occasionally with Democratic rhetoric, but—except for the lawyers who lived in the village—most of the players came from the outlying districts. The Clover Hill Tavern still entertained some excited party adherents on those court days that fell in the political season; Nathaniel Ragland's store, still in the old Raine tavern but sitting now on the lot nearest the courthouse, attracted an adequate clientele. Ragland's home, the scene of the surrender, struck the passerby as "forlorn," with its deteriorating porch and upper balcony, but the house was very much alive inside. Ragland's daughter Sallie and her husband still lived in the house with her parents; they already had three children running through the halls where Union officers' swords had rattled, ten years before. The same walls that had seen the death of the Confederacy had also witnessed the birth of the new generation.[27]

A decade later, the old McLean house stood with wide bands of black crepe wrapped around its porch columns. When Ulysses Grant died on July 23, 1885, Ragland draped his home in mourning for one of the two most famous men ever to pass through its front door. Though his presidency had been rent with scandals—including one involving Colonel Babcock, who had accompanied him to the McLean parlor—Grant was kindly remembered at Appomattox Court House. Now that the issues of emancipation and suffrage had been overcome, and especially since they had been overcome in a manner not entirely unsatisfactory to the white population, Southerners could admire Grant once more for his generosity at the moment of victory. Twenty years after the war, the good will that some Union and Confederate generals had shared in April of 1865 was beginning to infect the public at large. Politicians in search of regional coalitions were starting to pretend that these sentiments had flourished the instant Lee departed from McLean's dooryard. During Grant's second term Congressman Washburne, who had been so pleased with the resignation shown by surrendering Confederate generals, began to compose an inflated interpretation of their acquiescence, implying that they had harbored an underlying patriotic devotion to the nation they had fought so hard to leave.

"There was one sentiment among all these men," he informed a Southern correspondent nearly ten years after Appomattox, "which seemed to crop out in spite of themselves, and that was that after all the bloody struggle of the past, they were still all Americans."[28]

Washburne's observation was a little premature even for 1874, but in years to come others would attempt to create that retroactive atmosphere of instantaneous brotherhood. A quarter of a century after the surrender veterans would begin to write of Appomattox with a fraternal, bipartisan air. After a war with a foreign power and the turn of the century, it would become Joshua Chamberlain's Appomattox — a place where Union soldiers had presented arms to their enemies, opened their haversacks, and welcomed the South back into the union.[29] That spirit did not yet prevail: too many men remained alive who had preserved a different image of their time at Appomattox, and of the years that followed, but at the time of his death General Grant, at least, owned the gratitude of the people of Clover Hill.

Grant's visit there had given the village what, by then, remained its only hope for economic revival. The community had begun to show its decay, both physically and on paper. In 1882 William Hix surrendered his last interest in the village, selling the old Moffitt place to William Layne's widow, who had been living there since shortly after the war. In 1883 his brother Edward followed suit, liquidating his father's village parcels. He sold the empty Raine stable lot on the outskirts of town to George Peers, and William Trent's old saddle shop to Charles Sackett; like his predecessor, Judge Parrish, Sackett used the little building as a law office. The next year, Hix sold the tavern itself and moved out of town. Beside the tavern stood Robertson & Glover's big brick store, still empty and increasingly dilapidated. Meeks's store had become the Presbyterian parsonage, with an assessed value that had dropped half again from the depression year of 1870.[30]

Residents always stood ready to guide visitors around the scenes of the surrender, and hope remained for cultivating some tourist traffic that might attract some cash or even increase property values. If Nathaniel Ragland held such hopes, though, he would not realize them in his lifetime. He died early in 1888, leaving everything to Martha. On January 1, 1891, she signed a purchase agreement for the property with Myron Dunlap of Niagara Falls, New York. Dunlap agreed to pay her $10,000 for the property, which he said he planned to move to Chicago for the World's Columbian Exhibition of 1893. Five weeks later Dunlap sold half his interest in the house to another man, and each of them enlisted other partners in the Appomattox Land Improvement Company, of Niagara Falls.[31]

These entrepreneurs planned to transport the disassembled building to Chicago, where thousands of people could see it daily. Not even a fraction of such visitors would have made the arduous trek to its original site, where several miles of bad road separated it from a railroad station that offered few other excuses for a traveler to stop.

Even residents disliked the journey to the courthouse, which they had to make for virtually every legal transaction. That necessity ended on February 2, 1892. County clerk George Peers went home to lunch that day as usual, leaving a cozy fire in his office stove to ward against the winter chill: Peers had recently been reelected to his old position, which George W. Abbitt had held in the interim. Soon after Nathaniel Ragland's death, Peers had assumed the postmastership of the village; he retained that sinecure, and perhaps he spent a long lunch hour sorting mail. Some of the coals must have dropped through holes in the courthouse stove, for by the time Peers had finished his lunch the court clerk's office was ablaze. Loose papers and old, dry volumes of records nearby quickly fueled an inferno that caught the entire building. Buckets of well water stood no chance against the flames, and by midafternoon the roof collapsed, leaving the charred brick walls standing guard over the smoldering rubble. Peers had recently sent the county land books to Richmond for binding, and these tax assessments alone survived. Every deed, every will, and the records of every criminal case since Coleman May's murder trial had been destroyed.

The fire spelled the end of Appomattox Court House as an active community. Construction soon began on a new courthouse on a knoll overlooking the railroad, and by June the name of Appomattox Court House had disappeared from the rolls of the U.S. Post Office. Henceforth the surrender scene would be known simply as Appomattox, and Peers would remain postmaster over a much-abridged clientele.[32]

The destruction of that famous building inspired one Confederate veteran to come to Appomattox and photograph the remaining historic sites before they, too, disappeared. Adam Plecker, of Lynchburg, brought his camera to the courthouse sometime that summer, taking views of the tavern, the courthouse ruins, Peers's house, some of the more obscure cabins, and one broad image of the entire village as seen from the west. He spun his lens from the courthouse to the McLean house, capturing that handsome building standing cold and empty, and then the old artilleryman made so bold as to walk into the house, arranging a flash that allowed him to snap the only photograph ever taken of the room where Lee and Grant met. Before returning to Lynchburg, he went into the valley of the Appomattox to shoot the ground where Robert E. Lee and his army waited to surrender.[33]

Plecker's images north of the courthouse site included some crude wooden signs. Cast even farther into the hinterlands by the fire and the relocation of the county seat, local landowners had made one last effort to capitalize on the historic events their village had seen, marking the surrender sites with makeshift signs for the benefit of would-be tourists. Robert Poore, still practicing law in the neighborhood, may have been thinking both of tourist revenue and the value of his own family property in the fall of 1892, when he wrote to Walter Taylor, of Norfolk. He asked Taylor, who had been Robert E. Lee's adjutant, whether the general held a council of war at Appomattox, and if so where it took place. Edward Pollard's 1867 history of the war referred to such a council, Poore pointed out; he did not add that Pollard had mistakenly claimed the rear of the army then lay "within four miles of Appomattox Court House," or that the Flood family (to which Poore belonged) owned nearly all the land within four miles of Appomattox Court House.

"If this be so I am very anxious to know where this meeting was held," Poore explained. He also mentioned that a party of Northerners had bought the McLean house with some vague notion that they would "fit up" the surrender room. Perhaps he hoped to hear that the council took place at Pleasant Retreat, where he may have been living. Colonel Taylor, who had been away from headquarters on the night of April 8, could not have told Poore where the conference was held: that, or some hearsay from other staff members, may have been his response, which does not survive. It was about that time, though, that a wooden sign arose on the Flood land across from the Conner farm, indicating Lee's last headquarters, and eventually that site also became known as the scene of the final council of war.[34]

Other signs sprang up around the village then, marking the real or imagined locations of various episodes in the surrender legend, which the inhabitants had been relating in conflicting versions for nearly three decades. Prompted by Horace Porter's reminiscence and George Peers's subsequent claim to have been a witness, a sign remembering the April 10 meeting between Lee and Grant appeared across the road from Peers's house—rather than down by the North Branch, where Charles Wainwright described it in 1865. Across the branch, on Flood land, another sign identified the spot where Lee allegedly read his farewell address to his army—perhaps the place where he spoke to them on his way back from the

McLean house, on April 9. Another went up in Peers's side yard, marking the ground from which the last Confederate cannon offered violence to the enemy. More signs marked Grant's headquarters, the infamous apple tree, and the flanks of Bartlett's division as it accepted the Confederate arms.

In the fall of 1893, after months of correspondence with Appomattox residents, the War Department replaced all the wooden signs with iron tablets. Hoping to encourage visitation, local promoters saw to it that the major newspapers knew of the project. Within days after the iron tablets had been completed, readers in Washington and New York read about it.

"It is thought that the scene of the surrender," wrote a correspondent for the *New York Tribune*, "now that it has been accurately marked, will be the objective point of many trips by veterans of the war."

By then government officials had to amend the tablet for the McLean house, noting that it had been dismantled for transport to Washington. The Chicago exhibition had wound down by then, so the New York syndicate that owned the wreckage of the house was thinking of a more permanent location in the nation's capital, but the framework and bricks of John Raine's dream tavern still lay in heaps in the yard. There they would remain for half a century longer, steadily diminishing in volume under the attrition of wind, rain, and souvenir hunters.[35]

The harbingers of another Confederate legion appeared on the ridge by the Oakville Road before the setting sun of Saturday, April 8, 1905. They turned onto the lane that led to the old Trent place, lingered briefly, and then returned to the depot. On the morrow scores of others followed them, stepping down from the train at what the station sign told them was West Appomattox. Old veterans in grey Stetson hats and Prince Albert coats carried their satchels into the dusk of another Appomattox night, a few accompanied by wives and sons and daughters. Some of them had seen this place before, in the springtime of their lives. Now they came to remember those days, and to require that others remember what they had done here. They scattered to find their lodging in private homes, to spend one last Sunday in a place they once despised but which had shed at last its awful connotation. The inevitable, vigorous few made their way to the old village that evening for a private encounter with the ground where they had bid farewell to the nation of their youth, to commune in the darkness with the ghosts of comrades long departed.

They would have no privacy on Monday. Just after noon that day a crowd of some 3,000 thronged Trent's lane with the governors of both Virginia and North Carolina to dedicate a couple of tons of North Carolina granite. The principal monument, claimed the veterans, marked the spot from which Bryan Grimes's division fired the last volley from the infantry of the Army of Northern Virginia. Tarheel veterans had lobbied for little gifts of land and a thousand dollars from their legislature to mark the old battlefield with this and other claims supportive of their state's Confederate motto: "First at Bethel, farthest to the front at Gettysburg and Chickamauga, and last at Appomattox." Virginians had taken special offense at this phrase, which seemed to disparage the Old Dominion's contribution to the Confederate cause in particular. There had been talk of changing the inscription on the North Carolinians' memorial, and violent rejoinders that it should be pounded to dust before the chisel altered a single letter. The Appomattox chapter of the United Confederate Veterans, including survivors of Pickett's Charge who especially disputed the Carolina claim, voted not to attend the ceremony. Some had feared unpleasant demonstrations this fine spring day, but Virginians in the crowd offered no retort as one North Carolinian after another recounted a war history in which their own generals and regiments had played the most prominent part. Then the daughter of General Grimes released the canvas covering from the biggest monument, and the Rebel yell echoed one final time over the hilltop, thin but shrill as ever.

Afterward some of the crowd wandered down the hill toward the old village, stopping at a smaller stone that marked the capture of the last Union battery—a feat now exclusively claimed by a tiny brigade of North Carolina cavalry. Closer still to the village, not 500 yards from the courthouse, Wilson T. Jenkins introduced the final monument. Here, he told those who joined him, General William Cox had withdrawn the last two regiments of his brigade, leaving twenty-five volunteers from the 4th and 14th North Carolina to "take position behind some houses on the right of the road" and keep the enemy at bay. Those buildings—the Raine stable and some nearby outbuildings—had all vanished, and when Jenkins came to locate the monument in 1904 he mistook their sites by 300 yards, but none of those he so proudly addressed that day knew or cared about such details. They applauded him as loudly as the rest before continuing on to see what had been the town of Clover Hill.

Brush and young trees had sprouted in the yard of the McLean house. Meeks's store, Wilson Hix's tavern, and the old Raine tavern greeted the visitors with closed shutters. The crumbling concern of Robertson & Glover was gone, finally—torn down for its bricks, to provide the foundation of a new building at the depot. The rubble of the courthouse stood amid a tangle of vegetation. The veterans who had trod this way in 1865 recounted for the others their dismal parade. From here they had begun the long march that had led them to this new century, with its clanking factories and sputtering automobiles and its bright promise, but here the past still lay, abandoned and neglected. With perhaps a nostalgic cluck of the tongue Captain Jenkins turned back to the town by the railroad, for a luncheon hosted by Joel Flood's oldest son, Congressman Henry D. Flood. Young Hal spread himself to welcome his guests. His father may not have come to the ceremony in protest of Carolinian gall, but the ladies of Appomattox presented a bouquet to ease the snub of local Confederates.[36]

The visit of the North Carolinians rekindled an effort by Appomattox residents to build their own Confederate monument, and that October they laid the cornerstone, but not at the old Appomattox Court House, where the companies had gathered to go to war. Instead they placed the memorial at the new Appomattox courthouse, which had been woods in wartime. In June of 1906 another crowd convened to cheer more enthusiastically for the dedication of this monument: Congressman Flood returned to speak, as did the county attorney, Sam Ferguson.[37]

At thirty-seven, Sam Ferguson exemplified the new South. His grandfather had been an Appomattox day laborer, and his father an overseer. The father had been one of Joel Flood's first volunteers, sticking with the colors until the Yankees wounded him at Sailor's Creek. Sam saw his future with the law, and like most Appomattox lawyers with political aspirations he began his career as county solicitor; eventually he won a seat in the state senate. Ferguson made much of his Confederate heritage, as did his neighbors, whose pension applications he often witnessed and helped to facilitate. Like a true politician, he made certain to emphasize his role in establishing their claims, asking the state pension clerk to send the checks directly to him, so he could distribute them.

"I would thank you to make out the check payable to this old lady," Ferguson wrote of Charles Wingfield's widow, "and I will take great pleasure in transmitting it to her in person."

"This old fellow is a neighbor of mine," he remarked of one man who had evidently forwarded a fraudulent application, "and I would be delighted to give him his check as a Xmas gift from the old Commonwealth." [38]

Virginia's Pension Act of 1888 and a revised act in 1900 benefited mostly Confederate widows and field-service veterans who were totally disabled. With the new act of 1902, pensions began going to men with nominal service in the Virginia Reserves, like Charles H. Coleman, or to those who had performed no service at all. Coleman, who served only in Buckingham County's company of the 3rd Virginia Reserves, claimed to have fought in the renowned 4th Virginia, of the Stonewall Brigade, but instead of helping his case he nearly scuttled it, for no such soldier appeared on the rolls of that regiment: a man by the same name, an Appomattox veteran of the 2nd Cavalry, had died six years previously, but the pension department already knew about him. Coleman still won a pension, drawing it for thirty-three years, and the state gave his widow one of her own after the Second World War, although in her application she confused her husband with the cavalryman.[39]

Fraud had become common among Confederate pensioners half a century after the war. Old men desperate for money appealed to states with limited resources for investigation, presenting vague claims of Civil War service and banking on the growing reverence for Confederate veterans to forestall any challenge. State officials nonetheless did challenge many applications, and when that happened Sam Ferguson was the man to see. He pulled one pension out of the fire for John H. Patteson, who had grown up a mile north of Appomattox Court House. Patteson asserted that he had enlisted in a Captain Payne's company of cavalry at Montgomery County in the fall of 1864, and then had been transferred to the "engineer corps." Army officials in Washington searched Confederate records, finding no such man.

"Mr. Patteson is a splendid man," Ferguson insisted, "and is well known to have served in the war for 10 months prior to the close of the war." He acknowledged that the state auditors could refuse a pension if a veteran's service proved less than honorable, but he argued that they had no cause to deny a claim for the lack of any records at all.

"Now you know as well as I do that the records are very incomplete everywhere of the services of our soldiers," Ferguson contended, "and this very law and section to which I referred you contemplates the incompleteness of the records." The auditors refused to listen to that sort of logic, but the appeal kept Patteson's application alive and he finally modified it to claim the service record of the late J. A. Patteson, who enlisted in the 4th Virginia Cavalry from Buckingham County in January of 1864. That yielded him $24 a month.[40]

Eventually any connection to the Confederate cause lifted an individual's reputation beyond reproach, and even desertion failed to disqualify an application. In 1932 a woman who had married Samuel Webb shortly before his death asked for a pension as a Confederate widow. The muster roll that proved Webb's desertion to the enemy in the final months of the war survived, but the state of Virginia still gave his widow $10 a month.[41]

{ THE RESURRECTION }

The Confederate cemetery became the conventicle for local worshipers of the Lost Cause, and the once-neglected graves saw fresh flowers now every April 9. On the fiftieth anniversary of Lee's surrender some three dozen citizens, young and old, came to lay wreaths upon the graves. Among them stood two or three who had worn Confederate grey, including Joel Flood, in his final year of life. They had mostly come from the west, toward the railroad; their journey would not have required them to pass through the ruins of the village.

By then the old town had degenerated to desolation. Trees had grown so tall on either side of the road that they darkened the old thoroughfare at midday and completely disguised the courthouse ruins. Brush choked the McLean lot. Vines climbed the sides of Meeks's store and the sagging Raine tavern; missing windows and rotting shingles invited rain into the Clover Hill Tavern. Withered trunks stood in place of trees that had shaded stagecoach passengers. Fence boards drooped at awkward angles. Clapboards curled paintless and porous on George Peers's house and Judge Isbell's, where shrubs and saplings threatened the yards; the Moffitt house lay vacant in a snarl of foliage, and within a year men with wrecking bars would take it down. Everywhere the broad, green pastures gave way to locust and briars, as the forest came back to claim what it had lost. Only William Rosser's big white house betrayed signs of life, with a little store in the ell to welcome those infrequent travelers who stopped on their way to or from Buckingham. Rosser still lived to greet them, stooped and wiry, lodging with his daughter's family in the house he had built nearly half a century before. Of all the Clover Hill residents who had heard the Sweeneys' banjos and seen the militia musters, he alone survived.[42]

The bustling town that Samuel McDearmon had envisioned, and for which he had sacrificed both his credit and a brother, had never come to be. Instead there had risen a quiet crossroads village that lived a life no longer than a man's, though feeling in its day a touch of fame such as few men ever know. Even that had failed to lend it immortality, for Appomattox had been but an interlude upon the endless odyssey out of the past. Like any of its more conscientious citizens, the village had served its generation; now there remained only the few years of lassitude beneath the sunshine, until the advancing shadows intertwined and blotted out the light.

EPILOGUE: THE DEDICATION

Still seeking to exploit the historic significance of the site in 1925, the chamber of commerce in Appomattox appointed the inevitable committee to pursue construction of a shrine at the old courthouse ruins. The businessmen chose a local minister, the publisher of the town newspaper, and their state senator, Sam Ferguson. These three—and probably the last of them, in particular—caught the attention of their representative in the U.S. Senate, and five years later the War Department authorized the Appomattox Battlefield Site. Five years after that, the site was designated a National Historic Monument, and in 1936 the federal government began buying up the old village lots and surrounding acreage. By then the preponderance of the parcels belonged to Adalia C. Ferguson—widow of the late state senator.[1]

The scene of the surrender might have been commemorated with nothing more ambitious than an art deco obelisk like Gettysburg's peace memorial, but preservationists in both Appomattox County and the National Park Service finally steered government efforts toward restoration of the entire village. Archaeologists and historic preservationists descended on the site, digging up the foundation of the McLean house, tearing down unsalvageable buildings, cutting back the encroaching vegetation, and restoring everything they could save. The Second World War slowed the restoration, but with the end of the war attention turned to rebuilding the McLean house. By the spring of 1949 the building had seen its first visitors. On April 16, 1950, a crowd nearly as large as Lee's army gathered in the reopened field behind Francis Meeks's store, spilling around his son's grave, to hear Robert E. Lee's most famous biographer dedicate the building.

Douglas Southall Freeman, whose own father had stacked his musket in the stage road in the same depleted regiment with Thomas Tibbs, told his audience his father's story of Appomattox, in which the Lynchburg soldier crested the hill by the Conner farm on the night before the surrender and saw an ominous sea of Union campfires to the west, south, and east. Like most of the stories flourishing that long after the war, this one raised an odor of embellishment, for if Private Walker Burford Freeman had seen those campfires they would have been equally visible to General Lee, and the Miles Macons and Ivy Ritchies who died on April 9 would have been allowed to live out their lives. Freeman the historian throve on such burnished recollections, however, and his father's tale released the atmosphere of despair that he wished to cast. Then he swept the gloom away with the remembrance of Grant's generosity, and dedicated the scene as a monument to "the reunion of brothers who never must permit the strife of class to take the place of the strife of states." [2]

Freeman spoke to an audience composed almost exclusively of white people who probably never considered what his words implied, and he may not even have intended that implication. During his lifetime legal segregation and voting restrictions had reduced half the citizens of his native state to a facsimile of the bondage that had supposedly been abolished in the wake of Lee's surrender. That would soon begin to change, but the struggle—the strife of class—would last longer than the war that had ended across the road from Freeman's rostrum.

Freeman would not see the battle begin. He died in 1953, and that same year another writer filled his place as the preeminent historian of the Civil War with a book that ended at Appomattox. *A Stillness at Appomattox* won the Pulitzer Prize in history, and Bruce Catton began retelling the story of the conflict with a slightly Northern flavor.

The old ways died hard, and no harder than in Appomattox. Before another decade passed, hometown congressman Watkins Abbitt, a great-grandson of Captain George W. Abbitt, would assail the federal government's efforts to integrate Virginia schools under an education aid program. While arguing successfully for his constituents' tobacco subsidies, Abbitt simultaneously condemned federal school aid as neither needed nor wanted, and when integration of public schools became inevitable he helped lead an effort to abolish the public school system. [3]

Then, on the centennial of the surrender, that same congressman met Catton at Appomattox to dedicate the reconstructed courthouse. The sentiments they voiced did not differ greatly from those Freeman had expressed fifteen years previously, touching on the common national heritage and the theme of brotherhood, but they spoke to a nation still struggling with the issue of civil rights. Catton urged the crowd to remember the spirit of reconciliation that he felt had marked the surrender.

"As far as Lee and Grant were concerned," he said, "the nation could begin healing its wounds."

Virginia governor Albertis Harrison Jr. replied that Virginians could, indeed, look back on the surrender without bitterness.

"We can do it," he explained, "because the beliefs and principles for which the Confederate forces fought are still with us. They are still very much alive."

The ensuing applause implied that the audience heard the historian and the governor speak with the same voice. The throng appeared to miss the ominous contrast between their comments: along with millions who later read about the ceremony, the celebrants supposed that they were commemorating the hundredth anniversary of an event that represented unity, unanimity, and the national adoption of all the revolutionary principles of liberty, equality, and fraternity. With their limited perspective, they could not comprehend that those lessons had only begun to be absorbed.[4]

NOTES

ABBREVIATIONS

ACHNHP   Appomattox Court House National Historical Park

CSRCSV   Compiled Service Records of Confederate Soldiers Who Served in Organizations from the State of Virginia, M-324, RG 109, National Archives

LOV   Library of Virginia

NA   National Archives

OR   *War of the Rebellion: Official Records of the Union and Confederate Armies,* 128 vols. Washington: Government Printing Office, 1880–1901 (All citations to OR are to series 1, unless otherwise noted.)

RG   Record Group

SHC   Southern Historical Collection, University of North Carolina

USAMHI   U.S. Army Military History Institute

UVA   University of Virginia, Alderman Library

VHS   Virginia Historical Society

CHAPTER ONE

1. John Raine tombstone, Raine cemetery, Route 24, Appomattox County; *Lynchburg Republican,* March 17, 1845.

2. Bradshaw, *History of Prince Edward County,* 308; Deed Book 23, 274–75, Prince Edward County Courthouse.

3. *Lynchburg Virginian,* March 17, 1845, and May 5, 1851; Deed Book 23, 456, Prince Edward County Courthouse.

4. *Richmond Enquirer,* December 16, 1824; Legislative Petitions, Buckingham County, February 21 and March 13, 1839, LOV; Deed Book 23, 274–75, Prince Edward County Courthouse.

5. Legislative Petitions, Buckingham County, January 30, 1841, with polls of April 25, 1841, and April 28, 1842, LOV; Deed Book 23, 456, Prince Edward County Courthouse.

6. *Richmond Whig,* January 16 and 23, 1844.

7. Ibid., January 17 and February 9, 1844, February 5, 6, and 8, 1845; *Lynchburg Vir-*

ginian, September 19, 1844, and February 13, 1845; Legislative Petitions, Buckingham County, December 3, 1844, LOV; Stewart, *American Place-Names*, 19.

8. *Lynchburg Virginian*, March 10, 1845; Thomas W. Johns to "Dear Col." [presumed to be Benjamin Walker], March 7, 1845, photocopy tipped into Cauble, "Cultural History as of 1865," ACHNHP; *Acts of the General Assembly*, 1845, 38–41.

9. *Lynchburg Republican*, March 17 and May 5, 1845.

10. *Acts of the General Assembly*, 1845, 39; Journal of the Council of State of Virginia, 1845–46, 24, 31, 46, LOV; *Lynchburg Virginian*, June 5 and July 14, 1845.

11. *Lynchburg Virginian*, June 9, 1845.

12. Deed Book 26, 302, Prince Edward County Courthouse; *Lynchburg Virginian*, September 19, 1844, and May 1, 1845; *Acts of the General Assembly*, 1845, 46. McDearmon's beneficent uncle was Samuel J. Daniel.

13. Seventh Census of the United States, M-432, reel 933, 354–55, 413–14, and Slave Schedule for Appomattox County, reel 983, RG 29, NA; McDearmon marriage records, Farrar Family Papers; Land Book, 1845, Appomattox County Circuit Court. According to the Appomattox County Land Books for the late 1840s, McDearmon owned a sawmill near his father's plantation, and such a sawmill appears near Evergreen Station on the "Hotchkiss map" of Appomattox and Buckingham Counties (*Atlas to Accompany the Official Records*, plate 135, map 5); the Industrial Schedule of the 1850 census, T-1132, reel 4, RG 29, NA, also lists McDearmon and his brother-in-law as the owners of the largest grain mill in the county, at Bent Creek, with no capacity for milling timber.

14. Deed Book 26, 300, 302, Prince Edward County Courthouse; Land Books, 1845, 1846, and 1851, Appomattox County Circuit Court. Samuel J. Walker, who was married to Mary F. P. McDearmon's sister, served as security for the notes on the Clover Hill tract.

15. *Lynchburg Virginian*, September 8, 1845; George Peers recollections, undated newspaper clipping, ACHNHP.

16. *Lynchburg Virginian*, November 3 and 17, 1845, December 14, 1854; *Lynchburg Republican*, November 10, 1845.

17. *Lynchburg Virginian*, November 27 and December 1, 1845.

18. Ibid., December 1, 1845, and June 1, 1846. While most sources agree that Thomas S. Bocock was named Appomattox County's commonwealth attorney on May 12, 1845, the *Richmond Whig* of May 22, 1845, reported that Daniel A. Wilson Jr. had been appointed to that same position by his father. Loss of Appomattox County records in the 1892 courthouse fire leaves resolution of that conflict difficult, but the younger Wilson may have been appointed as an assistant. No written evidence has turned up to document whether the county commissioners chose the log jail or one of the two masonry alternatives; the dimensions of the excavated jail foundation more closely match the advertised specifications for the log jail, rather then the brick or stone versions, but Timothy O'Sullivan's 1865 photo of the courthouse reveals a glimpse of a brick structure where the original jail should have been (see Miller, *Photographic History of the Civil War*, 9:127).

19. Law Order Book, 1844–49, 278, 288, 290–98, Amherst County Circuit Court; *Lynchburg Virginian*, September 7, 1846. May's name does not appear on any state's

census index from 1850: a chest wound and long confinement in a damp, unheated jail cell may have sealed his fate.

20. *Lynchburg Virginian*, December 18, 1845.

21. Ibid., December 11, 1845.

22. Davis, "Swinging Sweeneys," 3–10; Seventh Census of the United States, M-432, reel 933, 314, and Eighth Census of the United States, M-653, reel 1332, 465, RG 29, NA. Davis quotes the recollection of Judge Robert B. Poore, the grandson of Dr. Joel Walker Flood, who spent his early years at his grandparents' home a mile and a half northeast of the Sweeney place; Sweeney's money belt is still in the hands of a descendant in Appomattox, and his original banjo has been preserved by the Los Angeles County Museum (see Woodward, "Joel Sweeney and the First Banjo," 7–11).

23. Land Book, 1846, Appomattox County Circuit Court. The new tavern was open for business by April 20, 1846, which would imply that construction must have begun as soon as the deal was struck between McDearmon and Raine.

24. *Lynchburg Virginian*, December 15, 1845, and January 26, 1846.

25. Legislative Petitions, Appomattox County, January 29, 1846, LOV. The controversy over precinct elections had been broiling for more than a dozen years: a Buckingham County delegate submitted a legislative petition on February 5, 1833, arguing that precinct balloting would rob the courthouse election of the spirited debate and candidate speeches that helped the voters to make their decisions.

26. *Lynchburg Virginian*, February 2 and 12, 1846.

27. Seventh Census of the United States, M-432, reel 933, 313, 315, and Slave Schedule for Appomattox County, reel 983, RG 29, NA; Land Books, 1845 and 1846, Appomattox County Circuit Court; Personal Property Tax Lists, Appomattox County, 1845 and 1846, reel 23, LOV. Flood Family Papers in the possession of Mrs. Virginia Tyler, of Appomattox, indicate that Henry D. Flood married his second wife, Mary Elizabeth Flood, the daughter of Thomas H. Flood, on July 15, 1842 (the author in conversation with Mrs. Tyler, January 11, 1997).

28. Land Book, 1846, Appomattox County Circuit Court; *Lynchburg Virginian*, September 13, 1846.

29. *Richmond Enquirer*, April 19, 1845.

30. *Lynchburg Virginian*, February 16, March 16 and 30, and May 4, 1846.

31. *Lynchburg Virginian*, April 20, 1846.

32. Reniers, *Springs of Virginia*, 25–26, 183.

33. *Lynchburg Virginian*, July 13, 1846; Results of the Election of Field Officers, 174th Regiment, July 4, 1846, Executive Department, Militia Commission Papers, 1777–1858, LOV.

34. *Lynchburg Virginian*, July 13, 1846.

35. Ibid., June 18, 1846. The longest-serving court clerk recalled the courthouse as standing forty feet square: see George Peers pencil map of the village, ACHNHP.

36. Land Books, 1846 and 1847, Appomattox County Circuit Court; Seventh Census of the United States, M-432, reel 933, 353, RG 29, NA.

37. Deed Book 26, 299–301, Prince Edward County Courthouse; Land Books, 1846–51, Appomattox County Circuit Court.

38. Land Books, 1848 and 1849, Appomattox County Circuit Court; *Lynchburg Vir-*

ginian, September 24, 1849; Seventh Census of the United States, M-432, reel 933, 351–52, RG 29, NA. The story of the brickmaking at the Raine house comes from the recollections of Branch Walker, a nephew of Major Samuel Walker, in the *Lynchburg News* of March 6, 1901.

39. Deed Book 26, 299, 301, Prince Edward County Courthouse; Seventh Census of the United States, M-432, reel 933, 353–55, RG 29, NA. McDearmon sold this house to Jacob Tibbs in 1854; a U.S. Signal Corps detachment established an observation post on the top of that building on the morning of April 9, 1865, and one of those signalmen described it as having a "mansard" (hipped) roof. See *OR* 46(1):1178, and Pray, "Recollections of Appomattox," 19. While Pray mistook the Tibbs house for the John Sears house, which had a traditional pitched roof, Chris Calkins reconciles the error (Calkins, *Battles of Appomattox Station and Appomattox Court House*, 137).

40. Seventh Census of the United States, M-432, reel 933, 355, RG 29, NA. Building locations are taken mainly from Nathaniel Michler's 1867 survey of the vicinity of Appomattox Court House (*Atlas to Accompany the Official Records*, plate 78, map 2), in conjunction with census information and Land Book records.

41. Seventh Census of the United States, M-432, reel 933, 313, 314, RG 29, NA; Land Book, 1851, Appomattox County Circuit Court; Davis, "Swinging Sweeneys," 7.

42. Seventh Census of the United States, M-432, reel 933, 354, 368, 369, RG 29, NA; gravestones of Susan LeGrand Sears and Martha Nowlin Sears, Sears family cemetery, Route 616, Appomattox County; Land Books, 1854–66, Appomattox County Circuit Court. The 1850 census gives Archibald and Caroline LeGrand eleven children between the ages of two months and twenty years; the gravestone of their daughter "A. C.," who died in 1845, stands in the Archibald A. LeGrand cemetery on Route 631 in Appomattox County; the *Lynchburg Virginian* of October 25, 1847, reports the marriage of another daughter; and the 1860 census lists two more children born between 1851 and 1856 (Eighth Census of the United States, M-653, reel 1332, 357, RG 29, NA). Perhaps worn out with a quarter century of nearly constant reproduction, Mrs. LeGrand herself died of heart disease in 1857 (Vital Statistics of Appomattox County, Deaths, 1857, reel 3, LOV).

43. Seventh Census of the United States, M-432, reel 933, 331, 340–41, 368–69, 413, RG 29, NA; Martha D. Trent gravestone, now removed to Route 618, Appomattox.

44. Seventh Census of the United States, M-432, reel 933, 313, 314, 316, 317, 361, RG 29, NA.

45. Ibid. The white population of Appomattox County in 1850 was 4,209, with 4,799 slaves and 184 free blacks; the census tallies 185, but the "mulatto" boy Joseph Staples on page 322 is actually white.

46. Nonpopulation Schedules for Virginia, 1850–80, T-1132, reel 1, RG 29, NA.

47. Ibid.; Personal Property Tax Lists, Appomattox County, 1845–50, reel 23, LOV.

48. Elections of field and company officers, 174th Regiment Virginia Militia, July 4, 1846–October 29, 1853, Executive Department, Militia Commission Papers, 1777–1858, LOV; Seventh Census of the United States, M-432, reel 933, 314–15, 328, 354–55, 384, RG 29, NA; Eighth Census of the United States, M-653, reel 1332, 445, RG 29, NA.

49. Elections of company officers, 174th Regiment Virginia Militia, April 22, 1848,

and May 4, 1850, Executive Department, Militia Commission Papers, 1777–1858, LOV; *Lynchburg Virginian*, July 2, 1848.

50. Election of field officers, 174th Regiment Virginia Militia, May 2, 1848, Executive Department, Militia Commission Papers, 1777–1858, LOV.

CHAPTER TWO

1. Land Books, 1850–54, Appomattox County Circuit Court; Seventh Census of the United States, M-432, reel 933, 315, 365–66, RG 29, NA; *Lynchburg Virginian*, January 17 and May 2, 1850. Upon the creation of Appomattox County, the General Assembly charged the school commissioners of the parent counties with the responsibility of educating poor Appomattox children (*Acts of the General Assembly*, 1845, 138), but the Prince Edward County commissioners failed to pay Barbara Wright for her efforts to teach the indigent at the Court House: see Legislative Petitions, Appomattox County, January 27, 1847, LOV.

2. *Richmond Enquirer*, January 10, 21, and April 17, 1850; *Republican General Advertiser*, May 13, 1850.

3. Phillips, *Yonder Comes the Train*, 155; *Lynchburg Virginian*, December 9, 1850; *Acts of the General Assembly*, 1849, 107, and 1851, 62, 81.

4. *Lynchburg Virginian*, February 13, March 24, April 24, and November 24, 1851.

5. *De Bow's Review* 10 (January 1851): 106–7; *Richmond Enquirer*, September 1, 1855.

6. *Lynchburg Virginian*, April 24 and May 5, 1851; Raine family gravestones, Raine cemetery, Route 24, Appomattox County.

7. Vital Statistics of Appomattox County, Deaths, 1857, reel 3, LOV.

8. Nonpopulation Schedules for Virginia, 1850–80, T-1132, Appomattox County Mortality, 1850, reel 1, RG 29, NA.

9. Flood family gravestones, Flood cemetery, Route 616, Appomattox County; *Lynchburg Virginian*, May 26, 1845, and April 6, 1846.

10. Susan LeGrand Sears gravestone, Sears cemetery, Route 616, Appomattox County; *Lynchburg Virginian*, June 26, 1846; Vital Statistics of Appomattox County, Deaths, 1857, reel 3, LOV; Seventh Census of the United States, M-432, reel 933, 368, 369, and 395–96, RG 29, NA.

11. Vital Statistics of Appomattox County, Deaths, 1857, reel 3, LOV.

12. Seventh Census of the United States, M-432, reel 933, 315, 352–53, 368, and 395–96; Eighth Census of the United States, M-653, reel 1332, 439, 472–73, and 482, RG 29, NA.

13. Seventh Census of the United States, M-432, reel 933, 315, 317, 338, 353, 361, and 395–96; Eighth Census of the United States, M-653, reel 1332, 474–75, 483, and 509, RG 29, NA; Vital Statistics of Appomattox County, Marriages, 1854–60, reel 4, LOV; gravestone of Mary Elizabeth Trent Flood, Flood family cemetery, between Routes 616 and 24, Appomattox County; Flood family marriage records, Mrs. Virginia Tyler, Appomattox. The Pryor Wright house was described as an "old brick residence" by a man who grew up in the village in the years after the war (see map notes in Featherston, *History of Appomattox*, 26).

14. Seventh Census of the United States, M-432, reel 933, households 332, 354, and 357, RG 29, NA; *Lynchburg Virginian*, October 11, 1852; Land Book, 1851, Appomattox County Circuit Court.

15. Deed Book 26, 302–4, Prince Edward County Courthouse; Land Book, 1851, Appomattox County Circuit Court.

16. Deed Book 26, 302, Prince Edward County Courthouse.

17. *Lynchburg Virginian*, April 24 and September 1, 1851; Phillips, *Yonder Comes the Train*, 155; Hubbard, *Encyclopedia of North American Railroading*, 35–36.

18. *Lynchburg Virginian*, September 15 and October 23, 1851.

19. Ibid., October 13 and 16, November 24 and 27, 1851, and March 1, 1852; Edward Sears to "Dear Sir," February 7, 1852, photocopy tipped into Cauble, "Cultural History as of 1865," ACHNHP.

20. Shade, *Democratizing the Old Dominion*, 281; *Lynchburg Virginian*, October 30 and December 11, 1851.

21. *Lynchburg Virginian*, January 26, 1852, and November 28, 1853; Legislative Petitions, Appomattox County, March 12, 1852, LOV; *Acts of the General Assembly*, 1851, 218.

22. The ownership of the two stores in 1852 is established by McDearmon's references to them early the next year in Deed Book 26, 299, Prince Edward County Courthouse, and by the Land Books for 1851 and 1854, Appomattox County Circuit Court.

23. *Lynchburg Virginian*, August 10, 1852; Land Books, 1853–55, Appomattox County Circuit Court.

24. *Acts of the General Assembly*, 1852, 341; Plunkett-Meeks Store ledger, December 3, 1853, ACHNHP; Deed Book 26, 303, Prince Edward County Courthouse; *Lynchburg Virginian*, October 11, 1852.

25. Deed Book 26, 302–4, Prince Edward County Courthouse.

26. *Lynchburg Virginian*, January 8, 1853; Henry D. Flood to Thomas S. Bocock, July 20, 1854, box 7, Bocock Papers, UVA.

27. Deed Book 26, 298–305, Prince Edward County Courthouse; Personal Property Tax Lists, Appomattox County, 1850–54, reel 23, LOV.

28. Deed Book 26, 298–305, Prince Edward County Courthouse.

29. *Lynchburg Virginian*, May 2, 1853.

30. Ibid., June 8 and 25, 1853; Land Books, 1851–53, Appomattox County Circuit Court; Vital Statistics of Appomattox County, Deaths, 1853, reel 3, LOV; Sarah Ann Eliza Horner gravestone, Raine cemetery, Route 24, Appomattox County.

31. *Lynchburg Virginian*, April 22, 1853; Election of Company Officers, 174th Regiment Virginia Militia, May 14, 1853, Executive Department, Militia Commission Papers, 1777–1858, LOV; Records of Appointments of Postmasters, M-841, reel 130, RG 28, NA.

32. Plunkett-Meeks Store ledger, October 1, 1853–January 7, 1854, ACHNHP.

33. Ibid.; Eighth Census of the United States, M-653, reel 1332, 528, and Seventh Census of the United States, M-432, reel 933, 385, RG 29, NA; Nathaniel Michler map of Appomattox Court House, *Atlas to Accompany the Official Records*, plate 78, map 2; Records of Appointments of Postmasters, M-841, reel 130, RG 28, NA.

34. *Lynchburg Virginian*, December 12 and 22, 1853, January 12 and 23, and February 2, 1854.

35. *Richmond Enquirer*, March 9, 1854. Douglas's biographer, Robert Johannsen,

examines the complicated motives behind the Senator's bill (*Stephen A. Douglas*, 390–434), but he focuses on political reasoning rather than indirect personal interest.

36. *Richmond Enquirer*, March 2, 1854.

37. Perdue et al., *Weevils in the Wheat*, 39; *Lynchburg Virginian*, January 5, June 21, and July 10, 1854.

38. *Lynchburg Virginian*, January 1, August 13, 18, and 21, and October 9, 1854, January 26, July 20, August 24, and November 12, 1855.

39. Land Books, 1854 and 1855, Appomattox County Circuit Court; *Lynchburg Virginian*, October 2, 1854.

40. Land Books, 1854–57, Appomattox County Circuit Court. Although the house in which Tibbs lived at the end of the war is generally identified as McDearmon's former home, no buildings appear on the Land Books for Tibbs's lot until 1857; the transaction itself was not recorded until 1856. The correspondent of the *Lynchburg Virginian* who recorded his rail journey on July 10, 1854, identified the owner of the hotel at Appomattox Station as "William" McDearmon, but the only William McDearmon living in the county at that time was Samuel McDearmon's twelve-year-old son.

41. Land Books, 1854–63, Appomattox County Circuit Court; notes on the McDearmon-Atwood house, Farrar Family Papers; Records of Appointments of Postmasters, M-841, reel 130, RG 28, NA. McDearmon's postal salary is reflected in his report of $120 annual "fees of office," Personal Property Tax List, Appomattox County, 1855, reel 23, LOV.

42. *Richmond Whig*, November 11, 1854; *Lynchburg Virginian*, January 23, 1855.

43. *Lynchburg Virginian*, February 23, 1855. For an account of the decline of the Whigs and the parabolic rise of the Know Nothings, see Holt, *Political Parties and American Political Development*, 237–90, and Potter, *Impending Crisis*, 240–50. For an excellent comprehensive account of the Whig Party, see Holt, *Rise and Fall of the American Whig Party* (and especially 856–57, for insight into the Southern Whigs at this juncture).

44. *Lynchburg Virginian*, March 26, 1855.

45. Ibid., April 16, 1855; Land Books, 1855–65, Appomattox County Circuit Court; *Acts of the General Assembly*, 1851, 81.

46. *Lynchburg Virginian*, December 10, 1855.

47. Ibid., December 12, 1855.

48. Rawley, *Race and Politics*, 112–14; *Lynchburg Virginian*, April 14, 1856.

49. Samuel G. Lewis to Drury Woodson, December 9, 1857, and to Elvira Woodson, December 13, 1858, Woodson Papers, Duke University; Joel T. Cawthorn to John H. Cawthorn, July 6, 1864, ACHNHP; *Lynchburg Virginian*, February 13, 1856.

50. Seventh Census of the United States, M-432, reel 933, 368, and Eighth Census of the United States, M-653, reel 1332, 533, RG 29, NA; Tweedy family headstones, Sears and Tweedy cemeteries, Route 616, Appomattox; Vital Statistics of Appomattox County, Deaths, 1862, reel 3, LOV.

51. Deed Book 26, 303, Prince Edward County Courthouse; Land Books, 1855–56 and 1860, Appomattox County Circuit Court; Vital Statistics of Appomattox County, Deaths, 1854, reel 3, LOV; Eighth Census of the United States, M-653, reel 1332, 483, RG 29, NA.

52. Land Books, 1855–56, Appomattox County Circuit Court.

53. Ibid., 1856; Vital Statistics of Appomattox County, Deaths, 1857, reel 3, LOV. The 1942 ACHNHP master plan's interpretive statement alludes to Dr. Abbitt's deed for this property dated April 11, 1855 (Deed Book 1, 449–50, Appomattox County Circuit Court), and it first appears in the Land Book of 1856 as a one-acre tract with an $800 building. Published National Park Service handbooks confuse this Dr. Abbitt with Dr. William H. Abbitt, who was seven years younger: both married young women named Sarah (William B. Abbitt married Sarah LeGrand, daughter of widow Nancy LeGrand, while William H. Abbitt married Sarah Plunkett, daughter of John Plunkett and sister of David Plunkett). Dr. William B. Abbitt died in the typhoid epidemic of 1857; Dr. William H. Abbitt served briefly in the Confederate army, contracted typhoid, and resigned his commission based on supposed long-term effects of that acute disease, although he lived until 1907.

54. Eighth Census of the United States, M-653, reel 1332, 425, 492, RG 29, NA; *Lynchburg Virginian*, February 13, 1856.

55. Land Books, 1854–63, Appomattox County Circuit Court; Seventh Census of the United States, M-432, reel 933, 331–32; Eighth Census of the United States, M-653, reel 1332, 450, 474–75; Vital Statistics of Appomattox County, Marriages, 1858, reel 4, LOV.

56. *Lynchburg Virginian*, May 4, 1855, September 6, 1856, May 23 and 25, 1860; notes on claims and judgments against administration of Eliza D. Raine, and chancery suit of Ella Raine and Horner infants against Charles A. Raine and others, Virginia Court of Appeals docket book, 1856–62, Jones Memorial Library; family headstones, Raine cemetery, Route 24, Appomattox County.

CHAPTER THREE

1. *Statistical Gazeteer of the States of Virginia and North Carolina*, 165–67; *Lynchburg Virginian*, September 1, 1853; Legislative Petitions, Appomattox County, January 10, 1854, LOV; Records of Appointments of Postmasters, M-841, reel 130, RG 28, NA; Robert J. Boaz to Thomas S. Bocock, November 1, 1856, box 7, Bocock Papers, UVA.

2. Eighth Census of the United States, M-653, reel 1332, 425, RG 29, NA; *Lynchburg Virginian*, November 11, 1856. The 1860 census records only four children in Henry Bocock's family born between 1848 and 1855; a fifth, eight-year-old "Janie," died in 1859 and is buried in the Bocock family cemetery at Wildway, on Route 616.

3. *Lynchburg Virginian*, December 16, 1856, January 28 and March 28, 1857; Willis P. Bocock will, July 13, 1885, Will Book 1, 153–56, Appomattox County Circuit Court.

4. *Lynchburg Virginian*, January 13 and May 29, 1857; Student Register, August 21, 1856, Emory and Henry College; Flood Papers, Mrs. Virginia Tyler.

5. Land Books, 1856–60, Appomattox County Circuit Court; Peers house documentation, Appomattox Court House National Historic Monument Master Plan, Interpretive Statement, ACHNHP; Legislative Petitions, Appomattox County, January 10, 1854, LOV; Records of Appointments of Postmasters, M-841, reel 130, RG 28, NA; Wilson Hix to "Postmaster General," February 1, 1857, box 7, Bocock Papers, UVA; Eighth Census of the United States, M-653, reel 1332, 464, and Slave Schedule, reel 1386, RG 29, NA. The Land Books do not record Hix's ownership of the tavern

until 1859, but his 1857 letter indicates that he left Bent Creek then; he, too, may have leased the business for a year before buying it. Wilson Hix's first wife was Martha Bocock.

6. *Lynchburg Virginian*, April 14, 1857, and July 26, 1858.

7. Nonpopulation Schedules for Virginia, 1850–80, T-1132, reels 1 and 5, RG 29, NA; *Lynchburg Virginian*, August 7, 1857. The Flood prizery is still preserved, in its final incarnation, on National Park Service land.

8. See Berlin, *Many Thousands Gone*, 109–41, and Elkins, *Slavery*, 44–47.

9. Stampp, *America in 1857*, 82–83; *Richmond Enquirer*, May 1, June 12 and 16, and October 9, 1857. For the far-reaching effects of the Dred Scott decision, see Fehrenbacher, *Dred Scott Case*.

10. Helper, *Impending Crisis of the South*, 10–11, 240, 246; Fitzhugh, *Cannibals All*, 15–21.

11. Shade, *Democratizing the Old Dominion*, 107, 196–97, 209–10; Vital Statistics of Appomattox County, Deaths, 1857–60, reel 3, LOV. From respective populations of 4,118 and 4,600, 57 white citizens and 117 slaves died in 1860, besides 2 of the county's 171 free blacks. That yielded mortality rates of 1.4 percent for whites, 2.5 percent for slaves, and only 1.2 percent for free blacks.

12. Vital Statistics of Appomattox County, Deaths, 1857, reel 3, LOV; George Peers recollections, undated newspaper clipping, ACHNHP; Amanda Woodson to Elvira Woodson, July 27, 1857, Woodson Papers, Duke University.

13. Vital Statistics of Appomattox County, Deaths, 1857, reel 3, LOV; *Lynchburg Virginian*, November 4, 1857.

14. Vital Statistics of Appomattox County, Deaths, 1857, reel 3, LOV; Personal Property Tax List, Appomattox County, 1857, reel 24, LOV; George Peers recollections, undated newspaper clipping, ACHNHP.

15. Huston, *Panic of 1857*, 1–14, 17–22; *Acts of the General Assembly*, 1856, 270.

16. *Richmond Enquirer*, October 16 and November 20, 1857.

17. Ibid., October 16, 1857; *Richmond Whig*, November 27, December 18 and 25, 1857; *Lynchburg Virginian*, November 23, 1857.

18. *Lynchburg Virginian*, February 3 and March 26, 1858; Legislative Petitions, Appomattox County, January 20 and 25, 1860, LOV.

19. *Lynchburg Virginian*, February 5 and 8, 1858; Land Books, 1855–60, Appomattox County Circuit Court.

20. *Lynchburg Virginian*, March 17 and 18, April 7, and June 14, 1858.

21. *Richmond Enquirer*, December 8, 1857, and March 5, 1858.

22. Eggleston, *Rebel's Recollections*, 37–38.

23. Ibid., 34.

24. *Lynchburg Virginian*, March 23 and May 3, 1858; Records of Appointments of Postmasters, M-841, reel 130, RG 28, NA; Land Books, 1856–65, Appomattox County Circuit Court. An abstract of John H. Flood's November 7, 1859, deed for an adjoining parcel (ACHNHP) indicates that David Plunkett and Joseph Abbitt Jr. owned the store at that time.

25. Sallie B. Markham to Elvira L. Woodson, September 6, 1858, Woodson Papers, Duke University; *Lynchburg Virginian*, April 28, 1858; Seventh Census of the United States, M-432, Slave Schedule, reel 983, RG 29, NA.

26. Eighth Census of the United States, M-653, Slave Schedule, reel 1386, RG 29, NA; Virginia Court of Appeals docket book, 1856–62, Jones Memorial Library.

27. Eighth Census of the United States, M-653, Slave Schedule, reel 1386, 227, 244–46, 251–52, 254, RG 29, NA; Scarborough, *Diary of Edmund Ruffin*, 1:25.

28. Nonpopulation Schedules for Virginia, 1850–80, T-1132, Appomattox County Mortality, 1850, reel 5; Seventh Census of the United States, M-432, reel 933, particularly 321; and Eighth Census of the United States, M-653, reel 1332, particularly 493, all in RG 29, NA. The instances of smothering among slave babies may have been the result of sudden infant death, or—particularly since it only seems to have occurred among slaves—could have been the deliberate acts of desperate mothers who wished to spare their children a life of bondage, but the tally of two deaths in October 1859, one in November, and one in January 1860 suggests that the two-, three-, and four-month-old children perished as their mothers huddled in the same bed to keep them warm.

29. Land Book, 1854, Appomattox County Circuit Court; Eighth Census of the United States, M-653, Slave Schedule, reel 1386, 241, RG 29, NA; Vital Statistics of Appomattox County, Births, 1855–62, reel 4, LOV; Perdue et al., *Weevils in the Wheat*, 30, 34.

30. Perdue et al., *Weevils in the Wheat*, 30, 36, 48–49; Eighth Census of the United States, M-653, reel 1332 (especially 526), RG 29, NA. Since a child was born slave or free depending upon the status of the mother, the two free children in the home of those white women would appear to have been their own.

31. Eighth Census of the United States, M-653, Slave Schedule, reel 1386, 227–55, RG 29, NA. The slave schedules offer no names for slaves, instead identifying them by owner, age, gender, and color.

32. Perdue et al., *Weevils in the Wheat*, 35; *Lynchburg Virginian*, September 23, 1859.

33. *Lynchburg Virginian*, June 2, 1858.

34. Elkins, *Slavery*, 211; Craven, *Coming of the Civil War*, 406; Maddex, *Virginia Conservatives*, 16–17; Seventh Census of the United States, M-432, Slave Schedule, reel 983, and Eighth Census of the United States, M-653, Slave Schedule, reel 1386, RG 29, NA; Perdue et al., *Weevils in the Wheat*, 32–33, 71.

35. *Richmond Enquirer*, June 4, 1858.

36. Ibid., June 13, 1859.

37. *Lynchburg Virginian*, April 6, 11, and 22, May 28, August 17, and September 12, 1859; Nonpopulation Schedules for Virginia, 1850–80, T-1132, Appomattox County Mortality, 1860, reel 5, RG 29, NA.

38. U.S. Congress, Senate, *Report of the Select Committee of the Senate*, 40–45; *Lynchburg Virginian*, October 19, 1859; *New York Tribune*, October 19, 1859; *Richmond Enquirer*, October 20 and November 5, 1859, January 5, 11, and 21, 1860.

39. *Lynchburg Virginian*, December 14, 1859; Susan Leigh Blackford, *Letters from Lee's Army*, 1.

40. *Lynchburg Virginian*, December 8 and 13, 1859.

41. Ibid., December 7–10, 1859.

42. Ibid., December 12, 13, 24, and 26, 1859, January 3, 4, 11, 19, and 31, 1860.

43. Ibid., February 1 and 3, 1860.

44. Ibid., January 17, 1860; Nonpopulation Schedules for Virginia, 1850–80, T-1132, Appomattox County Mortality, 1860, reel 5, RG 29, NA.

45. Eighth Census of the United States, M-653, reel 1332, 426, 482–83, RG 29, NA.

46. Wilson Hix to James Seddon, received July 8, 1862 (including a certified excerpt of the circuit court's approval of deputies William Daniel Hix and Daniel W. Gills), item 632-H-1862, Letters Received by the Confederate Secretary of War, 1861–65, M-437, reel 51, RG 109, NA.

47. *Lynchburg Virginian*, August 14, 1857, April 6, 1860, September 28, 1859, and June 2, 1858; Nonpopulation Schedules for Virginia, 1850–80, T-1132, Appomattox County Mortality, 1860, reel 5, and Seventh Census of the United States, M-432, reel 933, households 234 and 330, RG 29, NA; Vital Statistics of Appomattox County, Deaths, 1857, reel 3, LOV.

48. *Lynchburg Virginian*, May 23 and 25, 1860; Seventh Census of the United States, M-432, reel 933, household 313, RG 29, NA.

49. *Lynchburg Virginian*, May 26 and August 3, 1860; Land Book, 1860, Appomattox County Circuit Court.

50. Land Books, 1857–60, Appomattox County Circuit Court; Nonpopulation Schedules for Virginia, T-1132, 1860, Appomattox County Industrial Schedule, reel 8, RG 29, NA; Eighth Census of the United States, M-653, reel 1332, 425, 450, 475, 483, RG 29, NA; Vital Statistics of Appomattox County, Marriages, 1860, reel 4, LOV. Jones's law office has long been confused with the Kelly house because of an ostensibly original 1876 deed rerecorded after the courthouse burned down in 1892; all other records indicate that the law office occupied lot 30, at the southwestern corner of the intersection of the Buckingham Court House and Prince Edward Court House Roads. George Peers, who bought the Inge cabin in 1880, locates it near the southern line of lot 29 on his 1894 pencil map of the village, ACHNHP. The saddler's shop, meanwhile, is clearly identified in E. G. Hix's deed of December 14, 1883, to Charles H. Sackett (Deed Book 1, 451, Appomattox County Circuit Court) as the fifteen-by-eighteen-foot plot just north of what had been the Plunkett-Meeks Store, where now sits a building the National Park Service has identified as John W. Woodson's law office; copies of Francis Meeks's deed from William Trent and to Wilson Hix dated October 16, 1863, in the ACHNHP holdings, corroborate the site of the saddler's shop; Woodson's law office was on lot 20, west of the Raine tavern and house.

51. Land Books, 1854–63, Appomattox County Circuit Court; Eighth Census of the United States, M-653, reel 1332, 475, RG 29, NA. Because of the confused or fraudulent deed referred to in note 50, the actual site of the Kelly house has never been identified. Land Books indicate that Kelly bought two parcels from town lots that Samuel McDearmon had converted back to open acreage after his bankruptcy proceedings; in 1862, however, the Land Book notes that Kelly's larger tract was "entered with town lots" again, and thereafter it is identified as lot 3, which would place it north of the dwelling house for which Isbell and Flood were trustees. No archaeology has been conducted in that vicinity, but Nathaniel Ragland Featherston's 1948 map of the village locates a "frame house" there (*History of Appomattox*, 26, 27); the house in question is labeled #22 on Featherston's map.

52. Land Books, 1854–60, Appomattox County Circuit Court; Eighth Census of

the United States, M-653, Slave Schedule, reel 1386, 241, RG 29, NA; Featherston, *History of Appomattox*, 26, 28.

53. This enormous stable, the location of which has been a mystery, is referred to in an 1883 deed (Deed Book 2, 540, Appomattox County Circuit Court) as being on lot 11, on the western edge of the village just north of the stage road. The constricted configuration of adjacent lot 19, which the brick blacksmith shop shares with lot 20, suggests that the stable sat farther west than the blacksmith shop. That would place it near where the National Park Service now recognizes Charles Diuguid's blacksmith shop to have sat. The only building on Diuguid's lot disappears from the Land Books in 1857 and none reappears until 1871, when a more substantial one is erected; it lasted only one year that time, and no building resurfaces on that lot again until 1877.

54. *Lynchburg Virginian*, May 30, June 7, 26, and 27, 1860.

55. Ibid., September 4, 1860; *Acts of the General Assembly*, 1860, 91; Consolidated Index to Compiled Service Records of Confederate Soldiers, M-253, reel 1, RG 109, NA. The other field officers were Lieutenant Colonel James E. Robertson, Major Joel Walker Flood Jr., and Major William H. Abbitt.

56. *Lynchburg Virginian*, September 4, 1860; Eighth Census of the United States, M-653, households 520, 734, 761, and 808, RG 29, NA.

57. *Lynchburg Virginian*, September 4, 1860; Nonpopulation Schedules for Virginia, 1850–80, T-1132, Appomattox County Mortality, 1860, reel 5, RG 29, NA; Vital Statistics of Appomattox County, Deaths, 1860, reel 3, LOV; Eighth Census of the United States, M-653, reel 1332, household 292, RG 29, NA.

CHAPTER FOUR

1. *Lynchburg Virginian*, September 3 and 26, October 10 and 29, 1860.

2. Ibid., November 10 and December 7, 1860.

3. Ibid., December 4, 1860; John H. Bocock to James Henley Thornwell, December 22, 1860, James Henley Thornwell Collection, South Caroliniana Library, University of South Carolina.

4. *Lynchburg Virginian*, January 9, 17, and 29, February 9 and 27, and April 9, 10, and 15, 1861; Sarah Evelyn Gilliam to John B. Moseley, December 30, 1861, Moseley Papers, VHS. Flood's supporters included Dr. William D. Christian, Allen Conner, Samuel A. Glover, Archibald LeGrand, and John Sears. For a thoughtful account of Virginia's extensive unionism at this period, see Crofts, *Reluctant Confederates*, 37–49, 136–44, 277–83. Crofts poses the original argument that Lincoln's confrontational policy at Fort Sumter and his resulting call for troops worsened the magnitude of the conflict that ensued, and that a more conciliatory policy might have exerted better effect had it been given an earnest attempt.

5. William Matthews Blackford diary, April 6 and 14, 1861, Blackford Papers, Emory University; *Lynchburg Virginian*, April 20, 1861.

6. *Lynchburg Virginian*, May 4, 1861; Amanda Daniel to Elvira Woodson, April 16, 1861, Woodson Papers, Duke University.

7. See muster rolls of April–June 1861, Company A, 44th Virginia Infantry, reels

877–83, CSRCSV. Regimental muster rolls are kept alphabetically by member, rather than by company.

8. *Lynchburg Virginian*, April 22, 1861.

9. Richard Radford letter of recommendation, April 23, 1862, Robert B. Poore file, reel 22, CSRCSV.

10. Muster roll of Company H, 2nd Virginia Cavalry, June 30, 1861, reels 16–24, CSRCSV.

11. Vital Statistics of Appomattox County, Births, 1861, LOV; muster roll of Company H, 2nd Virginia Cavalry, June 30, 1861, reels 16–24; muster rolls of June 30, 1861, Robert W. Martin file, reel 880; and James E. Overton file, reel 881, CSRCSV; *Richmond Examiner*, June 3, 1861. By 1870 Charles Diuguid's son was known simply as Davy (Ninth Census of the United States, M-593, reel 1633, 29, RG 29, NA).

12. *Lynchburg Virginian*, January 9 and April 15, 1861; William Matthews Blackford diary, April 16 and July 17, 1861, Blackford Papers, Emory University; C. W. Jones file, reel 226, CSRCSV; George Peers recollections, undated newspaper clipping, ACHNHP.

13. *OR* 1:944; muster roll, June 30, 1861, Charles C. Gilchrist file, reel 603, CSRCSV.

14. *OR* 1:457–58, 926. Driver and Howard, *2nd Virginia Cavalry*, 11, quote (without citing the source or date of) a report by Captain Flood that every member of the company was armed with an old saber, while thirty-four men bore ancient, single-shot, flintlock pistols "about worthless," and forty more carried double-barreled shotguns. Charles W. Blackford (Susan Leigh Blackford, *Letters from Lee's Army*, 7) describes similar armament in another company of Radford's regiment.

15. *OR* 1:240, 269, 273–85.

16. *Lynchburg Virginian*, September 4, 1860, April 15 and June 8, 1861; *Richmond Enquirer*, June 7, 1861; muster roll of Company B, 46th Virginia Infantry, June 30, 1861, reels 892–905, CSRCSV.

17. Record of Events, reel 70, Compiled Records Showing Service of Military Units in Confederate Service, M-861, RG 109, NA; *Lynchburg Virginian*, July 25, 1861.

18. *OR* 1:450, 452, 458, 537–38.

19. Ibid., 446; Gallagher, *Fighting for the Confederacy*, 45–46; voucher for rent of McLean's property, July 17–December 31, 1861, Wilmer McLean file, reel 638, Confederate Papers Relating to Citizens or Business Firms, M-346, RG 109, NA.

20. *OR* 1:537.

21. Ibid., 474–77, 546–48.

22. Ibid., 538–39, 548; list of killed, wounded, and missing in the battle of Manassas dated August 29, 1861, files of Elijah Chism, reel 599, Andrew Leach and Thomas P. Mathews, reel 607, and Robert Meadows, reel 608, CSRCSV.

23. *Lynchburg Virginian*, July 25, 1861; *OR* 1:291–92; Lowry, *Battle of Scary Creek*, 162–63.

24. *OR* 1:292; Sarah Evelyn Gilliam to John B. Moseley, August 23, 1861, Moseley Papers, VHS; muster roll of August 31, 1861, Henry H. Dickinson file, reel 599, muster rolls of June 30 and October 31, 1861, James A. Calhoun file, reel 601, muster rolls of September–December, files of John Farrar, Robert W. S. Hannah, and Presley R. Wooldridge (reels 895, 896, and 905), and register of deceased soldiers, William N.

Beckham file, reel 892, CSRCSV; Vital Statistics of Appomattox County, Deaths, 1862, reel 3, LOV.

25. Muster rolls of July–October 1861, files of Joel W. Flood, reel 18, and Lafayette W. Meeks, reel 21, CSRCSV. The muster roll of Company H, 2nd Virginia Cavalry, dated October 31, 1861, indicates that Meeks died September 4, but on July 8, 1862, William D. Hix and George Peers signed affidavits swearing that the funeral was held October 6, and that they had been informed that Lafayette had died on October 4 (Lafayette Meeks file, ibid.).

26. *OR*, ser. 2, 1:463–79; Sarah Evelyn Gilliam to John B. Moseley, December 30, 1861, VHS; Robert Bell to Mrs. Bell, "April" [May] 21, 1865, "Civil War Letters of Capt. Robert Bell," ACHNHP.

27. Hix submitted separate vouchers for conveying both "Sep Roundar, a German," and "Sep Rosendat, a Yankee," to Richmond, and he received payment for both: Wilson Hix file, reel 450, Confederate Papers Relating to Citizens or Business Firms, M-346, RG 109, NA.

28. Marvel, *Battles for Saltville*, 14–16; *Lynchburg Virginian*, October 13, November 14 and 19, and December 16, 1861; George Peers recollections, undated newspaper clipping, ACHNHP.

29. Land Books, 1861–63, Appomattox County Circuit Court.

30. *OR* 5:456–68; *Lynchburg Virginian*, December 31, 1861; muster roll of December 31, 1861, James T. Dickerson file, reel 601, and register of deceased soldiers, Peter R. Pamplin file, reel 609, CSRCSV.

31. Sarah Evelyn Gilliam to John B. Moseley, December 30, 1861, Moseley Papers, VHS; regimental returns and muster rolls, November 1861–February 1862, John B. Moseley file, reel 640, CSRCSV; *OR* 5:389, 460.

32. *OR*, ser. 4, 1:837, 869.

33. Ibid., 9:179; muster roll of Company B, 46th Virginia Infantry, January and February 1861 (reels 892–905), CSRCSV; Sarah Evelyn Gilliam to John B. Moseley, February 8, 1862, Moseley Papers, VHS.

34. Muster roll of January and February 1862, Joel W. Flood file, reel 18, and Sampson D. Sweeney file, reel 23, CSRCSV; Sarah Evelyn Gilliam to John B. Moseley, February 8, 1862, Moseley Papers, VHS; memorandum book, March 4 and 19, 1862, Bocock Papers, UVA; "Proceedings of First Confederate Congress," *Southern Historical Society Papers* 44 (1916): 10–11.

35. Vital Statistics of Appomattox County, Births, 1862, reel 4; muster rolls of January–April 1862, Company B, 46th Virginia Infantry (reels 892–905), and resignation of April 1, 1862, William H. Abbitt file, reel 892, CSRCSV.

36. Roster of Company I, 3rd Light Artillery (Local Defense), reel 226, CSRCSV.

37. *OR* 5:1097 and ser. 4, 1:965–66; John W. Woodson to Judah P. Benjamin, February 20, 1862, and Thomas S. Bocock to same, same date, Letters Received by the Confederate Secretary of War, 1861–65, M-437, reel 76, RG 109, NA; muster-in roll, March 6, 1862, Captain Robert K. Kyle's Company, reel 317, CSRCSV; Register of Appointments, John W. Woodson file, reel 273, Compiled Service Records of Confederate General and Staff Officers and Nonregimental Enlisted Men, M-331, RG 109, NA; muster roll of March and April 1862, Company A, 20th Battalion of Heavy Artillery, reels 249–53, CSRCSV.

38. Muster roll for March and April 1862, Company H, 18th Infantry, reels 597–615, CSRCSV. The 1870 census of Appomattox County (M-593, reel 1633, 73, RG 29, NA) lists Harvey's widow, Elizabeth Wooldridge, with eleven-year-old "Fanie" Harvey (Samuel G. Harvey) and nine-year-old Elvira B. Harvey. Thomas J. Wooldridge's motive for enlisting in the 18th Virginia is offered in a petition for his discharge signed by Wilson Hix and others dated March 25, 1862, only seventeen days after his enlistment: see item 575-W-1862, Letters Received by the Confederate Secretary of War, 1861–65 (M-437), reel 53, RG 109, NA.

39. Muster roll of March and April 1862, Company H, 2nd Cavalry, reels 16–23, CSRCSV.

40. *OR*, ser. 4, 1:1031, 1095–96; "Proceedings of First Confederate Congress," *Southern Historical Society Papers* 45 (1917): 26–29, 125, 130.

41. *OR*, ser. 4, 2:160–62; petition received April 18, 1862, item 575-W-1862, Letters Received by the Confederate Adjutant and Inspector General, 1861–65, M-474, reel 53, and petition of Robert P. Patteson et al., certified March 31, 1862, item 123-P-1862, Letters Received by the Confederate Secretary of War, 1861–65, M-437, reel 65, both in RG 109, NA.

42. Thomas Bocock to George W. Randolph, May 12, 1862; John W. McKinney's resignation, May 26, 1862; and muster roll of March 6, 1862, all in McKinney file, reel 317, CSRCSV.

43. *OR*, ser. 4, 1:1062; Registers of commissioned officers and muster rolls of March and April 1862, files of Joel W. Flood, reel 18, Robert B. Poore, reel 22, Thomas A. Tibbs, reel 23, Charles E. Webb, reel 24, Samuel H. Overton and James E. Robertson, reel 252, Thomas A. Gilliam, reel 603, James Glover Harvey and Edward B. Harvey, reel 604, George W. Abbitt, reel 892, William G. Coleman, reel 893, and William S. Hannah, reel 896, CSRCSV.

44. Roll of persons received as substitutes, James Robertson file, reel 901, CSRCSV (Robertson, Coleman's substitute, deserted in November); Mary Ann Coleman memoir, ACHNHP; Land Books, 1860–63, Appomattox County Circuit Court.

CHAPTER FIVE

1. *OR* 11(3):427, 481; 12(1):417, 498, 502; and 51(2):518, 525.

2. Ibid., 11(1):569, 51(2):564; muster rolls of March–August 1862, files of Drury G. Woodson, reel 248, and Leonidas Cralle, reel 249, CSRCSV. Drury Woodson served less than four months in Company A, 19th Virginia Heavy Artillery Battalion.

3. *OR* 51(2):542; files of Company I, 3rd Light Artillery (Local Defense), and particularly those of E. Boyd Faulkner, C. H. Jones, Thomas A. Landrum, and John J. Tibbs, reel 226, CSRCSV.

4. Files of E. Boyd Faulkner, Thomas A. Landrum, Samuel W. McDearmon, and John J. Tibbs, reel 226, CSRCSV; Samuel D. McDearmon to James Seddon, May 9, 1863, George W. Abbitt affidavit, same date, and Henry Wise to Seddon, May 23, 1863, all in S. D. McDearmon file, reel 624, Confederate Papers Relating to Citizens or Business Firms, M-346, RG 109, NA.

5. Vouchers for delivery of Noah Boothe and Michael Coplay, May 12, 1862, Wilson

Hix file, reel 450, Confederate Papers Relating to Citizens or Business Firms, M-346, RG 109, NA.

6. Muster roll of July and August 1862, files of Edward H. Cawthorn, reel 599, Thomas A. Gilliam, reel 603, Edward G. Lee, reel 607, and John H. Singleton, reel 611, and muster roll of March and April 1863, James D. Glenn file, reel 603, CSRCSV; *OR* 11(2):980.

7. Vital Statistics of Appomattox County, Deaths, 1860–62, reel 3, LOV.

8. Ibid.

9. Ibid., Births, reel 4.

10. Ibid., Marriages, reel 4.

11. Lizzie Maynard to Elvira Woodson, December 4, 1864, Woodson Papers, Duke University; Vital Statistics of Appomattox County, Marriages, 1866, reel 4, LOV.

12. Sarah Evelyn Gilliam to John B. Moseley, August 23, October 17, and December 30, 1861, and February 8, 1862, Moseley Papers, VHS; muster rolls of January–April 1862, Nathan Ford file, reel 637; regimental return of March 1862, and roster of March 1865, John B. Moseley file, reel 640, CSRCSV; Nonpopulation Schedules for Virginia, T-1132, Mortality Schedules, 1870, reel 10, RG 29, NA; Evelyn Ford headstone, Gilliam-Sears cemetery, Route 627, Appomattox County.

13. Eighth Census of the United States, M-653, reel 1332:437, 452–53, 459, 460, RG 29, NA; muster roll of May and June 1864, John D. "Patterson" file, reel 900, CSRCSV.

14. Family headstones, Thornhill cemetery, Route 615, Appomattox County; Ninth Census of the United States, M-593, reel 1633:47, RG 29, NA; Flood, "Flood Family History," ACHNHP; *OR*, ser. 4, 2:160.

15. *OR*, ser. 4, 2:161.

16. Muster roll of March–August 1862, and report of persons employed at government shops, John W. Oden file, reel 247; muster-in roll of Ordnance Department Battalion, William Rosser file, reel 371; muster roll of May and June 1863, Caswell Inge file, reel 845; Samuel D. McDearmon to James Seddon, and William G. Coleman to same, William J. McDearmon file, reel 899; and roll of conscripts at Camp Lee, August 14, 1862, John A. Rosser file (reel 1075), CSRCSV; Land Books, 1862–65, Appomattox County Circuit Court; Samuel D. McDearmon to James Seddon, May 9, 1863, Samuel D. McDearmon file, reel 624, Confederate Papers Relating to Citizens or Business Firms, M-346, RG 109, NA; William G. Coleman to James Seddon, February 17, 1864, William J. McDearmon file, reel 899, CSRCSV.

17. *OR*, ser. 4, 2:162.

18. Personal Property Tax List, Appomattox County, 1863, reel 24, LOV; *Confederate Veteran* 11, no. 9 (September 1903): 418; "List of Confederate Chaplains, Army of Northern Virginia," *Southern Historical Society Papers* 34 (1906): 313.

19. *OR* 12(2):253, 565–66, 626, 748.

20. Ibid., 778; Edward B. Harvey diary, August 30, 1862, ACHNHP; muster roll of March and April 1862, files of John T. and William R. Wooldridge, R. and Elizabeth M. Wooldridge affidavit, Thomas J. Wooldridge file, all on reel 615, CSRCSV. Lieutenant Harvey's widow later married another man named William Wooldridge.

21. Vouchers dated July 17, 1861, to March 1, 1862, Wilmer McLean file, reel 638, Confederate Papers Relating to Citizens or Business Firms, M-346, RG 109, NA.

Frank Cauble speculates (*Biography of Wilmer McLean*, 71) that McLean may have learned of the Raine house from Nathaniel Ragland, a Richmond merchant whose wife spent the war years in Appomattox County, and who later bought the house himself.

22. Land Books, 1862–63, Appomattox County Circuit Court; McLean to John C. Pemberton, March 19, 1863, Wilmer McLean file, reel 638, Confederate Papers Relating to Citizens or Business Firms, M-346, RG 109, NA.

23. *OR* 19(1):825–26; muster roll of September and October 1862, Thomas A. Tibbs file, reel 23, CSRCSV.

24. *OR* 19(1):894–95, 899–900.

25. Edward B. Harvey diary, September 14, 1862, ACHNHP; Eighth Census of the United States, M-653, reel 1332, 426, and Slave Schedule, reel 1386, RG 29, NA.

26. Sorrel, *Recollections*, 101–2.

27. *OR* 19(1):896–97, 900–901; Edward B. Harvey diary, September 17, 1862, ACHNHP. Sgt. Samuel Gilchrist, whose brother had been the first Appomattox man to die in the war, was killed in the fighting of September 17, and Thomas Cubby, or Cumby, died that night; Allen Martin died of his wounds October 6, while James O. Melton, who suffered a broken thigh as well as a wound in his other leg, died November 17, at Winchester.

28. Muster rolls of September–December 1862, Sampson D. Sweeney file, reel 23, CSRCSV.

29. Two Lynchburg brothers commented particularly on Sweeney's popularity at Stuart's headquarters. See W. W. Blackford, *War Years with Jeb Stuart*, 50–51, and 162, and Susan Leigh Blackford, *Letters from Lee's Army*, 140.

30. *OR* 19(2):140–45; *Lynchburg Virginian*, November 4, 1862; Susan Leigh Blackford, *Letters from Lee's Army*, 140.

31. Vital Statistics of Appomattox County, Deaths, 1862, reel 3, LOV.

32. Sarah Evelyn Gilliam to John B. Moseley, February 8, 1862, Moseley Papers, VHS; Charles E. Webb to Fannie Abbitt, December 1, 1862, and Clifton V. Webb to "Dear Sister," September 22, 1862, William Abbitt Collection; muster rolls for January and February and May and June 1862, Clifton V. Webb file, reel 24, CSRCSV.

33. Clifton V. Webb to "Dear Sister," September 22, 1862, William Abbitt Collection; voucher of $74.10 paid September 30, 1862, Joel W. Flood file, and bill of May 20, 1863, Thomas H. Flood file, reel 310; receipts of September 15 and 30, 1862, A. A. LeGrand file, and receipt of July 26, 1862, Nancy LeGrand file, reel 580; receipt of July 6, 1863, George Abbitt Sr. file, reel 1; pay receipts and affidavit, Robert J. Boaz file, reel 75; and voucher of March 2, 1863, for $357.32, Wilson and William D. Hix files, reel 450, all in Confederate Papers Relating to Citizens or Business Firms, M-346, RG 109, NA; memorandum book, September 1862, box 8, Bocock Papers, UVA; Land Books, 1858–63, Appomattox County Circuit Court; *Acts of the General Assembly*, 1863, 70.

34. Assorted vouchers, Wilson and William D. Hix files, reel 450, Confederate Papers Relating to Citizens or Business Firms, M-346, RG 109, NA; memorandum book, December 5, 1863, box 8, Bocock Papers, UVA.

35. *Acts of the General Assembly*, 1862, 3–4; *OR*, ser. 4, 2:166–67; *Lynchburg Virginian*, November 24, 1862.

36. *OR*, ser. 4, 2:133, 426–30.

37. Personal Property Tax List, Appomattox County, 1863, reel 24, LOV; vouchers of October 31 and December 2, 1862, Wilson Hix file, reel 450; and affidavits of David P. Robertson, Thomas L. Singleton, and J. Lamb, N. S. Vest to William P. Smith, February 28, 1863, and voucher of July 15, 1864, Joel W. Flood file, reel 310, Confederate Papers Relating to Citizens or Business Firms, M-346, RG 109, NA.

38. Ninth Census of the United States, M-593, reel 1633, 83, RG 29, NA; Flood, "Flood Family History," ACHNHP; *Lynchburg Virginian*, December 17, 1862. The census marshal visited the Flood family early in August of 1870, by which time the Flood's oldest child, "Eliza B. Flood," was already seven years old; she was later known as Eleanor Bolling Flood, and she would grow up to marry Admiral Richard E. Byrd, the arctic aviator. In 1900 she gave March as her birth month, although she deducted three years from her age; see Twelfth Census of the United States, T-623, reel 1709, enumeration district 29, sheet 1, RG 29, NA.

39. Session Book, Records of Union Academy, Chilton Papers, UVA.

40. Legislative Petitions, Prince Edward County, January 29, 1838, LOV; *Lynchburg Virginian*, January 9, 1845, and January 1, 1854; Eighth Census of the United States, M-653, reel 1332, 425–534, RG 29, NA; George W. Abbitt to Fannie Abbitt, November 28, 1863, William Abbitt Collection.

41. Regimental returns for November and December 1862, George W. Abbitt file, reel 892; John D. "Patterson" file, reel 900; muster rolls of October–December 1862, William G. Coleman file, reel 893; muster roll of February 28, 1863, John E. Williams file, reel 905; muster rolls of November and December 1862, John J. Hannah file, reel 896; and W. S. Hannah to R. T. W. Duke, November 22, 1862, James Robertson file, reel 901, all in CSRCSV.

42. Register of approved furloughs and register of deceased soldiers, Joseph A. Megginson file, reel 249, and Lorenzo D. Kelley file, reel 251; James M. Carson to T. O. Chestney, January 13, 1863, Carson file, reel 249; and muster rolls of January–April 1863, files of Thomas A. Gilliam, reel 603, all in CSRCSV; Edward B. Harvey diary, February 13 and March 2, 1863, ACHNHP.

43. Robert B. Isbell to Anna Isbell, March 18, 1863, Bound Volume 104, Chatham office, Fredericksburg and Spotsylvania National Military Park; *Lynchburg Virginian*, March 18, 1863, various dates in April 1863, and May 13, 1863; John W. Woodson to A. C. Myers, April —, 1863, Woodson file, reel 273, Compiled Service Records of Confederate General and Staff Officers and Nonregimental Enlisted Men, M-331, RG 109, NA.

44. Land Books, 1862 and 1863, Appomattox County Circuit Court; Samuel D. McDearmon to R. G. H. Kean and James Seddon, May 9, 1863, George W. Abbitt affidavit of same date, and Henry Wise to Seddon, May 23, 1863, all in S. D. McDearmon file, reel 624, Confederate Papers Relating to Citizens or Business Firms, M-346, RG 109, NA; register of payments, William J. McDearmon file, reel 899, CSRCSV; William G. Coleman to Henry Wise, December 12 and 19, 1863, Coleman file, reel 893, CSRCSV; William G. Coleman to James Seddon, February 17, 1864, William J. McDearmon file, reel 899, CSRCSV.

45. *OR* 25(1):478, 793, 1027; John B. Moseley to James Seddon, May 26, 1863, Moseley file, reel 640, CSRCSV; John D. Moseley obituary, Moseley Papers, VHS; Eighth Census of the United States, M-653, reel 1332, 443, RG 29, NA.

46. Clifton V. Webb resignation and muster rolls of April 30 and June 30, 1863, Webb file, reel 24, CSRCSV.

47. Eighth Census of the United States, M-635, reel 1332, 427, 460, 462, and Slave Schedule, reel 1386, RG 29, NA; Records of Appointments of Postmasters, M-841, reel 130, RG 28, NA.

48. *OR* 27(2):358–59.

49. Ibid., 385.

50. Ibid.

51. Ibid., 387.

52. Ibid., 386.

53. Ibid., 386–87.

54. Ibid.; muster roll of Company H, 18th Infantry, July and August 1863, reels 597–615, CSRCSV.

CHAPTER SIX

1. Edward B. Harvey diary, July 7–August 6, 1863, ACHNHP; Ninth Census of the United States, M-593, reel 1633, 73, RG 29, NA; Vital Statistics of Appomattox County, Marriages, 1861, 1866, 1868, reel 4, LOV. Lucy McCune Paulett married Thomas Martin on April 18, 1866, and Elizabeth Harvey married William P. Wooldridge on October 7, 1868.

2. Register of deceased soldiers, files of E. W. Durham, reel 894, and R. W. Johnson, reel 898; order of July 7, 1863, and John D. Patteson to Major Cheney, August 24, 1863, John D. "Patterson" file, reel 900, CSRCSV; Vital Statistics of Appomattox County, Births, 1864, reel 4, LOV; voucher of July 20, 1863, for keeping Richard M. Oliver, Wilson Hix file, reel 450, Confederate Papers Relating to Citizens or Business Firms, M-346, RG 109, NA.

3. Muster roll of August 31, 1863, Samuel W. McDearmon file, reel 21; Clifton V. Webb resignation, dated May 5, 1863, Webb file, reel 24; muster rolls of August 31 and October 31, Clifton V. Webb file, reel 904, and Thomas J. M. Cheatham file, reel 226; and muster rolls of August–December 1863, Cheatham file, reel 599, all in CSRCSV; George W. Abbitt to Fannie Abbitt, November 28, 1863, William Abbitt Collection; receipts for deposits in the Confederate States Treasury, dated between December 7, 1863, and February 9, 1865, S. D. McDearmon file, reel 624, Confederate Papers Relating to Citizens or Business Firms, M-346, RG 109, NA.

4. Memorandum book, October 12, 1863, box 8, Bocock Papers, UVA; muster rolls of January–December 1863, Thomas A. Tibbs files, reels 23 and 817, and muster roll of January and February 1863, E. Boyd Faulkner file, reel 301, CSRCSV; Thomas S. Bocock to James Seddon, January 23, 1863, E. Boyd Faulkner file, reel 91, Compiled Service Records of Confederate General and Staff Officers and Nonregimental Enlisted Men, M-331, RG 109, NA. No record of Crawford Jones's death has surfaced, but CSRCSV contains no mention of any military service by him save his command of a battery in the 3rd Artillery for Local Defense, and after the tax list that was recorded in the Land Books in the Appomattox County Circuit Court on June 30, 1863, all his property is listed under "Crawford Jones Est[ate]."

5. Assorted muster rolls, files of John J. Hannah, Robert S. Hannah, and William S. Hannah, reel 896, and W. G. Coleman to Henry Wise, December 12, 1863, William G. Coleman file, reel 893, CSRCSV.

6. *Acts of the General Assembly*, 1863, 20.

7. Decision of Appomattox County Circuit Court, March 17, 1863; certificate of John W. McKinney for the arrest of Robert Worley, James Beasley, Frederick Alwell, and James Chambers, August 24, 1863; vouchers for board of Richard W. Oliver, Beasley, Worley, Alwell, and Chambers, various dates; and voucher for summoning slaves to work on Lynchburg fortifications, October 30, 1863, all in Wilson Hix file, reel 450, Confederate Papers Relating to Citizens or Business Firms, M-346, RG 109, NA. Worley, who had enlisted with Captain Abbitt less than two months before, had deserted the company on the Peninsula in May of 1862 (muster rolls, Worley file, reel 905, CSRCSV).

8. Receipt of Samuel Wheeler, February 17, 1864, reel 1095, and correspondence of Sarah W. Woodson, with receipt of September 24, 1864, reel 1140, Confederate Papers Relating to Citizens or Business Firms, M-346, RG 109, NA; claims and correspondence of Pryor B. Wright, Caswell C. Wright file, reel 24, and claims and correspondence of Francis Meeks, Lafayette W. Meeks file, reel 21, CSRCSV. Pryor B. Wright should not be confused with his older cousin, Pryor Wright, who built the brick house alongside the courthouse and who died in 1854, leaving his widow, Mariah, with that house and the nearby farmhouse.

9. Land Books, 1861–65, Appomattox County Circuit Court; copy of Flood deed to Trent, November 7, 1859, Trent to Meeks, October 16, 1863, and Meeks to Hix, same date, ACHNHP. In his sketch map of the village (*History of Appomattox*, 26), Nathaniel Ragland Featherston locates a frame residence between Charles Diuguid's blacksmith shop and the Meeks store that was "said to have been occupied at the time of the surrender by the Landons [*sic*]." The chimney of that house was still standing in 1948, he noted, which identifies it as the building called the "Union Academy dwelling house" in the interpretive statement accompanying the park's 1942 master plan. The saddler's shop, which served in 1863 as Landrum's barroom, sat just to the north of Meeks's store, where stands the little building now identified as John W. Woodson's law office. The saddler's shop was used as a law office by Henry Tucker Parrish in the 1870s, and was bought for that same use by Charles Sackett in 1883 (see Featherston, *History of Appomattox*, 26, and Deed Book 1, 451, Appomattox County Circuit Court). Sackett sold the lot after the turn of the century (see Deed Book 6, 549, ibid.). John W. Woodson's law office was located on lot 20, west of the Raine taverns; according to county land books, Woodson's widow retained ownership of that lot and office until 1877, when she sold it to John Rawlings, of Lynchburg.

10. George W. Abbitt to Fannie Abbitt, November 28, 1863, William Abbitt Collection; and George W. Abbitt to J. M. Otey, December 7, 1863, Abbitt file, reel 892; W. G. Coleman to Henry Wise, December 12 and 19, 1863, William G. Coleman file, reel 893; and William S. Hannah to J. M. Otey, February 13, 1864, William S. Hannah file, reel 896, all in CSRCSV.

11. Muster roll of October 31, 1863, and Register of Medical Director's Office, September 16, 1863, Charles J. Raine file, reel 309, CSRCSV; *OR* 29(1):848, 895.

12. Sallie B. Markham to Elvira Woodson, February 22, 1864, Woodson Papers, Duke University.

13. Muster roll of June 30, 1862, Robert Worley file, reel 905, muster roll of February 29, 1864, Caswell F. Inge file, reel 845, registers of deceased soldiers, Morgan Powell file, reel 252, and surgeon's note of October 25, 1863, Reuben Staples file, reel 253, CSRCSV; Vital Statistics of Appomattox County, Deaths, 1864, reel 3, LOV; *Lynchburg News*, September 25, 1866.

14. Register of deceased soldiers, Sampson D. Sweeney file, and muster roll for January and February 1864, Robert M. Sweeney file, all on reel 23, and muster roll of January and February 1864, Charles H. Sweeney file, reel 338, CSRCSV.

15. Muster rolls of January–April 1864 and files of John H. Gordon, reel 896, John R. Patteson, reel 900, Charles T. Plunkett, reel 252, Amasa J. Isbell, reel 251, and James P. Webb, reel 904; muster roll of March and April 1862, file of William H. "Furguson," reel 895; muster roll of March and April 1864, file of J. D. "Furguson," reel 895; muster roll of July and August 1863, file of Daniel P. Ferguson, reel 602, all in CSRCSV. In a letter to "Dear Nannie," dated February 22, "1863" [1864], Calkins collection, Amasa J. Isbell describes escorting one of the first detachments of Union prisoners bound for the Andersonville stockade from Richmond to Gaston, North Carolina.

16. James L. Kemper to James Seddon, January 30, 1864; Flood's commission as first lieutenant and A.D.C., dated February 17, 1864, with endorsement of acceptance, March 7, 1864; and Flood's resignation, May 16, 1864, all in Joel W. Flood file, reel 95, Compiled Service Records of General and Staff Officers and Nonregimental Enlisted Men, M-331, RG 109, NA; *OR* 36(2):972, and ser. 2, 3:178–81.

17. *OR*, ser. 4, 3:179, 212, 223, 257, 378. The law referred to the "reserve class" as those citizens "between seventeen and eighteen" and "between forty-five and fifty" years of age, but the intent was to include seventeen-year-olds and those aged forty-six through fifty. Albert Webb is identified as Flood's overseer at Eldon by his role as informant in the birth of slave children there (Vital Statistics of Appomattox County, Births, 1861, LOV); he enlisted in the local company of the 46th Virginia on July 7, 1864, and died of typhoid on September 8 (muster roll of October 31, 1864, Albert Webb file, reel 904, CSRCSV).

18. Muster roll of December 31, 1863, Company I, 3rd Reserves, reels 399 and 400, and muster roll of March 6, 1862, Charles H. Wingfield and Leroy J. Rosser files, reel 317, CSRCSV.

19. Muster roll of December 31, 1864, John W. Johns and Samuel D. "McDearmond" files, reel 399, CSRCSV; Consolidated Index to Compiled Service Records of Confederate Soldiers, M-253, Wyatt Abbitt file, reel 1; and receipts dated between September 18, 1863, and October 28, 1864, Wyatt Abbitt file, reel 1, Confederate Papers Relating to Citizens or Business Firms, M-346, RG 109, NA.

20. Muster roll of December 31, 1864, Company I, 3rd Reserves, reels 399 and 400; and muster roll of October 31, 1862, Register of Farmville hospital, and R. A. Booker to Thomas S. Bocock, January 6, 1863, Richard A. Booker file, reel 598, CSRCSV.

21. George W. Abbitt to Fannie Abbitt, May 3 and 4, 1864, William Abbitt Collection.

22. Register of deceased soldiers, files of John W. Harris, reel 250, Morgan Powell, reel 252, and Reuben D. Staples, reel 253, CSRCSV; Confederate Pension application of Elizabeth Evans, June 7, 1888, reel 1, LOV; register of Farmville General Hospital cases examined, September 16, 1864, Lewis A. Megginson file, reel 251; report of casualties in W. H. Stephens's command, March 1, 1864, George W. Steel file, reel 253; and muster rolls, files of William A. Doss and Nathan D. Hancock, reel 250, Frederick M. Isbell, Lorenzo D. Kelly, Charles LeGrand, and Joseph A. Megginson, reel 251, and William J. Webb, reel 253, all in CSRCSV; *OR* 33:184–85, 212–13, and 36(3):809–11.

23. *OR* 36(1):20 and (2):34–35, 244.

24. Ibid., 36(2):196–98, 236–38; Holcomb P. Harvey journal, May 16, 1864, Harvey Papers, Duke University; muster roll for May and June 1864, files of Samuel H. Farrar, reel 602, and Thomas A. Gilliam, reel 603, CSRCSV; Seventh Census of the United States, M-432, reel 933, 408, and Eighth Census of the United States, M-653, reel 1332, 481, RG 29, NA; election of company officers, 174th Regiment Virginia Militia, May 15, 1852, Executive Department, Militia Commission Papers, 1777–1858, LOV.

25. *OR* 36(2):257–59, 261; Vital Statistics of Appomattox County, Births, 1864, reel 4, LOV; muster roll of May and June 1864, John D. "Patterson" and John R. Patteson files, reel 900, CSRCSV.

26. *OR* 36(1):790–93; muster roll of May and June 1864, files of George W. Carter, reel 16, John T. Crenshaw, reel 17, Samuel A. and William H. Glover, reel 18, and Peter L. Pankey, reel 21, CSRCSV.

27. *OR* 36(2):1012; resignation, Joel W. Flood file, Compiled Service Records of Confederate General and Staff Officers and Nonregimental Enlisted Men, M-331, reel 95, RG 109, NA; *Lynchburg Virginian*, May 24, 1864; records of events and muster rolls of December 31, 1864, companies C and I, 3rd Virginia Reserves, reels 399 and 400, CSRCSV.

28. Register of Chimborazo Hospital, file of Albion V. Gordon, reel 18; muster roll of May and June 1864, file of William T. Phelps, reel 22; and report of sick and wounded at General Hospital 4, Richmond, file of Charles E. Webb, reel 24, CSRCSV.

29. George W. Abbitt to Fannie Abbitt, June 1, 1864, William Abbitt Collection; muster roll of May and June 1864, George W. Abbitt file, reel 892, CSRCSV.

30. *OR* 36(2):261, 308, 312, and (3):891; muster roll of May and June 1864, James W. Moore file, reel 900, CSRCSV.

31. *OR* 40(2):655–56, 676–77; muster roll of May and June 1864, files of Thomas A. Tibbs, reel 817, and Clifton V. Webb, reel 904, CSRCSV.

32. *OR* 40(1):705, 721–22, and (2):656; muster roll of May and June 1864, files of Thomas G. Davidson, reel 894, and John E. Williams, reel 905, CSRCSV.

33. *OR* 40(2):659–60, 662–67; muster roll of May and June 1864, files of William B. Davidson, reel 894, Samuel P. Dickerson, reel 601, James H. Godsey, reel 896, H. L. Martin, reel 899, Richard T. Moss, reel 900, Samuel J. Richardson, reel 901, Marshall Simms, reel 902, Martin V. Webb, reel 904, and James R. and James W. Wilkerson and William Worsham, reel 905; and Report of Surgical cases at C.S. Hospital, Petersburg, for June, 1864, Gilliam R. Wright file, reel 258, all in CSRCSV.

34. *OR* 37(1):94–98, 146, 156.

35. Ibid., 99–100, 160.

36. Ibid., 346, 347–49, 766.

37. Ibid., 40(1):621–31, 764–65.

38. Joel T. Cawthorn to John H. Cawthorn, July 6, 1864, ACHNHP.

39. *Lynchburg Virginian*, July 4, 1864; receipt for cordwood dated June 1, 1864, John W. Woodson file, reel 273, Compiled Service Records of Confederate General and Staff Officers and Nonregimental Enlisted Men, M-331, RG 109, NA; Ninth Census of the United States, M-593, reel 1633, 47, RG 29, NA; Resolution in Court of Appomattox County, July 7, 1864, ACHNHP; John W. and Mary E. Woodson headstones, Patteson family cemetery, Route 687, Appomattox County.

40. Petition of April 14, 1862, muster rolls of August 31, 1862, May–August 1864, registers of General Hospital 9 and Chimborazo Hospital, and register of payments, Hubbard L. Martin file, reel 899, CSRCSV; George W. Abbitt affidavit of June 7, 1895, Hubbard Martin Confederate Pension application, reel 1, LOV; Ninth Census of the United States, M-593, reel 1633, 26, RG 29, NA.

41. Mattie J. Sweeney Confederate Pension application, reel 64, LOV; Vital Statistics of Appomattox County, Marriages, 1864, reel 4, LOV.

42. W. P. Robinson, "Artillery in the Battle of the Crater," 166; George W. Abbitt to Fannie Abbitt, August 5, 1864, William Abbitt Collection.

43. Muster rolls of May–December 1864, Hubbard L. Martin file, reel 899, CSRCSV.

44. George W. Abbitt to Fannie Abbitt, November 28, 1863, William Abbitt Collection.

45. *OR*, ser. 4, 3:159–61; bond certificates, Wilmer McLean file, reel 638, Confederate Papers Relating to Citizens or Business Firms, M-346, RG 109, NA.

46. David J. Abbitt affidavit, July 8, 1864, Bocock Papers, ACHNHP; George W. Abbitt to Fannie Abbitt, May 3, 1864, William Abbitt Collection.

47. Receipts for treasury deposits, December 7, 1863, to February 9, 1865, Samuel D. McDearmon file, reel 624, Confederate Papers Relating to Citizens or Business Firms, M-346, RG 109, NA; memorandum book, October 27, 1864, and January 2, 1865, box 8, Bocock Papers, UVA; James Moss's tax-in-kind receipt, August 26, 1864, ACHNHP.

48. Land Books, 1863, 1865, Appomattox County Circuit Court.

49. George W. Abbitt to Fannie Abbitt, October 8 and November "24" [26], 1864, William Abbitt Collection.

50. Muster rolls of September 1864–February 1865, files of Charles W. Arrington, reel 892, Thomas Conner, reel 893, Hegeccous Davenport, reel 894, and William Worsham, reel 905, CSRCSV; George W. Abbitt to Fannie Abbitt, November "24" [26], 1864, William Abbitt Collection; Charles W. Arrington to Catharine Arrington, November 26 and December 13, 1864, quoted in Collins, *46th Virginia Infantry*, 66–67; *Richmond Examiner*, January 6, 1865.

51. *OR* 42(3):1083, 1213, 1249; George W. Abbitt to Fannie Abbitt, November "24" [26], 1864, William Abbitt Collection; muster roll of November and December 1864, James Giles file, reel 895; register of prisoners received and register of oaths and deserters, files of Henry Johnson, reel 898, Calaway, Thomas, and Wyatt Mann, reel 899, and Samuel Webb, reel 905, CSRCSV. Webb enlisted March 29, 1865, in the 2nd Maryland Infantry under the name John Glover: see Eleventh Census of the United States, Schedules Enumerating Union Veterans and Widows of Union Veterans of the

Civil War, M-123, reel 106, Appomattox County, family 387, RG 29, and muster and descriptive roll of drafted men and substitutes, John Glover file, Compiled Service Records of Volunteer Union Soldiers Who Served in Organizations from the State of Maryland, M-384, reel 80, RG 94, NA.

52. *OR* 42(3):580, 623, 1213, 1249; muster roll of February 25, 1865, Hubbard L. Martin file, reel 899, CSRCSV.

53. *OR* 42(3):1259, 1272; record of events and muster roll of December 31, 1864, Company I, 3rd Virginia Reserves, reels 399 and 400, CSRCSV.

54. Petition of Samuel D. McDearmon and others, received November 30, 1864, item M-4576, reel 132; petition of C. H. Chilton and others, dated October 13, 1864, item 737-E-1864, reel 110; and William D. Hix affidavit, November 20, 1864, item M-4263, reel 132, Letters Received by the Confederate Adjutant and Inspector General, 1861–65, M-474, RG 109, NA; William D. Hix to Quartermaster Department, January 21, 1865, reel 450, Confederate Papers Relating to Citizens or Business Firms, M-346, RG 109, NA; cases of Lilburn P. Ferguson (claim 13704) and Preston Ferguson (claim 13701), Barred and Disallowed Case Files of the Southern Claims Commission, M-1407, RG 233, NA.

55. *OR*, ser. 4, 3:179; Session Book, Records of Union Academy, Chilton Papers, UVA; William McFall to Mrs. William Anderson, January 23, 1865, William McFall Letters, Emory University.

56. Rolls of prisoners, files of Jesse P. Harvey, reel 604, and Charles W. Cardwell, reel 249, and list of wounded, James M. Stratton file, reel 23, CSRCSV; pension application of Charles W. Cardwell, August 20, 1918, Confederate Pension Applications, reel 64, LOV.

57. George W. Abbitt to Fannie Abbitt, February 19 and March 4, 1865, William Abbitt Collection; *OR* 46(2):1075, 1143, 1229–30, 1254, 1265.

58. *OR* 46(1):388–90; George W. Abbitt to Fannie Abbitt, February 19, 1865, Wilam Abbitt Collection.

CHAPTER SEVEN

1. *Richmond Examiner*, March 18, 24, and 27, 1865.

2. *OR* 46(1):345–48, 382–83, 388–90.

3. *Richmond Examiner*, March 27, 1865.

4. *OR* 46(1):1286–88; Holcomb P. Harvey journal, March 31, 1865, Harvey Papers, Duke University; Vital Statistics of Appomattox County, Deaths, 1865, reel 3, LOV. The Appomattox men from the 46th Virginia killed March 29 were David M. Coleman, David Davidson, and Sergeant William A. Gordon; Spotswood S. Stewart and William A. Jennings of the 18th Virginia were mortally wounded on March 31.

5. *OR* 46(1):1288–89, 1300; Benjamin H. Sims journal, April 1, 1865, North Carolina Department of Archives and History; roll of prisoners, Joseph Abbitt file, reel 498, CSRCSV.

6. *OR* 46(1):1264–65, 1293–94, 1296.

7. Ibid., 321, 388–90, 1105, and 46(3):1354.

8. Ibid., 46(1):1107, 1265, 1296. Though his staff members dismissed the idea, there

was some question whether General Lee himself was not among those responsible for the oversight. See Walter H. Taylor to W. Gordon McCabe, December 8, 1906, and D. S. Freeman to Walter H. Taylor III, June 14, 1933, Taylor Papers, Kirn Memorial Library.

9. Benjamin H. Sims journal, April 1–7, 1865, North Carolina Department of Archives and History; George Peers recollections, undated newspaper clipping, ACHNHP.

10. Durkin, *John Dooley*, 176–77; *OR* 46(1):851–52, 1149.

11. *OR* 46(1): 1265, 1294, 1296–97.

12. Ibid., 1107, 1265, 1294, 1296–97; John and Richard W. Waldrop diaries, April 5 and 6, 1865, SHC; Edmund K. Russell to "Dear Mother [and] Sisters," April 17, 1865, Russell Letters, Marye's Heights office, Fredericksburg and Spotsylvania National Military Park.

13. *OR* 46(1):682, 1265, and (3):597–99, 1386–87; Edmund K. Russell to "Dear Mother [and] Sisters," April 17, 1865, Russell Letters, Marye's Heights office, Fredericksburg and Spotsylvania National Military Park.

14. *OR* 46(3):1386–87.

15. Ibid., 46(1):1294, 1297; Holcomb P. Harvey journal, April 6, 1865, Harvey Papers, Duke University.

16. *OR* 46(1):1107, 1120, 1142, 1294, 1297; Holcomb P. Harvey journal, April 6, 1865, Harvey Papers, Duke University.

17. Wise, "Career of Wise's Brigade," 16–17; *OR* 46(1):1142, 1302.

18. *OR* 46(1):1294, 1297.

19. Ibid., 1294, 1297–1302.

20. Basinger, "Crutchfield's Artillery Brigade," 39; *OR* 46(1):1295, 1297; Howard, "Closing Scenes of the War," 141. Basinger's article was published directly from his report of the battle, which was written the following winter.

21. *OR* 46(1):1125, 1132, 1295; Wise, "Career of Wise's Brigade," 17–18.

22. *OR* 46(1):906, 1297; Basinger, "Crutchfield's Artillery Brigade," 40–41.

23. Basinger, "Crutchfield's Artillery Brigade," 42–44; *OR* 46(1):906, 914, 1297.

24. Rolls of prisoners and wounded, Company H, 18th Virginia Infantry, reels 597–615; Company A, 19th Battalion Virginia Heavy Artillery, reels 244, 247, 248; Company A, 20th Battalion Virginia Heavy Artillery, reels 249 and 252; and files of George L. Ferguson, reel 18, William Bocock Megginson, reel 21, and James M. Stratton and William A. Thornhill, reel 23, CSRCSV; Breckinridge, "Second Virginia Cavalry," filed with James Ellis Tucker letter to Cary Breckinridge, May 6, 1910, VHS; "Paroles of the Army of Northern Virginia," 437–39.

25. *OR* 46(1):682; Harwell, *Confederate Diary of the Retreat from Petersburg*, 14; Dayton, *Diary of a Confederate Soldier*, 134; George A. Bowen diary, April 6, 1865, BV 228, Chatham office, Fredericksburg and Spotsylvania National Military Park; John B. Gordon to Robert E. Lee, 5:00 P.M., April 6, 1865, section 8, folder 11, R. E. Lee Headquarters Papers, VHS.

26. *OR* 46(1):389, 1279; J. E. Whitehorn diary, April 6, 1865, SHC.

27. *OR* 46(1):1161–62.

28. Ibid., 46(1):1167–69, 1215, 1220, 1302–3.

29. William M. Owen journal, April 6–7, 1865, McIntosh Papers, VHS; Harwell,

Confederate Diary of the Retreat from Petersburg, 14–15; J. E. Whitehorn and John and Richard W. Waldrop diaries, April 6–7, 1865, SHC; Dayton, *Diary of a Confederate Soldier*, 134–35.

30. *OR* 46(1):1290; Wise, "Career of Wise's Brigade," 19.

31. *OR* 46(1):1266; Pearce, *Diary of Captain Henry A. Chambers*, 261; diary of anonymous Confederate officer, April 7, 1865, James B. Blackford Collection, UVA; J. E. Whitehorn and Richard W. Waldrop diaries, April 6, 1865, SHC.

32. *OR* 46(1):1278, 1291. By April 12 returned stragglers and detached men had increased Ransom's brigade to 435 officers and men, while 2,277 were paroled from Johnson's division on that date.

33. J. E. Whitehorn diary, April 7, 1865, SHC; Roller, "Incidents of Our Retreat to Appomattox," Museum of the Confederacy; Mohr and Winslow, *Cormany Diaries*, 535; *OR* 46(1):758.

34. Harwell, *Confederate Diary of the Retreat from Petersburg*, 15; J. E. Whitehorn diary, April 7, 1865, SHC; Caldwell, *History of a Brigade of South Carolinians*, 294; Gallagher, *Fighting for the Confederacy*, 525; Channing Smith diary, April 7, 1865, Museum of the Confederacy. Caldwell wrote much of his history of Samuel McGowan's brigade during the final months of the war, and completed the closing episodes soon afterward, publishing the book in 1866.

35. *OR* 46(1):683, 758–59, 1143; Osmun Latrobe diary, April 8, 1865, VHS; Gallagher, *Fighting for the Confederacy*, 525–26; Caldwell, *History of a Brigade of South Carolinians*, 294–95.

36. Osmun Latrobe diary, April 8, 1865, VHS; Chief Quartermaster John L. Coley to Robert E. Lee, April 15, 1865, series 8, folder 14, R. E. Lee Headquarters Papers, VHS. Coley counted approximately 1,000 four-horse wagons, 50 two-horse and 50 six-horse wagons, and 300 ambulances in the train that left Petersburg; he reported 480 four-horse wagons and 160 ambulances surrendered at Appomattox, and all of the two- and six-horse vehicles.

37. *OR* 46(1):683–84, 1142, 1155; J. E. Whitehorn diary, April 7, 1865, SHC.

38. *OR* 46(1):684, 686, 715–16; J. E. Whitehorn diary, April 7, 1865, SHC.

39. J. E. Whitehorn diary, April 7, 1865, SHC; *OR* 46(1):604–5, 1109, 1162.

40. Harwell, *Confederate Diary of the Retreat from Petersburg*, 15; John Willis Council diary, April 7–8, 1865, North Carolina Department of Archives and History; *OR* 46(1):1281–82; Richard W. Waldrop diary, April 8, 1865, SHC.

41. *OR* 46(3):619; John Waldrop and J. E. Whitehorn diaries, April 8, 1865, SHC; John Bell Vincent diary, April 8, 1865, VHS; Longstreet's general order, dated April 8, 1865, Latrobe Papers, VHS.

42. John Willis Council diary, April 8, 1865, North Carolina Department of Archives and History; New Store ledger, ACHNHP; *OR* 46(1):1152, 1155; Mohr and Winslow, *Cormany Diaries*, 537. Holladay's Creek is now known as Holiday Creek.

CHAPTER EIGHT

1. "Paroles of the Army of Northern Virginia," 82, 432, 434–39. Government clerks transcribing the paroles copied "W. T. Hubbard, Co. H," thus leading to con-

fusion between William J. Hubbard of Company H (the Appomattox Grays) and William T. Hubbard of Company I: see their respective compiled service records, reel 605, CSRCSV. Dozens of other Appomattox soldiers had either made their way home previously through legitimate or illegitimate means, or arrived with the army and immediately went to their homes, coming in after the surrender to pick up their paroles.

2. "Paroles of the Army of Northern Virginia," 69–449; Pearce, *Diary of Captain Henry A. Chambers*, 262; Caldwell, *History of a Brigade of South Carolinians*, 296–97.

3. Stephen W. Gordon diary, April 9, 1865, Chatham office, Fredericksburg and Spotsylvania National Military Park; Racine, *Unspoiled Heart*, 268; Harwell, *Confederate Diary of the Retreat from Petersburg*, 17–19; John Richardson Porter diary, April 7 and 8, 1865, Duke University. While other sources suggest that the road from New Store to Walker's Church crossed the Appomattox at a ford called Cut Bank Ford, A. H. Campbell's 1863 map of Appomattox and Buckingham Counties (*Atlas to Accompany the Official Records*, plate 135, map 5) and John Richardson Porter's diary entry for April 8, 1865, both indicate that there was a bridge there.

4. Walters, *Norfolk Blues*, 221; Mary Ann Coleman memoir, ACHNHP. The presence of a ford over the Appomattox, rather than a bridge, is mentioned by Louisiana artilleryman Eugene Henry Levy in his diary entry for April 8 (Levy Family Papers, SC#7005, American Jewish Archives). Robert E. Lee's military secretary, Charles Marshall, remembered a bridge there, but Marshall's memoir is littered with inaccuracies: just three sentences before mentioning the bridge, for instance, he describes cavalry general James Dearing being killed at Appomattox Court House on April 9 rather than mortally wounded at High Bridge on April 6 (see Maurice, *Aide-de-Camp of Lee*, 266–67). Alexander C. M. Pennington, a Federal cavalry colonel, remembered a bridge as well, but that recollection also came more than thirty years later (Schaff, *Spirit of Old West Point*, 170).

5. Walters, *Norfolk Blues*, 221–22.

6. Hannaford, "Diary," April 8, 1865, Cincinnati Historical Society. A number of persons labeled "insane" or "idiotic" inhabited Appomattox County in 1860 and 1870, but census records do not clearly identify either of these families.

7. Charles Marshall (for Lee) to Longstreet, April 8, 1865, Latrobe Papers, VHS. Lee's 3:00 P.M. message was written alongside an unnamed watercourse "about half a mile south of Day's house" and "two miles and a half" before "a small branch beyond the stream mentioned." A Confederate map drawn late in 1863 (*Atlas to Accompany the Official Records*, plate 135, map 5) shows two Day families in the area, one of whom (John Day) lived on the road from New Store half a mile before Webb's Creek; according to that map, Webb Creek lay about two and a half miles short of Fishpond Creek, and it was the first water on the road from New Store. The creek was generally west of Day's house, but the road did take a turn to the south there.

8. Silliker, *Rebel Yell and the Yankee Hurrah*, 263; Reed, *Civil War Diary of Private Robert Scott Moorhead*, 5; Ellis C. Strouss to "Dear Mother," April 8, 1865, *Civil War Times Illustrated* Collection, USAMHI; *OR* 46(1):1292; George K. Griggs and Channing Smith diaries, April 8, 1865, Museum of the Confederacy; G[orman], *Lee's Last Campaign*, 37–38; J. E. Whitehorn, Richard W. and John Waldrop, and William D. and E. P. Alexander diaries, April 8, 1865, all in SHC; John Bell Vincent and James Eldred

Phillips diaries, April 8, 1865, VHS; Caldwell, *History of a Brigade of South Carolinians*, 297. The campsites occupied by Wilcox, Heth, and Field were revealed to the commander of the Union Second Corps by a deserter from Field's division the next morning: see *OR* 46(3):670–71. Chaplain Abner Hopkins, of John B. Gordon's staff, located that general's bivouac that night "about" three miles east of Appomattox Court House (Hopkins memoir, VHS).

9. *OR* 46(1):1132, 1282; John Willis Council diary, April 8, 1865, North Carolina Department of Archives and History; Walters, *Norfolk Blues*, 222; Hannaford, "Diary," April 8, 1865, Cincinnati Historical Society. Hannaford's detailed "diary," written almost five years after the campaign, is so remarkably consistent with contemporary accounts that its description as an expanded diary seems credible—something that cannot be said for most of that genre.

10. Hannaford, "Diary," April 8, 1865, Cincinnati Historical Society; John A. Clark to "My kind Friend," April 16, 1865, Clements Library, University of Michigan; *OR* 46(1):1282; Eri D. Woodbury to "Dear Father," April 25, 1865, and diary, April 8, 1865, Woodbury Collection, Dartmouth College Library; diary of anonymous Confederate officer, April 8, 1865, James B. Blackford Collection, UVA; James W. Albright diary, April 9, 1865, SHC.

11. *OR* 46(1):1139, 1282; David Gregg McIntosh journal, April 8, 1865, VHS; John Richardson Porter diary, April 8, 1865, Duke University.

12. Channing Smith diary, April 8, 1865, Museum of the Confederacy; Pearce, *Diary of Captain Henry A. Chambers*, 262; William D. Alexander diary, April 8, 1865, SHC; Eugene Henry Levy diary, April 8, 1865, Levy Family Papers, American Jewish Archives.

13. *OR* 46(1):1139. An 1880s interview with Edward G. Hix and George T. Peers that appeared in newspapers across the country (*Portsmouth* [N.H.] *Journal* of July 16, 1887, for instance), alleged that Colonel Root was killed by a man from the 5th Alabama Battalion. Hix, a seventeen-year-old member of the Appomattox Reserves who claimed to have later joined the Appomattox Rangers of the 2nd Virginia Cavalry, insisted that he saw the shooting; if he did, he was clearly absent from his command.

14. *OR* 46(1):1291, 1292; Lovell, "With Lee after Appomattox," 40. Although the order itself never turned up, Lee's chief of staff, Walter Taylor, insisted that the general relieved Richard Anderson, George Pickett, and Bushrod Johnson of their commands on the evening of April 8 (see, for instance, Taylor to Robert E. Cowart, November 10, 1908, and Cowart to Thomas T. Munford, September 17, 1909, both in box 14 of the Munford-Ellis Family Papers, Duke University). The following year Anderson acknowledged that he had received orders for his own relief, but neither Johnson nor Pickett ever did. Anderson's corps had disintegrated, but the divisions of the other two remained sufficiently numerous to have justified their retention, although Pickett's 800 survivors were almost entirely unarmed. See Anderson to Lee, June 15, 1866, and Pickett's report of May 1, 1865, both in series 5, R. E. Lee Headquarters Papers, VHS. Taylor appears to be the principle source for the story about the relief of Johnson and Pickett, but Fitz Lee seemed to question it, at least in the case of Pickett. See Fitzhugh Lee to Taylor, January 9 and 16, 1904, and Taylor's reply of January 15, 1904, Taylor Papers, Kirn Memorial Library.

15. Mahone, "On the Road to Appomattox," 43–44.

16. *OR* 46(1):1303 and (3):641; Dowdey and Manarin, *Wartime Papers of Robert E. Lee*, 937. The exact location of this final council of war has not been positively identi-fied. Lee's headquarters after the surrender were located at the top of the hill opposite the Conner farm, and that seems to have been accepted as the site of his headquarters on the night of April 8, but manuscript evidence suggests otherwise. In his memoirs, written three decades later, Longstreet recollected that Lee "made his head-quarters near the rear-guard" that night. The rearmost fragments of Longstreet's corps lay that night somewhere beyond Joseph Abbitt's, at least four miles back from the Conner farm and nearly five miles from the village. Longstreet remarked that Lee "spread his couch about a hundred feet from the saddle and blanket that were my pillow and spread for the night" (*From Manassas to Appomattox*, 623). Longstreet's Appomattox head-quarters are purported to have been at Pleasant Retreat (see John Watts DePeyster, quoted in Calkins, *Battles of Appomattox Station and Appomattox Court House*, 285–86), but DePeyster's source was a New York colonel with the Second Corps, who could only have known the whereabouts of Longstreet's headquarters after the late morning of April 9. Though it is a recollection recorded three decades later, Longstreet's com-ment about sleeping on his saddle the night of April 8 hints that he had not yet reached the comfortable—and perhaps unoccupied—home of the late Mrs. Flood. Even more compelling is the diary of Longstreet's adjutant general, Osmun Latrobe, transcripts of which are held by the Virginia Historical Society: under the date of April 8, 1865, Latrobe estimated that Longstreet's military family camped six miles from Appomat-tox Court House and mentioned that they "supped" with General Lee, with whom his chief was "in consultation." They resumed the march at midnight, Latrobe added. As previously noted, Chaplain Abner Crump Hopkins of Gordon's staff placed Gordon's bivouac "about" three miles east of Appomattox Court House—thus, anywhere from Pleasant Retreat to the other side of New Hope Church—with Longstreet camping two or three miles beyond that. In his postwar memoir (VHS), Hopkins also noted that Gordon returned from the council at Lee's headquarters around 10:00 P.M.

17. *OR* (1):841, 1175, 1215, 1239; Styple, *With a Flash of His Sword*, 216; Hugh C. Perkins to Herbert Frisbie, April 19, 1865 (*Christian Science Monitor*, April 7, 1983); Jacob Ogden Wilson diary, April 8, 1865, Calkins collection; Silliker, *Rebel Yell and the Yankee Hurrah*, 263; Robertson, *Civil War Letters of General Robert McAllister*, 607.

18. *OR* 46(1):1303 and (3):670–71; G[orman], *Lee's Last Campaign*, 39; John B. Gordon's report of April 11, 1865, R. E. Lee Headquarters Papers, series 5, VHS; Richard W. and John Waldrop diaries, April 9, 1865, SHC. The units that General Gordon commanded that morning surrendered 7,313 officers and men (*OR* 46[1]: 1277–78).

19. *OR* 46(1):1278, 1291, 1292; Kena King Chapman diary, April 9, 1865, SHC; William Wiatt diary, April 9, 1865, Calkins collection; "Paroles of the Army of North-ern Virginia," 432–34. General Johnson estimated that 250 of Moody's men and 80 of Ransom's escaped Sailor's Creek, while Wallace said he could gather only 350 of his brigade at the beginning of the retreat and lost a few of those during the cam-paign. Wise's effective strength on April 9 is not known, though the count of 20 men in the 26th Virginia suggests his brigade was probably not as large as Moody's. De-spite fielding fewer than 1,000 men that day, Johnson's division accounted for 2,253 of the officers and men paroled at Appomattox, of whom exactly 600 belonged to Wise.

The diary of Lieutenant Chapman, formerly Stapleton Crutchfield's ordnance officer, mentions the consolidation of the remnants of Crutchfield's brigade with Wise's.

20. Grimes, "Surrender at Appomattox," 94–95; Henry Carter Lee diary, April 9, 1865, Museum of the Confederacy; *OR* 46(1):1303. A Union officer with the Signal Corps later described what he thought was the Sears house but could only have been the Tibbs—and formerly the Samuel McDearmon—house, as having a "mansard" (hipped) roof (Pray, "Recollections of Appomattox," 19–20); see also *OR* 46(1):1178.

21. James Longstreet's report of April 11, 1865, series 5, R. E. Lee Headquarters Papers, VHS; J. E. Whitehorn diary, April 9, 1865, SHC; *OR* 46(1):713, 759; E. K. Russell to "Dear Mother [and] Sisters," April 17, 1865, Edmund K. Russell Letters, Marye's Heights office, Fredericksburg and Spotsylvania National Military Park; Lothrop Lincoln Lewis diary, April 9, 1865, Library of Congress. Longstreet later wrote that he stopped at New Hope Church because the wagon train was blocking the road, implying that his progress was slowed so that he feared the enemy would catch up with him (*From Manassas to Appomattox*, 623).

22. *OR* 46(1):1159, 1245–46, 1303; Grimes, "Surrender at Appomattox," 95.

23. Isaac H. Ressler diary, April 9, 1865, *Civil War Times Illustrated* Collection, USAMHI; *OR* 46(1):1155, 1162, 1187, 1196, 1215; Mohr and Winslow, *Cormany Diaries*, 537–38; Robert Larimer diary, April 8 and 9, 1865, UVA.

24. William B. Stark diary, April 9, 1865, Massachusetts Historical Society; *OR* 46(1):852, 877–78, 1132, 1138, 1139, 1215, 1218, 1220, 1236, 1243; Robert Larimer diary, April 9, 1865, UVA; Vital Statistics of Appomattox County, Deaths, 1865, reel 3, LOV; William T. Livermore diary, April 9, 1865, VHS; David J. Scott to "Dear Maud," April 10, 1865, *Civil War Times Illustrated* Collection, USAMHI; Hannaford, "Diary," April 9, 1865, Cincinnati Historical Society.

25. Gordon's report of April 11, 1865, and Cadmus Wilcox's report of the same date, both in series 5, R. E. Lee Headquarters Papers, VHS; J. E. Whitehorn diary, April 9, 1865, SHC; E. P. Alexander to James Longstreet, October 26, 1892, North Carolina Department of Archives and History.

26. Longstreet's report of April 11, 1865, series 5, R. E. Lee Headquarters Papers, VHS; Longstreet, *From Manassas to Appomattox*, 626–27; Agassiz, *Meade's Headquarters*, 356–57; Maurice, *Aide-de-Camp of Lee*, 262–65; *OR* 46(3):664–66.

27. Robert Larimer diary, April 9, 1865, UVA; *OR* 46(1):852, 878; Newsom Edward Jenkins to "Mamie & Mattie," April 9, 1906, Jenkins-Aikens Papers, Duke University.

28. All the accounts of Custer meeting Sims and speaking to Gordon and Longstreet came two decades and more after the fact, when Custer was dead; they vary in details, and this interpretation represents a reconciliation of the conflicting versions. Sims gave his story to a Union veteran in the 1880s (Survivors' Association, *History of the 118th Pennsylvania*, 590–91), while Gordon's rather confused recollection appeared in 1903 (*Reminiscences of the Civil War*, 438–40). In 1896 Longstreet recorded the incident in softer tones (*From Manassas to Appomattox*, 627), but his staff officers remembered him offering Custer a stinging rebuke: see Thomas Jewett Goree to E. P. Alexander, December 6, 1887, Alexander Papers, SHC, and Alexander to Longstreet, October 26, 1892, North Carolina Department of Archives and History. It was Goree who identified the location of the exchange between Longstreet and Custer.

29. A bronze plaque honoring these North Carolina skirmishers lies a few hundred

yards west of the site of the Raine stable, but that does not appear to be the scene of this encounter. Their precise location, on lot 11 of the old village plat, is determined mostly from postwar sources, but all of them seem to agree and they are corroborated by the official report of the commander of the Union skirmish line. Newsom Edward Jenkins, the sergeant major of the 14th North Carolina, wrote that he and about twenty-five comrades took cover "behind some houses nearby" as they backed into the village (Jenkins to "Mamie & Mattie," April 9, 1906, Jenkins-Aikens Papers, Duke University); First Sergeant Julius Schwab, of the 14th, recalled in 1900 that his regiment was deployed as skirmishers with "its left resting at a barn, the last building on the outskirts of the town, on the main street we had been in part of the previous night" ("Some Closing Events at Appomattox," 71). Of the same incident, E. R. Harris claimed in 1923 that he and another private of the 14th took refuge "behind an old barn," from which they continued firing even after the flags of truce went out ("First— and Last," 438). That location is corroborated by the T. J. Watkins memoir (Bound Volume 85, Chatham office, Fredericksburg and Spotsylvania National Military Park). The old Raine stable (bought from the Raine estate about 1864 by Wilson Hix) would have been the last building at that end of the village in 1865, as no structure stood on Charles Diuguid's lot from 1857 until 1871. An 1867 map (*Atlas to Accompany the Official Records*, plate 78, map 2) shows an isolated, unidentified building near the junction of Sears Lane, but that building may have been a postwar structure and did not match Jenkins's reference to multiple "houses"; nor would it have been considered on the outskirts of the village or on the "main street," as Schwab described it. Colonel Joseph B. Pattee, whose men composed the Federal skirmish line and captured the Carolinians, located their lair within the village itself: he reported that his line was sweeping down the ridge into the village "and when about entering the town a flag of truce came forward and passed through my line. The enemy still maintained a fire, however, from the cover of the houses, killing a cavalryman; whereupon some twenty of my men . . . entered the town and drove the enemy beyond it and sending some twenty prisoners to the rear." Other cover might have been offered in that vicinity by the brick blacksmith shop, the late James W. Woodson's little law office, outbuildings belonging to Wilmer McLean, and the house Thomas Landrum's family occupied north of the road, on lots owned by the trustees of Union Academy: see Land Books, 1865, Appomattox County Circuit Court.

30. Hannaford, "Diary," April 9, 1865, Cincinnati Historical Society; Talcott, "From Petersburg to Appomattox," 72; Gordon, *Reminiscences of the Civil War*, 441; M. Porter Snell diary, April 9, 1865, Warren Papers, VHS; Hugh C. Perkins to Herbert Frisbie, April 19, 1865 (*Christian Science Monitor*, April 7, 1983); OR 46(1):1178.

31. Agassiz, *Meade's Headquarters*, 356–57; Meade, *Life and Letters*, 2:271; OR 46(3): 666.

32. J. E. Whitehorn diary, April 9, 1865, SHC; James Eldred Phillips diary, April 9, 1865, VHS; Mahone, "On the Road to Appomattox," 45.

33. E. P. Alexander to James Longstreet, October 26, 1892, North Carolina Department of Archives and History.

34. OR 46(3):665; Grant, *Personal Memoirs*, 2:488; Maurice, *Aide-de-Camp of Lee*, 267–68. The dubious reliability of this last source, Colonel Marshall's posthumously published memoir, has already been discussed, but almost all the details of the sur-

render conference are derived from doubtful and conflicting reminiscences. Marshall recalled that two "orderlies" accompanied them to the village. Although he has been cited as the origin of the information that Sergeant G. W. Tucker was the Confederate orderly, Marshall simply wrote that "one of our orderlies" rode along. Since Marshall had made particular and detailed comment on Tucker as the orderly who accompanied them to the truce conference at New Hope Church that morning (262), his generic reference to their afternoon escort would suggest it was not Tucker; otherwise, he would simply have named him again. Sylvanus Cadwallader, a newspaper reporter who rode with Grant, identified the Confederate orderly as "Johns"—Joshua O. Johns of Lynchburg, a trooper of Company C of the 39th Virginia Cavalry Battalion, which was Lee's escort (*New York Herald*, April 14, 1865). Another private in the 39th Battalion, Lewis B. Ellis, also identified the orderly as "Special Courier Johns" in a newspaper article near the twelfth anniversary of the surrender ("The Appomattox Apple Tree," in the Hawkinsville, Ga., *Dispatch*, April 5, 1877). Cadwallader also identified Babcock's "orderly" as one of Grant's aides, Lieutenant William M. Dunn Jr. (*Three Years with Grant*, 323), and Dunn was included in a list of conference witnesses compiled by Grant's military secretary only seventeen days later: see Adam Badeau to "My dear Sir," April 26, 1865, Dartmouth College Library.

35. Maurice, *Aide-de-Camp of Lee*, 268–69; *New York Herald*, April 14, 1865.

36. Maurice, *Aide-de-Camp of Lee*, 269–74; Grant, *Personal Memoirs*, 2:486–95; Sheridan, *Personal Memoirs*, 2:200–202; *OR* 46(3):665. No comprehensive list of those present in the McLean parlor has ever been agreed upon, nor any sequence of arrivals and departures. All accounts thus far have relied almost exclusively on conflicting memoirs such as those above, and none have cited what appears to be the earliest attempt by a participant to document the attendance. Barely a fortnight after the event Colonel Adam Badeau, Grant's military secretary, counted at least seventeen men in the room during the discussion of the surrender: Lee, Grant, Sheridan, Ord, Marshall, four generals assigned to Grant's headquarters—John Rawlins, Rufus Ingalls, Seth Williams, and John Barnard—and eight members of Grant's personal staff, including Horace Porter, Ely Parker, Theodore Bowers, Frederick Dent, Peter Hudson, Dunn, Babcock, and himself. He added that the chief "quartermaster" (commissary) for all the Union armies, Lieutenant Colonel Michael Ryan Morgan, may also have been present. Badeau also said that an unspecified number of Ord's and Sheridan's staff officers "were afterwards brought into the room," but he did not remember them being present during the formal conference. See Badeau to "My dear Sir," April 26, 1865, Dartmouth College Library. Colonel George H. Sharpe included himself in the roomful of officers (*Philadelphia Weekly Times*, June 30, 1877). Contrary to Badeau, other sources, and most of the artistic depictions of the scene, Sheridan claimed in his memoirs that he and Ord were ushered out of the room while Grant and Lee discussed the terms, and were reinvited afterward.

37. Sheridan, *Personal Memoirs*, 2:202; Frank Potts to unidentified correspondent, April 1865, and Channing Smith diary, April 9, 1865, both in the Museum of the Confederacy; E. P. Alexander to James Longstreet, October 26, 1892, North Carolina Department of Archives and History; Giles B. Cooke diary, April 9, 1865, VHS; William Wiatt diary, April 9, 1865, Calkins collection; Welch, *Confederate Surgeon's Letters to His Wife*, 118–19; John Bell Vincent diary, April 9, 1865, VHS; John Kennedy Cole-

man diary, quoted in antique catalogue, Krick collection. For Wilmer McLean's own account of the loss of his furniture, see Dennett, *South as It Is*, 68. Captain Thomas W. C. Moore appropriated the doll, which his grandson retained eighty-six years later ("The Silent Witness," *Saturday Evening Post*, April 7, 1951).

38. Styple, *With a Flash of His Sword*, 217–18; Lyon, "Letter from Appomattox," 74; William H. Berrier to "My Dear Beloved Companion," April 10, 1865, Berrier Letters, Calkins collection; David J. Scott to "Dear Maud," April 10, 1865, *Civil War Times Illustrated* Collection, USAMHI.

39. Agassiz, *Meade's Headquarters*, 358; Clement E. Warner memoir, Warner Papers, State Historical Society of Wisconsin; Thomas Wilson to Mrs. Wilson, April 1865, Library of Congress.

40. Robertson, *Civil War Letters of General Robert McAllister*, 607–8; John R. Brincklé to "My Dear Brother," April 14, 1865, Brincklé Papers, Library of Congress; George Blotcher diary, April 9, 1865, Calkins collection; Stephen W. Gordon diary, April 9, 1865, Chatham office, Fredericksburg and Spotsylvania National Military Park.

41. Lothrop Lincoln Lewis diary, April 9, 1865, Library of Congress; Henry Keiser diary, April 9, 1865, Calkins collection.

42. *OR* 46(1):1304; Henry Carter Lee diary, April 9, 1865, Museum of the Confederacy; Eighth Census of the United States, M-653, reel 1332, 528, RG 29, NA.

43. *OR* 46(1):1146, 1155–56, 1246; Isaac H. Ressler diary, April 9, 1865, *Civil War Times Illustrated* Collection, USAMHI; John A. Sharrah diary, April 9, 1865, ACHNHP; Thomas T. Munford to Samuel Griffin, April 30, 1906, box 14, Munford-Ellis Family Papers, Duke University.

44. John Richardson Porter diary, April 9, 1865, Duke University; Henry Carter Lee diary, April 9, 1865, Museum of the Confederacy; Harwell, *Confederate Diary of the Retreat from Petersburg*, 17; Report of Charles E. Lightfoot, series 8, folder 11, R. E. Lee Headquarters Papers, VHS; diary of anonymous Confederate officer, April 9, 1865, James B. Blackford Collection, UVA; John Willis Council diary, April 9, 1865, North Carolina Department of Archives and History; James W. Albright diary, April 9, 1865, SHC.

45. David Gregg McIntosh and Osmun Latrobe diaries, April 9, 1865, VHS; John Paris diary, April 9, 1865, SHC; Fitzhugh Lee to Robert E. Lee, April 17, 1865, series 8, folder 11, R. E. Lee Headquarters Papers, VHS.

46. T. J. Watkins memoir, BV 85, Chatham office, Fredericksburg and Spotsylvania National Military Park; Dayton, *Diary of a Confederate Soldier*, 136; Kena King Chapman diary, April 9, 1865, SHC; John Richardson Porter diary, April 9, 1865, Duke University; Walters, *Norfolk Blues*, 224.

47. John Bell Vincent and James Eldred Phillips diaries, April 9, 1865, VHS; J. E. Whitehorn diary, April 9, 1865, SHC.

48. Lyon, "Letter from Appomattox," 74; J. W. Warr diary, April 9, 1865, ACHNHP; Channing Smith diary, April 9, 1865, Museum of the Confederacy; Robert Larimer diary, April 11, 1865, UVA.

49. Billings, "Union Officer's Diary of Appomattox Campaign," 23.

50. William T. Livermore diary, April 9, 1865, VHS; William D. Alexander diary, April 9, 1865, SHC; John Richardson Porter diary, April 9, 1865, Duke University.

CHAPTER NINE

1. Walters, *Norfolk Blues*, 224.

2. William T. Livermore diary, April 10, 1865, VHS; Isaac H. Ressler diary, April 10, 1865, *Civil War Times Illustrated* Collection, USAMHI; Walters, *Norfolk Blues*, 224; John Richardson Porter diary, April 10, 1865, Duke University; Pearce, *Diary of Captain Henry A. Chambers*, 263–64.

3. James Eldred Phillips and John Bell Vincent diaries, April 10, 1865, VHS; J. W. Warr diary, April 10, 1865, ACHNHP. In a 1914 article for the *Confederate Veteran* ("Surrender of Mahone's Division," 312–13), Surgeon H. A. Minor seemed to confuse the less formal stacking of arms on April 10 with the final ceremony of April 12.

4. *Richmond Whig*, April 10, 1865; *OR* 46(3):683; "George" (last name unknown) to "Dear Mother," April 10, 1865, Brown University; Alonzo V. Richard diary, Richard Papers, April 10, 1865, State Historical Society of Wisconsin.

5. Radclif Lawrence to "Dear Brother," April 10, 1865, Museum of the Confederacy; George E. Farmer to "Dear Father," April 14, 1865, Farmer Letters, Gilder-Lehrman Collection, Pierpont-Morgan Library; Kena King Chapman diary, April 10, 1865, SHC; William Wiatt diary, April 9, 1865, Calkins collection.

6. William T. Livermore diary, April 10, 1865, VHS; Styple, *With a Flash of His Sword*, 220; Chaplain O. B. Clark to his son, April 13, 1865, quoted in Civil War paper catalogue, Krick collection; Rhodes, *All for the Union*, 230; William Howard to "My Dear Mother," April 24, 1865, Howard Papers, Library of Congress.

7. William Wiatt diary, April 11, 1865, Calkins collection; J. L. Smith to "Dear Mother," April 18, 1865, Smith Letters, Historical Society of Pennsylvania.

8. Douglas J. Cater to "Dear Cousin Laurence," May 16, 1865, Rufus W. and Douglas J. Cater Papers, Library of Congress; George W. Munford to Mrs. E. T. Munford, April 21, 28, and May 9, 1865, box 5, Munford-Ellis Family Papers, Duke University.

9. Nevins, *Diary of Battle*, 523; Elihu Washburne diary, April 11, 1865, Washburne Papers, Yale University; *OR* 46(3):763.

10. Grant, *Personal Memoirs*, 2:496–98; Nevins, *Diary of Battle*, 523; Gibbon, "Personal Recollections of Appomattox," 940; Robert Larimer diary, April 10, 1865, UVA; *OR* 46(3):695. A plaque near the Peers house, at the top of the hill overlooking the valley of the Appomattox, has long marked the supposed site of this second meeting between Grant and Lee, but that supposition appears to be based on Horace Porter's undependable memoir (*Campaigning with Grant*, 490) and the confused recollections of George Peers (Washington *Evening Star*, April 5, 1890). Porter's recollection that "they met on a knoll that overlooked the lines of the two armies" does not quite match the diary entry of Colonel Charles Wainwright, who was also present: Wainwright (Nevins, *Diary of Battle*, 523) recorded that "the meeting took place near a small stream, in the road, and all were mounted." It does not seem likely that Wainwright would have referred to their gathering as "near a small stream" if they had been atop the hill, fully a quarter of a mile away from it. *New York Herald* correspondent Sylvanus Cadwallader (*Three Years with Grant*, 334) claimed that Lee was accompanied by a single orderly on this visit, and that observation was corroborated by a Confederate sergeant of the 1st Engineer Regiment, which camped in the vicinity of

the Sweeney house (John Thomas Gibson to Jubal A. Early, January 24, 1888, Early Papers, Jones Memorial Library). Captain Oscar Heinrich, an engineer in Early's old division, nevertheless suggested that he went with Lee on this visit (Heinrich diary, April 10, 1865, Krick collection); General Meade also met Lee just as he returned from this conference, and one of Meade's staff officers noted that Lee was attended by "three or four Staff officers" (Agassiz, *Meade's Headquarters*, 360). The conflicting observations could be reconciled by supposing that Lee left in haste with one attendant, while two or three staff members followed him soon thereafter.

11. Agassiz, *Meade's Headquarters*, 359; Silliker, *Rebel Yell and the Yankee Hurrah*, 266; William D. Alexander diary, April 10, 1865, SHC; *OR* 46(3):674, 691. The legendary mingling of Confederate and Union rank and file immediately after the surrender appears to have been greatly exaggerated. Many diaries refer to visitors traveling back and forth on April 10, especially in Joseph Bartlett's division of the Fifth Corps, but those visitors appear to have been almost entirely officers (see William T. Livermore diary, VHS; Jacob Ogden Wilson diary, Calkins collection; Spear, *Recollections*, 272; and Robert P. Myers diary and T. F. McCoy to Hon. S. Casey, April 12, 1865, both in Museum of the Confederacy). T. F. McCoy, a full colonel, specifically mentioned that the "stream" of traffic on April 10 consisted of officers. A West Virginia bugler in John Turner's division of the Twenty-fourth Corps reported Confederates "running around through our camps with our boys" on April 11, when his division lay in the village to oversee the surrender of the artillery, and the Confederates to whom he referred may well have been paroled already (Wirt Phillips to Richard Phillips, April 11, 1865, published in the unpaginated *Thirteenth Report of the Descendants of the French Creek Pioneers*). William Livermore mentioned enlisted men passing the pickets as well, but not until April 11, when his brigade had been posted in the village in place of Turner's; there the business of surrender was still being conducted, with paroled prisoners by the hundreds and Union ordnance and quartermaster details passing in all directions. William D. Alexander's diary attests to the stringent separation of the opposing camps; in an 1876 reminiscence that he reprinted in 1914, H. A. Minor, a surgeon in Mahone's division, insisted that "we were not allowed to wander about" (H. A. Minor Collection, UVA), and a number of Union field officers and acting field officers appeared to consider themselves lucky to obtain permission for passage through the lines, usually in the company of generals: see, for instance, Nevins, *Diary of Battle*, 523, and McCoy to Casey, above. Alfred Waud, the *Harper's Weekly* artist traveling with the Army of the Potomac, made a sketch of Union and Confederate soldiers sharing rations, and that sketch survives in the Library of Congress: these were probably Gordon's pickets and their counterparts from the Fifth Corps, who—judging from their lack of issued rations and the numerous reports of their rampant foraging—had probably stolen that food from nearby farms.

12. Agassiz, *Meade's Headquarters*, 360–62; Meade, *Life and Letters*, 2:270; Field, "Campaign of 1864 and 1865," 562.

13. Nevins, *Diary of Battle*, 523; Longstreet, *From Manassas to Appomattox*, 630; Gibbon, "Personal Recollections of Appomattox," 941; Grant, *Personal Memoirs*, 2:498.

14. *OR* 46(3):685–86, 709–10.

15. Walters, *Norfolk Blues*, 224; Ellis Spear diary, April 10, 1865, Spear, *Recollections*,

272; Ely S. Parker to Chief Ordnance Officer, Army of the Potomac, April 9, 1865, Webb Papers, Yale University; *OR* 46(1):1277–78 and (3):696.

16. William T. Livermore, James Eldred Phillips, and John Bell Vincent diaries, April 10, 1865, all in VHS; Kena King Chapman diary, April 10, 1865, SHC.

17. *OR* 46(3):688–89, 694–95.

18. Maurice, *Aide-de-Camp of Lee*, 278; Norfolk *Virginian-Pilot*, May 21, 1951; "Paroles of the Army of Northern Virginia," 28, 458, 472.

19. Walters, *Norfolk Blues*, 224.

20. Dayton, *Diary of a Confederate Soldier*, 136; Nevins, *Diary of Battle*, 523.

21. Henry Felix Wilson diary, April 11, 1865, Alabama Department of Archives and History; Thomas P. Devereux, "Recollections, December, 1864 to April, 1865," Devereux Papers, SHC.

22. Walters, *Norfolk Blues*, 225; *OR* 46(1):1278–79.

23. Ellis Spear diary, April 11, 1865, Spear, *Recollections*, 272; Alexander, *Military Memoirs of a Confederate*, 613. Alexander estimated that the surrendered artillery column was "about a mile" long: allowing for a space of ten feet between each of seventy-four six-horse teams, limbers, cannons, and caissons that would have measured about fifty feet apiece, the column would run 4,400 feet from head to tail; the distance from the Peers house to the site of the Conner house, by the present road, is almost exactly one mile.

24. Lovell, "With Lee after Appomattox," 42; Norfolk *Virginian-Pilot* clipping, May 21, 1951, Bell Papers, SHC; undated statement of Walter Taylor regarding the return to Richmond, Taylor Papers, Kirn Memorial Library; Styple, *With a Flash of His Sword*, 219–20. Perhaps because his report to Davis is dated "Near Appomattox Court House" on April 12 (Dowdey and Manarin, *Wartime Papers of R. E. Lee*, 935), others who have written of Appomattox have maintained that Lee left his army on April 12. Lieutenant Samuel Lovell, who led the cavalry escort, noted it in his diary under April 11, however. So did Lee's assistant adjutant and inspector general, Giles B. Cooke, who accompanied the party (Giles B. Cooke diary, VHS). E. P. Alexander (Gallagher, *Fighting for the Confederacy*, 541) recalled that "Gen. Grant started for Washington City at noon on Monday the 10th. Gen. Lee started for Richmond early on the 11th." Joshua Chamberlain, in describing the circumstances under which he was directed to command the surrender ceremony, twice recorded that Lee had left the area by noon of April 11 (*Passing of the Armies*, 258, and "Appomattox," 274). Douglas Southall Freeman, who did not have access to the Lovell diary, did not cite Alexander, and discounted Cooke's diary in favor of several ex post facto recollections, dated Lee's departure April 12 (*R. E. Lee*, 4:158).

25. J. E. Whitehorn diary, April 11, 1865, SHC; Walters, *Norfolk Blues*, 225; Robert Larimer diary, April "10" ["11"], 1865, UVA; Field returns of the Artillery corps, Army of Northern Virginia, April 8, 1865, series 8, folder 13, R. E. Lee Headquarters Papers, VHS; *OR* 46(3):710; William B. Stark diary, April 11, 1865, Massachusetts Historical Society. In his *Military Memoirs of a Confederate* (613) Alexander claimed that the army surrendered sixty-three guns, probably by counting the pair of Union guns brought in on April 9.

26. James L. Corley to Robert E. Lee, April 15, 1865, series 8, folder 14, R. E. Lee Headquarters Papers, VHS; *OR* 46(3):710.

27. Kena King Chapman diary, April 10, 1865, SHC; James Eldred Phillips diary, April 11, 1865, VHS; J. E. Whitehorn diary, April 11, 1865, SHC; John Bell Vincent diary, April 11, 1865, VHS; William D. Alexander diary, April 11, 1865, SHC. Francis and Maria Meeks still owned the general store but seem not to have bought the house on lot 12 of Clover Hill until 1866; a woman named Lucinda Bryant often shared their household, and they may have lived with her and her brother, who occupied a home owned by Joel Flood half a mile south of Pleasant Retreat. That house lay in the midst of Longstreet's half of the army, which included Mahone's division. See *Atlas to Accompany the Official Records*, plate 78, map 2, and Giddens, "Recollections of the Battle of Appomattox Court House," 233.

28. William T. Livermore diary, April 11 and 14, 1865, VHS.

29. Henry J. Millard to "Dear Parents," April 10, 1865, Henry J. Millard Letters, and William B. Stark diary, April 8, 1865, both in the Massachusetts Historical Society.

30. George Blotcher diary, April 9, 1865, and William H. Berrier to "Dear Mamly," April 12, 1865, Berrier Letters, both in Calkins collection.

31. Like most other Appomattox residents, Willis Inge was refused any compensation for his losses on the grounds of disloyalty. The county's unanimous vote for secession left little room for claims of antebellum union devotion, but Inge plied the usual excuse that he had voted for secession against his own principles, through fear of retaliation. Federal officials still rejected his claim because his adult son, Caswell, served in the Confederate army (which Inge also insisted had been against his wishes). While Caswell's service may not have offered a reliable indication of Inge's loyalty, he did choose the name Stonewall Jackson Inge for the son his wife bore in 1862. See Barred and Disallowed Case Files of the Southern Claims Commission, M-1407, RG 233, NA: case files of Willis Inge (#10150), William Trent (#2129), York Wright (#11591), Louisa Morgan (#2126), Mary Dickerson (#17157), Samuel Baldwin (#15703), and Frances St. Clair (#17158). Inge's youngest son appears as Thomas J. Inge on the 1870 census, about the time Inge was preparing his damage claim, but he also had an older son named Thomas S. Inge; the younger boy was always known as Stonewall Jackson or S. J. Inge in Appomattox County (Ninth Census of the United States, M-593, reel 1633, 24, RG 29, NA; Vital Statistics of Appomattox County, Marriages, 1886, reel 4, LOV; Featherston, *History of Appomattox*, 192–93).

32. James Eldred Phillips diary, April 12 and 13, 1865, VHS.

33. *OR* 46(3):706; Jacob Ogden Wilson diary, April 11, 1865, Calkins collection; Ellis Spear diary, April 11, 1865, Spear, *Recollections*, 272.

34. Richard W. Waldrop diary, April 11, 1865, SHC; John Paris diary, April 11, 1865, SHC; William B. Stark diary, April 11, 1865, Massachusetts Historical Society; notes from Crumpler, "War Diary," April 11, 1865, Calkins collection; Elihu B. Washburne diary, April 11, 1865, Washburne Papers, Yale University.

35. John Paris diary, April 11, 1865, SHC; Jacob Ogden Wilson diary, April 11, 1865, Calkins collection; Ellis Spear diary, April 11, 1865, Spear, *Recollections*, 272. The diary references to an April 11 surrender of arms by Gordon's entire corps (Waldrop, Paris, Stark, Crumpler, and Washburne, above) make sense only when combined with the information that Gordon objected so strongly to the more formal affair that eventually took place on April 12. In at least two written accounts Joshua Chamberlain referred to this dispute, the details of which he learned from General Griffin (*Passing*

of the Armies, 248, "Appomattox," 273), and a captain in Chamberlain's original regiment noted just after the April 12 surrender ceremony that "General Gordon objected very strongly to this but was brought to it" (Styple, *With a Flash of His Sword*, 220). No extant record has surfaced of a meeting of the surrender commission on the evening of April 11, but some official encounter would have been necessary to force a repetition of the surrender of arms on April 12. Furthermore, Gordon's objection would have had to come after his Confederates-only parade of April 11, and it likely arose in his capacity as a commissioner.

36. Confederate infantry officers spent much of the night of April 11 filling out parole papers: see, for instance, John Bell Vincent and James Eldred Phillips diaries, April 11, 1865, VHS; Pearce, *Diary of Captain Henry A. Chambers*, 264.

37. Joshua L. Chamberlain to Sarah B. Chamberlain, April 13, 1865, Chamberlain Papers, Bowdoin College.

38. Ibid.; Chamberlain, "Appomattox," 272–74, "Last Salute of the Army of Northern Virginia," 360–61, and *Passing of the Armies*, 254–59. Chamberlain was the only original source of the claim that he commanded the surrender ceremony; he offered no witnesses or documentation, and none has been found. Regimental histories published as early as 1880 named him as commander of the Union forces, but those histories came from regiments within his own brigade, and his private claim may have influenced those references. One of those histories (*Under the Maltese Cross*, 367) asserts that Chamberlain, who was reassigned to command of the veteran third brigade on the night of April 10 (*OR* 46[3]:691), had claimed that assignment by virtue of his seniority within the division, with the implication that he did so because that brigade was then expected to receive the surrender. Circumstantial evidence points to Bartlett commanding the parade formation, including Chamberlain's own reference to Bartlett retaining the division flag. Chamberlain told his sister on April 13 that he and his staff had gathered around "the old flag, the red maltese cross on the white field with blue border." In the Army of the Potomac a red emblem on a white field designated the first division of a corps, while a blue border identified the third brigade of that division: see unpaginated plates in Billings, *Hardtack and Coffee*. The commander of the Fifth Corps, Charles Griffin, died in 1867; General Grant died in 1885, and General Bartlett in 1893. The two other brigade commanders in Bartlett's division, Edgar Gregory and Alfred Pearson, died respectively in 1871 and on January 6, 1903. Pearson was the last man besides Chamberlain who would have had to know who was in command of the troops at the surrender, and the first time Chamberlain claimed to have been that person in a national forum seems to have been in an address to the Military Order of the Loyal Legion of the United States on October 7, 1903—nine months after Pearson's death. A similar Chamberlain story appeared in the *Southern Historical Society Papers* in 1904, and his book on the Appomattox campaign came out in 1915. He appears to have made local references to his role at Appomattox in interviews prior to 1903, including in the *New York Times* of May 4, 1901, and a Boston *Journal* article in May of 1901 that was reprinted as the 1904 *SHSP* piece. In the *SHSP* article (363) he took the opportunity to correct exaggerations that he said had been mistakenly attributed to him. In "Reminiscences of Petersburg and Appomattox" (180), Chamberlain complained that "some persons" had charged that he was not even present at the surrender ceremony, suggesting that his role in the ceremony had indeed been challenged, at

least privately. He undoubtedly was present, but evidently not in formal command, and he certainly was not designated for that service by General Grant.

39. Joshua L. Chamberlain to Sarah B. Chamberlain, April 13, 1865, Chamberlain Papers, Bowdoin College; J. L. Smith to "Dear Mother," April 15, 1865, Smith Letters, Historical Society of Pennsylvania; James Eldred Phillips diary, April 12, 1865, VHS; J. W. Warr diary, April 12, 1865, ACHNHP.

40. Styple, *With a Flash of His Sword*, 220.

41. Chamberlain, "Last Salute of the Army of Northern Virginia," 361–62; Gordon, *Reminiscences of the Civil War*, 444–45.

42. Joshua L. Chamberlain to Sarah B. Chamberlain, April 13, 1865, Chamberlain Papers, Bowdoin College; Chamberlain, *Passing of the Armies*, 249; Hardee, *Rifle and Light Infantry Tactics*, 31, 130–31.

43. Elihu B. Washburne diary, April 12, 1865, Washburne Papers, Yale University; William T. Livermore diary, April 12, 1865, VHS; J. L. Smith to "Dear Mother," April 15 and 18, 1865, Smith Letters, Historical Society of Pennsylvania.

44. John Paris and Kena King Chapman diaries, April 12, 1865, SHC; William Wiatt diary, and notes from Crumpler, "War Diary," April 12, 1865, Calkins collection; Dayton, *Diary of a Confederate Soldier*, 137; Richard W. Waldrop diary, April 12, 1865, SHC. In a reminiscence for the *Shepherdstown* (W.Va.) *Register* of December 1, 1883, Chaplain John Paris of the 54th North Carolina, whose diary noted that the order of march was "by Brigades and divisions," wrote that his division (Walker's) marched at the front; even in 1883 he made no mention of any salute by the attending Union forces.

45. J. W. Warr diary, April 12, 1865, ACHNHP; Joshua L. Chamberlain to Sarah B. Chamberlain, April 13, 1865, Chamberlain Papers, Bowdoin College.

46. *OR* 46(3):731; George K. Griggs diary, April 12 and 13, 1865, Museum of the Confederacy; Pearce, *Diary of Captain Henry A. Chambers*, 264; Walters, *Norfolk Blues*, 226; Channing Smith diary, April 12, 1865, Museum of the Confederacy.

47. Elihu B. Washburne diary, April 12, 1865, Washburne Papers, Yale University; Elihu Washburne to John L. Winston, June 17, 1874, UVA; E. P. Alexander diary, April 12, 1865, Alexander Papers, SHC. General Wise was supposed to have been very surly at Appomattox, according to both General Chamberlain and the historian of the regiment that held the post near the McLean house. Chamberlain (*Passing of the Armies*, 267), who had no opportunity to converse with any of the Confederate officers that morning, claimed that he and Wise (whom he described without naming) engaged in an acerbic exchange in which Wise remarked, "You may forgive us but we won't be forgiven. . . . We hate you, sir." The main contributor to Survivors' Association, *History of the 118th Pennsylvania*, 596, described Wise as snapping at his men, who supposedly turned viciously on him, with the Pennsylvanians chiming in with taunts about John Brown; this source describes Wise wearing a new blue uniform coat with gold braid, however, while everyone else who saw Wise at Appomattox found his best attire "shabby."

48. In his letter to Sarah B. Chamberlain (April 13, 1865, Chamberlain Papers, Bowdoin College), Joshua Chamberlain noted that the three divisions of the old Third Corps surrendered last; J. E. Whitehorn remarked in his diary entry of April 11 (SHC) that his division (Mahone's) would be the last paroled, as it may have been. Wilcox's

appearance at the McLean house well before noon (Washburne diary, above) indicates that his was not the last division surrendered, since the ceremony lasted until 1:00 P.M., leaving either Heth's or Mahone's until last.

49. Compiled Service Records of Confederate Soldiers Who Served in Organizations from the State of Alabama, M-311, RG 109, NA; Hoar, *South's Last Boys in Gray*, 463–66. Though a dozen others made false claims of having been Confederate soldiers after he died, Pleasant Riggs Crump of the 10th Alabama was the last surviving Confederate soldier when he died on December 31, 1951. See Marvel, "Great Impostors," 33.

50. Agassiz, *Meade's Headquarters*, 362.

CHAPTER TEN

1. Elihu Washburne diary, April 12, 1865, Washburne Papers, Yale University; Fitzhugh Lee to Robert E. Lee, series 8, folder 11, R. E. Lee Headquarters Papers, VHS; *OR* 46(3):719.

2. E. P. Alexander, Kena King Chapman, and Richard W. Waldrop diaries, April 12, 1865, SHC; [Corbin], *Letters of a Confederate Officer to His Family in Europe*, 93–94; William Wiatt diary, April 12, 1865, Calkins collection; Dayton, *Diary of a Confederate Soldier*, 137; Cutrer, *Longstreet's Aide*, 143–45. James E. Hall, the Confederate adjutant of the 31st Virginia whose diary constitutes Dayton's *Diary of a Confederate Soldier*, hailed from the same vicinity as Wirt Phillips, a Union bugler in the 10th West Virginia, who remarked upon paroled Confederates wandering through his camp: see Wirt Phillips to Richard Phillips, April 11, 1865, *Thirteenth Report of the Descendants of the French Creek Pioneers*, unpaginated.

3. J. E. Whitehorn diary, April 12 and 13, 1865, SHC; George K. Griggs diary, April 13, 1865, Museum of the Confederacy; William Wiatt diary, April 13, 1865, Calkins collection; William T. Livermore diary, April 13, 1865, VHS; Jacob Ogden Wilson diary, April 13, 1865, Calkins collection.

4. J. E. Whitehorn diary, April 13, 1865, SHC.

5. William T. Livermore diary, April 13, 1865, VHS; *OR* 46(3):731.

6. "Reminiscences of Berry Greenwood Benson," 669, Benson Papers, SHC. Benson includes his own and his brother's diary entries in this manuscript.

7. Marvel Ritchie to A. H. Boyden, September 14, 1923, North Carolina Department of Archives and History. North Carolina veterans made a lot of claims to having been responsible for the last this or that at Appomattox—members of Ritchie's own regiment insisted that they fought the last skirmish and fired the last shot—and Marvel Ritchie asserted in his letter that his brother had been the last man killed.

8. The minutes of the Ladies Memorial Association of Appomattox for May 18, 1866 (VHS), mention a letter from Captain Macon's mother, thanking "Mr. E. G. Hix and citizens of the Court House" for giving her son a decent burial.

9. See Chris Calkins's list of casualties, compiled from various sources, in *Battles of Appomattox Station and Appomattox Court House*, 233–34, and Goldsborough, *Maryland Line in the Confederate Army*, 225.

10. Elvira L. Woodson to Mariam Wall, June 5, 1865, Mrs. Wall's reply of Janu-

ary 10, 1866, and Spencor Adams to Elvira L. Woodson, all in Woodson Papers, Duke University.

11. Session Book, Records of Union Academy, Chilton Papers, UVA.

12. Spear diary, April 15, 1865, Spear, *Recollections*, 273; Joseph Wheeler to Joseph E. Johnston, April 18, 1865, Gilder-Lehrman Collection, Pierpont-Morgan Library; Ellen Maria Ravenel to Rosa Pringle, April 23, 1865, South Caroliniana Library, University of South Carolina; *OR* 46(3):763.

13. Sparks, *Inside Lincoln's Army*, 496; Richard W. Waldrop diary, April 16, 1865, SHC.

14. J. Warren Keifer to Mrs. Keifer, April 15, 1865, Keifer Papers, Library of Congress; Unidentified Union soldier to "Dear Parents," April 18, 1865, Gilder-Lehrman Collection, Pierpont-Morgan Library; Edmund K. Russell to "Dear Mother [and] Sisters," April 17, 1865, Russell Letters, Marye's Heights office, Fredericksburg and Spotsylvania National Military Park.

15. Blair, *Politician Goes to War*, 241; Rawleigh William Downman to Mary Alice Downman, April 23, 1865, section 10, Downman Family Papers, VHS.

16. *OR* 46(3):796, 813, 1157; William D. Hix letter of authorization to John M. Harris, April 25, 1865, ACHNHP.

17. George W. Munford to Elizabeth T. Munford, April 21 and 30, 1865, box 5, Munford-Ellis Family Papers, Duke University.

18. Thomas S. Bocock memorandum of May 1865, box 8, Bocock Papers, UVA.

19. *OR* 46(3):1137–39, 1156–57; Louis Stevenson to Orlando Brown, January 31, 1867, Narrative Reports of Criminal Cases Involving Freedmen, Entry 3806, RG 105, NA.

20. *OR* 46(3):1156; J. Irvin Gregg to S. M. B. Young, May 20, 1865, Letters Received, May–July 1865, Entry 1475, and General Order No. 6, Letters Sent, Entry 1476, RG 393, NA.

21. S. M. B. Young memorandum, May 31, 1865, Letters Sent, May–July 1865, Entry 1475, RG 393; Robert Bell to Mrs. Bell, "April" [May] 21, 1865, Robert Bell Letters, ACHNHP. The two children Captain Bell noted were Eleanor Bolling Flood and Henry De La Warr Flood. Eleanor, born in 1863, married Admiral Richard Evelyn Byrd, the arctic explorer, while "Hal" Flood went to Congress, where he introduced the resolution declaring war on Germany in 1917. An informal family history compiled by their half-brother Joel West Flood (ACHNHP) dated Hal's birth on September 2, 1865, but Captain Bell's letter clearly indicates that the second child was born by late May of 1865. Joel and Ella Flood had only one other child, Holmes Boyd Flood, whose birth date is recorded on his tombstone as April 28, 1866, which would have been nearly impossible had an older brother been born the previous September. The births of neither Eleanor nor Henry D. Flood were recorded in the county register, and the third child's birth is incorrectly recorded under the date of September 21, 1866, as "Hunter B." Flood (Vital Statistics of Appomattox County, reel 4, LOV). According to the minutes of the Ladies Memorial Association of Appomattox (VHS), Ella Flood announced on July 28, 1866, that she would be traveling abroad, and she remained absent through the subsequent winter; it would have been highly unusual in 1866 for a woman who was seven months pregnant to embark upon so extended a journey.

22. *OR*, ser. 2, 8:578–80, and ser. 1, 46(3):1170, 1275–76; Thomas S. Bocock to

Susan Bocock, June 23, 1865, UVA. Orlando Brown's advocacy of "extensive confiscation" and distribution of plantation land is documented by Eric Foner in *Reconstruction,* 158–59.

23. J. D. Aiken to Wyatt Aiken, May 20, 1865, David Wyatt Aiken Collection, South Caroliniana Library, University of South Carolina; Gallagher, *Fighting for the Confederacy,* 547–49; Merli, "Alternative to Appomattox," 210–19; Dennett, *South as It Is,* 64.

24. Applications of Henry F. Bocock, reel 57, Henry D. Flood, Joel W. Flood, and John H. Flood, reel 61, Case Files for Presidential Pardons, M-1003, RG 94, NA. Henry D. Flood's assertion that he did not serve in the army contradicts a family tradition that he served as a staff officer: that story may have confused his son's appointment to Kemper's staff.

25. *OR* 46(3):1282; W. K. Gillespie to L. D. Phelps, June 16, 1865, Letters Sent, Entry 1475, RG 393, NA.

26. W. K. Gillespie to L. D. Phelps, June 20 and July 10, 1865, Endorsement Book, Entry 1477, RG 393, NA; John Sears petition, May 30, 1866; Isaac P. Wodell to R. S. Lacey, July 10 and September 10, 1866; A. H. Terry to Lacey, August 6, 1866; John Kendall petition with endorsements, October 9, 1866; Louis Stevenson to Lacey, January 15, 1867, August — and August 28, 1867; and Stevenson to Samuel G. Chalfin, September 24, 1867, all in Letters Received, May 31, 1866, to January 9, 1867, and Letters Sent, January 14, 1867, to August 12, 1868, Entry 4082, RG 105, NA.

27. Simpson, Graf, and Muldowney, *Advice after Appomattox,* 44–46; *Lynchburg Republican,* June 3, 1865; Vital Statistics of Appomattox County, Marriages, 1866, reel 4, LOV; Louis Stevenson to Samuel G. Chalfin, September 24, 1867, Letters Sent, Entry 4082, RG 105, NA.

28. James Geiser to Charles E. Dibble, July 28, 1865, with endorsement, Reports Received, Entry 7005; J. H. Jewett to Geiser, September 23 and 27, 1865, Letters Sent, Entry 7000; and Geiser's reports of August 30 and September 15, 1865, Register of Letters Received, Entry 7004, all in RG 393, NA.

29. R. S. Lacey to Orlando Brown, July 29, 1865, Unregistered Telegrams and Letters Received, Entry 3799, RG 105, NA; Dennett, *South as It Is,* 50; James Geiser to Charles E. Dibble, August — and August 14, 1865 (2), and to H. H. Jewett, September 14, 1865, Reports Received, Entry 7005, RG 393, NA.

30. James C. Briscoe to E. W. Smith, August 13, 1865, Letters Sent, Entry 7000, RG 393, NA; James Geiser to Charles E. Dibble, August 18, 1865, and to J. H. Jewett, August 31 and September 8, 1865, Reports Received, Entry 7005, RG 393, NA; Richmond *Times,* October 24, 1865, quoted in Carter, *When the War Was Over,* 149; Thomas S. Bocock memorandum book, August 1865, box 8, Bocock Papers, UVA; Edmund Wilcox Hubard, memorandum of contracts, 1865–66, Hubard Family Papers, SHC.

31. James C. Briscoe to Charles E. Dibble, September 3, 1865, and to E. W. Smith, August 13, 1865, Letters Sent, Entry 7000, RG 393, NA; Returns for Appomattox Court House, July and August 1865, Returns, Rosters, and Reports of Changes of Officers, Enlisted Men, and Civilians, Entry 3813, RG 105, NA.

32. Copies of the Collett sketch and Frankenstein's paintings are preserved in the files of Appomattox Court House National Historical Park. Two of the O'Sullivan photographs, showing Mr. and Mrs. McLean on the porch of their house (NWDNS-165-SB-99) and the supposed scene at Appomattox Station (NWDNS-165-SB-97)

survive in the National Archives' Still Picture Branch, while the Prints and Photographs Division of the Library of Congress holds three of the others: the McLean house view from the northwest (LC-B817-7292), the Clover Hill Tavern scene (LC-B817-7189), and the scene of the courthouse in which McLean appears (LC-B817-7169). An alternate view of the courthouse, without McLean and with George Peers standing more prominently in the front, appears only in Miller's *Photographic History of the Civil War*, 9:127, and a third image of the courthouse with no civilians or officers seems to have been published only in Calkins, *Battles of Appomattox Station and Appomattox Court House*, 193; the left background of this last shot more clearly depicts the brick wall of what is probably the original county jail.

33. Dennett, *South as It Is*, 63–68.

34. James Geiser to Charles E. Dibble, August 18, 1865, and to J. H. Jewett, August 31 and September 8, 1865, Reports Received, Entry 7005, and Jewett to Geiser, September 11, 1865, Letters Sent, Entry 7000, all in RG 393, NA; Eighth Census of the United States, M-653, reel 1332, 454–55, and Ninth Census of the United States, M-593, reel 1633, 18, RG 29, NA; *Lynchburg News*, September 22, 24, and 26, 1866. Wilson survived the assault, and five years later the couple had three more children.

35. James Geiser to Charles E. Dibble, August 14, 1865, and to J. H. Jewett, September 8, 1865, Reports Received, Entry 7005, RG 393, NA; Endorsement on the inside front cover of Letters Received, May 31, 1866–January 9, 1867, and Letters Sent, January 14, 1867–August 12, 1868, Entry 4082, RG 105, NA. William T. Johnson was elected sheriff and H. H. Marshall county judge; neither previously appeared on the county census. Captain Geiser dated the reorganization of the court September 7, but that was a Saturday; court day was traditionally the first Thursday of the month, and the *Lynchburg Virginian* recorded it as September 5.

36. Internal Revenue Assessments for Virginia, 1865–66, M-793, reel 1, RG 58, NA; Land Book, 1866, Appomattox County Circuit Court.

37. *Acts of the General Assembly*, 1865, 6; *Lynchburg Virginian*, September 10, 12, 17, 19, 23, and October 19, 1865.

38. Circular, September 27, 1865, General Orders, Special Orders, Circulars, and Circular Letters, Entry 3800, and R. S. Lacey to Orlando Brown, October 16, 1865, and Lacey's Report on Civilian Agents, both in Unregistered Telegrams and Letters Received, Entry 3799, all in RG 105, NA.

39. James Geiser to J. H. Jewett, September 14, 21, 28, and October 11, 1865, and Henry J. Cogan to Jewett, October 20, 1865, Reports Received, Entry 7005, RG 393, NA.

40. Circular, November 4, 1865, General Orders, Special Orders, Circulars, and Circular Letters, Entry 3800, and R. S. Lacey to Cogan, November 20, 1865, Press Copies of Letters Sent, Entry 4072, RG 105, NA; *Lynchburg Virginian*, November 9 and 10, 1865.

41. Vital Statistics of Appomattox County, Deaths, 1860 and 1865, reel 3, Births, 1861–69, reel 4, and Marriages, 1854–66, reel 4, LOV; *Lynchburg Virginian*, November 8, 1865; *Lynchburg News*, January 3, 1867.

42. Vital Statistics of Appomattox County, Marriages, 1866, reel 4, LOV; Records of Appointments of Postmasters, M-841, reel 130, RG 28, NA; Twelfth Census of the United States, T-623, reel 1381, enumeration district 63, sheet 2, RG 29, NA. See also

Geiser's appointment as county registrar, Louis Stevenson to Geiser, August 17, 1867, Letters Sent, Entry 4082, RG 105, NA.

43. Dennett, *South as It Is*, 35–37; *OR*, ser. 3, 5:73; *Sixteenth Annual Report of the South Side Railroad Company*, 5, cited in Johnston, *Virginia Railroads in the Civil War*, 250, 309; *Lynchburg Republican*, November 30, 1865.

44. *Lynchburg Virginian*, December 9, 1865, and January 30, 1866.

45. *Acts of the General Assembly*, 1865–66, 91–93; *Lynchburg Virginian*, December 30, 1865, and February 16, 1866. For a good synopsis of this period in Virginia history, see Maddex, *Virginia Conservatives*, 39–45.

46. James A. Bates to R. S. Lacey, March 18, 1866, and George G. White to Lacey, December 18, 1866, Letters Received, Entry 4084, and Lacey to Orlando Brown, March 9 and 22, 1866, Press Copies of Letters Sent, Entry 4072, RG 105, NA. From 1865 until 1868 black schools, scholars, and their teachers became particular targets for arson and assault throughout the South: see Butchart, *Northern Schools, Southern Blacks, and Reconstruction*, 186–90.

47. R. S. Lacey's report of the Akers case, District 7, Folio 87, Descriptive List of Reports of Outrages, March to June 1866, Records Relating to Murders and Outrages Against Freedmen, M-1048, reel 59, RG 105, NA. Bureau records do not include the outcome of the Akers case, and any criminal file would have been burned in the 1892 fire that destroyed the courthouse.

48. Isaac P. Wodell to Orlando Brown, March 31, April 30, May 31, July 31, August 31, September 30, and November 30, 1866, and Louis Stevenson to Brown, January 31 and February 28, 1867, all in Narrative Reports of Criminal Cases Involving Freedmen, Entry 3806, RG 105, NA.

49. Assorted muster rolls, John H. Cumby file, reel 872, CSRCSV; original application and surgeon's affidavit, John H. Cumby Pension File, certificate 149511, RG 15, NA; Ninth Census of the United States, M-593, reel 1633, 60, RG 29, NA.

50. Muster-out roll, July 17, 1865, John Glover file, Compiled Service Records of Volunteer Union Soldiers Who Served in Organizations from the State of Maryland, M-384, reel 80, RG 94, NA; Eleventh Census of the United States, Schedules Enumerating Union Veterans and Widows of Union Veterans of the Civil War, M-123, reel 106, Appomattox County, RG 29, NA; Declaration for Pension, November 1, 1890, affidavits of March 16, 1894, and December 24, 1896, and Samuel Webb to Commissioner of Pensions, February 19, 1892, and November 12, 1897, John Glover Pension File, application 840103, RG 15, NA.

CHAPTER ELEVEN

1. Minute book of the Ladies Memorial Association of Appomattox, May 18, 1866–May 10, 1870, VHS. A Union soldier's grave was later found in the neighborhood, and his body was reinterred alongside his former enemies.

2. Session Book, Records of Union Academy, Chilton Papers, UVA; Vital Statistics of Appomattox County, Marriages, July 19, 1866, reel 4, LOV.

3. Vital Statistics of Appomattox County, Marriages, June 27, 1866, reel 4, LOV; "Paroles of the Army of Northern Virginia," 453; Ninth Census of the United States,

M-593, reel 1633, 29, RG 29, NA. The house in question, identified in National Park Service literature as the "Union Academy dwelling house," was built in 1857 by Samuel McDearmon, apparently on speculation. Nathaniel Ragland Featherston, who was born and raised in the McLean house immediately opposite this one, recorded that this house was "said to have been occupied at the time of the surrender by the Landons [*sic*]" (*History of Appomattox*, 27).

4. Thomas Harvey file, reel 604, CSRCSV; T. H. to "My Dear Ella," August 17, 1866, Woodson Papers, Duke University; Vital Statistics of Appomattox County, Marriages, October 23, 1866, reel 4, LOV; Thomas and Elvira Harvey headstones, Harvey family cemetery, Route 24, Appomattox.

5. Vital Statistics of Appomattox County, Marriages, October 3 and November 14, 1866, reel 4, LOV; Jennings Conner file, reel 893, and Daniel F. Ferguson file, reel 602, CSRCSV.

6. Land Books, 1866–69, Appomattox County Circuit Court. This is the same house discussed in note 3, above.

7. *Lynchburg News*, January 1, 1867; Louis Stevenson to Charles W. McMahon, January 5 (with McMahon's endorsement of January 8) and 9, 1867, Letters Received, Entry 4082, RG 105, NA. The site of the freedmen's school is not specified in Freedmen's Bureau correspondence beyond that it was "at Appomattox Court House." In the Land Books of the Appomattox County Circuit Court no single village lot shows a sudden change of building value that might suggest the presence of a schoolhouse that was first heavily damaged and then reconstructed. The old and new schools probably occupied two different sites, however, and the new building may have been constructed on a single acre owned by John Rosser across the Prince Edward Court House Road from the southeast corner of the village. That lot, long identified as the "Academy & Hall" lot and taxed for a $1,100 building, had been owned in the 1850s by Samuel McDearmon, John Woodson, and finally by John West, the keeper of the county poorhouse. That building disappeared from the Land Books after 1857 (the same year that John Moffitt's house burned down, next door), and the vacant lot was acquired by the trustees of Union Academy, who sold it to Rosser in 1865. The lot was not again taxed for a building until 1867, when Rosser built a $400 structure on it; the next year he sold a three-quarter interest in it to the trustees of the Clover Hill Presbyterian Church. Those taxes were based on a building that would have been completed by the end of June 1867: Freedmen's Bureau correspondence (see n. 11, below) indicated that the schoolhouse authorized in January of 1867 was in use by July 26, 1867. In an interview with National Park staff in the 1940s (see Appomattox Court House National Historic Monument Master Plan, Interpretive Statement, 1942, ACHNHP), Nathaniel Ragland Featherston remarked that this building had been an odd one for a church, having two stories, and that it measured about thirty by forty feet. That coincidence with the dimensions of the school, and the more institutional style of architecture, suggests that the church had originally been the school building, which Rosser may have built in collaboration with McMahon: the three-quarter interest that he later conveyed precisely equalled the $300 McMahon had been authorized to spend.

8. Louis Stevenson to R. S. Lacey, January 31, 1867, Letters Received, Entry 4080, RG 105, NA.

9. Maddex, *Virginia Conservatives*, 45.

10. *Lynchburg News*, February 1, April 26, and June 8, 1867, and June 15, 1899; *Lynchburg Virginian*, April 14, 1856, November 16, 1859, and May 13, 1863; John H. Flood to Andrew Johnson, July 19, 1865, Case Files for Presidential Pardons, M-1003, RG 94, NA.

11. Louis Stevenson to John J. Purvis, June 13, August 2, and August 17, 1867, and Stevenson to Anthony "Norton" and Charles W. McMahon, July 26, 1867, Letters Received, Entry 4082, RG 105, NA. See also A. A. North's rejected application for pardon, July 6, 1865, reel 63, Case Files for Presidential Pardons, M-1003, RG 94, NA.

12. George Peers recollections, undated newspaper clipping, ACHNHP.

13. *Richmond Enquirer*, October 8, 1867; *Lynchburg News*, October 28, 1867.

14. Louis Stevenson to Samuel G. Chalfin, December 7, 1867, Letters Received, Entry 4082, RG 105, NA; *Richmond Enquirer*, October 25, 1867. The black delegate from Prince Edward County, James W. D. Bland, actually proved more moderate in his proposals for former Confederates than some of the white Republicans: see Lowe, *Republicans and Reconstruction*, 137. The 500 rifles remained in the jail until at least June of 1869, when ex-sheriff William Daniel Hix asked if he could buy some of them for resale, wryly remarking, "I suppose they will have been imprisoned long enough for rebeling against the government, provided they will never do so any more." See Hix to the Lynchburg post commander, June 5, 1869, quoted in Moore, "Appomattox Court House—Community, Village, and Families" (ACHNHP), 121. A diligent search of relevant entries in RG 393, the supposed source of that document in the National Archives, has failed to uncover the original letter.

15. Entry of November 29, 1867, Minutes of the West Hanover Presbytery, 1861–77, Union Theological Seminary/Presbyterian School of Christian Education; Minute Book of Liberty Baptist Church, 1834–1926, LOV; Land Books, 1868, 1869, Appomattox County Circuit Court; "Some 'During the War' Experiences of M. W. Ragland," UVA. See Nathaniel Ragland Featherston's comments about the church building, n. 7, above.

16. *Lynchburg News*, May 14, 1869; Land Books, 1869–72, Appomattox County Circuit Court; Vital Statistics of Appomattox County, Marriages, 1869, reel 4, LOV; Terry, *Raglands*, 39.

17. Spotts & Gibson to Thomas S. Bocock, January 1, 1869, box 7, Bocock Papers, UVA.

18. Ninth Census of the United States, M-593, reel 1633, 18, 28–29, RG 29, NA; Land Books, 1869–70, Appomattox County Circuit Court; Vital Statistics of Appomattox County, Marriages, 1869, reel 4, LOV; Deed Book 2, 352, Appomattox County Circuit Court.

19. Maddex, *Virginia Conservatives*, 59, 63, 69, 76, 78; Lowe, *Republicans and Reconstruction*, 172–73, 177; Foner, *Reconstruction*, 412–13; *Richmond Whig*, July 12, 1869. Virginia newspapers (e.g., *Lynchburg News*, July 18, 1866, and *Lynchburg Virginian*, September 28, 1867) reported disparagingly on the marriages of black men to white women in Petersburg and Wytheville.

20. Appomattox County Industrial Output, reel 8, Nonpopulation Schedules for the State of Virginia, 1870, T-1132, RG 29, NA; Land Books, 1869, 1870, Appomattox County Circuit Court.

21. Appomattox County Mortality, 1870, reel 10, Nonpopulation Schedules for the

State of Virginia, T-1132, RG 29, NA; Records of Appointments of Postmasters, M-841, RG 28, NA; Land Books, 1871–81, Appomattox County Circuit Court.

22. Land Books, 1871, 1872, Appomattox County Circuit Court; Ninth Census of the United States, M-593, reel 1633, 30, RG 29, NA; Parrish to George W. Randolph, May 7, 1862, with Thomas S. Bocock's endorsement, and Bocock to John C. Breckinridge, March 21, 1865, Parrish file, reel 578, CSRCSV. Nathaniel Ragland Featherston, who grew up in the village, identified the buildings occupied by these attorneys in his *History of Appomattox*, 26–27, 87. William Rosser's daughter corroborated his recollections in interviews with the National Park Service in the 1930s and early 1940s: see the Appomattox Court House National Historic Monument Master Plan, Interpretive Statement, 1942, ACHNHP. James H. Featherston's manuscript history of Appomattox Court House Presbyterian Church (Union Theological Seminary/Presbyterian School of Christian Education) mentions Lewis D. Isbell being suspended as both an elder and a member in December 1870 for "conduct unbecoming a Christian and an officer."

23. Deed Book 2, 206–7, Appomattox County Circuit Court. This deed, which clearly confuses the law office with Lorenzo Kelly's house, was the mistake that convinced the National Park Service to misidentify the building for decades. Since it was rerecorded in county records after the courthouse fire of 1892, the confusion could have arisen either from sloppy 1870s research on Sackett's part or from fraud—his own, with the motive of bilking the illiterate Robertson, or Robertson's, in a later effort to protect his property by reconstructing a lost document. Since Robertson was still signing documents with an "X" in 1897, his complicity seems unlikely.

24. Vital Statistics of Appomattox County, Deaths, 1871, reel 3, LOV; Appomattox County Industrial Output, reel 8, Nonpopulation Schedules of the State of Virginia, 1870, RG 29, NA.

25. Vital Statistics of Appomattox County, Marriages, 1876, reel 4, and Deaths, 1876, reel 3, LOV; *Lynchburg Virginian*, May 23 and 24, 1876. Like all other criminal cases in the first forty-six years of Appomattox County's history, the records for this one were lost to fire.

26. Wilson Hix headstone, Patteson-Hix cemetery, ACHNHP; Land Books, 1875–80, Appomattox County Circuit Court. An example of William D. Hix's stationery survives in a letter of April 23, 1897, to the Virginia Department of Pensions, Samuel Hubbard file, Virginia Confederate Pension Applications, Warrant 914, Act of 1888, reel 1, LOV.

27. *Lynchburg Republican*, August 23 and 26, 1875, quoted in Moore, "Appomattox Court House—Community, Village, and Families," 127–28, ACHNHP; Vital Statistics of Appomattox County, Births, 1870–74, reel 4, LOV; Terry, *Raglands*, 40–41.

28. Elihu B. Washburne to John L. Winston, June 17, 1874, UVA. Adam H. Plecker, of Lynchburg, photographed the McLean house wrapped in mourning in 1885, and a copy appears in a collection of his work held by the Museum of the Confederacy.

29. See, for instance, Jones, "Last Days of the Army of Northern Virginia," 86–87, and Chamberlain, "Appomattox," 272–80.

30. Land Books, 1883–85, Appomattox County Circuit Court; Deed Book 1, 451, Deed Book 2, 352, 540, Appomattox County Circuit Court.

31. Will and deed abstracts, McLean House Study, ACHNHP.

32. Records of Appointments of Postmasters, M-841, RG 28, NA; *Lynchburg News,* February 2 and 3, 1892.

33. Plecker's photographs are now owned by the Museum of the Confederacy. Plecker was a member of the Botetourt Artillery.

34. Robert B. Poore to Walter H. Taylor, October 12, 1892, Taylor Papers, Kirn Memorial Library; Pollard, *Lost Cause,* 706; Taylor, *General Lee,* 287.

35. Washington *Post,* November 17, 1893; *New York Tribune,* November 23, 1893.

36. *Appomattox and Buckingham Times,* April 5 and 12, 1905; Raleigh *News and Observer,* April 8–12, 1905. Leonard E. Smith, son of saddler Thomas Smith, told National Park Service personnel that he tore the old Robertson & Glover store down about 1900: see Appomattox Court House National Historic Monument Master Plan, Interpretive Statement, 1942, ACHNHP.

37. "Confederate Monument at Appomattox," 464.

38. Sam L. Ferguson to John R. Johnson, August 30, 1915, Mary F. Wingfield file, and same to same, December 11, 1914, Patrick Henry Wooldridge file, both under Pension Act of 1902, reel 64, LOV.

39. Original application, November 20, 1911, W. P. Hall to Auditor of Public Accounts, April 30, 1912, Joseph V. Bidgood to Auditor of Public Accounts, June 25, 1912, and approval endorsement of December 4, 1912, Charles H. Coleman file; see also original application of Edmonia Coleman, August 28, 1945, all under Pension Act of 1902, reel 64, LOV.

40. Original application, March 30, 1912, Sam L. Ferguson to Edward L. C. Scott, July 23, 1912, and approval endorsement of August 31, 1912, all in pension file of John H. "Patterson," Pension Act of 1902, reel 64, LOV; muster rolls of Company K, 4th Virginia Cavalry, January–July 1864, J. A. Patteson file, CSRCSV.

41. Original application, January 21, 1932, with approval endorsement of February 13, 1932, Sarah Anne Webb file, Pension Act of 1902, reel 64, LOV; John Glover Pension File, application 840103, RG 15, NA.

42. The appearance of the village is documented by photographs in the ACHNHP files taken about 1914, where a photo of the 1915 wreath-laying also lies. The interpretive statement of the park master plan notes that L. E. Smith said he tore down the Moffitt-Layne house around 1915, but he did not buy it until November 11, 1916, and obviously demolished it later: Deed Book 17, 88, Appomattox County Circuit Court.

EPILOGUE

1. Crawley, "Surrender Grounds at Appomattox," 129; assorted deeds, May 21, 1936, to June 3, 1943, Deed Books 35–41, Appomattox County Circuit Court.

2. Hosmer, *Preservation Comes of Age,* 2:733–35; typescript of Freeman's speech, ACHNHP; Washington *Post,* April 16, 1950.

3. *Arlington* (Va.) *Daily Sun,* March 6, 1959, Suffolk (Va.) *News Herald,* October 9, 1957, *Lynchburg News,* February 11, 1959, and assorted clippings, 1957–59, Watkins M. Abbitt scrapbook, LOV.

4. Washington *Post,* April 10, 1965; *Lynchburg News,* April 10, 1965.

BIBLIOGRAPHY

MANUSCRIPTS

William Abbitt Private Collection, Appomattox, Va.
  George W. Abbitt Letters
  Clifton V. Webb Letters
Alabama Department of Archives and History, Montgomery, Ala.
  Henry Felix Wilson diary
American Jewish Archives, Cincinnati, Ohio
  Levy Family Papers
    Eugene Henry Levy diary
Amherst County Circuit Court, Amherst, Va.
  Law Order Book Number 4, 1844–49
Appomattox County Circuit Court, Appomattox, Va.
  County Supervisors' Records
  County Deeds
  Land Books
  Roll of Confederate Veterans, Volume 1
  Roster of Appomattox Units in Confederate Service
Appomattox Court House National Historical Park
  Appomattox Court House National Historic Monument Master Plan
    Interpretive Statement
  Robert Bell Letters (typescripts)
  Bocock Papers
  Lucius Bushnell letter (photocopy)
  Frank Cauble, "Cultural History as of 1865 of the Village Green at Appomattox
    Court House"
  Joel T. Cawthorn letter
  Census of Persons in Clover Hill District Aged 5 to 21, 1870
  Mary Ann Coleman memoir
  Deed copies (saddler's shop)
  Joel West Flood, "Flood Family History"
  Douglas Southall Freeman speech, April 16, 1950
  Edward B. Harvey diary
  Ed Hedden letter

Edward G. Hix bond, with endorsement
William D. Hix letter (photocopy)
Inge Family History
    Marriage Certificate of Caswell and Martha Inge
McLean House Study
Moore, John H., "Appomattox Court House—Community, Village, and Families"
James Moss tax statement, with E. G. Hix endorsement
New Store ledger
George T. Peers, "The Dawn of Peace"
————, 1894 sketch map
————, undated newspaper clipping
Plunkett-Meeks Store ledger
John A. Sharrah diary (photocopy)
J. W. Warr diary
J. O. Williams Papers
John W. Woodson, resolution in Court of Appomattox County regarding
        ————, July 7, 1864
Bowdoin College, Brunswick, Maine
    Joshua Lawrence Chamberlain Papers
Brown University, Providence, R.I.
    Anonymous letter, April 10, 1865
Chris Calkins, private collection, Petersburg, Va.
    William H. Berrier Letters (transcripts)
    George Blotcher diary (transcript)
    R. M. Crumpler, "War Diary of ————"
    Amasa J. Isbell Letters (photocopies)
    Henry Keiser diary (transcript)
    William E. Wiatt diary (transcript)
    Jacob Ogden Wilson diary (photocopy)
Cincinnati Historical Society, Cincinnati, Ohio
    Roger Hannaford, "Diary of ————"
Dartmouth College Library, Hanover, N.H.
    Adam Badeau letter
    Eri D. Woodbury Collection
Duke University, Durham, N.C.
    William Clifton Harvey Papers
        Holcomb P. Harvey journal
    Jenkins-Aikens Papers
    Munford-Ellis Family Papers
    John Richardson Porter diary
    Elvira M. Woodson Papers
Emory and Henry College, Emory, Va.
    Student Register
Emory University, Atlanta, Ga.
    W. H. Adams Reminiscence-in-verse
    William Matthews Blackford Papers

William McFall Letters

Stuart McDearmon Farrar Family Papers, Pamplin, Va.

    McDearmon-Walton marriage records

    Notes on historic Appomattox houses

Fredericksburg and Spotsylvania National Military Park

    Chatham office, Falmouth, Va.

        George A. Bowen diary (typescript)

        Stephen W. Gordon diary (photocopy)

        Robert B. Isbell letter (photocopy)

        T. J. Watkins memoir

        John James Woodall diary (typescript)

    Marye's Heights office, Fredericksburg, Va.

        Edmund K. Russell Letters (typescripts)

Historical Society of Pennsylvania, Philadelphia

    John L. Smith Letters

Historical Society of Wisconsin

    Clement Warner memoir

Jones Memorial Library, Lynchburg, Va.

    Jubal A. Early Papers

    Virginia Court of Appeals docket books

Kirn Memorial Library, Norfolk, Va.

    Walter Herron Taylor Papers

Robert K. Krick, private collection, Fredericksburg, Va.

    Civil War antique, artifact, and paper catalogues

    Oscar Heinrich diary (transcript)

Library of Congress

    John R. Brincklé Papers

    Rufus W. and Douglas J. Cater Papers

    William Howard Papers

    Joseph Warren Kiefer Papers

    Lothrop Lincoln Lewis diary

    Thomas Wilson letter

Library of Virginia, Richmond

    Watkins M. Abbitt scrapbook

    Confederate Pension Applications, Appomattox County

    Executive Department

        Militia Commission Papers, 1777–1858

    Journal of the Council of State of Virginia, 1845–46

    Legislative Petitions

        Appomattox County

        Buckingham County

        Prince Edward County

    Minute Book, Liberty Baptist Church, 1834–1926

    Personal Property Tax Lists, Appomattox County, 1845–63

    R. E. Lee Camp Confederate Soldiers' Home

        Applications for Admission

Vital Statistics, Appomattox County
Louisiana State University, Baton Rouge, La.
    Minutes of the Appomattox Baptist Association Meetings
Massachusetts Historical Society, Boston
    Henry J. Millard Letters
    William B. Stark diary (transcript)
Museum of the Confederacy, Richmond, Va.
    Eleanor S. Brockenbrough Library
        George K. Griggs diary
        Radclif Lawrence letter
        Henry Carter Lee diary
        Thomas F. McCoy letter
        Robert P. Myers diary (transcript)
        Frank L. Potts letter
        John E. Roller, "The Incidents of Our Retreat to Appomattox"
        Channing M. Smith diary
National Archives, Washington, D.C.
    Record Group 15, Records of the Pension Office
        Pension Applications
    Record Group 28, Records of the Postmaster General
        Records of Appointments of Postmasters, M-841
    Record Group 29, Records of the Bureau of the Census
        Schedules Enumerating Union Veterans and Widows of Union Veterans of
            the Civil War, M-123
        Sixth Census of the United States, M-704
        Seventh Census of the United States, M-432
        Eighth Census of the United States, M-653
        Ninth Census of the United States, M-593
        Eleventh Census of the United States, T-9
        Twelfth Census of the United States, T-623
        Thirteenth Census of the United States, T-624
        Nonpopulation Schedules for the State of Virginia, T-1132
            Industrial Schedules, 1850, 1860, 1870
            Mortality Schedules, 1850, 1860, 1870, 1880
    Record Group 58, Records of the Internal Revenue Service
        Internal Revenue Assessments for Virginia, 1865–66, M-793
    Record Group 92, Records of the Quartermaster General
        Claims, John Sears file 83-36
    Record Group 94, Records of the Adjutant General
        Register of Enlistments in the U.S. Army, 1798–1914, M-233
        Compiled Service Records of Former Confederate Soldiers Who Served in
            the 1st through 6th U.S. Volunteer Infantry Regiments, 1864–66, M-1017
        Compiled Service Records of Volunteer Union Soldiers Who Served in
            Organizations from the State of Maryland, M-384
        Case Files for Presidential Pardons, 1865–67, M-1003

Record Group 105, Records of the Bureau of Refugees, Freedman, and
    Abandoned Lands, Seventh District, Lynchburg, Virginia
    Unregistered Telegrams and Letters Received, Entry 3799
    General Orders, Special Orders, Circulars, and Circular Letters, Entry 3800
    Records Relating to Murders and Outrages against Freedmen, Descriptive
        Lists of Reports of Outrages, M-1048, Reel 59
    Narrative Reports of Criminal Cases Involving Freedmen, Entry 3806
    Returns, Rosters, and Reports of Changes of Officers, Enlisted Men, and
        Civilians, Entry 3813
    Press Copies of Letters Sent, Entry 4072
    Ration Returns for Appomattox Court House, Entry 4080
    Letters Received, May 31, 1866–January 9, 1867, and Letters Sent,
        January 14, 1867–August 12, 1868, Entry 4082
    Letters Received, November 1865–May 1867, Entry 4084
Record Group 109, War Department Collection of Confederate Records
    Consolidated Index to Compiled Service Records of Confederate Soldiers,
        M-253
    Compiled Service Records of Confederate Soldiers Who Served in
        Organizations from the State of Tennessee, M-268
    Compiled Service Records of Confederate Soldiers Who Served in
        Organizations from the State of Alabama, M-311
    Compiled Service Records of Confederate Soldiers Who Served in
        Organizations from the State of Louisiana, M-320
    Compiled Service Records of Confederate Soldiers Who Served in
        Organizations from the State of Virginia, M-324
    Compiled Service Records of Confederate General and Staff Officers and
        Nonregimental Enlisted Men, M-331
    Confederate Papers Relating to Citizens or Business Firms, M-346
    Index to Letters Received by the Confederate Adjutant and Inspector
        General and the Confederate Quartermaster General, M-410
    Letters Received by the Confederate Secretary of War, 1861–65, M-437
    Letters Received by the Confederate Adjutant and Inspector General,
        1861–65, M-474
    Compiled Records Showing Service of Military Units in Confederate
        Organizations, M-861
Record Group 233, Records of the United States House of Representatives
    Barred and Disallowed Case Files of the Southern Claims Commission,
        M-1407
Record Group 393, Records of U.S. Army Continental Commands
    Letters Received, 1865, Entry 1475
    Letters Sent, 1865, Entry 1476
    Endorsements Sent, 1865, Entry 1477
    Reports of the Brigade Officer of the Day, Entry 1497
    Inspectors Reports, Entry 1499
    Letters Sent, Entry 7000

Register of Letters Received, Entry 7004
Reports Received, Entry 7005
North Carolina Department of Archives and History, Raleigh
John Willis Council diary, Collection #1169
James Longstreet letter
Marvel Ritchie letter
Benjamin H. Sims journal
Petersburg National Military Park, Petersburg, Va.
Solomon Russell diary
Pierpont-Morgan Library, New York, N.Y.
Gilder-Lehrman Collection
George E. Farmer Letters
Unidentified Union soldier's letter
Joseph Wheeler letter
Prince Edward County Courthouse, Farmville, Va.
County Deeds
State Historical Society of Wisconsin, Madison, Wis.
Clement E. Warner Papers
Alonzo V. Richard Papers
Mrs. Virginia Tyler, private collection, Appomattox, Va.
Flood Family Papers
Union Theological Seminary/Presbyterian School of Christian Education,
Richmond, Va.
James H. Featherston, "Sketch of Appomattox Court House Church"
Minutes of the West Hanover Presbytery, 1867–68
U.S. Army Military History Institute, Carlisle Barracks, Pa.
Civil War Miscellaneous Collection
Daniel Faust letter
Civil War Times Illustrated Collection
Isaac H. Ressler diary
David J. Scott letter
Ellis C. Strouss Letters
University of Michigan
Clements Library
John A. Clark letter
University of North Carolina, Chapel Hill
Southern Historical Collection, Wilson Library
James W. Albright diary
E. P. Alexander Papers
William D. Alexander diary
Norman Bell Papers
Berry Greenwood Benson Papers
Kena King Chapman diary
Thomas Pollock Devereux Papers
T. P. Devereux, "Recollections, December, 1864 to April, 1865"
Hubard Family Papers

Kinnison Papers
    H. M. Doak, "Surrender at Appomattox Courthouse"
John Paris diary
John Waldrop diary
Richard W. Waldrop diary
J. E. Whitehorn diary
University of South Carolina
  South Caroliniana Library
    David Wyatt Aiken Collection
    Ellen Maria Ravenel letter
    James Henley Thornwell Collection
University of Texas, Austin, Tex.
  Center for American History
    Mrs. E. M. Schiwetz Papers
University of Vermont, Burlington, Vt.
  William Wells Papers
University of Virginia, Alderman Library, Charlottesville
  James B. Blackford Collection
    Diary of an Anonymous Confederate Officer
  Thomas S. Bocock letter
  Thomas S. Bocock Papers
    George W. Leyburn memoir
  Chapman Hunter Chilton Papers
  Giles B. Cooke diary (typescript)
  John Warwick Daniel Papers
    C. B. Fleet memoir
  Robert Larimer diary and letter
  H. A. Minor Collection
  M. W. Ragland, "Some 'During the War' Experiences of ———"
  Elihu B. Washburne letter
Virginia Historical Society, Richmond
  Cary Breckinridge Papers
    "The Second Virginia Cavalry Regt. from Five Forks to Appomattox"
  Thomas Henry Carter Papers
  Giles B. Cooke diary (original)
  Downman Family Papers
  John Price Kepner diary (transcript)
  Abner Crump Hopkins memoir
  Ladies Memorial Association of Appomattox minute book
  Osmun Latrobe Papers (diary and letter transcripts)
  R. E. Lee Headquarters Papers
  William T. Livermore diary
  David Gregg McIntosh Papers
  John Baxter Mosley Papers
  James Eldred Phillips diary
  Llewelyn Traherne Basset Saunderson diary (transcript)

John Bell Vincent diary
Governor K. Warren Papers
M. Porter Snell diary
Yale University, New Haven, Conn.
Ulrich Bonnell Phillips Papers
Elihu B. Washburne Papers
A. S. Webb Papers

NEWSPAPERS

Appomattox and Buckingham Times
Arlington (Va.) *Daily Sun*
Atlanta *Journal*
Christian Science Monitor
De Bow's Review
Hawkinsville, Ga., *Dispatch*
Lynchburg News
Lynchburg *News and Advance*
Lynchburg Republican
Lynchburg Virginian
New York Herald
New York Times
New York Tribune
Norfolk *Virginian-Pilot*
Raleigh *News and Observer*
Richmond Enquirer
Richmond Examiner
Richmond *Republican and General Advertiser*
Richmond *Times*
Richmond Whig
Shepherdstown (W.Va.) *Register*
Suffolk (Va.) *News Herald*
Washington *Evening Star*
Washington *Post*

PUBLISHED SOURCES

Abstract of Virginia's Militia Laws. Richmond: Ritchies and Dunovant, 1861.
Acts of the General Assembly of Virginia Passed at the Session Commencing December 2,
    1844, and Ending February 22, 1845. Richmond: Samuel Shepherd, 1845.
Acts of the General Assembly of Virginia Passed at the Session Commencing December 4,
    1848, and Ending March 19, 1849. Richmond: Samuel Shepherd, 1849.
Acts of the General Assembly of Virginia, Passed at the Extra and Regular Sessions of 1849
    and 1850. Richmond: William F. Ritchie, 1850.

Acts of the General Assembly of Virginia, Passed at the Session of 1850 and 1851. Richmond: William F. Ritchie, 1851.

Acts of the General Assembly of Virginia Passed in 1852. Richmond: William F. Ritchie, 1852.

Acts of the General Assembly of Virginia Passed in 1852–53. Richmond: William F. Ritchie, 1853.

Acts of the General Assembly of Virginia Passed in 1855–56. Richmond: William F. Ritchie, 1856.

Acts of the General Assembly of Virginia Passed in 1859 and 1860. Richmond: William F. Ritchie, 1860.

Acts of the General Assembly of Virginia Passed in 1861. Richmond: William F. Ritchie, 1861.

Acts of the General Assembly of Virginia Passed at the Called Session of 1862. Richmond: William F. Ritchie, 1862.

Acts of the General Assembly of Virginia Passed at Adjourned Session, 1863. Richmond: William F. Ritchie, 1863.

Acts of the General Assembly of Virginia Passed at Session of 1863–64. Richmond: William F. Ritchie, 1864.

Acts of the General Assembly of the State of Virginia Passed at the Extra Session (June 1865). Richmond: Republic Book and Job Office, 1865.

Acts of the General Assembly of the State of Virginia Passed in 1865–66. Richmond: Allegre and Goode, 1866.

Acts of the General Assembly of the State of Virginia Passed in 1869–70. Richmond: James E. Goode, 1870.

Agassiz, George R., ed. *Meade's Headquarters, 1863–1865: Letters of Colonel Theodore Lyman from the Wilderness to Appomattox.* Boston: Atlantic Monthly Press, 1922.

Alexander, Edward Porter. *Military Memoirs of a Confederate: A Critical Narrative.* New York: C. Scribner's Sons, 1907.

Atlas to Accompany the Official Records of the Union and Confederate Armies. Washington: Government Printing Office, 1891–95.

Basinger, William S. "Crutchfield's Artillery Brigade." *Southern Historical Society Papers* 25 (1897): 38–44.

Berlin, Ira. *Many Thousands Gone: The First Two Centuries of Slavery in North America.* Cambridge, Mass.: The Belknap Press of Harvard University Press, 1998.

Bernard, George S. *War Talks of Confederate Veterans.* Dayton, Ohio: Morningside Bookshop, 1981.

Billings, E. E., ed. "A Union Officer's Diary of Appomattox Campaign." *Civil War Times Illustrated* 1, no. 3 (June 1962): 22–23.

Billings, John D. *Hardtack and Coffee, or the Unwritten Story of Army Life.* Boston: George M. Smith and Co., 1887.

Blackford, Susan Leigh. *Letters from Lee's Army.* New York: Charles Scribner's Sons, 1947.

Blackford, W. W. *War Years with Jeb Stuart.* New York: Charles Scribner's Sons, 1945.

Blair, William Alan, ed. *A Politician Goes to War: The Civil War Letters of John White Geary.* University Park, Pa.: The Pennsylvania State University Press, 1995.

Botkin, B. A. *Lay My Burden Down: A Folk History of Slavery.* Chicago: University of Chicago Press, 1945.

Bradshaw, Herbert Clarence. *History of Prince Edward County, Virginia.* Richmond: Dietz Press, 1955.

Butchart, Ronald E. *Northern Schools, Southern Blacks, and Reconstruction: Freedmen's Education, 1862–1875.* Westport, Conn.: Greenwood Press, 1980.

Cadwallader, Sylvanus. *Three Years with Grant, as Recalled by War Correspondent Sylvanus Cadwallader.* Edited by Benjamin P. Thomas. New York: Alfred A. Knopf, 1955.

Caldwell, J. F. J. *The History of a Brigade of South Carolinians First Known as "Gregg's" and Subsequently as "McGowan's Brigade."* Philadelphia: King and Baird, 1866.

Calkins, Chris M. *The Battles of Appomattox Station and Appomattox Court House, April 8–9, 1865.* Lynchburg, Va.: H. E. Howard, Inc., 1987.

Carter, Dan T. *When the War Was Over: The Failure of Self-Reconstruction in the South, 1865–1867.* Baton Rouse: Louisiana State University Press, 1985.

Cauble, Frank P. *Biography of Wilmer McLean.* N.p.: National Park Service, 1969.

Chamberlain, Joshua L. "Appomattox." *Personal Recollections of the War of the Rebellion: Addresses Delivered before the Commandery of the State of New York, Military Order of the Loyal Legion of the United States,* Vol. 3, 260–80.

———. "The Last Salute of the Army of Northern Virginia." *Southern Historical Society Papers* 32 (1904): 355–63.

———. *The Passing of the Armies.* New York: G. P. Putnam's Sons, 1915.

———. "Reminiscences of Petersburg and Appomattox: October, 1903." *War Papers Read before the Commandery of the State of Maine, Military Order of the Loyal Legion of the United States,* Vol. 3, 161–82.

Cilley, Jonathan P. "The Dawn of the Morning at Appomattox." *War Papers Read before the Commandery of the State of Maine, Military Order of the Loyal Legion of the United States,* Vol. 3, 263–78.

Collins, Daniel L. *46th Virginia Infantry.* Lynchburg, Va.: H. E. Howard, Inc., n.d.

"Confederate Monument at Appomattox." *Confederate Veteran* 14, no. 10 (October 1906): 464.

Congressional Globe. 36th Cong., 1st sess. Washington: Government Printing Office, 1861.

[Corbin, Richard W.] *Letters of a Confederate Officer to His Family in Europe.* Paris: Neal's English Library, [1902].

Craven, Avery. *The Coming of the Civil War.* Chicago: University of Chicago Press, 1957.

Crawley, L. "The Surrender Grounds at Appomattox." *Confederate Veteran* 34, no. 4 (April 1926): 128–29.

Crofts, Daniel W. *Reluctant Confederates: Upper South Unionists in the Secession Crisis.* Chapel Hill: University of North Carolina Press, 1989.

Cutrer, Thomas W., ed. *Longstreet's Aide: The Civil War Letters of Major Thomas J. Goree.* Charlottesville: University Press of Virginia, 1995.

Davis, Burke. "The Swinging Sweeneys." *The Ironworker* 33, no. 4 (Autumn 1969): 3–11.

Dayton, Ruth Woods, ed. *The Diary of a Confederate Soldier, James E. Hall.* [Charleston, W.Va.: n.p., ca. 1961].

Dennett, John Richard. *The South as It Is: 1865–1866.* New York: Viking Press, 1965.

Devin, Thomas C. "Didn't We Fight Splendid." *Civil War Times Illustrated* 17, no. 8 (December 1978): 38–40.

"Diary of W. M. Davis." *Report of the Annual Reunion of the Sixth Ohio Veteran Volunteer Cavalry Association,* Vol. 48, October 1913.

Dowdey, Clifford, and Louis H. Manarin, eds. *The Wartime Papers of Robert E. Lee.* New York: Virginia Civil War Commission, 1961.

Driver, Robert J., Jr., and H. E. Howard. *2nd Virginia Cavalry.* Lynchburg, Va.: H. E. Howard, Inc., 1995.

Durkin, Joseph T., ed. *John Dooley, Confederate Soldier: His War Journal.* Georgetown, D.C.: Georgetown University Press, 1945.

Eggleston, George Cary. *A Rebel's Recollections.* Baton Rouge: Louisiana State University Press, 1996.

Elkins, Stanley M. *Slavery: A Problem in American Institutional and Intellectual Life.* New York: Grosset and Dunlop, 1963.

Featherston, Nathaniel Ragland. *The History of Appomattox, Virginia.* Appomattox: American Legion Post 104, 1948.

Fehrenbacher, Don E. *The Dred Scott Case: Its Significance in American Law and Politics.* New York: Oxford University, 1978.

Field, Charles W. "Campaign of 1864 and 1865." *Southern Historical Society Papers* 14 (1886): 542–63.

Fitzhugh, George. *Cannibals All! Or Slaves without Masters.* Cambridge, Mass.: Harvard University Press, 1960.

Foner, Eric. *Reconstruction: America's Unfinished Revolution, 1863–1877.* New York: Harper and Row, 1988.

Freeman, Douglas Southall. *An Address, April, 1950, Appomattox Court House, Virginia.* N.p.: Eastern National Park and Monument Association, 1964.

———. *R. E. Lee, A Biography.* 4 vols. New York: Charles Scribner's Sons, 1943.

Gallagher, Gary W., ed. *Fighting for the Confederacy: The Personal Recollections of General Edward Porter Alexander.* Chapel Hill: University of North Carolina Press, 1989.

Gibbon, John. "Personal Recollections of Appomattox." *The Century Magazine* 58, no. 6 (April 1902): 936–43.

Giddens, Paul H. "Recollections of the Battle of Appomattox Court House." *Tyler's Quarterly Historical and Genealogical Magazine* 33, no. 4 (April 1952): 233–41.

Goldsborough, W. W. *The Maryland Line in the Confederate Army, 1861–1865.* Baltimore, Md.: Guggenheimer, Weil and Co., 1900.

Gordon, John B. *Reminiscences of the Civil War.* New York: Charles Scribner's Sons, 1903.

G[orman], J[ohn] C. *Lee's Last Campaign.* Raleigh, N.C.: Wm. B. Smith and Company, 1866.

Grant, U. S. *Personal Memoirs of* ———. 2 vols. New York: Charles L. Webster and Company, 1886.

Greenough, Mark H. "Aftermath at Appomattox: Federal Military Occupation of Appomattox County May–November 1865." *Civil War History* 31, no. 1 (March 1985): 5–23.

Grimes, Bryan. "The Surrender at Appomattox." *Southern Historical Society Papers* 27 (1899): 93–96.

Hardee, W[illiam] J. *Rifle and Light Infantry Tactics, for the Instruction, Exercises and Manoeuvres of Riflemen and Light Infantry.* New York: J. O. Kane, 1862.

Harwell, Richard Barksdale, ed. *A Confederate Diary of the Retreat from Petersburg, April 3–20, 1865.* Atlanta: Emory University, 1953.

Harris, E. R. "First—and Last." *Confederate Veteran* 31, no. 11 (November 1923): 438.

Helper, Hinton Rowan. *The Impending Crisis of the South.* New York: Collier Books, 1963.

Helvestine, Frank. "The Development of a Great Railroad." *Norfolk and Western Magazine,* July 1923 (no vol. or no.), 12–14, 73–75, 77.

Hoar, Jay S. *The South's Last Boys in Gray.* Bowling Green, Ohio: Bowling Green State University Popular Press, 1986.

Holt, Michael. *Political Parties and American Political Development from the Age of Jackson to the Age of Lincoln.* Baton Rouge: Louisiana State University Press, 1992.

———. *The Rise and Fall of the American Whig Party: Jacksonian Politics and the Onset of the Civil War.* New York: Oxford University Press, 1999.

Hosmer, Charles B., Jr. *Preservation Comes of Age: From Williamsburg to the National Trust, 1926–1949.* 2 vols. Charlottesville: University Press of Virginia, 1981.

Howard, McHenry. "Closing Scenes of the War About Richmond." *Southern Historical Society Papers* 31 (1903): 129–45.

Hubbard, Freeman. *Encyclopedia of North American Railroading.* New York: McGraw-Hill Book Company, 1981.

Huston, James L. *The Panic of 1857 and the Coming of the Civil War.* Baton Rouge: Louisiana State University Press, 1987.

Jamerson, Vicki, Clyde Nash, and Edith Nash. *Appomattox County Marriages, 1854–1890.* N.p.: Privately published, 1979.

Johannsen, Robert W. *Stephen A. Douglas.* New York: Oxford University Press, 1973.

Johnston, Angus James, II. *Virginia Railroads in the Civil War.* Chapel Hill: University of North Carolina Press, 1961.

Jones, Thomas G. "Last Days of the Army of Northern Virginia." *Southern Historical Society Papers* 21 (1893): 57–103.

Longstreet, James. *From Manassas to Appomattox.* Philadelphia: J. B. Lippincott Co., 1896.

Lovell, Samuel C. "With Lee after Appomattox." *Civil War Times Illustrated* 17, no. 7 (November 1978): 38–43.

Lowe, Richard. *Republicans and Reconstruction in Virginia, 1856–1870.* Charlottesville: University Press of Virginia, 1991.

Lowry, Terry. *The Battle of Scary Creek.* Charleston, W.Va.: Pictorial Histories Publishing Co., 1982.

Lyon, Farnham. "A Letter from Appomattox." *Twice Told Tales of Michigan and Her Soldiers in the Civil War*, 73–75. N.p.: Michigan Civil War Centennial Observance Commission, 1966.

McCalmont, Alfred B. *Letters of* ————. Privately printed, n.d.

McGill, John. *The Beverley Family of Virginia*. Columbia: R. L. Bryan Company, 1956.

McKim, Randolph H. *A Soldier's Recollections: Leaves from the Diary of a Young Confederate*. New York: Longman, Green, and Co., 1910.

McMillen, Sally G. *Motherhood in the Old South: Pregnancy, Childbirth, and Infant Rearing*. Baton Rouge: Louisiana State University Press, 1990.

Maddex, Jack P., Jr. *The Virginia Conservatives, 1867–1879: A Study in Reconstruction Politics*. Chapel Hill: University of North Carolina Press, 1970.

Mahone, William. "On the Road to Appomattox." *Civil War Times Illustrated* 9, no. 9 (January 1971): 5–11, 42–47.

Majeske, Penelope K. "Virginia after Appomattox." *West Virginia History*, 1982, 95–117.

Marshall, Charles. "Appomattox Courthouse." *Southern Historical Society Papers* 21 (1893): 353–60.

Marvel, William. *The Battles for Saltville*. Lynchburg, Va.: H. E. Howard, Inc., 1992.
————. "The Great Impostors." *Blue and Gray Magazine* 8, no. 3 (February 1991): 32–33.

Mattox, Henry E., and Robert W. Mattox. "Appomattox Court House Revisited." *Southern Historian*, 1987, 8:64–73.

Maurice, Sir Frederick, ed. *An Aide-de-Camp of Lee: Papers of Colonel Charles Marshall*. Boston: Little, Brown and Company, 1927.

Meade, George. *The Life and Letters of George Gordon Meade*. 2 vols. New York: Charles Scribner's Sons, 1913.

Merli, Frank J., ed. "Alternative to Appomattox: A Virginian's Vision of an Anglo-Confederate Colony on the Amazon, May, 1865." *Virginia Magazine of History and Biography* 94, no. 2 (April 1986): 210–19.

Miller, Francis Trevelyan. *The Photographic History of the Civil War*. 10 vols. New York: Review of Reviews Co., 1912.

Minor, H. A. "Surrender of Mahone's Division." *Confederate Veteran* 22, no. 7 (July 1914): 312–13.

Mohr, James C., and Richard E. Winslow III, eds. *The Cormany Diaries: A Northern Family in the Civil War*. Pittsburgh, Pa.: University of Pittsburgh Press, 1982.

Mooney, Charles C., ed. "A Union Chaplain's Diary." *Proceedings of the New Jersey Historical Society* 45, no. 1 (January 1957).

Moore, John Hammond. "Appomattox: Profile of a Mid-Nineteenth-Century Community." *Virginia Magazine of History* 88, no. 4 (October 1980): 478–82.

Nevins, Allan, ed. *A Diary of Battle: The Personal Journals of Colonel Charles S. Wainwright, 1861–1865*. New York: Harcourt, Brace and World, 1962.

"Paroles of the Army of Northern Virginia." *Southern Historical Society Papers* 15 (1887): 1–487.

Pearce, T. H. *Diary of Captain Henry A. Chambers*. Wendell, N.C.: Broadfoot's Bookmark, 1983.

Perdue, Charles L., Jr., Thomas E. Barden, and Robert K. Phillips. *Weevils in the Wheat: Interviews with Virginia Ex-Slaves.* Charlottesville: University Press of Virginia, 1976.

Phillips, Lance. *Yonder Comes the Train.* New York: A. S. Barnes and Co., 1965.

Pollard, Edward A. *The Lost Cause: A New Southern History of the War of the Confederates.* New York: E. B. Treat and Co., [1867].

Porter, Horace. *Campaigning with Grant.* New York: Century Co., 1897.

Potter, David M. *The Impending Crisis, 1848–1861.* New York: Harper and Row, 1976.

Pray, J. L. "Recollections of Appomattox." *First Maine Bugle* 3, no. 3 (July 1893): 19–20.

Racine, Philip, ed. *Unspoiled Heart: The Journal of Charles Mattocks of the 17th Maine.* Knoxville: University of Tennessee Press, 1994.

Rawley, James A. *Race and Politics: "Bleeding Kansas" and the Coming of the Civil War.* Philadelphia and New York: J. B. Lippincott Co., 1969.

Reed, George E., ed. *Civil War Diary of Private Robert Scott Moorhead of Erie County, Pennsylvania.* Harrisburg, Pa.: Privately printed, n.d.

Reniers, Percival. *The Springs of Virginia.* Kingsport, Tenn.: Kingsport Press, 1955.

Rhodes, Robert Hunt, ed. *All for the Union: A History of the 2nd Rhode Island Volunteer Infantry in the War of the Great Rebellion as Told by the Diary and Letters of Elisha Hunt Rhodes.* Lincoln, R.I.: Andrew Mowbray Incorporated, 1985.

Robertson, James I., Jr., ed. *The Civil War Letters of General Robert McAllister.* New Brunswick, N.J.: Rutgers University Press, 1965.

Robinson, W. P. "Artillery in the Battle of the Crater." *Confederate Veteran* 19, no. 4 (April 1911): 164–66.

Scarborough, William Kauffman, ed. *The Diary of Edmund Ruffin.* 3 vols. Baton Rouge: Louisiana State University Press, 1972–89.

Schaff, Morris. *The Spirit of Old West Point, 1858–1862.* Boston: Houghton, Mifflin Co., 1909.

Schwab, Julius L. "Some Closing Events at Appomattox." *Confederate Veteran* 8, no. 2 (February 1900): 71.

Shade, William G. *Democratizing the Old Dominion: Virginia and the Second Party System, 1824–1861.* Charlottesville: University Press of Virginia, 1996.

Shaw, William H. *A Diary as Kept by Wm. H. Shaw during the Great Civil War, from April, 1861, to July, 1865.* N.p.: n.d.

Sheridan, P. H. *Personal Memoirs of* ———, 2 vols. New York: Charles L. Webster and Co., 1888.

Silliker, Ruth L., ed. *The Rebel Yell and the Yankee Hurrah: The Civil War Journal of a Maine Volunteer.* Camden, Maine: Down East Books, 1985.

Simpson, Brooks D., Leroy P. Graf, and John Muldowney, eds. *Advice after Appomattox: Letters to Andrew Johnson, 1865–1866.* Knoxville: University of Tennessee Press, 1987.

Smith, Ethel Marion. "Clover Hill: Early History of an Old Appomattox Landmark." *Virginia Magazine of History and Biography* 57, no. 3 (July 1949): 269–73.

Sorrel, G. Moxley. *Recollections of a Confederate Staff Officer.* Jackson, Tenn.: McCowat-Mercer Press, 1958.

Sparks, David S., ed. *Inside Lincoln's Army: The Diary of Marsena Rudolph Patrick, Provost Marshal General, Army of the Potomac.* New York: Thomas Yoseloff, 1964.

Spear, Ellis. *The Civil War Recollections of General* ———. Orono: University of Maine Press, 1997.

Stampp, Kenneth M. *America in 1857: A Nation on the Brink.* New York: Oxford University Press, 1990.

Statistical Gazeteer of the States of Virginia and North Carolina. Richmond: The Proprietor, 1856.

Stewart, George R. *American Place-Names.* New York: Oxford University Press, 1972.

Styple, William B., ed. *With a Flash of His Sword: The Writings of Major Holman S. Melcher, 20th Maine Infantry.* Kearny, N.J.: Belle Grove Publishing Co., 1994.

Survivors' Association. *History of the 118th Pennsylvania Volunteers: Corn Exchange Regiment.* Philadelphia: J. L. Smith, 1905.

Talcott, T. M. R. "From Petersburg to Appomattox." *Southern Historical Society Papers* 32 (1904): 67–72.

Taylor, Walter H. *General Lee: His Campaigns in Virginia, 1861–1865, with Personal Reminiscences.* Dayton, Ohio: Morningside Press (reprint of 1906 edition), 1975.

Tenney, Luman H. *War Diary of Luman Harris Tenney, 1861–1865.* Cleveland: Evangelical Publishing House, 1914.

Terry, Thomas Ragland. *Appomattox County: A Pictorial History.* Norfolk: Donning Company, 1984.

———. *Raglands: Facts and Legends of an Old Virginia Family.* Appomattox, Va.: Privately printed, 1984.

Thirteenth Report of the Descendants of French Creek Pioneers. Buckhannon, W.Va.: The Buckhannon Record, 1962.

Trout, Robert J. *With Pen and Saber: The Letters and Diaries of J. E. B. Stuart's Staff Officers.* Mechanicsburg, Pa.: Stackpole Books, 1995.

Trout, William E., III, ed. *Appomattox River Seay Stories: Reminiscences of James Washington Seay, Last of the Appomattox River Batteaumen.* Petersburg, Va.: Petersburg Foundation, Inc., 1992.

Under the Maltese Cross, Antietam to Appomattox, the Loyal Uprising in Western Pennsylvania, 1861–1865: Campaigns 155th Pennsylvania Regiment, Narrated by the Rank and File. Pittsburgh, Pa.: 155th Regimental Association, 1910.

U.S. Congress. Senate. *Report of the Select Committee of the Senate Appointed to Inquire into the Late Invasion and Seizure of the Public Property at Harper's Ferry.* 36th Cong., 1st sess., 1860. Washington: Government Printing Office, 1860.

Walters, John. *Norfolk Blues: The Civil War Diary of the Norfolk Light Artillery Blues.* Shippensburg, Pa.: Burd Street Press, 1997.

Welch, Spencer Glasgow. *A Confederate Surgeon's Letters to His Wife.* Marietta, Ga.: Continental Book Company, 1954.

Wise, Henry. "The Career of Wise's Brigade." *Southern Historical Society Papers* 25 (1897): 1–22.

Woodward, Arthur. "Joel Sweeney and the First Banjo." *Los Angeles County Museum Quarterly* 7, no. 3 (Spring 1949): 7–11.

SOURCES & ACKNOWLEDGMENTS

Twice now have I begun the acknowledgments of one of my own books by citing the early influence of MacKinlay Kantor. His *Andersonville*, which I read in high school, offered the epic treatment in fiction of a subject that had not, curiously enough, been similarly documented in history, and some years ago I undertook to correct that omission. Perhaps the first book I ever read about the Civil War (one of several I received for Christmas in 1960) was Kantor's *Lee and Grant at Appomattox*. Meant to interest youthful readers in historical events, it did just that for me: the book's illustrations and some of Kantor's phrases came back to me as I undertook further research on his topic. Often, as in studying Andersonville, that happened as I discovered that Kantor had been mistaken about this incident or that, but he had not been a historian. His job had been more to inspire than to educate, and he succeeded. Four decades later the interest survives.

Without a doubt the most useful resource for this study was Appomattox Court House National Historical Park. An extremely knowledgeable staff offered unlimited assistance and endlessly useful suggestions from the beginning of the research for this book until the completion of the manuscript. Historian Ron Wilson, who dutifully answered my first inquiries about Appomattox in 1985, remained just as diligent in providing information and assistance when I reappeared a decade later to resume the neglected project. Curator Joe Williams sacrificed much of his professional energy as well as his personal time helping me find documents in the park's extensive collection, double-checking information and sources, and duplicating photographs. Always cheerfully helpful was Ranger Tracy Chernault, a native of the county who gave me a guided tour of the outlying districts; the park lost a valuable asset in his transfer to Petersburg National Battlefield. Many of the revisionist insights that appear in the chapters on the surrender had their genesis in observations made by the historical staff: it was, for instance, Ron Wilson who first detected that the courier who rode to the McLean house with Robert E. Lee and Charles Marshall was not the renowned Sergeant Tucker.

The National Park Service also provided a great deal of assistance indirectly through another Petersburg veteran, historian Chris Calkins. Chris conducted the most extensive previous research on the fighting around Appomattox Court House: it was his sources that formed the core of my own bibliography, and when I was unable to track some of those sources down he generously shared them with me. The subsequent appearance of other sources sometimes led me to different conclusions, but my way was made much easier by his earlier work.

There is always one other Park Service fixture to thank. Chief historian Robert K. Krick, of Fredericksburg and Spotsylvania National Military Park, manages to assist just about every student of Virginia's battlefields through his intimate knowledge of source material. Appomattox and I proved no exception, and Bob came up with some surprise sources and some good advice about that, too. Among other things, evidence from his collection helped to confirm the identity of the orderly who accompanied Lee and Marshall on the ride to see Grant.

The National Archives provided the preponderance of material for this work, and as usual Michael Musick and Michael Pilgrim found the most obscure manuscripts for me. Both suggested troves of out-of-the-way records pertaining to local history. First one and then the other of them guided me through the cavernous stacks to documents that never appeared in the bibliography because they only disproved a story that I doubted anyway: Appomattox legend has it that Confederate veteran Thomas Tibbs enlisted in the 7th U.S. Cavalry soon after the war and was killed fighting with Custer at the battle of the Washita, but Regular Army enlistment certificates and the original casualty list from the Washita cast much doubt on that, unless Tibbs was able to pass himself off as an Irish or German immigrant.

Virginia repositories hold a wealth of manuscripts concerning Appomattox—particularly the Virginia Historical Society and the Museum of the Confederacy, where historian John Coski offered an assortment of boxes that turned out to contain numerous Confederate diaries from Appomattox. The Library of Virginia—which, like much of the National Archives, underwent a major relocation while I researched Appomattox—yielded birth, marriage, and death records, legislative records, militia papers, pension applications, and tax lists, besides duplicate copies of Confederate military records and pardon applications from the National Archives. The University of Virginia holds an assortment of papers relevant to Appomattox, too, as well as helpful staff members like Margaret Hrabe, Special Collections director Michael Plunkett, and the Special Collections Department's own Civil War expert, Ervin L. Jordan Jr.

Outside Virginia, the most productive collections for events in and around Appomattox are held by the Southern Historical Collection, at the University of North Carolina, and by Duke University, where senior reference librarian Bill Erwin remains as conversant with the collection and as accommodating as ever. Judith Ann Schiff, the chief research archivist for Yale University, came through once again by determining ahead of time not only what Yale held but what numerous other institutions retained that might be of use to me, and most of it was.

Other archivists and research assistants who made special efforts on my behalf include Peter Drummey, of the Massachusetts Historical Society; Jennie Rathbun, at Harvard's Houghton Library; Mark Brown, at Brown University; Susan Ravdin, at Bowdoin College; Ken Tilley, at the Alabama Department of Archives and History; William Richter, at the University of Texas at Austin; Kathy Shoemaker, of Emory University; Henry Fulmer, of the University of South Carolina; Harold Miller, from the State Historical Society of Wisconsin; Cathy Price, at the William L. Clements Library of the University of Michigan; and Sandra Trenholm, in the Gilder-Lehrman Collection at the Pierpont-Morgan Library. Roy Mayo, clerk of Amherst County Circuit Court, helped me find the records of Coleman May's 1846 murder trial. In Appomattox, Betty Drinkard provided me with a copy of the out-of-print cemetery records that she helped compile, while Clyde Nash did the same with the marriage records that he, his wife, and Vicki Jamerson published.

Harold Howard, who lives within shouting distance of the old village (at least if he is doing the shouting), frequently hosted my research trips there. It was he who introduced me to Virginia Tyler, who now lives in Eldon, the old home of Joel W. Flood Jr. Mrs. Tyler, whose files contain much of the Flood family history, offered some of that material for this project.

Perhaps my greatest thanks are due my partner in a morning walk down the old stage road, whose fondness for the reconstructed village occasionally helped revive my determination to complete this book in spite of endless distractions. Little did she know how much her enthusiasm rekindled my own early fascination with the place.

INDEX

Manassas campaign, 112–13; in Maryland campaign, 115–16; in Gettysburg campaign, 128, 130–32, 163; depleted ranks of, 165, 221; at Petersburg, 178, 183, 200; at Sailor's Creek, 209

Appomattox Invincibles (Company A, 44th Virginia Infantry and Company A, 20th Battalion Virginia Heavy Artillery), 85–86, 94, 105, 123

Appomattox Land Improvement Company, 309

Appomattox militia, 15, 86; organization of, 11; description of, 21–23; musters of, 76–77; drained by volunteers, 87, 99

Appomattox Rangers (Company H, 2nd Virginia Cavalry), 95, 109, 124, 182, 348 (n. 13); organized, 85; at First Manassas, 88–89, 90; disease in, 91; election of officers in, 102; screens retreat of army, 105; in Overland campaign, 179; at Five Forks, 201; at Sailor's Creek, 212; at Farmville, 218; at Appomattox Court House, 221, 227; armament of, 333 (n. 14)

Appomattox Savings Bank, 57

Appomattox States Rights Association, 26

Armistead, Lewis, 130, 131

Arrington, Charles, 192

Averell, 176–77, 179, 184

Babcock, Orville, 239–40, 281, 307

Back Street, 302

Bagby, Luke, 227

Baker, Ada (Mrs. John McDearmon), 306

Bartlett, Joseph, 258–59, 260–61, 264, 311

Beauregard, P. G. T., 88–89, 177–78, 180–83, 187

Bell, John, 75, 78

Bell, Norman, 253, 255

Berry, Fanny, 63, 64

Big Anderson (slave), 167

Bird, H. D., 126

Blackford, William M., 81–82, 85

Boaz, Robert, 44, 49, 93, 119

Bocock, Anna (Mrs. Thomas S. Bocock), 48, 92

Bocock, Charles, 12, 27

Bocock, Henry T., 10, 12, 15, 19, 30, 48, 69, 328 (n. 2); as county clerk, 5, 27, 36, 73; committee appeals to, 49–50; as slaveowner, 65; daughter dies, 67; as presidential commissioner, 78; principal of Union Academy, 122; seeks pardon, 274

Bocock, Rev. John, 51, 79–80, 95, 112

Bocock, John T., 5

Bocock, Thomas S., 10, 14–15, 19, 75, 267, 304; presents county bill, 3, 5; as commonwealth attorney, 12, 322 (n. 18); as congressman, 27, 33, 48, 67–68; and first wife, 30, 48; correspondence with Henry Flood, 35; and second wife, 48, 92; exerts political influence, 49, 102, 165, 166; and Wilson Hix, 52; as slaveowner, 62, 65, 271; as candidate for Speaker of the House, 70–71; as unionist, 78–80; calls for secession, 82; and donation to volunteers, 83; as Confederate congressman, 96; as Speaker of Confederate House, 97, 99, 106, 211; sells produce to government, 119; as private attorney, 190; fears prosecution, 273, 274; and labor shortage, 278; and tobacco prices, 301

Bocock, Willis, 12, 33, 45, 50–51, 282, 297

Breckinridge, John C., 46, 75, 78, 179, 184

Brown, John, 68–69, 70, 75, 114, 168

Brown, Orlando, 273, 284–85, 289

Bryant, Ellen, 286

Bryant, Lucinda, 304

Buchanan, James, 46, 59, 79–80

Burbridge, Stephen, 177, 179

Burnside, Ambrose, 96–97, 116, 118, 121

Garnett, Richard, 128, 130, 131
Geiser, James: as provost marshal, 276, 277, 278, 281–82, 283, 284; marriage of, 286; as registrar, 299, 363 (n. 35)
Gettysburg, battle of, 128–32, 163, 164, 165, 167, 169, 171, 186
Gibbon, John, 246, 255, 256, 259; as commissioner of surrender, 252; as commander at Appomattox Court House, 253, 258, 270, 279; and Cadmus Wilcox, 263
Gilliam, Sarah Evelyn, 95–96, 97, 109, 127, 166, 224
Gilliam, Spencer, 224
Gilliam, Thomas, 100, 102, 107, 124, 128, 130, 178
Glass, Robert, 32, 33
Glover, John. *See* Webb, Samuel
Glover, Samuel, 37, 85, 179; and postmaster's appointment, 38, 39, 61; and Clover Hill Tavern, 43, 47, 52; enlists, 83
Glover, William, 83, 179
Godsey, Joseph, 22
Gordon, John B.: at Fort Stedman, 199; on retreat, 204, 205, 219, 220; at Sailor's Creek, 207–8, 212–13; at Farmville, 217, 218; at Appomattox Court House, 226–27, 230, 231, 232, 233–35, 236, 237, 244–45, 251–52, 255, 258, 265, 350 (n. 28); and surrender ceremony, 259, 261, 263, 357–58 (n. 35)
Grant, Ulysses S., 242, 246, 256, 259–60, 311; and Overland campaign, 176, 179, 180; before Petersburg, 182–83, 191, 198, 199–200; and surrender overtures, 219, 231, 236, 238, 239; meets with Lee, 240, 241, 249–50, 251, 281, 351 (n. 10); surrender terms of, 249, 265, 318; and Longstreet, 252; leaves Appomattox Court House, 252–53; as president, 302–3; death of, 307; view of, in Appomattox, 308
Griffin, Charles, 235, 258, 259

Grimes, Bryan, 205, 212, 232, 233–34, 254, 262, 267, 312

Hannah, John J., 65, 123, 166
Hannah, Robert, 86, 91
Hannah, William M., 283, 284
Hannah, William S., 102, 110, 123, 166, 169, 221, 287
Harpers Ferry, [West] Virginia, 68–69, 70, 72, 75, 168, 114, 166
Harris, John, 109, 270
Harvey, Edward B.: as slaveowner, 62; enlists, 100; elected lieutenant, 102; at Second Manassas, 113; in Maryland campaign, 115, 116, 117; furlough, 124; economic situation of, 128; at Gettysburg, 130, 131; death of, 163, 186
Harvey, Elizabeth, 124, 163, 211, 335 (n. 38), 339 (n. 1)
Harvey, James G., Jr., 100, 102, 113, 124, 130, 131, 164
Harvey, Thomas, 295–96
Helper, Hinton Rowan, 54, 70
Henry (slave), 121, 123
Heth, Henry, 220, 235, 237, 251
Hill, Ambrose Powell, 116, 193
High Bridge: construction of, 31, 34–35, 37; completed, 41; strategic importance of, 180, 214; battle of, 213–14; passage over, 215–16; repairs to, 279–80, 287
Hix, Carrie, 294
Hix, Edward G., 174, 267, 293, 294, 306, 308, 360 (n. 8), 348 (n. 13)
Hix, Emma, 286
Hix, Martha (daughter of Wilson Hix), 294
Hix, Martha (first wife of Wilson Hix), 329 (n. 5)
Hix, William D.: as deputy sheriff, 91–92, 93, 119, 120–21; marriage of, 95–96; exemption from conscription, 101; as government contractor, 120, 194–95; as sheriff, 194, 270; arrested, 272; favoritism, 275; divested of

Williams, James, 18, 98

Williams, John, 123, 182

Wilson, Daniel, Jr., 8, 322 (n. 18)

Wilson, Daniel, Sr., 8, 322 (n. 18)

Wingfield, Charles, 173, 313

Wise, Henry, 69, 166; campaigns for governor, 43–44; elected, 45; retrenchment policy of, 60; recruits brigade, 86, 87; in western Virginia, 90–91, 93; in North Carolina, 96; and McDearmons, 111, 126; grants furloughs, 168–69; at Petersburg, 177, 178, 181–83, 187–89, 199–200; at Sailor's Creek, 207, 209, 211–12; at High Bridge, 215–16; at Appomattox Court House, 221, 222, 232, 262, 263; meets George Meade, 251; and Joshua Chamberlain, 359 (n. 47)

Woodson, Drury, 38, 56, 82, 267

Woodson, Rev. Drury, 38, 105, 170, 186, 187

Woodson, Elvira, 82, 109, 122, 170, 268, 296

Woodson, James H., 84

Woodson, John W., 69, 74; opens office at Appomattox Court House, 38–39, 47; as quartermaster, 99, 119, 125; as private attorney, 168; death of, 186; law office of, misidentified, 331 (n. 50), 340 (n. 9)

Woodson, Mary, 186, 304, 340 (n. 9)

Wooldridge, Thomas J., 100, 101, 335 (n. 38)

Wooldridge, William P., 336 (n. 20), 339 (n. 1)

Wooldridge, William R., 113

Wright, Caswell, 167–68

Wright, Fountain, 84, 293

Wright, Gilliam, 183

Wright, Horatio G., 208, 210, 220

Wright, Mariah, 47, 55, 84, 111, 183, 236, 340 (n. 8)

Wright, Pryor, 74; home of, 16, 17, 239, 279, 304, 327 (n. 40); children of, 29–30; death of, 47; identified, 340 (n. 8)

Wright, Pryor B., 167–68, 340 (n. 8)

Wright, William M., 42, 63

Young, Samuel M. B., 272

William Marvel has written a dozen books about the Civil War, including the award-winning *Andersonville: The Last Depot* and, most recently, *Mr. Lincoln Goes to War. Lincoln's Darkest Years* will be released in 2008.